HUMAN ADAPTATION
AND POPULATION GROWTH

HUMAN ADAPTATION
AND POPULATION GROWTH
A Non-Malthusian Perspective

DAVID S. KLEINMAN

ALLANHELD, OSMUN & CO. / Montclair
UNIVERSE BOOKS / New York

ALLANHELD, OSMUN & CO. PUBLISHERS, INC.
Montclair, New Jersey

Published in the United States of America in 1980
by Allanheld, Osmun & Co., 19 Brunswick Road, Montclair, N.J. 07042
and by Universe Books, 381 Park Avenue South, New York 10016
Distribution: Universe Books

Copyright © 1980 by David S. Kleinman

LIBRARY OF CONGRESS CATALOGING IN PUBLICATION DATA

Kleinman, David S.   1920–
  Human adaptation and population growth.

    Bibliography: p.
    Includes index.
    1. Population.   2. Fertility, Human.
3. Human ecology.   I. Title.
HB871.K59   301.32   78-59176
ISBN 0-916672-18-2

Printed in the United States of America

To G. D. K.

Contents

Preface

I undertook the study of population many years ago, believing that population growth was a major threat to our future and expecting that I might help in halting its advance. With time and study, it became apparent that population had little to do with humanity's ills, that human reproductive behavior is part of the repertoire of coping with adverse natural and social circumstances, and that fertility is controlled indigenously when it threatens to diminish the significant values of a people.

Yet population concerns have been undeservedly and mistakenly prominent in considerations of social policy related to poverty, scarcity, aggression and the like. It appeared important to me to help lay these concerns to rest. In the process some of the real sources of social ills are noted but not treated in the detail they deserve. I consider this book a prelude to a more extended discussion of the origins of social ills and of what might be done to at least mitigate them.

The past failures of social scientists to predict population trends, the direction of other social changes and the effects of various social interventions are almost proverbial. A reason frequently given is that our knowledge of social processes is incomplete, that more research is needed. My personal view is that while more knowledge is, as always, desirable, the basic deficit lies not with the paucity of information but with its fragmentation and frequent misconstruction.

A variety of disciplines examine many different facets of social and behavioral phenomena, while a durable, integrated perspective of the human condition eludes us. Many social scientists try to model their work on the more exact "hard" sciences, where specialty areas based on paradigms derived from innovative discoveries have been highly productive. But they lack the foundation discoveries upon which the structure of the "hard" sciences rest. Thomas S. Kuhn, in his book, *The Structure of Scientific Revolutions*, authoritatively distinguished between the process of innovative science responsible for discoveries and that of "normal" science given over to ramifying and otherwise exploiting established paradigms. Sooner or later existing paradigms are fully exploited and new ones are required. But normal science, employing a bureaucratic ethos to maintain its authority, may inhibit the excercise of innovative or revolutionary science and actually obstruct the development of new paradigms. This lesson has yet to be learned.

The various social and behavioral sciences have experienced successions of fads and fashions. But only a very few of their paradigms have stood the tests of time and the proliferation of a reliable fund of generally accepted and eventually useful information. Yet social scientists, particularly the more parochial among them, often behave as if they possessed powerful and true paradigms, defending the primacy and autonomy of their specialties and confusing a plethora of pseudo-technical jargon and pretentious, arcane conceits with knowledge inaccessible to the outsider. They ignore the admonition of Occam's razor, that entities, abstractions and assumptions introduced to explain something should not be multiplied beyond necessity. Unnecessary entities constrict and stultify thought, narrowing vision, and obscuring realities which might otherwise become apparent. Many social phenomena, particularly those containing significant moral or normative components, may not be amenable to study and processing in the same manner as are the more material phenomena whose various aspects can be studied separately and at different levels, micro to macro, without apparent loss or distortion of information.

The foundations, oriented to social betterment, policy analyses and applied research, could help balance the sectarian tendencies of academic social science. Several forces militate against this, not the least of which are the close ties between many of the foundations with a research component and the academic milieu from which they draw their talent. In addition the foundations are quite responsive to the wants, including the ideological needs, of sponsors, government agencies, private pressure groups, corporations and the wealthy. Their executive officers have outlooks similar to those of corporate-level executives in industry, academia and government, from which groups many of them were drawn. Though they may sound like reformers, and are in some respects, many are also committed to the established order in other respects and particularly with regard to the status and authority of the learned elites.

The point is that knowledge and ideas which could guide and facilitate solutions to our social problems may be slow in coming from the existing institutional settings. The tragedy is that the educated public and even the erudite, finding the guidance of experts to be unreliable, place increased credence in the sensational, alarming and simplistic versions of social developments. There emerges a tendency to see people as meaner and less competent than they actually are, because the circumstances with which people must cope and which should be changed are not clearly seen. I hope to render these circumstances as they relate to demographic behavior more visible than they may have been.

The scholarly work of our time is performed largely within the framework of academic specialties and associated institutions and much of our information must, perforce, come therefrom. Despite the institutional constraints and imperatives, much of this work does exhibit considerable insight, particularly when freed of parochial commitments. I've selected material without regard to discipline in this effort to elucidate the place of fertility behavior and population growth in human adaptation to various social processes and societal developments. I have tried to make the issues involved comprehensible and the material accessible to nonspecialists. I hope that specialists will forgive me if, in this effort, I have, here and there, presented matters which appear elementary to them (I trust not to all), or neglected favored works (some out of ignorance, others with deliberation). They may find virtue and value in other parts and aspects of the book and the argument worth pondering.

The extensive critical discussions and editorial assistance of my wife, Goldy D. Kleinman, helped sharpen my ideas and contributed significantly to the development and realization of this work. The detailed critical commentaries and queries, at the instance of the publisher, of an anonymous reader-reviewer and a nameless editor, are also much appreciated and valued. No one can be held in any way responsible for or agreeable to the ideas and opinions expressed herein, for errors of commission or omission or for other inadequacies; these must be laid entirely to me. Nonetheless the book was greatly improved from what it would have otherwise been because of the intervention of those acknowledged above.

Cecilia Paul gave unstintingly of herself and her talents in the arduous tasks of typing and retyping the manuscript, and helped in many other ways as well, all out of friendship.

My son, Jesse A. Kleinman, provided valued research assistance. My daughter, Leah S. Kleinman, provided a sustaining interest which was much appreciated.

Charles W. Brown, Virginia L. Richmond and Gordon Bermant furnished early encouragement and counsel and exerted more tangible efforts to further the realization of this work. Over the years during which the theses of the book were being formulated and the book written, I've received encouragement from friends and colleagues and other assistance as well. In addition I am indebted to many other people, teachers, colleagues and friends, without whose influence on my intellectual development, this work would have never been. But I would presume too much on the indulgence of readers and publisher, if I have not already done so, were I to acknowledge these debts in detail here.

D. S. K.

Seattle, Washington
March 1979

1

The Malthusian Model

Introduction

This book is in the tradition of radical anti-Malthusianism. Malthusians view population growth and size as significant contributors to a variety of social ills, depletion of resources, debasement of environments and the like. It is the purpose of this book to reexamine the purported population problems in historic and contemporary times, and to argue that the Malthusian views do not reflect the realities of human behavior, the conditions with which people must cope, nor the manner in which people adapt. Malthusian views of fertility behavior and population problems reflect the ethnocentric and class biases of their proponents, giving rise to myths that distract attention from the sources of social ills.

This examination will indicate that the problems attributed to population were, and are, problems immanent in the social order, manifesting themselves without regard to population size or growth. Fertility behavior is shown to be adaptive in most circumstances, compensating for deficiencies in social structure and economic relations, providing for the security of individuals and families, but also responding to limitations of resources and other constraints. The accommodation of population growth requires the expansion of resources, at which humans have shown considerable proficiency, but when the accommodation becomes difficult or children become onerous, fertility is reduced and population growth decreases. The basic problems of humans historically, and currently as well, have derived not from a scarcity of resources but from their relationships with each other.

The conclusions are that population is not now and has rarely, if ever, been an issue relevant to the survival of people or even to their comfort; that it is tangential to issues of societal development, the unequal distribution of

1

power and wealth, and the underlying social, economic, and political processes. If these issues are attended to and resolved, the problems erroneously attributed to population growth and density would diminish, if not vanish altogether. Discouraging population growth will not significantly improve human welfare.

Fertility serves not only to assure the continuation of the species and to gratify a variety of psychological needs, but it is also a way of coping with social conditions. For the greater part of history, and in most of the world today, the security of most individuals stemmed not from the society at large but from the family. What passes for welfare services and mutual assistance in modern America and Europe is provided by families in most of the world. Many writers have held that large families and the resulting population growth lead to a crisis of resources. However, the mutual aid provided within large families has frequently maintained the integrity of society, holding off crises arising from social malfunction, and providing time for the evolution of social and economic change.

Many analysts start with the view that high fertility and population growth result from some cultural or psychological compulsion or from a pursuit of personal interest and gratification that is heedless of social consequences. Thus, population growth is seen as a blind process. Further a terrifying vision of the multiplicative effects of even such a slowly reproducing species as homo sapiens is easily evoked. At present there are around four billion people on earth, and they are increasing at a rate of almost 2 percent a year. If present birth and death rates continue, the human population will double every 35 to 40 years to reach 32 billion before the end of the 21st century. Since there appears to be difficulty in supporting a large segment of the world's population today, the prospects appear grim.

A number of closely reasoned theses have been presented that purport to demonstrate that the rates of population growth found in most of the world today are detrimental to society. The theme is not new, having been raised many times in the past, most notably by Malthus with whose name this gloomy perspective is associated. Some contemporary economists have asserted that population growth prevents industrialization and economic development which would increase the living standards in the developing countries. These economists hold that the potential savings, which might be applied to increase the per capita productive capacities of a society, go instead into supporting increasing numbers of people (see Chapter 13).

These theses have been of little use in the past as guides to the relationship between population growth, national resources, and social welfare. Nor do they explain today's problems. The statement that were there fewer people, the average income would represent a greater fractional share of the produce of society, can be made with mathematical certitude. But this does not mean that the average would be larger. The size of the economic product of a society is adjusted to the size of its population.

The critical weakness in the arguments of those who predict ultimate disaster is their assumption that human fertility will maintain its momentum regardless of consequences. An alternative view is that fertility behavior is adaptive, that people have children to enhance their security and their chances for survival, as well as for personal satisfaction. When children no longer perform these functions, when population pressures restrict the opportunities for and magnitude of livelihoods, and the costs of rearing children increase while their anticipated contribution to family welfare decreases, fertility tends to diminish.

The development of this theme involves more than a consideration of resources and technology. The unequal distribution of social and economic power has dominated human behavior and limited human options as much as physical resources and technology and often more. They must adapt to these social and economic constraints or change them, as they must live within the limits of resources and technologies or expand them. In the past, societies' failure to provide adequate personal and economic security has been compensated for by families and by high fertility, population growth and economic expansion.

Some analysts interpret human behavior including fertility behavior in the framework of a mathematical system. The materials of demography in particular lend themselves to this effort. The precision and logical coherence of mathematical formulations make them the language of choice for scientific communication as well as the basic framework for scientific investigation. However, the validity of any system depends ultimately on how well it reflects reality, enhances understanding, and predicts behavior. Counting births and deaths, enumerating population by age and sex, and establishing mathematical relations between them are important for the description of population events. But they do not inform us *why* humans behave in such a manner as to bring about these events.

The adaptive aspects of fertility behavior are not as easily expressed in mathematical fashion as are the demographic events themselves. Analysts frequently ignore these adaptive aspects, or simplify them in order to accommodate a mathematical framework. The simplification often does not account for the principal facet of human adaptiveness, namely, the ability to change behavior or to alter external conditions in response to circumstances. Instead the trends of the past and present are projected into a future in which circumstances may or may not be quite different. A brief review of the more or less mechanical approaches to population growth may provide a useful contrast to the examination of the actual experience of population growth that follows.

The Model of "The Dismal Science"

Nearly two centuries ago, Malthus proposed that while population tends to increase in geometric or exponential fashion (doubling over a certain number of years depending on the rate of growth), its subsistence can at best increase in arithmetic fashion (increasing by some constant increment in that same period). Thus, a population of two will increase in a geometric series such as 2, 4, 8, 16, while subsistence will increase in an arithmetic series such as 1, 2, 3, 4. Whatever the constant increment of the arithmetic series, or its starting value, the values of the geometric series must soon outrun those of the arithmetic series. A growing population must sooner or later exceed the capacity of its resources to sustain it.

After an optimal amount of labor is applied to a finite piece of land, additional labor results in lesser and lesser additional output, as described by the law of diminishing returns. Thus, if land resources are severely limited, a growing population may not be able to increase its subsistence even arithmetically. To this, Ricardo added the observation that the best resource is exploited first: The most fertile and favorably located lands will be cultivated first, and then as need be, less productive land will be brought into use.[1] If straitened circumstances do not induce people to delay or forego marriage and reduce their fertility, and population continues to grow, the positive checks to population growth—war, pestilence, famine and undernutrition—intercede to increase mortality. Population and its rate of growth are thus controlled, not by people, but by limited resources and mortality.

Even if an economic advance (such as the opening of virgin territories), or increased productivity (through new technologies and industrialization), extends the frontier of available subsistence, relief is only temporary. The tendency for population to grow to the limits of subsistence levels, in time, brings humankind to the same pass. Thus, for most periods and in most places, most people have been obliged to live at a bare subsistence level because of the press of population.

Private property helps keep a miserable humanity from expanding to the ultimate limit of resources. Since the proprietors of agricultural land will not grow food unless there is a profit in it, much land is withheld from cultivation. This keeps humanity from reaching that state where everybody is reduced to scrabbling for bare survival. Thus, the existence of private property, and its associated economic inequality, allows at least some fortunate few to live above the subsistence level, to enjoy a high culture, and to promote the progress of society.[2] Such were the views of Malthus.

At the time Malthus wrote, a large proportion of Englishmen lived in the squalor of town and rural slums despite a total population of only nine million people. The misery which prevailed for the overwhelming number of people seemed to give the lie to the promise of progress held out by Adam Smith on the one hand and William Godwin on the other, neither of whom were troubled by population growth. But in the almost two hundred years since Malthus and Ricardo proposed that the misery of their times was inherent in the reproductive capacities of humans, Britain's population has increased some five-fold, as have those of other European nations, and the people are better housed, better fed, better clothed and longer lived now than they were then. The horrifying slums of eighteenth- and nineteenth-century Liverpool, Manchester, London and other cities in Europe are largely gone. However in the United States, which is among the least densely populated and best endowed with natural resources, considerable urban and rural slum conditions still exist. At the same time, birth rates among modern Europeans and Americans have declined and at present writing they are tending toward less than a population replacement level. The logical explanations offered by Malthus and Ricardo have been inadequate, at least to describe the events of the last two centuries.

The less rigorous and looser arguments of Godwin and Smith, stemming almost from a blind faith in the adaptive capacity of humans and their ingenuity in coping with the limitations of their environment, have better described the history of European populations in the last 200 years.

Godwin, Malthus' older contemporary and antagonist, based his views on a faith in man's rationality, moral nature, and utopian future. He held that fertility and population growth would not exceed the capacity of resources, that intelligence and diligence would enable Europe to satisfactorily support many times its then current population and that "... the men whom we are supposing to exist, when the earth shall refuse itself to a more extended population will probably cease to propagate."[3] He thought by that time humans would learn to extend life indefinitely, and they would no longer need to propagate. They could learn to live in a dignified and utopian style. His supporting arguments were diffuse and frequently based on underestimates of the population growth, overestimates of the wealth then available for distribution, and other claims whose flaws obscured the value of observations that otherwise might have provided a stronger response to the Malthusian position.

Adam Smith, on the other hand, saw overpopulation as a problem for the remote future which did not warrant serious consideration in his time. Increasing division and specialization of labor, making for better organization of the productive process and stimulating the development of technology, would increase the productivity of labor, thereby getting around the immediate constraints of the law of diminishing returns. These changes would permit wages to increase and capital investment to remain highly profitable until that point is reached when the country is fully stocked with capital and labor. Then competition would cause profits and wages to decline. But Smith did not see any sign of that occurring for some time to come.

Since Malthus's time the economies of the industrialized nations have followed the trend predicted by Smith and Godwin, circumventing the law of diminishing returns and increasing the productivity of land, labor and capital. New technologies and labor converted inferior into superior resources; reclaimed marshland became highly fertile farmland. Output has increased faster than population, and with time the rate of population growth declined through a decline in fertility.

Malthus revised his *Essay on the Principles of Population* many times, taking into account some of the objections to his thesis. The dismal tenor of his first edition (1798) was modified as he explored the possibility of a way out of the Malthusian trap. He thought that humans could escape their economic fate by restraining their concupiscence, and he cited instances when such restraint had occurred. He opposed governmental policies which would encourage the proliferation of people, such as the Speenhamland decision that provided for a sort of guaranteed income at a low level. (See pp. 67-68). He also expressed the opinion that if people became accustomed to a higher standard of living, they might be more inclined to restrain themselves to protect what they had. Education and civil liberty, providing people with a share in society, would encourage them to limit their concupiscence, and a good polity could insure that resources were appropriately developed. But the tenor of his philosophy that the "passion between the sexes is necessary and will remain nearly in its present state...," and his view that birth control was a vice from which no good could come, promised a poor prospect for humanity.

Indeed, Malthus did not and perhaps could not think of birth control practices except in the context of illicit and depraved sexual liasons.

Moral restraint in application to the present subject may be defined to be, abstinence from marriage, either for a time or permanently, from prudential considerations, with a strictly moral conduct towards the sex in the interval. And this is the only mode of keeping population on a level with the means of subsistence which is perfectly consistent with virtue and happiness. All other checks, whether of the preventive or the positive kind, though they may greatly vary in degree, resolve themselves into some form of vice or misery. The remaining checks of the preventive kind, are the sort of intercourse which renders some of the women of large towns unprolific; a general corruption of morals with regard to the sex, which has a similar effect; unnatural passions and improper acts to prevent the consequences of irregular connections. These evidently come under the head of vice.[4]

To Malthus, promiscuity and birth control went together.

The effect of anything like a promiscuous intercourse, which prevents the birth of children, is evidently to weaken the best affections of the heart, and in a very marked manner to degrade the female character. And any other intercourse would, without improper arts, bring as many children into the society as marriage. . .[5]

The principle of population and the prescription of chastity had the same origins for Malthus. Both derived from the wisdom of the Deity. The purpose of the principle of population was not to assure the misery of humankind but to be as a goad to humans to labor. If the earth were so underpopulated that humans could satisfy their needs with little labor, a major incentive to industry would be lacking and indolence would triumph. And if the passions were easily ignored or satisfied and celibacy was not a state of privation, the ends of nature would be defeated.

It is clearly the duty of each individual not to marry till he has a prospect of supporting his children; but it is at the same time to be wished that he should retain undiminished his desire of marriage, in order that he may exert himself to realize this prospect, and be stimulated to make provision for the support of greater numbers.[6]

Himmelfarb quotes Walter Bagehot as aptly observing: "In its first form the *Essay on Population* was conclusive as an argument, only it was based on untrue facts; in its second form it was based on true facts, but it was inconclusive as an argument."[7]

In Malthus's later revisions, there was some recognition that humans had to face troubles whose origins lay in the organization and structure of society, and that these conditions led to high fertility and population growth that further exacerbated social problems. Attempts have been made to revise the popular conception of Malthus as a prophet of doom by pointing to the high valuation Malthus placed on universal education, good government and other measures which promised hope for the future. For example, the following from the 7th edition of the *Essay on the Principles of Population:* "In most countries, among the lower classes of people, there appears to be something like a standard of wretchedness, a point below which they will not continue to marry and propagate their species. . . . The principle circumstances which contribute to raise this standard are liberty, security of property, the diffusion of knowledge and a taste for the comforts of life.

Those which contribute principally to lower it are despotism and ignorance."[8]

Malthus did not see high fertility as an adaptation to circumstances. He underestimated the capacities of people to expand their resources or to control their fertility. The simple Malthusian version of the relationship between population growth and misery too often prevails in the popular mind.

The Limits to Growth

The recent revival of the Malthusian spectre was largely due to the unprecedented increases in the rate of growth of the world's population and of the economy after World War II. (In the decade of the Great Depression prior to World War II, the prevailing concern was the stagnation of population and economic growth rates.) Recent decades have seen an increase in the rate of world population growth to around two per cent per year and a still greater rate of growth in the use of resources and in the generation of pollution. Growth in the developing countries resulted from a decline in mortality following a general improvement in living conditions and the application of health technology measures such as malaria control, immunization, and improved sanitation.

In many of the economically developed countries, birth rates which had reached a low point during the 1930s increased in the post-World War II decade, causing a spurt in population growth. In the United States, population increased by some 50 percent from around 140 million in 1946 to 210 million people in 1970. Income per capita increased about 60 percent so that the total national product in 1970 was almost two and one-half times as large as that of 1946. Moreover, the new technologies that contributed significantly to increased productivity also increased pollution, generating less degradable types of pollution with considerable toxicity which spread and accumulated with increasing concentration in the environment, air, water and soil.

Analysts examining the consequences of the combination of population and economic growth, added the detrimental effects of pollution resulting from increased industrialization and use of chemical technologies in agriculture to the limits imposed by diminishing resources. The mathematics and analytic methods used to predict consequences are more sophisticated than those used by Malthus, and make extensive use of computer technology. But the basic approach and philosophy remain the same. The bad—population, pollution, diminution of resources, increase exponentially; the good—pollution control technology, knowledge, adaptation, increase at a much slower pace. The end predicted—sooner or later—is disaster.

Among the more recent and more ambitious models of the future, based on the continuation of present trends, are those developed by a team of scientists at the Massachusetts Institute of Technology and summarized in the book *The Limits to Growth*.[9] These scientists used a "systems dynamics" approach to plot on a computer the future course of the world under the impetus of "accelerating industrialization, rapid population growth, widespread malnutrition, depletion of nonrenewable resources, and a deteriorating environment." At any given point in time, the world is described by such characteristics as the amount of nonrenewable natural resources, food production per capita, industrial output per capita, pollution, and population. The model simulates the changes in these characteristics as people go about their business. They procreate, and if fewer die than are born, population grows. They invest capital and they produce industrial and agricultural goods. In the process they deplete nonrenewable resources and generate pollution. Each characteristic of the condition of the world is related mathematically to the other characteristics, and each succeeding state to that which preceded it.

Thus, changes from year to year are derived from a set of interacting subsystems which together comprise a dynamic system. Built into these subsystems are lags or delays in adaptation. These assure that population increase will exceed the food supply and pollution will rise to deadly levels before effective action is taken to prevent these disasters. The authors propose that, on the basis of what they discern from current trends, population and pollution will continue to increase, nonrenewable resources will be depleted and food production per capita will further diminish. Corrective action will be too slow and too late to affect the outcome. There will thus be an "overshoot" of population and pollution and a collapse of the system. This collapse is projected to occur towards the end of the 21st century unless growth is stopped.

The dynamic relationships of the factors determining the operation of the subsystems are expressed mathematically. In some cases the expression is based on fitting curves to limited empirical data. Growth, of course, is represented as being exponential. Resource availability and capacity to manage pollution are presumed to increase at a lesser rate. Estimates of nonrenewable resources and such other characteristics of the environment as the capacity to withstand and neutralize pollution before toxic levels are attained and the effects of pollution on health are based on limited data. Future technological development is accounted for implicitly by extending the limits of resources and decreasing the rate of pollution per unit of industrial output but not enough to prevent eventual collapse of the system. No account is taken of new and unforeseen developments addressed specifically to resolve the problems of the future.

The authors recognize that their model, despite its complexity, is still an oversimplification and that estimates of the various parameters involved are fairly gross and may be inaccurate. Nonetheless, they feel that their model is robust. Even if resources are twice the amount estimated, and the pollution carrying capacity of the environment should be several times greater, or if the rate of pollution diminished for a given industrial output, the exponential growth attributed to population, industrial development, resource depletion, need for food, and pollution generation will still cause the system to break down, if not in 100 years then in 120 or 150 or 200. The ultimate limit— which comes into play if the collapse of energy, pollution control and industrial output systems are delayed—is the food supply, which brings us back to Malthus.

The Limits to Growth models have been widely praised and just as widely criticized, one of the most comprehensive critiques being that of a team from the Science Policy Research Unit of the University of Sussex.[10] Some of the criticisms relate to the quality and sufficiency of the data used by the M.I.T. team to establish resource and environmental limitations and to their failure to recognize that as old resources are depleted, technological developments lead to the discovery of new resources and ways to handle pollution. Other criticisms relate to lumping the whole world and all industry into a single system. Economies and populations in different parts of the world behave differently, and within a given economy different industrial activities and sectors have their own unique patterns of development and pollution. By dealing with the sectors separately, analysts would be better able to identify the sources of the problem more clearly; and they could provide for the development of responses and changes in less apocalyptic terms than that growth must stop if disaster is to be averted. A more recent work of the same genre as the *Limits to Growth* takes the latter criticism into account. In this work the world is divided into ten regions, each with its own model. These models are linked with each other by trade and aid. Nonetheless, as might have been expected, the world collapses in the absence within the model of provision for suitable adaptation and change.[11]

Members of the Sussex group, making different assumptions, arrive at world models indicating stability rather than collapse when projected to the year 2200. What comes out of such computer models is what one puts in.

The "Limits to Growth" model is not necessarily invalidated by the lack of precision of its measurements and parameters. Measurements may be made more precise, but it is the internal structure of the model that is crucial. The "Limits to Growth" model, in effect, postulates the failure of humans to adapt, to recognize threats to their survival and values, and to modify their behavior to avoid disaster. The projections of the model are based on trends during a relatively short period of time, the last century. During this period, conditions of life, including longevity, improved for most peoples in the western world. The fact that the improvements were bought at a price, namely some level of deterioration in some aspects of the environment which, nonetheless, was on the whole rendered healthier and more congenial, is no indication that people will be willing to continue paying this price or a higher one to the point where their survival is threatened.

People have generally been aware, at some level, of what was happening to their environment, that forests were disappearing, that the air and waters were becoming foul, that certain trades and workplaces were dangerous. Plato, in the *Critias*, noted regretfully that the hills of Attica had been denuded of their trees within the memory of some still living and that the soil was eroding. Elizabethan London tried to prohibit the burning of 'sea coal' because it was a particularly obnoxious pollutant. The mad hatter, poisoned by mercury, and the chimney sweep with scrotal cancer were well known figures as were the maimed miners and those suffering from black lung and other diseases. Societies either did not care about their depredations or this was a cost they were willing to pay. The Athenians invested many of their trees in building a large navy so that they could rule an empire. Being expert arboriculturalists, they could have reforested their hills had they wished. (On Cos, sacred to the Greeks, it was a crime to cut a tree in antiquity.) The lower classes may be obliged to accept the nasty conditions under which they work and live for the sake of livelihood if not by compulsion, aware of the risks to health and safety.

The question is what are the forces behind growth, and how can people, under these circumstances, effectively respond to protect their interests and to forestall disaster. This question will not be answered by projecting their behavior under current circumstances to a future with different circumstances, while denying the continuation of the adaptive capacities they have shown in the past and which are very much evident in the present.

Few will dispute that in a finite world, there must be limits to growth. At issue is the location of these limits, but this is not the only issue. Even if these limits are still far off and continued growth were feasible, according to the opponents of growth further expansion can only result in squandered resources and pollution and detract from the quality and aesthetics of life. Economic striving may debase human existence.

The dilemma is that population growth and economic growth arise from needs for security not otherwise satisfied in most societies. In our own industrialized and highly productive society, where high levels of fertility serve little purpose, economic growth is still essential to the orderly operation of our society. The demands on resources and resulting pollution far exceeds that which can be attributed to population growth. Growth compensates for a want of equity and justice. Since we do not know how to live happily in a steady state economy, economic growth buys time in which to develop the more equitable yet workable social and economic relations which would increase the possibility of stability (see Chapter 13).

One can match pessimistic experts with other equally qualified experts who are quite optimistic about the potential for resources and the management of pollution at reasonable costs under conditions of growth. W. Beckerman, the noted economist, and J. Maddox, the respected and widely knowledgeable scientist and editor are but two examples.[12]

Experts can not know the extent of resources that will be available to humans for aeons to come. The abstract argument that in any case resources are finite and thus limited may be indisputable. But it is little more significant today than it would have been to the small bands of prehistoric hunters who hurried the mammoth and the mastodon to extinction. What matters is how humans recognize their economic limitations and how they cope with them.

Estimates of resources and their utilization rates are biased not only by gaps in our information, but by business interests who stand to profit by controlling access. However, the process of resource estimation is useful because it provides a framework for discussion, research, and evaluation of the factors that need consideration in planning. Plans can only be tentative and subject to correction as new information is developed.

In the past, economic conditions often led to technological developments in which new, cheaper and more plentiful resources could be used, and the recovery of old resources were rendered more practical.[13] The past history of technology does not guarantee the future. Technological capabilities are also limited. But neither can it be presumed that technological innovation will not keep up with the needs of economic growth in the foreseeable future; nor, if technological innovation is not forthcoming, growth will nonetheless continue to ultimate catastrophe.

Though the growth of population, depletion of resources and degradation of the environment are often described as explosive, they do not occur instantaneously. They occur over a period of time during which detrimental effects make their presence felt in gradual stages. The response to these effects will depend on how they impinge on the daily lives of people and on the consequences of the various responses, including reduced fertility, lower standards of living, and perhaps even different forms of social organization. Experts can not locate the limits, and they cannot know how they will affect peoples' lives. In effect, the limits to growth will be determined by the aggregate of people as they cope with the problems of living.

Population Prospects

Even as the authors of "The Limits . . . " were writing, the fertility trend in the United States, on which their population subsystem was partly based, had changed. This change occurred rapidly, and it was in the opposite direction to the one postulated in the model.

The model presumes that the relationship between desired family size and per capita product is as follows. Among those countries with per capita incomes of $1000 (1960) or less, the poorer the country the larger the proportion of families wanting 4 or more children. But among the countries with larger per capita incomes, the wealthier the country, the larger the proportion of families wanting 4 or more children. It was also presumed that fertility would follow these trends as per capita income increased.

The explanation presented (following a model familiar to economists) is that families weigh the value and cost of each additional child against the resources available for rearing them. As industrial output increases (accompanied by changes in life style), the value of many additional children decreases and the costs of raising them increase making children less desirable. At the same time, the resources available to raise them also increase, and at some point the increase in income more than compensates for the increased cost of raising children. At this point the model presumes that fertility will increase. The curve describing the relationship of desired family size with increased industrial output is a composite, or resultant, of the curves of the value and cost of children against the available resources represented by industrial output per capita.

The data on which the above considerations were based reflect to some degree the fertility experience of the 1950's, the years of the so-called baby boom. In the decade following World War II, fertility, which had previously reached a low point in the United States and in Western European countries, increased. This increase in fertility occurred at the same time these nations were recovering from both the war and the earlier economic depression. In the United States, whose per capita industrial output was highest, the increase in fertility was sharpest, and a large proportion (40 percent) of the population expressed a desire for four or more children.[14] This seemed to establish a trend with a positive relationship between desired fertility and income in developed countries where contraception was well established. But during the 1960's, though per capita real income in the United States and Europe continued to grow markedly, actual, expected, and desired fertility declined. In the inflationary 1970's the lowest of fertility levels observed in history were reached. The long term trend of decreasing fertility in modern industrial nations was resumed. This phenomenon is considered in greater detail in later sections.

Logistic curves have been used to describe the growth of various organisms in closed environments. Among humans, the use of growth curves to project trends has generally been unsuccessful. Humans can live in a greater variety of conditions than can other species and respond to changes in a greater variety of ways, including changing their resource conditions or their fertility behavior. After a marked lack of success in the use of curves, even superimposition of one curve on another to reflect changing circumstances, several analysts concluded, some time ago, that there is no evidence of a unique mathematical law or curve of human population growth.[15]

However, the fertility patterns of the past few generations will affect population growth for some generations to come by determining not only population size but its age structure as well. At any one time, the natural growth rate is equal to the crude birth rate minus the crude death rate. Changes in population growth may be best projected by examining the more refined age-specific birth and death rates and the distribution of age in the population. Suppose there is a relatively high proportion of young people in the population, as was true in 1970 for the United States as a result of the baby boom of the late 1940's and 1950's. Suppose again that the fertility of women dropped suddenly so that women on the average expected to have 2.1 children, just enough to replace themselves and their husbands, rather than 3 children as formerly. The immediate switch to replacement level fertility will not keep the population from growing. There will still be a disproportionate number of young people in the population who will tend to keep fertility high enough and mortality low enough to result in continuing growth. Fifty years of replacement level fertility may be needed before the age distribution rights itself so that births equal deaths, though in the latter part of this period, growth will be slow indeed.

The inertia exercised by the age structure is one of the forces making for delays in the adjustment of population growth rates, and one cannot argue the mathematics of this. But there is nothing magical about replacement level fertility. If people feel so constrained, fertility can drop even lower. From 1967 to 1974 in the United States, the total fertility rate dropped from over 3 children per woman to 1.8 children which, if continued, would mean negative growth rates. In many European countries, zero or almost zero growth rates were achieved in relatively short periods of time, despite the mathematical inertia exercised by the age structure with which these countries started out on the latest fertility decline. (As will be shown later, the assumption that fertility decline in very poor countries such as India depends on increased income is also wrong. In these countries, people are likely to respond to resource limitations as do all people within the context of their way of life.)

In the greater part of the world, population growth rates are high, so that world population is increasing at a rate slightly less than 2 percent per year. This growth rate if continued would result, as noted earlier, in a doubling of population every 35 years; there would be more than 32 billion people by 2080.

Starting with the beginning of time, the human population first reached one billion in 1850. A second billion was added by 1930, after 80 years. The third billion, reached about 1960, took only 30 years and the fourth was reached in 1975, some 15 years later. From 1950 to 1975 the population had increased from 2½ billion to 4 billion. There are indications, however, that the increase in population growth rates has peaked and in many areas of the world growth rates are beginning to decline, albeit slowly in the eyes of some.

Tomas Frejka has computed the numbers of people there would be if present mortality experience continued and people reduced their fertility to replacement level at various times in the future. If world fertility had dropped to the replacement level between 1970 and 1975, population would increase to about 4.7 billion in the year 2000, 5.6 billion in the year 2050 and stabilize at around 5.7 billion thereafter. If fertility were to decline and reach replacement level between 2000 and 2025, the population would stabilize at 8.4 billion and if replacement level fertility were reached between 2040 and 2045, population would stabilize shortly after 2100 at a little more than 15 billion people.[16] If people are slower in controlling their fertility, population may increase to large numbers unless prevailing death rates increase in the interim. At present there is no sign that this is occurring.

The issue in the minds of many is whether the world can sustain such large numbers of people until some happy equilibrium between people and resources is reached. What conditions will intervene in the interim? The future cannot be expected to repeat the past. But the past (and present) can teach us something about human behavior in various contexts that may permit us to visualize what is important and what is not so important to human welfare, and how this may affect the future.

The most recent doubling of population, from 2 to 4 billion, occurred between 1930 and 1975, an interval of 45 years, with the period of most rapid growth starting in 1950, when world population stood at around 2.5 billion people. This has been the period of the most rapid rate of growth history has seen and may ever see, yet the conditions of life for most people have not deteriorated. And for many—mostly those in developed nations, but also a fair number in the developing nations—the conditions of life and incomes improved more rapidly during the latter part of this period, when growth rates were high and world population was approaching 4 billion, than during the earlier part, when population stood at around 2 billion and population growth rates were relatively low. The world at that time was in an economic depression that ended only with the outbreak of a world war. The argument is raised that conditions would likely have been better without population growth, particularly in the developing nations where economic and industrial development policy and investments are presumed thwarted by population growth. The facts are that when growth was low, there was little progress; and currently there is little relationship between population growth and growth in per capita income among developing nations (see Chapter 13). Regardless of protestations of general welfare objectives and even socialism, economic development policies in many third world countries operate to advance the interests of the elite, at the expense of the poor majority if need be. Foreign aid policies operate to the benefit of donor nations as well as to the benefit of the elite in recipient countries; meanwhile, the failure to improve the condition of the poor is blamed on population. Demonstrable potential increases in food production are thwarted by policy, not population.[17] (see Chapters 5, 6, 12.)

It is impressive that the world, which in this period had gone through the most devastating war in history, was able to absorb a doubling of population in so short a time. Many of the problems attributed to population such as pollution and resource depletion, civil disorder, and violence were for the most part due to other factors as will be discussed in the chapters directed to these issues.

Notes

1. D. Ricardo, *The Principles of Political Economy and Taxation* (London: J. M. Dent and Sons, Ltd., 1948), p. 37.

2. See T. R. Malthus, "A Summary View of the Principle of Population," (1830), in D. V. Glass, ed., *Introduction to Malthus* (London: Frank Cass and Co., 1959).

3. Quoted by J. J. Spengler, "Malthus on Godwin's 'Of Population,'" *Demography* 8:1 (February 1971), pp. 1--12.

4. Malthus, "A Summary View . . . ," op. cit. p. 153.

5. T. R. Malthus, *On Population*, G. Himmelfarb, ed., Seventh Edition of the *Essay* (New York: Modern Library, 1960), p. 489.

6. *Ibid.* pp. 477--494.

7. *Ibid.*, p. xxxiii.

8. See T. R. Malthus, *An Essay on the Principles of Population.* Seventh Edition (London: Reeves and Turner, 1872) pp. 436--41, cited by W. Petersen, "The Malthus-Godwin Debate, Then and Now," *Demography 8:1 (February 1971), pp. 13--26; also T. R. Malthus, On Population,* op. cit., p. 543.

9. D. H. Meadows, D. L. Meadows, J. Randers and W. W. Behrens III, *The Limits to Growth* (New York: Universe Books, 1972).

10. H. S. D. Cole, C. Freeman, M. Jahoda and K. L. R. Pavitt, eds., *Models of Doom, A Critique of the Limits to Growth* (New York: Universe Books, 1973).

11. M. Mesarovic and E. Pestel, *Mankind at the Turning Point: The Second Report to the Club of Rome* (New York: Dutton, 1974).

12. W. Beckerman, *Two Cheers for the Affluent Society* (New York: St Martin's Press, 1975); also *Pricing for Pollution: An. analysis of market pricing and governmental regulation in environmental consumption and policy* (London: Institute for Economic Affairs, 1975). See also J. Maddox, *The Doomsday Syndrome* (New York: McGraw-Hill, 1972).

13. G. Hueckel, "A Historical Approach to Future Economic Growth", *Science* 187 (March 1975), pp. 925--31. See also Hueckel's critics, Letters to *Science* 189, pp. 410--14; D. B. Brooks and P. W. Andrews, "Mineral Resources, Economic Growth and World Population," *Science* 185 (July 1974), pp. 13--19; H. E. Goeller and A. M. Weinberg, "The Age of Substitutability," *Science* 191 (February 1976), pp. 683--89.

14. See B. Berelson, "KAP Studies on Fertility," in B. Berelson et al., eds., *Family Planning and Population Programs* (Chicago: University of Chicago Press, 1966), Table 5, p. 665.

15. See. E. B. Wilson and R. R. Puffer, "Least Squares and Laws of Population Growth," *Proceedings of the American Academy of Arts and Sciences* 68 (9) (August 1933), pp. 285--382; L. Hogben, *Genetic Principles in Medicine and Social Science* (London: Williams and Norgate, 1931), pp. 177--84, cited in H. S. Shryock and J. S. Siegal, *The Methods of Demography*, U. S. Bureau of the Census (May 1973) 2 vols., pp. 384--85.

16. T. Frejka, *The Future of Population Growth: Alternative Paths to Equilibrium* (New York: Wiley, 1973); T. Frejka, "The Prospects for a Stationary World Population," *Scientific American*, 223:3 (March 1973), pp. 15--23.

17. See S. George, *How the Other Half Dies: The Real Reasons for World Hunger* (Montclair, N.J.: Allanheld Osmun and Co., 1977), and F. Lappe Moore and J. Collins, *Food First* (Boston: Houghton Mifflin, 1977).

2

The Social Historical Context

Introduction

The early hominids who began to use fire, fashion tools and communicate with symbols more versatile than the signs used by animals, established the direction of human evolution.[1] Those hominids, who had the capacity to develop and use tools, to manipulate objects, to incorporate the experience of generations into the learning process, and to coordinate efforts with those of others in a social unit, were more likely to survive. No longer did adaptation have to wait upon slowly evolving genetic and physical change; it could occur through more rapid cultural changes. The result is that humans can not long survive outside a social context. People had not only to cope with a physical environment but also with a social milieu which while supportive was also oppressive for many. Change to a more congenial social environment is restrained by powerful beneficiaries of the status quo and fear of unknown consequences of change.

For most of history and in much of the world today, society has been dependent on families, not only to socialize children, but to act as the basic economic unit of production and consumption, and the principal support of individuals. Before the industrial revolution, production, except in some relatively few communities, took place largely within the household. The few establishments in the ancient world that employed large numbers of individuals rather than families—in quarrying, building, farming, transporting, and even in enterprises that might have passed as factories—were often manned by slaves. In rural areas, where the bulk of the population resided, households produced practically all their needs with the help of village artisans whose work was also largely a family affair. In pre-industrial and even later periods, many of the products handled by large commercial

15

firms were often manufactured in home workshops, in which the entire family was employed in weaving or other crafts while the raw materials were distributed and the final products collected by entrepreneurs. (This system survived even into the 20th century United States.) Security came from membership in a family for most people. By meeting needs not otherwise provided for, the family helped maintain the integrity of the society, and in times of social breakdown maintained the continuity of the community. The family has been a "Haven in a Heartless World," (as Christopher Lasch has called it) even in times when it was a cruel institution.

Family structure and relationships within and between kinship groups come in many forms, but in all cultures the need for viable familial ties has been recognized. The universal prohibition of incest, with the exception of prescribed brother-sister marriages in the royal family of some few societies of the past, is generally taken as a recognition of this need. By prohibiting sexual access within the immediate family, and often to other relations as well, a source of competition among family members, often associated with strong contentious emotions, is eliminated. The choice of a marriage partner from outside the family group serves to cement alliances between families. (Other explanations for the origins of the incest taboo have been proposed. These include the prevention of inbreeding defects and matings between incompatible persons presumed to have developed a sexual antipathy to each other in the course of living or being reared together. Nonetheless the utility of the incest taboo in keeping the peace and cementing ties between distant families remains.) Sahlins' conclusion that in early times human culture brought sex under control in the interests of cooperation within and beyond family groups, appears reasonable.[2]

The Rise of Hierarchy

Sahlins concluded on the basis of the similarities between the few extant, widely separated hunting and gathering societies, that social dominance—the power and authority of individuals, groups or classes over others—is at its lowest among hunters and gatherers, including those of prehistoric times.[3] He believes status and prestige were accorded to the generous and giving rather than to the aggressive and taking. The more proficient shared their produce with those less fortunate. This may well have been the case, but the fact remains that the few remaining communities of hunters and gatherers, generally relegated to undesirable parts of the world, experienced a different history from our ancestors. Some observers of the prehistoric scene, such as Dart and his popularizer Ardrey, believe that our early hominid ancestors excelled in aggression, a theory that has been the subject of considerable controversy.

However idyllic the social relations of our hunting-gathering ancestors may or may not have been, these relationships did not survive the advent of civilization and social classes. Civilization requires some degree of urbanization, a larger population aggregate than can be sustained by small bands of hunters and gatherers ranging over extensive areas in search a livelihood. The most common view is that civilization, the urban revolution was made possible by the development and adoption of agriculture.

What caused prehistoric or preliterate people to make the transition to agriculture must remain speculative. While we know something about their material accomplishments through archeology, we know little about their reasons. Some would say that population pressure induced people to turn from hunting and gathering to the more disciplined, more intensive and more productive work of agriculture; others that the invention of agriculture and expansion of resources caused the increase of population. Cohen, a proponent of the population pressure hypothesis, does not consider agriculture an invention but the application, when required, of an accumulation of known techniques of plant manipulation.[4] Still others maintain that both agriculture and subsequent political and economic developments were the consequences of ongoing cultural processes.

Jacobs hypothesized, not without a basis, that in some areas at least, agriculture may have been invented by creative crafting and trading communities fortunate enough to have access to a valued material, for example, obsidian, which when shaped into knives could be traded for captured animals, seeds, and other food items.[5] The storage of varieties of seeds and animals then led to an intimate knowledge of their character and how to manipulate them. Jacobs presented her account of the origins of agriculture, illustrated by inferences drawn from some archeological findings, as a supportive part of her theory of the primacy of urban communities in the development and diffusion of innovations.

Cohen (see above) addressed the origin of agriculture in prehistory as the central focus of his study. In that enterprise he performed a comprehensive examination of the pertinent archeological and anthropological research, concluding as was noted that population pressures led to the adoption of agriculture. The conclusion was not, however, readily ascertainable from the physical evidence but required the mediation of a number of suppositions about the nature of archeological indicators of population pressure. Thus he presumed that in the absence of other possible evidential explanations, increasing sedentism (the settling down of nomadic hunters and gatherers), various changes in food habits, increases in the ranges of food gatherers, skeletal indications of malnutrition, and a variety of other circumstances which may be discerned from the archeological record may be taken to indicate population pressure.

Factors other than population pressure (changes in taste, religion, social organization, etc.) may have caused the indicator conditions, and as we shall see, it can be very difficult to ascertain a reasonable sequence of causes and effects in historic times. To attempt to do so for prehistory, where the basis for ascertaining, much less interpreting, the character of human behavior and thought is meager, is hazardous though worthwhile. Several facts are clear. The practice of agriculture did not begin to an appreciable extent until almost all habitable areas of earth were occupied in some fashion, around 10,000 years ago. Within several thousand years, a relatively short interval in human existence, the people of a large part of the world had taken to cultivation, the practice having been developed and adopted independently in some areas and spread by diffusion in others. Whether people turned to argiculture to support a growing population or for other reasons, some minimal level of population density was apparently required or was at least associated with the process.

Whatever the reasons for people turning to agriculture, the archeological and early literary record indicates that many of the earliest Neolithic agricultural communities were democratically organized. There are no signs of hierarchical structure, either by differences in the size of the houses and graves of these early settlements, or in the later legends of their descendents.[6] But with time, the appearance of hierarchies and social classes become apparent in both the archeological and written records.

Durkheim proposed that population growth and often (not always) associated social interactions led to a social density that resulted in the division of labor. Individuals thus avoided the conflict which might have ensued if everybody did the same thing and competed for the same resources. The resulting interdependence of those performing different functions served not merely as an economic advantage but, more importantly, it assured a level of social solidarity.[7]

Carneiro proposed that the state and political hierarchy arose from the conflicts within and between agricultural villages as a result of population growth, and pressure on available land. As villages grew, they split and supernumerary people went off to develop new lands and found new communities. There came a time when this alternative was circumscribed by geographic barriers such as mountains and deserts or even by the presence of a ring of other villages that hemmed in potential migrants. Land, being no longer available, was prized and fought over. Previously, violence had been sporadic and of small scale, directed towards revenge and the like. Now, according to Carneiro, it became organized and directed at either eliminating occupants of coveted land or bringing them under submission as tributaries, a condition not feasible when the prospective victims could escape to empty lands and find refuge beyond the reach of aggressors. War leaders and organizers became the nucleus of the upper class.[8] As villages were aggregated into petty states and kingdoms into empires with attendant needs of coordination, the class of administrators, tax collectors, and other functionaries burgeoned.

Adams hypothesized that the rise of hierarchy in ancient Sumer, perhaps the oldest civilization, was born of conflict between communities, between nomads and settled cultivators, and between craft and related groups within growing urban complexes. In the protoliterate period of that culture, the term "king" is not mentioned in the texts, and if the ancient myths about the gods reflected the experience of men, the early communities were governed by assemblies of the adult males of the communities. Their functions were largely to select war leaders when conflicts with other communities arose. Eventually successful war leaders were retained in times of peace, and eventually these took unto themselves greater authority, taxing the citizenry, and organizing a standing army of soldiers and retinues of personal retainers and palace officials. The resulting demand for weaponry and luxury goods stimulated the development of specialized crafts and trade. Whatever the origin of the early Mesopotamian city states and the constant wars between them, the historic record also shows, according to Adams that once they were established, the Mesopotamian kingships and hierarchies took on purpose of their own, expanding their power and military capabilities, often against the wishes of those they ruled.[9]

Ruling groups did not limit themselves to war but were intimately involved in maintaining and expanding the economic bases of their states. In Ancient Egypt, Mesopotamia, China and elsewhere, the economy rested on intricate irrigation systems. The management and coordination and construction of these systems were among the responsibilities of government. This was so significant that Wittfogel proposed that it was the basic reason why ancient peoples "subordinated themselves to a directing authority," hence for the establishment of the state.[10] Others, including Carneiro and Adams, disagree. They note from the archeologic and historic record that while cities and states grew more powerful with expanded irrigation systems, they did not originate in them. Indeed, it was the rise of the state, the source of coordination and direction which made the complex irrigation systems possible. But people could not be kept in subjection very long unless some benefit accrued from it. Peasants gave of their labor and surpluses not only because of compulsion but to assure the power of the king or pharoah as divinity or intercessor with the gods, and particularly in their stewardship of the irrigation and water systems.[11]

A problem not easily resolved in studies of political organization and population is the direction of cause and effect. It is certainly difficult if not impossible to discern in the dim sequences of the distant past whether it was institutional processes that caused the population to grow, or population growth that was responsible for institutional developments.

The relationships between population density and political development are not always clear. Fortes and Evans-Pritchard found little relationship between population density and complexity of political systems among six African societies. While Fortes and Evans-Pritchard looked at these societies synchronically, as they existed at a given time, the present, Stevenson examined these societies diachronically, in the perspective of their history.[12] He concluded that the political systems of these societies were related to the conditions of their past history, contacts with and influences of other peoples, former economies and previous population densities, and related characteristics. Thus the Bemba, now sparsely settled, were, until the British broke their power at the turn of the century, conquerors and slavers with a strong political and military organization, with concentrated population centers in contact with the Arabs. What remained after their defeat and dispersion was an anachronistic political organization which did not really function as it once did, the chiefs being relatively powerless despite outward forms remaining from former days of grandeur.

Stevenson demonstrated that the formal structure of political institutions, though unrelated to current population conditions, could be related to the population characteristics of the past. These, however, were in turn related to the political and historic experience and the prevailing economy. As these changed, so did the substance if not the form of the political structure and so did the density and organization of the population.

Sahlins questioned the validity of tracing such developments as the state or social economic systems and associated technologies to demographic pressures. He noted that there is no evidence that archaic peoples tended "to reach, let alone exceed, the population capacity of their means of production." Indeed Sahlins' examination of the economies of several primitive societies indicates quite the contrary, that regardless of the level of technology, resources were abundant relative to the number of people to be supported. Pressure on land by primitives was not in his view a function of population, land, or technology, but of the cultural specification of access to the means of livelihood, rules of land tenure, relations within and between groups regarding property, systems of production and distribution of goods and services, and so forth. He concludes that explanations, of warfare, of the origin of the state, and of other events, which do not take into account the social and cultural structures, are suspect.[13]

The important point is that however they started, once hierarchies and social classes were instituted, they developed their own momentum. The troubles attributed to population growth are likely in fact to reflect the workings of social structure, status, and associated roles.

The establishment of elites with the power to enforce demands on those of lower social orders presented families with a new set of circumstances to which they had to adapt. No longer were families to contend with other families of approximately equal force, but against the overwhelming power of a state or its agents. Childe, in writing about the beginnings of urban communities and classes, asserted that farmers were compelled or persuaded to produce a surplus that was appropriated by the state to support craftsmen, merchants, priests, officials and clerks.[14] That the term "surplus" is ambiguous has not escaped the scrutiny of some scholars. Is the "surplus" extracted from the immediate producers really superfluous to their needs, and how are those needs determined? Do not the non-food producing activities, which the surpluses sustain, also fulfill human needs? Did the appropriated surplus in fact exist, or was it brought into existence by the expropriators who not only forced people to work harder, but also coordinated work and supervised the development and deployment of technologies that increased productivity? Was the surplus actually a form of savings (and investment), even though forced? A series of discussions by a few scholars indicated little but that the term "surplus" has no absolute referent, and its meaning depends on the context in which it is used.[15] (For want of a convenient alternative, we must continue to use this term. Hopefully, the context will make its meaning clear.) In summary, with the agricultural and urban revolution, families were subject not only to the needs of their members, but also to the demands for part of their production and labor by elites too powerful to resist.

The Family - Power and Security

The economics of producing a maximum surplus over subsistence are different from that of producing a maximum income per capita, a common economic index of welfare. This difference was outlined by Sauvy, the eminent French economic demographer, who distinguished between the optimum population size required to produce maximum welfare, and that required to produce maximum power.[16] He demonstrated that with a given level of resources and technology, the population size which produces the maximum surplus or power is larger than that which would produce the optimum welfare under the circumstances.

If the objective of the state is to produce a maximum income per capita (that is, optimum welfare) the optimum population size for a given level of resources and technological capacity would be where the marginal product of the last worker added to the work force is equal to the average product. With a work force smaller than optimum, the average product per worker would be less than the marginal product because there are not enough workers to take full advantage of division of labor and economies of scale or size. In a work force larger than optimum, the marginal product would be less than the average product because diminishing returns exceed the advantages of scale.

If, on the other hand, the state wishes to maximize its power, it must maximize the means at its command, the source of these means being the surplus that can be extracted from the work of its people. For any given level of resources, technology and subsistence, the maximum surplus (that is, power) is determined by the point at which the marginal product of additional workers is equal to the designated level of subsistence (provided that it is not so low as to seriously affect productivity, a problem discussed in Chapter 7). The size of population at this point is larger than that of the maximum welfare population. A larger population can be supported still, but only by decreasing accumulated surpluses to provide subsistence.

Sauvy's model illustrates the cardinal economic theorem that different objectives cannot be maximized simultaneously; a balance must be struck. With the appearance of hierarchy, competition, exploitation, and contention, power becomes a prime consideration in the lives of people and states, detracting from concerns for welfare and comfort. Mary Douglas noted that many primitive people practice birth control to conserve resources that confer status and prestige. In the process the basic subsistence resources will also be conserved. She also noted, however, that such primitive communities as are engaged in political competition with others are eager to maintain or increase their number even in the face of diminishing resources.[17] In the face of threats from others the needs of power become paramount.

Where the family is the principal source of security, the welfare of individual members tends to be subordinated to the maintenance of the family's status, lowly though it may be. The sweepers of the Indian village in which the Wiser's lived were much concerned that their family rights to the filthy and distasteful tasks which gave them a mean livelihood were not jeopardized by the attempts of their children to better themselves.[18] The small living of poor families in peasant societies has long depended on their ability to muster relatively large labor forces. In traditional agrarian societies, peasant families were obliged to produce considerable surpluses over their own subsistence because of the imposition of taxes, rents, high interest indebtedness, labor dues, and other exactions not readily resisted.

Polgar suggested that the exactions of western colonial powers, taxation in money, produce, or forced labor, induced peasants to increase their family size and labor force to better be able to meet these exactions. This and the disapproval by western governors of indigenous population control practices such as infanticide and abortion are presumed to account for much of the increase in growth rates of many colonial countries under European domination.[19] However, exploitation of peasants in colonial countries did not begin with western powers; the indigenous rulers were not known for their benevolence. Nonetheless, the colonial powers did nothing to mitigate this force for fertility while maintaining order and controlling epidemics, thus mitigating the force of mortality.

In fluid situations where a poor family might enhance its status by the purchase of land or the education of one of its members, such can be achieved only by the surpluses of a number of family laborers. The wealthy family may think in terms of educating all its members, easier to accomplish if there were fewer of them. The poor family can only hope to educate but one or two, and that would take the surpluses from the labor of several others to accomplish. The smaller the earnings per family member, the more members needed to generate a sufficient surplus for any family purpose. A corollary is that the smaller the earnings, the younger the entry of children into work to augment the family's labor force. (The early factory system in Europe was built on low wages and child labor.)

Children and Old Age Security

Children have not only helped parents—whether engaged in cultivation, domestic industry, or outside work—to maintain the family household, but also have been the source of old age security. In many societies, rearing children is the only way the poor can save for the future. Where mortality levels are appreciable, even if only moderately so, parents can not be sure that a number of their children will survive to the parents' old age. Thus parents may have had to accept the risk of having more children than they needed or could have comfortably supported to minimize the risk of being left with too few.

M. Anderson[20] estimated, on the basis of the United Kingdom census reports for 1851, that in the town of Preston, almost all persons 65 years or older who had surviving children were living with one or another of them. However, around 30 to 35 percent of the people who were 65 years of age and older did not have a surviving child; some of these may have never married; others may have lost their children to death. By the middle of the 19th century, death rates had fallen. In earlier times, when death rates were higher, the probability of being left with no child to support one in old age was greater still.

By means of a computer simulation, Heer and Smith described the levels of fertility that would be needed if parents wished to be assured that at least one son would survive to support them in later years. The simulation showed that even at moderate levels of mortality (such as expectation of life of around 50 years), parents need to beget at least five children if they are to be very sure (with a 95 percent probability) that they will have at least one son who will survive to their old age. If they would like to be sure of more than one son they would need even more children. To achieve this level of assurance parents would have to have spare sons, and since each birth is almost as likely to result in a daughter as in a son, the parents will have many daughters as well. The result is considerable population growth.[21] Actually fertility did fall in some societies before a significant drop in mortality (see Chapter 9). In some societies high infant mortality was aggravated by neglect and even less subtle forms of infanticide. Heer and Smith's model is attractive but should be taken with some reservation.

Parents in third world countries have, when surveyed, often expressed the expectation that their children will provide old age security and those parents who have experienced the loss of children express greater anxiety in this regard. However, data from studies of fertility behavior in less developed countries do not indicate that most parents who have a requisite number of surviving sons (and daughters) early in life go on to limit their fertility, though among early groups of acceptors of clinical birth control services, women with many sons are over-represented compared to the general population. Repetto, who reviewed some of these data, concludes that broader economic considerations than just old age security, enter into fertility behavior.[22] These considerations include more immediate family welfare concerns, the contribution children's labor can make to the household economy, and the costs and trouble of bearing and rearing them.

Caldwell has generalized the dependence of parents on children for economic security to be but one aspect of the intergenerational flow of wealth from the younger to the older in many preindustrial societies. In contemporary western societies, parents invest heavily in children, receiving little in the way of an economic return. In many pre-industrial societies, parents do not need to wait until children are adults to receive benefits; even as children, their work adds to the parents' wealth, or more accurately diminishes the parents' poverty. Where large extended kinships exert strong influence or control over the reproductive family unit (as they did among the Yoruba Caldwell studied) the senior members amass considerable power and wealth from the work of the junior members. Caldwell anticipates that the impetus for high fertility in such societies will diminish, even without industrialization, as western cultural values diffuse among them.[23]

Western values will not (and probably could not) diffuse as ideas alone. Senior members did not amass wealth in the past simply because they were valued elders. They were also the business and political executives whose power, perquisites and the deference owed them derived from their status in the social economic order as do the privileges of western elites. Changes in the direction of the intergenerational flow of wealth follow social economic changes. Such changes were initiated in Africa by the colonial powers and are being continued by those who control and benefit from the expansion of the modern sector of the economy. The degree to which changes in ideas and values facilitate social economic changes or simply reflect and serve them is difficult to determine.

Family and Kinship

Elemental conjugal units (husband, wife, children) belong to larger kinship networks defined not only by relationship but also by obligations, rights, and living or household arrangements among members and between groups. Family structure appears to bear some relationship to the type of economy which prevails as well as to the social patterns. Independent nuclear families are reported to predominate in hunting and gathering societies as well as in modern industrial societies; extended families or households that include more than one married couple and their children are most often found in traditional agricultural societies.[24]*

(Much of our information about family types, particularly in complex societies, relates to household arrangements. One or more conjugal units or single adults and children live together, consuming and sometimes producing as a unit. Information about how related units interact would add to our knowledge of family function but is often lacking).

Extended and joint family arrangements would appear to have some advantage in providing security. But there are disadvantages. The stronger units in the family may feel that they would be better off without the weaker, while the weaker units may be oppressed and feel put upon. There is a historic tendency in even agricultural societies for joint and extended families to break into smaller units as opportunity warrants and regardless of ideological committment. While the ideal family may be joint, the prevailing type may be nuclear.

Linton, comparing the Tanala of Madagascar with the Betsileo, a closely related neighboring group, concluded that as the functional significance of the joint family changed, so did it break up. The joint family prevailed among the Tanala, whose swidden forest dry rice cultivation techniques were best managed by the joint efforts of several families. The neighboring Betsileo, apparently with the same origins as the Tanala, cultivated wet rice, which could easily be managed by a single family settled on a plot of marshy land. The former joint family arrangements had therefore broken down among the Betsileo and the nuclear family prevailed. The settled life also led to the establishment of powerful chiefdoms and hierarchies.[25]

The vast extended kinships that provided protection and some security for their members disappeared in western Europe (except in some fringe areas as in Scotland) during the Middle Ages as feudal lords took over the governance and economies of local communities.[26] In Scotland the clans received their formal death blow at Culloden in 1745. But the end of the clan's pretensions to family came with the acceptance by the clan chiefs of the role of landlord in which capacity they proceeded to enclose lands and evict tenants, those who in former times they considered kinsmen. All over Europe the span of recognized relations narrowed. Even household units became smaller if they were not small to begin with. Extensive examination of sources from which household lists were reconstituted showed that nuclear families dominated household structure for at least the last 300–400 years in much of Europe. The restricted nuclear family was the predominant form in England by 1500.[27]

In China from ancient times and India in the past 100 years at least, household sizes as reported in censuses were not very large, averaging around four to six persons. This number is consistent with nuclear or only slightly extended families (parents and married son) being the predominant household units. This was true despite the organization of families into clans on the basis of descent (as in China) or emphasis on kinship obligations (as in

*In the author's study of the 1961 Indian Census (see Chapter 10) it was estimated that no more than a third of rural households included one or more married male relatives of the "head of household." Many may have been aged dependents and many must have been very young married sons, too young to make it on their own, but who would do so in time.

India). Many conjugal pairs, particularly when young, may have spent some time in a joint family relationship, usually with the husband's parents and brothers. This arrangement was often temporary and with the death of the father, nuclear families were often thrown on their own resources, though they might enjoy some claim to the income of their common patrimony.* Data for several Arab lands, some dating back 100 years, indicate that in these societies most households were also small.[28] The few rich could and did organize into larger households.

In China, the solidarity among families of the same clan, presumably descended from a common ancestor, was often fragile. While the clan could unite effectively against a common enemy—sometimes the state itself—the clan gentry did not hesitate to exploit and oppress the poorer and weaker of its families. With time the clan lost its importance. The province of Kwangtung, where the clan system was most intact, witnessed the most violent peasant uprising from 1924 to 1927 with smallholders and laborers of different clans united to fight their clan brothers and class enemies, the landlords and merchants.[29]

Tribal and family solidarities exist largely in the face of a common threat or challenge. People appear to give up the constraints of traditional tribal and family obligations when the advantages and benefits are gone. Breakdown in the relations among extended kindreds were not limited to complex societies but occurred among primitives as well. Sahlins, in his examination of the economies of primitive societies, saw a potential conflict between the household, the basic economic unit of production and consumption, and the larger kindred of which it was a member; the kindred had a claim on the household and vice versa. Though this conflict was rarely open and obvious, it became apparent in periods of economic crises. Sahlins illustrated the solidarity of the elementary family as opposed to that of kith and kindred by citing the description presented by Firth, of the manner in which the Tikopians, primitive cultivators of a Pacific island, coped with a famine caused by hurricanes. Mutual aid between households of the same kindred broke down while members of the same household held fast to each other.[30]

Sklar[31] proposed that the reason for the high fertility and relatively young married ages in the Balkans of the late 19th century, as contrasted with the lower fertility of western Europe and Baltic countries, can be found in differences in family structure.

The families of western Europe and the Baltic were nuclear, conjugal units living independently. A new family unit could not be formed until a livelihood was available for it. In the Balkans a type of family structure and household economy, labeled the Zadruga, was common though by no means universal. The Zadruga was a large extended family group, a father and his married sons or married brothers living together; sometimes other relatives and even non-relatives joined the group. The group farmed the family lands or herded the family flocks in collective fashion. Some of these groups were reported to have included as many as 20 adult males who with their families comprised as many as 100 persons, though agglomerations of such size were rare. Most included a total of 10 to 20 persons in all, and many were smaller still. Marriages did not need to be delayed in the Balkans because of the lack of a holding or livelihood as in western and Baltic Europe.

Hammel[32] suggested that the Zadruga in Serbia be regarded as a process rather than as a permanent relationship. The Zadruga waxed as father and increasing numbers of sons and perhaps other relatives worked their land together, and waned as the members of the group decided to split into smaller independent households. Conditions, such as being in a frontier situation, may have given rise to the need for adult males to band together in co-residence for more effective defense. Taxes and labor dues on households made it economical for households to be large, and to include within them a large labor force. Hammel noted that at times some Zadrugas were mythical entities; the families within them operated independently in clandestine fashion. On the surface they were organized as Zadrugas to fool the tax collector and minimize the feudal labor dues which could be exacted on the households. The Turks who ruled Serbia at one time had no objection to the Zadruga household form, but were concerned if it led to a diminution of taxes. (In another context, 300 years before Christ, Shang Yang, a Chinese legalist, advised the duke of the state of Ch'in to double the taxes on families that included two adult males unless the family was divided.)[33]

The internal structure and relations of Zadrugas are still to be detailed.[34] There is little reason to think that the high fertility of such households was due to their structure rather than to the circumstances that made this form of organization functional, namely the need to concentrate and maintain high levels of family manpower in a turbulent region that had not been pacified, nor order established among contending ethnic groups, clans, and the like until recently.[35]

A number of studies of the relationship between family structure and fertility have been reviewed by Burch and Gendell.[36] Various mechanisms had been proposed to explain the possibility of fertility differences between extended or joint families and nuclear families. On the one hand, the responsibilities for child care and child rearing are shared in joint families and such families can otherwise exercise pressure to encourage high fertility. However, if there is a lack of privacy within the joint family, frequent intercourse may be inhibited. Families can, of course, discourage or encourage fertility in other ways according to inclination. Which force will prevail? Burch and Gendell observed that there is no consistent evidence for differences in fertility between women living in extended and those living in nuclear families. Two problems must be noted, however. Although residence in the same domicile or household is an important consideration in classifying families, it does not tell us anything about the interactions between related family units living in different domiciles. Also, the significance of family structure to fertility may have been different in the past than in recent times when the studies were carried out. The findings of the author's own research on the relationship between the prevalence of joint households in the rural districts of India in 1961, and the fertility of these districts are discussed later (see Chapter 10). These findings indicated that it was not family structure that was related to fertility so much as the economic resources in the areas where the different family structures were found.

The foregoing treatment of family and kinship, necessarily brief, cannot begin to describe the rich variety of family relations designed to sustain people in different circumstances. The slave family and the family headed by a female attest to the capacity of people to develop and maintain family relations even under the most oppressive and poverty stricken conditions. Undoubtedly, new or modified family relationships are being developed today to better fit changing circumstances, not only in modern society but in contemporary non-industrial societies as well. Analysts will likely look for a relationship between the fertility patterns of such families and the peculiarity of their structure, for example, to the continuity of sexual relations and other such factors. But whatever the form of relations, if the fertility outcome is not consistent with the conditions of life, it is likely to be changed.

Population Growth—A Preliminary Overview

Ten thousand years ago, prior to the appearance of the earliest known farming communities, there were an estimated 5 million humans and these had spread over most of the earth. It had taken a million years from the appearance of early hominid types for humans to attain this number. Thereafter, population increased more rapidly, its growth accelerating, according to many observers, as mortality declined in the west during the past three centuries, and much more as mortality declined in the non-industrial countries in the last few decades.[37]

Deevey criticized the impression left by smoothed population growth curves that growth was a continuous phenomenon. In Deevey's view, population growth took place in a series of surges following technological revolutions, the very early toolmaking cultural revolution, the agricultural revolution and the scientific-industrial revolution. Following each surge population stabilized, albeit at a higher level. In between these great revolutions, there occurred other conditions leading to population surges in various parts of the world at various times, for example, the population surge in western Europe from 1000 to 1300 A.D., and in early Manchu China from 1650 to 1750 A.D.

The classic Malthusian explanation for the changes in population growth rates focuses on changes in death rates. Agriculture can support a larger number of people in a given area than can hunting and gathering; the greater availability of food results in a lesser mortality and an increase in population. Similarly, industrial technology can sustain a growing population more readily than can traditional agriculture, in addition to which modern technology includes a repertoire of public health and medical practices which can effectively intervene in the prevention and mitigation of many diseases.

A number of anthropologists and investigators from other disciplines have objected to the Malthusian formulation that population growth in the past has been largely controlled by death, and to the "neo-Malthusian" notion that the widespread use of birth control is of recent modern origin.[38] These anthropologists question the likelihood that the death rates of archaic hunters and gatherers were so much higher than those of the agriculturalists who followed them in history as to account for the difference in population growth rates. If anything, the death rates of hunters and gatherers should theoretically have been lower, consistent with the findings that mortality rates among contemporary primitive societies are generally lower than among peasant societies only 50 to 100 years ago (see pp. 32, 60-61). These considerations, and evidence that contemporary hunters and gatherers as well as other primitive people appeared to practice birth control (through infanticide and abortion as well as contraception) and experienced long intervals between births, supports the claim that the very low rates of growth before the development of agriculture were due largely to birth control. (See also pp. 32, 139-140.)

The paltry and fragmented evidence used to estimate life expectancy in prehistory contains more male remains than female for the Paleolithic period. This may indicate the practice of female infanticide since infant remains are not likely to withstand the ravages of time. But the sex ratio is equalized among the few remains of Mesolithic people. Mortality was high but not so much different from that of cultivators as to account for the differences in population growth rates.[39]

Dumond suggested that the independent nuclear family structure which predominates in hunting and gathering societies helped to motivate birth control practices. One reason hunters and gatherers found it necessary to space children with long intervals between them is that women had to carry their infants and toddlers on the march along with other possessions, and it was impracticable to carry more than one child at a time. The more settled agricultural life eliminated this problem. Families became larger and more extended, including many people who could help care for children and thus the responsibility for rearing and supporting their children did not fall wholly on an individual couple. Dumond suggested analagous pressures operating to keep the fertility of nuclear families low in both early and modern societies.[40]

As has been noted, the prevalence of extended family households may be small in many agrarian societies, while there appears to be little if any consistent difference in fertility between joint and single family units. Kinship support, however, may not depend so much on co-residence as on relationships and exchanges not easily discerned or evaluated. The source of these relationships as well as the determinants of fertility behavior and change may be best sought in the conditions with which people must cope. For while much of human behavior is in good part determined by culture, a more important facet of human behavior is that it is adaptive, that behavioral change does not need to wait on cultural change and indeed may precede it. In peasant societies of the past and present, fertility has been controlled, in one manner or another, when important for welfare.

The motivating forces behind fertility behavior are obscured and the consequences of the resulting state of population are misconstrued by the focus on society-resources relationships. Societies, except among some primitive folk, are not unitary entities. Though their members may be moved by common sensibilities, they are also riven by conflicting interests and groups. We can not know much about prehistoric societies but the record of historic societies is replete with conflict, between groups within a society and between societies. The problems of people in coping with their environments were small compared to the problems of coping with each other. Fertility behavior provided one way of coping.

The argument that people tend to reproduce to fill their environments explains neither the motive forces behind population growth nor, for that matter, the expansion of the human population into almost every area of the earth. The cessation of population growth whether because of fertility control or the positive checks, as Malthus called inordinate increases in death rates, tells us nothing about the limits of resources or carrying capacity of the environment even relative to existing technologies and standards of living. Access to resources is mediated by social structure. The positive checks, war, pestilence, famine and hunger, are related to the ways societies are organized, the ways they relate to each other and to the ways in which their members live, and have little or no relation to what has been called population pressure.

Notes

1. See C. Geertz, "The Impact of the Concept of Culture on the Concept of Man", *Bulletin of the Atomic Scientists XXII-4* (April 1966), pp. 2–8. See also S. L. Washburn, "Tools and Human Evolution," *Scientific American* 203:3 (September 1960), pp. 63–75.

2. M. D. Sahlins, "The Origin of Society", *Scientific American* 203:3 (September 1960), pp. 76–86.

3. Ibid.

4. M. N. Cohen, *The Food Crisis in Prehistory: Overpopulation and the Origins of Agriculture* (New Haven: Yale University Press, 1977).

5. J. Jacobs, *The Economy of Cities* (New York: Random House, 1969), pp. 3–48.

6. See G. Childe, *Man Makes Himself* (New York: Mentor Books, 1951), pp. 84–85; S. Piggott, *Ancient Europe* (Chicago: Aldine, 1965), p. 44.

7. E. Durkheim, *The Division of Labor in Society* (1893), trans. G. Simpson (Glencoe, Ill.: Free Press, 1949) pp. 256–63, 266–75.

8. R. L. Carneiro, "A Theory of the Origin of the State", *Science* 169 (August 1970), pp. 733–38.

9. R. M. Adams, "The Origin of Cities," *Scientific American* 203:3 (September 1960), pp. 153–68.

10. K. Wittfogel, *Oriental Despotism* (New Haven: Yale University Press, 1957).

11. See. S. Moscati, *The Face of the Ancient Orient* (English translation, New York: Doubleday Anchor, 1962), pp. 18–24; also J. A. Wilson, *The Culture of Ancient Egypt* (Chicago: University of Chicago Press, 1956), pp. 8–18.

12. M. Fortes and E. E. Evans-Pritchard, eds., *African Political Systems* (London: Oxford University Press, 1948), Introduction, pp. 7–10; R. F. Stevenson, *Population and Political Systems in Tropical Africa*, (New York: Columbia University Press, 1968).

13. M. Sahlins, *Stone Age Economics* (Chicago: Aldine Atherton, 1972), p. 49.

14. G. Childe, *What Happened in History* (New York: Penguin Books, 1946), p. 18.

15. For a discussion of the argument about the nature of surpluses, which in some respects appears to be semantic, see M. Harris, "The Economy Has No Surpluses?" *American Anthropologist* 61 (April 1959), pp. 185–99; G. Dalton, "A Note of Clarification of Economic Surplus", *American Anthropologist* 62 (1960), pp. 483–90; and the article which started the discussion: H. Pearson, "The Economy Has No Surplus," in K. Polanyi, C. Arensberg and H. Pearson, eds., *Trade and Market in the Early Empires* (Glencoe, Ill.: Free Press, 1957).

16. A. Sauvy, *General Theory of Population* (English translation, New York: Basic Books, 1969), pp. 42–59.

17. M. Douglas, "Population Control in Primitive Groups", *Brit. J. of Sociology* 17 (1966), pp. 263–73.

18. W. and C. Wiser, *Behind Mud Walls* (1930–1960) 2nd Ed. Berkeley: University of California Press, 1967.

19. S. Polgar, "Culture, History and Population Dynamics," in S. Polgar, ed., *Culture and Population* (Cambridge, Mass: Schenckman, 1970), pp. 3–8; "Population History and Population Policies from an Anthropological Perspective," *Current Anthropology*, 13: 2 (April, 1972), 203–11.

20. M. Anderson, "The Study of Family Structure," E. A. Wrigley, ed., *Nineteenth Century Society* (Cambridge: Cambridge University Press, 1972), pp. 47--81.

21. D. M. Heer and D. O. Smith, "Mortality Level, Desired Family Size and Population Growth," *Demography* 5:1 (1968), pp. 104--21.

22. See R. Repetto, "Son Preference and Fertility Behavior in Developing Countries", *Studies in Family Planning* 3:4 (April 1972), pp. 70--76.

23. J. C. Caldwell, "Toward a Restatement of Demographic Transition Theory," *Population and Development Review* 2:3, 4 (September--December 1976), pp. 321--66.

24. See M. F. Nimkoff and R. Middleton, "Types of Family and Types of Economy," in R. F. Winch and L. W. Goodman, eds., *Selected Studies in Marriage and the Family* (New York: Holt, Rinehart and Winston, 1968), pp. 35--43; also E. A. Hoebel, *Anthropology: The Study of Man*, 4th ed. (New York: McGraw-Hill, 1972), chapters on family and kinship.

25. R. Linton, "The Tanala of Madagascar," in A. Kardiner, *The Individual and His Society* (New York: Columbia University Press, 1939), pp. 251--90.

26. See M. Bloch, "Kinship and Lordship," from M. Bloch, *Feudal Society*, (English Translation, Chicago: University of Chicago Press, 1961), reprinted in B. Tierney, *The Middle Ages* 2nd ed. (New York: Alfred A. Knopf, 1974), Vol. II, *Readings in Medieval History*, pp. 94--106.

27. P. Laslett, *Household and Family in Past Time*, Cambridge: Cambridge University Press, 1972). See also L. Stone, *The Family, Sex and Marriage in England 1500--1800* (New York: Harper & Row, 1977).

28. See W. J. Goode, *The Family* (Englewood Cliffs, N.J.: Prentice-Hall, 1964), pp. 46--50.

29. See E. R. Wolf, *Peasant Wars of the Twentieth Century* (New York: Harper & Row, 1969), pp. 108--11.

30. M. Sahlins, *Stone Age Economics* op. cit., pp. 123--30; R. Firth, *Social Change in Tikopia* (New York: Macmillan, 1959).

31. J. Sklar, "The Role of Marriage Behavior in the Demographic Transition, The Case of Eastern Europe around 1900," *Population Studies* 28:2 (July 1974), pp. 231--49.

32. E. A. Hammel, "The Zadruga as a Process," in P. Laslett, ed., *Household and Family in Past Time*, (Cambridge: Cambridge University Press, 1972), pp. 335--74.

33. H. G. Creel, *Chinese Thought from Confucius to Mao Tse Tung* (Chicago: University of Chicago Press, 1953), p. 119 (Mentor edition).

34. See Hammel and other papers on Zadrugas in Laslett, op. cit.

35. See M. Djilas, *Land Without Justice* (New York: Harcourt, Brace, 1958).

36. T. K. Burch and M. Gendell, "Extended Family Structure and Fertility: Some Conceptual and Methodological Issues," in S. Polgar, ed., *Culture and Population* (Cambridge, Mass.: Schenckman Publishing Co., and Chapel Hill, N.C.: University of North Carolina, 1971), pp. 87--104.

37. For estimates of world population at various periods of history see J. D. Durand, "Modern Expansion of World Population," *Proceedings of the American Philosophical Society III* (June 1967), pp. 137, 139. For an alternate set of estimates see E. S. Deevey Jr., "The Human Population," *Science American* 20:3 (September 1960), pp. 195--204.

38. See S. Polgar, "Population History and Population Policies," op. cit., pp. 203--11; "Culture History and Population Dynamics," op. cit., pp. 3--8; D. E. Dumond, "The Limitation of Human Population: A Natural History," *Science* 187 (February 1975), pp. 713--21; M. Nag, "Anthropology and Population: Problems and Perspectives," *Population Studies* 27:1 (March 1973), pp. 59--78. Ethnographic studies attesting to the practice of birth control, abortion and infanticide by primitive people abound.

39. H. V. Valois, "The Social Life of Early Man: The Evidence of Skeletons," in S. L. Washburn, ed., *The Social Life of Early Man* (Chicago: Aldine, 1961).

40. Dumond, op. cit.

3

War and Civil Disorder

Introduction

War, brigandage and rebellion, often accompanied by pestilence, famine and a breakdown of social order, have at times checked population gowth and even on occasion temporarily reversed it. While no observer would claim that all wars involve population pressures, Malthusians regard population as a contributing factor in many wars and the principal cause of some, sufficient to place population pressures among the more important causes of war.

The instances where population pressures are often cited as important causes of war also include manifestations of lust for power and dominion, greed and economic conflict, hunger for glory, political rivalry and a host of other incitements sufficient in themselves to explain the occurrence of war. Population does not appear to influence the presence or intensity of these classic causes of war. Yet if war occurred when there appeared to be too many people, population pressure is likely to be blamed though there existed other causes which would carry the onus were it not possible to evoke overpopulation. If population pressures were indeed a significant factor, then wars should be more frequent and intense during times of population pressure, however that is defined, than during times of population decline, stagnation or when population pressures are not apparent. This does not appear to be the case. The pressures of other social, economic and political forces far outweigh those stemming from population and fertility behavior. Indeed, the latter is responsive to the conditions inducing and induced by war rather than being causative; high fertility may well compensate for social tensions which could otherwise lead to disorder.

A Primitive People and War

Consider J. V. Neel's sympathetic report on a primitive people.[1] These people, the Yanomamo, practice abortion, infanticide, prolonged lactation, and intercourse taboos which reduce their population growth. They are reported to live in harmony with their environment though not with each other. Infant and child mortality are relatively low compared to that of peasant societies of the not too distant past; their nutrition and health are good. But mortality among adults, particularly men, is unusually high, a consequence of village warfare, albeit on a primitive level, and even violence within villages.

Some primitive peoples depending on swidden cultivation of forest plots have been reported to fight each other over territory though, as shown later, they can increase the production of their lands by more intensive cultivation if needed. But the Yanomamo forest cultivators do not need to do either. Chagnon, an anthropologist and colleague of Neel, regards them as a pugnacious people who fight for glory and for women—even though there is sufficient food and there could be sufficient women if they did not practice female infanticide so intensively.

Female infanticide is more widely practiced among the Yanomamo than is male infanticide, so that the sex ratio of children is 1.4 males to 1.0 females As the children grow older the males die off in fighting and the sex ratio approaches 1.2 males for every female. One-third of adult male deaths recorded (109 out of 337) were due to violence, but violence was involved in only one-twentieth of female deaths (14 out of 273). In addition, a large number of male deaths (16 percent) and females (11 percent) were attributed by the Yanomamo to hostile witchcraft. Female children are not valued as they contribute little to the defense of the community and the men steal wives from other villages who thus have the expense of rearing them for the benefit of others. Despite the artificial shortage of women, the fiercer of the Yanomamo males have several wives.[2]

The Yanomamo, numbering between ten to fifteen thousand and slowly increasing, practice primitive cultivation in a remote forest region of Venezuela. They live in villages of 50 to 150 persons. If villages get larger, a split occurs, frequently accompanied by hostility, which is a regular feature of village life. Just as the Yanomamo do not live peacably within the precincts of their villages, the villages carry on frequent raids against each other, so that too small a village may not be a viable unit for defense. In some of the peripheral areas settled by groups forced from the "hot" interior, conflicts are less frequent, possibly, as Chagnon noted, because distances between villages are greater than in the interior and contact less easy. However, even in the interior areas, distances between villages are quite large; considerable travel is necessary for one village to raid another. Chagnon observed that sufficient territory and food is available; thus, the fighting appears due to ferocity, having no economic purpose.

Marvin Harris proposed a contrary explanation. The aggressiveness and female infanticide of the Yanomamo is due to overpopulation and scarcity, not of calories, for these are readily available, but of protein.[3] The tropical forests can provide only a limited amount of game, and killing each other limits the number of hunters. Harris notes that the Yanomamo distinguish between simply being hungry and having a craving for meat. Moreover, he notes that refugee Yanomamo, who fled the bloody interior and settled on the banks of the Orinoco, got plenty of protein by fishing; they are peaceable, and do not practice female infanticide. Harris proposes further that in previous times, when the Yanomamo were fewer, they depended more on hunting, and less on primitive cultivation. He doesn't say, however, how they managed to keep their numbers down. Nor does he entertain the possibility that the refugee Yanomamo may have been more peaceful types to begin with, and transmitted their peaceful ways to their children. Also, the craving for meat may have been a craving for prestigious food, particularly because it was scarce. Far from suffering protein deficiencies, they obtain as much or more animal proteins than does most of the world's population.

Social phenomena are often amenable to a variety of conflicting interpretations while observations can be adduced to support any thesis. The mountain Arapesh of New Guinea practice a primitive form of cultivation, have little food, particularly protein, and are a peaceable people. The Kwakiutl and other Indians of northwest America lived amist an abundance of animal foods, ingested much protein, and were extremely warlike and competitive.[4] Shall we attribute the Kwakiutl's competitiveness to a high protein diet and the mountain Arapesh's temperament to the yam?

Similar considerations apply to the interpretation of more complex societies. Harris, following Harner, attributed Aztec wars and the taking of captives for human sacrifices, whose limbs provided cannibal feasts for nobles, to the paucity of large meat-supplying mammals.[5] Ortiz de Montellano challenged this thesis as highly presumptuous. He noted that food was plentiful with large amounts of meat from small animals supplied as tribute, that sacrifices and cannibal feasts increased during the harvest season when food and tribute were most plentiful, that cannibalism was not practiced with the bodies of enemies slain in battle even in times of famine, and that in any case only a small portion of the diet of a small proportion of the population was comprised of human flesh. He concluded on the basis of research on Tenochtitlan (on the site of Mexico City), an Aztec city about which much information is available, that sacrifice and cannibalism was not due to a meat shortage, but was rather a quest for communication with the gods, and for the status therefrom.[6]

In view of the often insatiable and wasteful characteristics of human wants, scarcity can be located in almost any context. And since access to even abundant resources can be denied to segments of a population, scarcity does not necessarily signify environmental limitations. Thus scarcity is too facile an explanation to link population pressure to war. The argument must show that if there were fewer people in the same environment, they would have been richer, more peaceful, and their governments less aggressive. This is not evident from lessons of history. One can only say—and this on the basis of limited information—that humans were most peaceful when they were so few that unrelated groups rarely came across one another, and when their material needs were so simple that there was no need to covet another's wealth.

Migrants and Raiders

While continual conflicts and assassinations may keep the population of
some primitive groups at a low level, these conflicts are not necessarily a
response to overpopulation. Often little attempt is even made to appropriate
the enemy's resources. In contrast, the large-scale migrations of peoples who
overran the Americas, Europe, and Asia, did involve the expropriation of
other peoples, or at least moving in with them and sharing their resources.
While much of the movement and interpenetration of peoples even in the
ancient and medieval world was accomplished peacefully, history is dominated by the movements of such fighting tribes as the Huns, Goths, Mongols
and Turks. The fact that the conflict between the Visigoths and Rome was
not over territory but over compensation for military services, injustice, and
other complaints is often forgotten. Ardener noted that to the settled peoples,
the fighting tribes appeared to periodically expand and swarm out of steppe,
desert or elsewhere, and often they disappeared as rapidly as they came.[7] He
noted further that the apparent swarming of these invading nomads were
frequently due to their mobility and to the accretions of other peoples to their
ranks; their disappearance to their rapid assimilation into the conquered
people. The swarming of peoples is thus not necessarily due to increases of
population. Many of those who pressed on the borders of the great population enclaves such as Rome, Byzantium, China, and India were nomads.
Whether an increase in population, or an aggregation of many small tribes
under aggressive leadership eventually made these nomads so formidable,
population growth also provided the manpower for settled people to resist
nomadic incursion and provided the nomads with incentive to settle down.

After the Turkic Mongol peoples were united politically by Ghengis Khan
in the thirteenth century (enabling more devastating attacks on Europe,
India, and China), they enjoyed a peace at home without precedent. Before
the time of the Great Khan, the steppes of Asia were scenes of constant
internecine warfare, in which tribal groups were wont to eliminate each
other. The tribal group of the future Khan was itself virtually eliminated in
one of these feuds. During his childhood and youth he and his immediate
family were forced to take refuge in the taiga. Perhaps this led him to devote
his life to the unification of the Turkic Mongol people under the harsh
moral law of the Yasaq which, while it did not recognize a universal
humanity, proscribed arbitrary aggression among the peoples of the steppes.
The foreign traveller permitted to enter the Khan's domain could traverse the
Mongol realm relatively unmolested by brigands or by tribesmen, a situation
that made possible the journeys of Marco Polo, and other land travellers to
Cathay.[8]

A clear relationship between population, migration, and war is to be
found in the Scandinavia of the first millenium, which spawned the Germans, the Burgundians, and Goths, the Normans, the Lombards, and other
peoples.[9] The rugged Scandinavian land, much of it inhospitable and
unproductive, poor in both arable and pasture land, was called by some
ancient historical writers the "factory" of peoples, and the "matrix" (vagina)
of nations. Peoples swarmed from this hive to populate those areas of Europe

where resistance was weak. Other peoples (for example, Celts) were frequently displaced in the process.

Gwyn Jones, on whose work much of this account is based, proposed that the great migrations resulted from land shortages, aggravated by an unfavorable change in climate at the beginning of the Iron Age (around 400–500 B.C.) and by periodic overpopulation.[10] This conventional view not only oversimplifies but distorts the nature of the processes involved. During the Bronze Age the Scandinavians enjoyed a prosperity to which trade and cultural interchanges with the Mediterranean civilizations of the Greeks and Etruscans contributed significantly. The routes over which these interchanges took place were blocked when the Iron Age Celts, a fierce warrior people, occupied the Rhine and Danube valleys and the Atlantic and Channel coasts. Jones considered this to be of secondary importance in depressing the economy of Scandinavia, a judgment which would be difficult to validate. For the Celts, wild and aggressive, had become the principal outside cultural and trade contact of the Scandinavians. To cope with these people and to survive, the Scandinavians had to learn iron weaponry and war, eventually surpassing the Celts and their descendents in both. In the process they discovered that war could not only satisfy the ego, but could also be remunerative to those who were successful. In barbaric warfare conducted at a low level of organization and discipline, success depends not only on strength and ferocity, but also on numbers. (During the ninth and tenth centuries, the clemency of weather enabled the Northmen to cross the seas and harry Europeans far afield.[11] Had the weather been foul, it might have been said that population pressure had forced the raiders out as in earlier times.)

The Northmen's warlike behavior soon developed a functional autonomy of its own. War and violence were valued for their own sake, and predation became the economic activity of choice, glorified in ideology, religion, and saga. The trader and merchant Viking was ever ready to turn pirate or raider when opportunity afforded. Although farming and fishing were the principal sources of sustenance, raiding and piracy were essential parts of the Scandinavian economy. Other communities, and other tribes were legitimate prey. The *strandhogg* or victualling raid, in which stores and cattle belonging to another group were carried off, was standard practice; justice depended on belonging to a strong kinship or band which could exact bloody vengeance for wrongs done, although kings and *things* (assemblies) tried to mitigate the violence of blood feuds through the institution of *wergeld*. (This was payment, based on the worth of the victim, by the perpetrators of manslaughter to the aggrieved kin.)

Before the development of the long ship in the eight century, which enabled the Vikings to prey more effectively on Europe, the Norsemen preyed on each other. Many chieftains and their bands were driven out, some to establish dominion elsewhere. To survive and prosper, a man needed many strong sons, "a quiver full," as Jones wrote in his history of the Vikings. Despite the apparent population press, large numbers of people were captured from Slavic and other lands and imported as thralls to perform the necessary tasks at home allowing the free farmer and his sons to go marauding.

Tacitus wrote of the earlier Germans, who were derived from the same stock as the Vikings, "Nay, they think it tame and stupid to acquire by the sweat of toil what they may win by blood." And perhaps in comparison with the Romans, "To limit the number of their children or to destroy any of their subsequent offspring is accounted infamous, and good habits are here more effectual than good laws elsewhere." And "The more relatives he has, the more numerous his connections, the more honored in his old age; nor are there any advantages in childlessness."[12]

To return to the question—were the wars, destruction, and migrations of the Northmen due to overpopulation, or was their high birth rate due to their commitment to war and violence? When violent aggression is acceptable, and feasible, and the attribution of humanity is circumscribed by membership in kinship group, community, tribe, or nation, war may become just another economic enterprise. The taking of slaves was akin to the domestication of animals. The displacement or despoilment of other peoples differed only in degree from the displacement of the wolf from its lair or the rabbit from its warren. Demographic behavior thus served the purposes of war, and not the other way around. A chief defense against displacement was to be of sufficient numbers and strength to resist attack.

In the end the Viking was tamed not be a reduction in population growth but by a change in circumstances. The principal chieftains established central authorities, formalized justice, and limited the power of band chieftains. They abolished such practices as the victualling raid; they helped introduce Christianity, which broadened the Northman's view of humanity and may have even made him uncomfortable about enslaving Christians. Perhaps most important was the fact that in the meantime the Europeans had increased their capacity to resist predation in part by a growth in numbers. The descendants of the Viking settlers in England, Normandy, Ireland, and elsewhere contributed significantly to the new order in Europe and to its defense against the depredations of their former relatives. Raiding was resisted and the farmer Viking made do with a smaller farm and patrimony at home, became a tenant, even hired out as labor or perhaps sought grazing land in more northerly and higher mountain areas. In short, he had to get along at home and in peace, which, like other peoples, he too often broke. The initiation of war was left to the principal chiefs.

Similarly the incursions of forest and desert nomads that kept the populations of China, India, Russia, and other areas in check in ancient times, stopped only when populations and civilizations grew strong enough to deal with these aggressors. The fate of North American Indians and Australian aborigines can be blamed only in part on population pressures in Europe. The social and economic pressures, regardless of population, the wealth to be gained in the new world, a salubrious climate and ecology, and the inability of the aboriginal inhabitants to effectively resist displacement sealed their fate. Were the American Indians as numerous as the Asiatic Indians, they would not likely have been displaced.

Violence in the Middle Ages

In western Europe, the cessation of the Viking raids, and the internal peace resulting from the stabilization of the feudal order relieved some of the force of mortality that prevailed prior to the eleventh century. Then population increased through the thirteenth century. New agricultural techniques were introduced; marshes were drained and land reclaimed. Towns grew, and with them newly developed manufacturing and commercial enterprises. A new class of urban citizens, the bourgeoisie, came into being, even then challenging the prerogatives of the feudal order in the management of urban life. The gains in population growth over these three centuries were partially reversed by the Plague (Black Death) of the mid-fourteenth century. But there are some indications that population growth had already begun to slow down earlier as the opportunity for the internal colonization of Europe became limited.

Norman Cohn attributed the unrest and violence associated with the millenarianism of the Middle Ages, in part at least, to excessive population growth. Superfluous workers and others from rapidly growing Flanders and Brabant were quick to espouse millenarianism and other protest movements, or to take up arms as mercenaries. The latter occupation, temporary and seasonal, often left armed men without employment who turned to brigandage. Industrialization and commerce, in part a response to the stimulus of population, loosened old ties and created a dislocated and uprooted population.[13] Cohn presumed that if populations had been much smaller or had grown less rapidly, people would have found more productive and peaceful employments.

In the eleventh to fourteenth centuries, revolutionary outbreaks occurred in northern France and Belgium (Flanders); in Germany such outbreaks occurred from the thirteenth to the sixteenth centuries, and then later in the sixteenth century spread to the Netherlands along with the Reformation and violent chiliasm born of the peasant wars in Germany. During this period of six hundred years, there were times of population growth, decline and depopulation, as well as stagnation and later repopulation, and, despite Cohn's attribution of violence to overpopulation, there appeared to be little relationship between the extent of violence and the state of population. The first 250 years of the second millennium in Europe, when population was increasing and the economy expanding, appeared less affected by revolutionary upheavals and war than the subsequent period, after a decline in population to lowered levels and relative stagnation. The outbreaks of revolutionary chiliasm can be traced to the dislocations involved in the expansion of commerce and industry more readily than to so-called population pressures. And as agriculture became more and more commercialized, the countryside was also subjected to similar dislocations resulting from economic depressions, changing technologies and consequent unemployment.

From around 1000 to 1250 or 1300 A.D., depending on place, both the population and sustaining economy of western Europe grew, though not uniformly or without setbacks. Towns were encouraged to grow, and their citizenries were permitted considerable independence by local lords interested in promoting enterprise, industry and commerce. Full rights and freedom were guaranteed by town charters to those who resided in the city for a year and a day. City air the saying went, makes men free. Nonetheless, the economy was still overwhelmingly agricultural and the peasantry comprised 80 to 90 percent of the population. Reclamation of old lands and the development of new lands, the expansion of old settlements and the establishment of new—in effect, internal colonization—expanded the productive land area. In some places lords remitted feudal dues in kind and labor to monetary rents, permitted freer access to markets and allowed new, less constricting forms of land tenure and the formation of a yeomanry in some areas and the establishment of free communes in others to encourage new settlements. Peasant prosperity reached a peak in the middle of the thirteenth century, while lords who were but thugs at the beginning of this era of growth had become magnates by its end.[14] The later phases of this era of growth was characterized by relative peace as well as prosperity. Cantor wrote that there were no important wars from 1214 to 1290.[15] The period was, of course, not completely free of violence and disorder but it was markedly peaceful compared to the times which preceded it and those which followed, when population pressures were considerably less.

After 1250, economic growth had apparently become increasingly difficult, and by 1300 western Europe was in an economic depression. The conventional explanation is, as might be expected, that the limits of growth for that time had been reached. The available land had been fully utilized, and the Mongols, Turks, Slavs, Arabs and Moors contained the outward expansion of Europe, even in the matter of trade.[16] The cities, which depended on trade, were the first to experience the resurgence of violence in the latter part of the thirteenth century. Factional rivalries, particularly between the patriciate of merchants and professionals and the proletariat of artisans and laborers, always endemic in the trading cities of Flanders, France, Italy and Germany and elsewhere, increased in intensity sometimes reaching the pitch of armed and violent riots and civil disorder. A sequence of wet years and floods resulted in food shortfalls and famine in the last quarter of the thirteenth century and the first quarter of the fourteenth imposed further restraints on the economy and deepened the depression.[17]

Thus, though population growth was involved in the previous period of peace and prosperity, the impasse at the end of the thirteenth century is often attributed to the resulting population pressure exacerbated by military failures in the east and bad weather in the west. It is difficult to judge the degree of population pressure; if the nobles of the preceding two centuries had resisted the settling of the marshes, forests or other lands because they wished to save them for hunting or for herding (as they would later), the resulting distress would have been laid to overpopulation. However, an examination of various other developments may help to place the population issue in perspective.

The closing of the external frontiers, the land and sea trade routes to eastern Europe and Asia Minor, was not due to population pressure, the Slavs or the Turks, but to the avariciousness of the westerners. Constantinople, the capital of the Byzantine Empire, the bulwark against the Turk and other marauding peoples for five centuries, was taken and plundered in 1204 by adventurous Crusaders suborned to do so by Venetians interested in destroying a rival. Although the Byzantines eventually regained control of their city, they were never again a match for the Turks, who eventually took over that area. In the north, the advance of the Teutonic Knights into Russia and along the Baltic was being slowed in the middle of the thirteenth century and had almost stopped by the end of the fourteenth. Advancing into Slavic lands, ostensibly to Christianize heathens, this religious military order had established Prussia and other principalities oriented to the German states and cities. The Order of Teutonic Knights had also a reputation for being oppressors, making no distinction between Christians and pagans. In time they invited a stout resistance such as that of the famed Alexander Nevsky, ruler of the merchant city of Novgorod, who submitted to the Mongols so as to be able to mount a stronger resistance to the Knights.

Population started to decline shortly after the middle of the thirteenth century. Genicot hypothesized that the decline in population started with a drop in birth rates, and was accelerated by the flood and famine deaths which, as was noted, came later. Herlihy, examining public records in Tuscany, one of the more densely populated areas of Europe at the time, concluded that in rural Pistoia, population had declined around 23 percent from 1244 to 1344, four years before the Black Death; various evidentiary material indicated that a fall in birth rates was involved (see Chapter 9). In other areas the decline in population started a little later. What was evident was that population pressure, if it existed, was being relieved rapidly by a decline in fertility rather than by mortality.[18] Towns stopped growing, settlements contracted or were abandoned while many tracts of farm land, much of it marginal, were taken out of production.[19] If there had been considerable population pressure on land, it is doubtful that much land, even marginal land, would have been taken out of production as population declined.

While the people responded to the economic constraints of the late thirteenth century by reducing their number, the elites became more aggressive. Lacking the windfalls formerly derived from population and economic growth, they turned on each other as well as attempting to squeeze as much as they could from the mass of common people.

A Malthusian would presume that were the population of Europe smaller at that time, the conflicts might well have been mitigated; or that had there been room for further expansion, peace would have likely continued. Rarely in history do events permit such suppositions to be examined. However, the event that subsequently removed a sizeable portion of the population indicated that what Europeans really needed was not a reduction in population but a change in social institutions and economic structure. In the middle of the fourteenth century the Bubonic Plague—the Black Death—struck Europe, killing between a quarter to a third of the population (and more in places) in about three years. The Black Death was followed by periodic lesser and more localized epidemics over the next several decades. The resulting depopulation assured that there would be little or no population pressure for two centuries to come. As Europe recovered from the plague, the survivors could have considered themselves quite fortunate. Empty farms were available for the taking. The capital stock was large, having been geared to the size of a larger population. Opportunities for advancement were easier than in the days of internal colonization when marshes had to be drained. Many peasants were able to achieve yeoman status as lords found it dificult to find people to work their domains. In England, real wages increased until the battle of Agincourt (1415) and held steady for a century thereafter.[20]Increased wages may have been due as much to the quantities of unused capital developed by the previous generation and to the demand, generated by wars, for military manpower and material, as to a dearth of labor. Despite the available opportunities in civilian life, there was little trouble in recruiting mercenaries as the tempo of war and domestic violence increased in a relatively underpopulated Europe, in which land and resources were plentiful.

Within depopulated England, a wave of internal violence was climaxed by the Rising of 1381, little more than a generation after the Black Death. While wages rose and feudal services and work dues were remitted to cash payments for some peasants, even to their achieving yeomen status, many lords attempted by force to reinstitute feudal dues, keep their peasants tied to the land in serfdom, and otherwise turn back the clock. Parliament enacted "Statutes of Laborers," setting ceilings on wages and limiting the rights of the laborers to leave one job for another.

The Rising of 1381, though it ended largely in failure, was as successful a peasant revolt as the English were to experience. Rustic rebels joined Londoners to take that capital city. They beheaded the Archbishop of Canterbury and massacred foreign artisans, the competitors of English artisans, who were in short supply. The revolt was pacified by the granting of royal concessions including the commutation of feudal servile dues. Most concessions were revoked when the leaders were slain and order was restored. But peace did not come to England. Though there remained a glut of land and a dearth of people for a century or two, internal disorder and violence, of which the campaigns of the Wars of the Roses were but a small part, characterized the times. The year 1450 saw another major peasants' revolt, led by John Cade. Brigandage was rife and even landed proprietors attacked each others' holdings. Recourse to court and jury provided no relief because these institutions were easily bought or intimidated.[21]

In depopulated France, a much more oppressive and rapacious nobility, less controlled by the crown than their English counterparts, drove peasants to engage in terrorism and destructive risings—called the Jacqueries—often without program or leadership.

The violence experienced by England and France was not limited to internal disorders. The Hundred Years War, which began in 1337, eleven years before the plague, was halted by a truce a few months before the Black Death, resumed soon after the plague ran its course, and continued well into the fifteenth century. In central Europe, the violence of the fifteenth century was epitomized by the rebellion of radical Hussites. These millenarians, part of the revolutionary chiliastic movement traced by Cohn (as noted earlier), defeated imperial armies and were responsible for much slaughter before they were overcome. They helped lay the foundation for the later Protestant Reformation and the peasant and religious wars which followed.

The increasing tendency to violence noted at the end of the thirteenth century, and attributed by some to the press of population on resources—the closing of the medieval frontier,[22] was not mitigated when population pressure was relieved, even after the shock and dislocations of the Black Death had run their course. One might argue that there were insufficient people remaining to staff the economy, witness the attempts to refeudalize peasants and restrict the freedom of workmen. Yet there were no fewer people in Western Europe than there were two or three centuries earlier when the population, with fewer endowments, had set out on the long course of growth. There is no indication that workers of the later more violent era were less productive than those of earlier more peaceful times. The surge of violence lay not in the state of population and resources to which people were adapting but to the social order and the aspirations of elites.

Social stress may thus be found when the population increases, decreases, or remains stationary. Indeed, as has been seen, economic expansion (and associated population growth) may incline to peace. When economic expansion slows, even as population levels fall below their former levels, as in the later Middle Ages in Europe, conflict ensues as lower classes attempt to hold their position, while the upper classes attempt to maintain their style. Peace depended on economic growth; a corrupted and exploitative nobility inhibited such growth while a stationary or declining population could not support it.

The Decline of Spain

A pattern often found in the history of various societies is that a period of economic and population growth is followed by a reversion to stagnation and disorder. A simple and facile Malthusian explanation might have it that the period of growth and order was due to technological innovation and discoveries that expanded the resource horizons of the society, and that eventually the population again pressed on resources causing stagnation and disorder.

A contrasting point of view is associated with historians such as the medieval Arab, Ibn Khaldun, and Arnold Toynbee, who saw history in terms of the cyclical rise and fall of civilizations. In the initial phases of a civilization, the elites were presumed to be enterprising and creative. The populace faced the future hopefully, population grew, and this growth sustained prosperity. With time and the accumulation of power and wealth, the elites became inept, oppressive, and corrupt. The general public became pessimistic when confronted by political decay, civil turbulence, and economic decline, and depopulation followed.

Consider Spain, the leading power of the sixteenth century, which with the rest of the Mediterranean region of that time was the subject of a monumental, detailed study by Braudel which is largely Malthusian.[23]

The marriage of Ferdinand and Isabella in 1469, in effect uniting the kingdoms of Aragon and Castille, paved the way for the unification of Spain. The wars with the Moors ended and the last of the Moors was expelled in 1492; internal wars among Christians were stopped; the power of nobles was limited; lawless nobles and other brigands who harassed the people were suppressed; taxation and coinage were reformed, and the stage was set for an economic expansion further enhanced by the discovery of America, a venture financed by the crown. The royal revenues of Castille, from customs duties, had increased six-fold between 1477 and 1482, indicating that economic growth had gained momentum even before the discovery of America. The revenues from Castillian commerce had increased thirty-fold during the three decades after 1474.[24]

Economic growth in Spain (and other Mediterranean lands) was accompanied by population growth during the sixteenth century. In the initial part of this period, there appeared to be considerable room for expansion. The population of Castille was estimated about three million in 1530, four million in 1541, (indicating in-migration as well as natural growth) and six million in 1591.[25] Poor as these estimates may be, there can be no doubt about the considerable growth of the Spanish population and economy during this century. The windfalls of economic growth were not sufficient to eliminate class conflict. During the early part of the sixteenth century, when there was still considerable room for the population expansion which was already gaining momentum, several rebellions occurred: the Comuneros in the towns of Castille (1521); the Germanias in Valencia (1525–26), and others in various Mediterranean regions including Italy. The revolts were short-lived and handily suppressed by the increasingly powerful states. The latter half of the sixteenth century, when population growth was more rapid, saw fewer revolts though vagrancy and banditry may have increased.[26]

If economic expansion did not eliminate class conflicts, it may have mitigated them though this would be difficult to demonstrate. However, the economic elites, finding their efforts profitably employed in expanding the economy, may have been less prone to oppress the lower orders. But in those days continued economic expansion depended, to a large extent, on the increase in population as well as on entrepreneurial abilities.

Banditry and brigandage always endemic in the Mediterranean, appeared to Braudel to increase during the close of the sixteenth century. Braudel interprets the increase in brigandage to be a consequence of "pauperization and oppression by the high and powerful," the underlying cause being "the correlation between overpopulation and economic depression, an unrelieved double burden which dictated social conditions."[27] The connection between "overpopulation" and "depression" is found in the inelasticity of agriculture, that is, in its inability to provide food for the Spanish population and at the same time satisfy the demands of the "high and powerful." Even towards the end of the century, the land did not appear densely populated; twelve out of eighteen provinces of Castille were estimated to have had densities ranging from 11 to 20 inhabitants per square kilometer, and two provinces had densities of less than 10. Since much of this land was arid, this may not mean much without knowing the potential productivity of the land relative to the available technology. While the productive capacity of land determines its carrying capacity, the productive capacity often depends on human works, such as irrigations systems, while the carrying capacity depends also on land use patterns. The fact is that the key economic decisions as to land use were the prerogative of the rich and powerful.

In the sixteenth century, precious metals from the New World enabled elites to import what they wanted, decreasing domestic employments and markets, disastrous to productive enterprise. The evidence is that the purported increase in brigandage was associated not with an inability of the economy to expand but with a marked contraction of the economy due to the oppressiveness of the ruling elites. Lands formerly tilled were left empty as peasants were evicted or left their holdings because they could not meet the increasing rents, taxes, and interest. Rather than being limited by physical resources, the population was denied access to those resources. The population of Spain declined as a response to these conditions, a decline which did not bring internal peace. In the seventeenth century Spain presented a paradox of land that was available for settlement and cultivation, but many people preferred to go overseas, or turn brigand and vagabond rather than work under the existing proprietorships. Rebellion was also seen in the depopulated Spain of the seventeenth century, the Catalan peasant rebellions of 1640–52 and again in 1705–14 being among the more notable.[28]

The mercantilists neglected food production for commercial and associated cash crops. But as the enterprisers grew rich and powerful, they became parasitic, incompetent and obstructive, a drag on the economy. With a population half the size of France, Spain is reputed to have had four times as many nobles, many of them former merchants who had purchased titles. The taxation and exactions required to support the governmental and private sector elites destroyed both the opportunity and the incentive of peasants to work.[29]In time, Spanish agriculture was refeudalized, with the peasants producing subsistence plus a surplus in rent, and population growth resumed its course in the eighteenth century.

Braudel has amassed a wealth of data on the social, economic, geographic, and demographic conditions of the sixteenth century Mediteranean world, but for all the data collected, the attempt to relate population pressure to social conflict is strained and circular. Thus, he noted, "Proof of overpopulation of Mediterranean Europe after the end of the fifteenth century is the frequent expulsion of the Jews, who were driven out of Castille and Portugal in 1492, from Sicily in 1493, from Naples in 1540 and 1541, from Tuscany in 1571 and finally from Milan in 1597." And again, "Christian intolerance, *the consequence of large numbers* [my italics] did not welcome strangers, it repelled them. And all those expelled from its lands—the Jews of 1492, the Moriscos of the sixteenth century and 1609–1614—joined the ranks of the voluntary exiles, all moving towards Islam where there was work and money to be had."[30]

The fierce hostility of Christians to Jews and Moslems (including the Marranos and Moriscos, former Jews and Moslems, respectively, who had converted to Catholicism but were accused of maintaining their old ways) had a long history. Intolerance did not wait on population pressure; it occurred even when the land was relatively underpopulated. Long before the expulsion in 1492, there were the anti-Jewish riots and civil disorders; the terrible pogrom that began on Ash Wednesday of 1391 took tens of thousands of lives and resulted in many more forced conversions. Persecutions occurred continuously. In 1473 there were widespread riots and disorders against converted Jews (Marranos) accused of secretly desecrating their adopted religion.[31] Widespread pogroms against Jews began when Europe was free of population pressures by any criterion. When the Jews were finally expelled in 1492, after the Christians had completed the conquest of the entire Iberian Penninsula, bringing peace and order, the land was, as noted earlier, entering an economic and population boom. On the other hand, the Moriscos were expelled from 1609 to 1614, depending on the region, during a period of depopulation that was of considerable concern to the royal councils. Much of the land farmed by the Moriscos was left vacant, thereby aggravating the agricultural decline in seventeenth-century Spain.[32]

In summary, internal disorders whether expressed in wars between nobles, brigandage, violence against minorities, and revolts, appeared to have little relation to the number of people or the amount of resources. These disorders are best understood in terms of the policies of those in power. Similarly with the wars of the Spanish against the Moors and Turks, and later against the British, French and Dutch. Wars raged before the population spurt of the sixteenth century, and during the sixteenth century, and into the seventeenth century when Spain faced problems of depopulation. An eighteenth century Spanish reformer wrote, "In Spain three things which must support the greatness and wealth of any powerful monarchy lie almost neglected: land, men, and money. . . . Ten thousand leagues of excellent land, two or three millions of idle hands, and many millions of pesetas buried in private hoards—is there a richer mine than this in the world?"[33]

Peasant War in China

In its long history, China has suffered through many periods of war, dynastic conflict, rebellion and internal disorder. During much of this time China's population was relatively small. A census conducted in the late Han period (100 A.D.) reported a population of 60 million.[34] Four hundred years before Christ, the Chinese philosopher Mo Tzu, optimistic about the potential accomplishments of humans under a wise and benevolent ruler, held that the quest for peace and order would be advanced by a growth in population and the wealth that it would generate. Mo Tzu concluded that the disorders of his day were the result of too many oppressive rulers and too few common people. A century and a half later, the legalist Han Fu Tsu, suspicious of human nature, which he regarded as basically evil, and exalting the role of rulers as keepers of the peace, blamed the violence of the times on there being too many people contending with one another while the rulers were lax and not sufficiently repressive.[35] China's population continued to grow, though not uniformly. During the first millennium after Christ, its size appeared to be stable. Yet, though many scholars are ready to discern a relationship between population pressure and violence in China, there is no evidence that times of low or stationary population levels brought peace.

The outbreak of peasant disorders in China at the end of the eighteenth century and culminating but not ending with the disastrous T'aiping Rebellion of 1850-64, followed a century of relative peace and population growth. Previously, the Chinese population had sometimes fluctuated widely because of famine, pestilence, and war. Estimates of the Chinese population in 1650 range from 113 to 150 million.[36] This was shortly after China was conquered (1644) by a small northern warrior tribe, the Manchus, who established a dynasty which, in the beginning, was capable of enforcing internal order and security against the Mongol incursions. This peace, and the diffusion of crops such as the sweet potato, peanuts, and corn, introduced earlier from the New World, permitted an extended period of prosperity, accompanied by an increase in population. By the end of the eighteenth century, the population of China reached about 300 million. Ping-ti Ho estimated that the optimum population for greatest economic benefits per capita was reached and passed sometime between 1750 and 1775.[37]

Ping-ti Ho's conclusion was based on changes in the standard of living, which, before the middle of the eighteenth century was rising with population growth but afterwards deteriorated along with social and economic conditions, while population continued to grow. Needless to say, overpopulation was considered the culprit. Ping-ti Ho did acknowledge, however, that the government and the economic elites had become corrupt and ineffective, and that this contributed to the ills of society. Still, while concluding that a more effective social order might have redressed some prevailing inequities and alleviated suffering, he did not believe that it would have stopped the decline in productivity. But oppression affects production as well as distribution.

The history of China under the Manchus conformed to the typical Chinese dynastic pattern which had been recurring since the times of the Chin and Han dynasties two hundred years before Christ. As dynasties aged, they lost their vigor and control over the officials and bureaucrats on whom depended the maintenance of order.[38] The more powerful groups in the public and private sectors competed viciously with one another and exploited the underclasses with little restraint. Corruption and oppression increased; the economy deteriorated; civil disorder and rebellion followed and opened the way for some enterprising warrior chief to establish a new dynasty. Then the same scenario would be acted out. Chinese demographic historians tend to attribute dynastic dissolution to population pressure but it is evident that other conditions, which were independent of population growth, were sufficient in themselves to account for the dissolution.

The early Manchus did not depend on naked force alone to maintain order but also lifted a great number of surtaxes which had lain heavily on the Ming peasantry. They froze other taxes, encouraged more intensive cultivation, and discouraged the production of non-cereal commercial crops such as tobacco while increasing public purchases and storage of rice. The apparent result of these policies was prosperity, an increase in population, and at the same time, for a while at least, an unprecedented increase in the standard of living, which by Pint-ti Ho's reckoning, lasted until the final quarter of the eighteenth century. Poor and sparsely populated counties became densely populated and included in their numbers several hundreds with small fortunes while wine, silk and meat, formerly rarely seen, became common articles of consumption. Cities became places of luxurious living, extravagant and wasteful. The demand of the rich for goods not available locally supported a large commerce and handicraft industry, remarkable by European standards of the time.

At the same time, the price of rice rose steadily without regard to the occurrence of bumper crops or reduction of public purchases. Again, the reason most frequently given for this trend is population growth although note was also taken of the levels of public extravagance, of rice hoarding, and of price manipulation by the rich. The fact that bumper crops and the reduction of large-scale government purchases of rice had little effect on the price trend would indicate that market forces were not operating freely, and that the inflation of those days may not have been due any more to a rising population than the inflation in modern western Europe and the United States is due to a relatively stagnant population.

The increased prosperity served, among other things, to whet the appetite of powerful individuals for more. Landowners vied to increase the size of their holdings. In late Ming times, the biggest landowners in the Sung-chiang area owned only a few thousand mou.* After the Manchus consolidated their power and prosperity ensued, the same prefecture contained many great landlords whose estates ranged from 10,000 to 50,000 mou and more. In Hunan, 50 percent of the crops went to rent, and the governor of the province in 1748 suggested, unsuccessfully, that land owned by a single household be limited to 3,000 mou. The landlords of Kwangtung were so oppressive that the poor were afraid to rent land from them. Provincial officials warned that unless security of tenure was guaranteed by the government, the fertile lands of west central Kwangtung would not be developed, even though the eastern part contained a surplus of people.[39]

The Manchus, who in their early reigns were concerned with the plight of the poor, protected the rights of property as a primary government obligation although the exercise of property rights by some resulted in the impoverishment of many. As prosperity increased the rich grew richer and more influential while the peasants lost whatever protection the government could provide. The official bureaucracy, obviously dissatisfied with the handsome salaries that were supposed to keep them honest were corrupted and allied themselves with the local elite to the detriment of government and populace. They found ways of circumventing the limitation of land taxes by increasing the number of surtaxes, a practice carried over by the warlords of republican China. By the middle of the eighteenth century, gross corruption was evident in the central administration as well as in the provinces.[40] The ultimate source of funds was, as usual, the peasantry.

The failure of the regime was hastened by the appearance of the colonial powers, though its eventual demise must be laid primarily to the stultification, corruption, and venality of the government and upper classes. Early in the nineteenth century, China was opened to imperialist domination and forced to allow foreign goods to enter local markets. England went to war with China to open that country to the opium trade which was so profitable to British interests in India, but so devastating to the Chinese. Opium cultivation displaced food production in some areas. Protected foreign goods displaced rural handicraft industries. Between 1860 and 1890, Lancashire textiles drove native cotton cloth entirely out of urban markets.[41] Indemnities levied against the government by the imperialist nations were passed down in the form of additional taxes to peasants already impoverished by increased demands on their surplus. That the population, as it grew, exceeded that which would have provided optimal economic welfare (as proposed by Ping-ti Ho) was, however, not unlikely. Recall the distinction made earlier between the optimum *welfare* population size and the optimum *power* population size. The optimum power population size produces the larger surplus even though the per capita output is less than

---

*The size equivalent for the mou is frequently given as 6½ to the acre. The mou, however, was not entirely an areal measurement, but was also—for purposes of taxation—a unit determined by productivity as well as size. Thus a mou of irrigated land capable of producing two or three crops a year could be smaller (say one sixth of an acre) compared to a mou of plateau land receiving little annual rainfall.

that of the optimum welfare population size. The social structure and relationship with powerful overlords obliged peasant families to produce large surpluses if they were to survive, and survival is, of course, a prerequisite to welfare.

The first Chinese rebellion in a hundred years broke out in Shantung in 1774 (around the time that widespread corruption was becoming evident). It was followed by others: Kansu in 1781 and 1784; Formosa in 1786–1787; Hunan and Kweichou in 1795–1797; Hupei, Szechwan and Shensi in 1796–1804.[42] Suppression of these uprisings devastated and impoverished whole provinces. The T'aiping Rebellion of 1850–1864 consumed some twenty million lives and was suppressed with the aid of western powers. Inspired by their interpretation of Christian ideology, the leaders of the T'aiping Rebellion proposed such social reforms as the abolition of the opium traffic, the improvement of the status of women, the establishment of communal economic organizations, and land tenure reforms.

Clubb, in an otherwise excellent book, states that the increase of the population of China from an estimated 60 million during the Ming dynasty to 300 million under the Manchus was not evidence of the capacity of the country to provide for an ever growing population. The increase was made possible by the peace enforced by the Manchu conquerors and a limited expansion of productive capacity. The rebellions and disorders at the end of the eighteenth century were, according to Clubb, the result of a growing imbalance between population and food supply.[43] Would conditions have been better without growth?

How is one to choose between this popular explanation of China's troubles and that proposed here? Ping-ti Ho, who did not hesitate to invoke Malthus in explaining the demise of the Manchus, found no evidence of population pressure during the latter part of the Ming dynasty. Yet the late Ming period was characterized by comparable corruption, oppression and rebellion which eventually laid it open to the disorders of bandit armies and conquest by the Manchus.[44] Common to both dynasties at the end were oppressiveness, corruption and incompetence: not the size of population.

To the contrary, what carried people through these periods were strong—albeit poor—families, capable of compensating for the deficiencies of government and formal society. Despite the intervening wars, famines, civil disorders, heavy taxation, warlords, and brigandage, and possibly even because of the heavy load these placed on the people, the population of China increased from the somewhat more than 300 million at the beginning of the nineteenth century to almost 600 million in 1950. And these millions did not appear to be any more wretched in their condition than was the smaller population of the previous century. Now the population of China had grown to about 900 million who are purported to be better off than fewer than half that number were a century earlier.

War in Recent Times

Not long ago, the aggressions of Germany and Japan were attributed to population pressures. But these nations were no less expansionist in the late nineteenth century when, with smaller populations, they embarked on an imperial policy, than they were in the 1930s and 1940s. Since then, with access to world markets and resources, these nations—even more densely populated now—have been among those most active economically and comparatively peaceful. Today, war and peace depend largely on the policies of the United States and the Soviet Union, both relatively sparsely populated and with considerable potential for self-sufficiency. Both are large enough to support the industry and technology on which their power is based, and both are using that power to maintain a dominant economic and political position worldwide. Many of the small-scale international conflicts which plague the world today are exacerbated by the involvement of these two nations.

Whatever the demographic condition of a society, it can be related in some fashion to the troubles of that society. When not troubled by war, South Vietnam had long been a rice surplus area. Nor was much labor required to produce that rice, except perhaps in the peak agricultural seasons. Stroup and Gift,[45] in analyzing a rural income and expenditure survey of the early 1960s hypothesize that more labor was used to produce the rice crop of South Vietnam than was actually necessary; the same crop could have been produced by a smaller work force. Thus, much of the agricultural labor force might as well have been unemployed, there being too many people for the work which needed to be done. (The concept of hidden unemployment from which this theme is derived is discussed later in other contexts.) Stroup and Gift stated, in a rejoinder to critics,

Hence, on many days during the year, the opportunity cost of leaving the fields for participation in revolutionary activities was low. This should be viewed in the light of the large number of days of overt idleness among the members of rice producing households. Taken together, disguised and overt underemployment formed a significant part of the resource base for revolutionary activity in particular and institutional change in general, in rural South Vietnam in 1964.[46]

Paradoxically, the provinces of South Vietnam which were most insurgent during the war against the United States supported government of South Vietnam (G.V.N.) were those which were less densely populated and where land was more equitably distributed. Frances Fitzgerald wrote, "the ideal province from the point of view of G.V.N. control would be one where inequality was the most severe, where there had been no G.V.N. land reforms and where the population density was highest and communications the poorest."[47] These conclusions were consistent with findings of a technical study by the Rand Corporation.[48] The Rand Corporation and its sponsor, the United States government were reported to have concluded that landlordism and land reform were not significant issues in the insurgency which was regarded as ideologically and politically motivated. Fitzgerald noted, however, that the military conflict had its source in a deep social conflict. In the so-called "peaceful" provinces where landlordism and inequality prevailed, the economy operated much in the way of a traditional subsistence peasant society. Landlords (including leaders of the Hoa Hao and Cao Dai sects) were paternalistic, providing peasants with help in times of trouble and gifts to help defray the costs of births, deaths, and the like. They settled disputes and administered justice. Though the landlords collected heavily in the course of performing these functions, they did maintain some modicum of stability and security. On the other hand, in those areas where land-holdings appeared to be more equitably distributed, a commercial or market economy prevailed. The frail security afforded the peasants by the tradi-tional way was gone. Without political or economic power, the peasants were subject to the exploitations of officials and profiteers, experiencing a condition of economic insecurity not reflected in the cold statistics of landholding patterns. Along with peasants, small tradesmen and service workers also felt themselves to be much abused and insecure under the then current regime and provided a source of support for the National Liberation Front rebels and their North Vietnamese supporters. For the purposes of our discussion, the vital point is that there was little connection between population density and the revolution in Vietnam.

One of the mathematical consequences of an increase in the rate of population growth is an increase in the proportion of young people. The result is pressure on society to provide increased places and employments to accommodate these youths. Moller has argued that an increase in the proportion of young adults is associated with civil commotion, citing a number of historical examples.[49]

The increase in the proportion of United States youth and the associated commotion in the 1960s may be taken as a case in point. But the proportion of young people in the United States is higher still in the 1970s and for the time being, they seem to be less inclined to challenge the establishment even though they face more difficulties economically. The end of the war in Vietnam and the removal of the possibility of forced military service was likely an important factor. France, with one of the lowest population growth rates of nineteenth-century Europe, saw more than its share of civil com-motion, while mid-Victorian England (with relatively high population growth) appeared to be a model of order. In Latin America of the recent past, Chile, Argentina and Uruguay, with relatively low fertility and growth, have been among the most unstable politically. Costa Rica, on the other hand, with very high growth rates and, until recently, with very high fertility, has been among the most politically stable of Latin American countries. Mexico was more politically unstable in the early part of the twentieth century when, due to higher death rates, its population growth rate was a fraction of its current rate, and the proportion of young people in its population was smaller.

The age composition of a population has a direct relationship to such problems as juvenile delinquency and violent crime, which young people are better able to perpetrate than old. But the contribution of age structure to such problems may be small as compared to that of social, economic, and cultural circumstances.

An Aside on a Different Opinion

A recent study by Nazli Choucri of violent conflicts in developing areas (including Cyprus, Ulster, and Bay of Pigs) between 1947 and 1973[50] would appear to contradict the theses presented here, and deserves comment. A summary by the author states,

Detailed analysis of 45 conflicts in Asia, Africa, and Latin America between 1945 and 1969 [sic] indicated that population factors played a role in 38 of the conflicts. Composition and distribution of population seem to play a larger role than sheer population size and changes in composition (ethnic, religious, racial, or tribal) appear both to exacerbate conflict and to affect the parameters of conflict situations.[51]

Choucri's listing of population factors is so inclusive that it is surprising that it was not possible to find a population factor for the remaining seven instances of violence. Each factor is so inclusive that a variety of social phenomena with different causes and dynamics are classed under a single rubric. Population movement covers political refugees, migrant workers and transhumant nomads. Population movement (migration) is credited as a minor irritant contributing to the Bay of Pigs invasion, but of central importance in the Palestine War of 1947–49 between the Arabs and Israelis. The war between El Salvador and Honduras in July 1969, over the Honduran expulsion of some 11,000 Salvadorean migrants, provoked by riots set off by a soccer match, was ended in a few days. And this was despite the tensions between these countries related to the population pressure in El Salvador and the low population density and the employment opportunities in Honduras. This war, however, is given the same weight by Choucri as the conflict between Ethiopia and Somalia. Although neither country is heavily populated, they have been fighting for more than a decade and a half over some desert lands, part of the range of Somali nomads claimed by Ethiopia. Population factors are credited by Choucri as being major irritants in the conflict but the factors in this case are classified by Choucri as population movements and ethnic divisional conflicts. These are hardly related to population pressure.

Population pressure is credited as a central cause in the takeover of West Irian (formerly Dutch New Guinea) by Indonesia. Although Java, the principal island of Indonesia, is densely populated, the outer islands, including Sumatra are not. The Indonesian government has had no more success than the Dutch in promoting emigration to the outer islands, which are certainly more attractive than New Guinea.

Population pressure is credited with being the sole determinant in the 1971 insurrectionary riots in Sri Lanka (Ceylon), a direct result of food shortages and large-scale unemployment which also exacerbated ethnic hostilities. The underlying presumption is that were the population smaller and growing at a less rapid rate, the relative number of jobs available and the rate of economic growth would be larger. This presumption is, as will be discussed later, unwarranted. Unemployment and economic stagnation arise from other factors to which Sri Lanka is particularly subject. Sri Lanka's economy is heavily dependent on the export of plantation crops— tea, coconuts, and rubber—which account for one-third of the net domestic product and are under private, and in large part, foreign, management. The plantations also severely limit the acreage available for food crops. Were it not for the resistance of the peasantry, the acreage given over to plantations might be larger still. Economic depression is induced by the lagging world demand for some export crops, and it is exacerbated by a stultified elite (in government, labor and business) incapable of reforming the economy, and all too ready to appeal to ethnic prejudice to maintain their position.[52]

Since population had been increasing, the stresses which occurred were predictably blamed on population growth; in a period of population stagnation and decline, the stresses leading to conflict might just as easily have been attributed to that. Nonetheless, population size and growth do not appear to have been as important, overall, as factors such as the distribution of peoples and the changes in ethnic composition. The period was one in which the countries of Asia and Africa were beginning to exercise their independence from colonial rule. This rule had kept the peace, and by subsuming under a single political administration those traditionally conflicting ethnic groups, it had minimized the possibility of a unified opposition. As colonial rule was lifted, conflicts broke out between ethnic groups struggling for position and power. Population redistributions and migrations of people, sometimes forced, were accompanied by violence. "Population factors," a term which includes growth, size, density, distribution, ethnic and age composition, and the like, is too broad, reflecting too many different dynamics for useful employment in the analysis of population problems. In a broader overview, there appears little indication that stationary populations or sparsely settled peoples are any more peaceful than rapidly growing populations or heavily settled nations. Were the nineteenth and early twentieth centuries in Latin America any more peaceful than recent times?

Summation

Quincy Wright, in his monumental study of war, its history, its causes, and its control, devoted relatively little space (fewer than 30 out of 1,500 pages) to population changes and war.[53] He regarded the relationship between population and war as indeterminate, depending on a host of other factors; under certain conditions population growth (or pressure) could lead to war; under other conditions to peace. All in all, the role of population size and increase in causing war did not appear as consistent or clear in Wright's analysis as did the role of a plethora of other social, economic, political, cultural, and historic factors.

Wars and civil disorder helped check the growth and size of populations in the past. But this cannot be taken as evidence that population growth and pressure caused the war. There appears to be little relation between the intensity of violence exhibited by a society and its rate of population growth, its density or even the availability of resources to support its people. Examples of violent societies living under conditions of scarcity can be matched by violent societies living under conditions of relative abundance, as can examples of peaceable peoples living under conditions of abundance be matched with those living under conditions of scarcity.

The purported link between population and war is scarcity. Standards of scarcity based more on psychological and socially derived values than on physiological needs may be defined into existence to suit any occasion. Yet in the history of war, population pressures, which implies scarcity, appeared to play a small part. The case might even be made that as population grew, and with it greater political order, the internecine local wars which plagued people were brought under control, while the risk of a people being driven from their lands, as were the American Indians by Europeans, diminished.

Notes

1. J. V. Neel, "Lessons from a Primitive People," *Science* 170 (November 1970), pp. 815–22.

2. N. A. Chagnon, "Tribal Social Organization and Genetic Microdifferentiation," in G. A. Harrison and A. J. Boyce, eds. *The Structure of Human Populations* (Oxford: Clarendon Press, 1972), pp. 252–82. See also N. A. Chagnon, *Yanomamo, The Fierce People* (New York: Holt, Rinehart and Winston, 1968).

3. M. Harris, *Pigs, Wars, and Witches: The Riddles of Culture* (New York: Random House, 1974).

4. See M. Mead, "The Arapesh of New Guinea," and I. Goldman, "The Kwakiutl of Vancouver Island," in M. Mead, ed., *Cooperation and Competition Among Primitive Peoples* (Boston: Beacon Press, 1961), pp. 20–50, 180–209.

5. M. Harris, *Cannibals and Kings: The Origins of Cultures* (New York: Random House, 1977), pp. 97–110.

6. B. R. Ortiz de Montellano, "Aztec Cannibalism: An Ecological Necessity?" *Science* 200 (May 1978), pp. 611–17.

7. E. Ardener, "Social Anthropology and Populations," in H. B. Parry, ed., *Population and Its Problems* (Oxford: Clarendon Press, 1974).

8. See R. Grousset, *The Empire of the Steppes: A History of Central Asia* (English translation, New Brunswick, N.J.: Rutgers University Press, 1970), pp. 252, 304–13.

9. This account of the Vikings leans heavily on Jones, *A History of the Vikings* (New York: Oxford University Press, 1968). The interpretation of that history is my own.

10. Ibid., pp. 19–20, 196–98.

11. R. A. Bryson and T. J. Murray, *Climates of Hunger* (Madison: University of Wisconsin Press, 1977), p. 67.

12. Tacitus, *The Agricola and Germany*, reprinted in part in B. Tierney, *The Middle Ages*, Vol. I, "Sources of Medieval History," 2nd ed. (New York: Alfred A. Knopf, 1973), pp. 34–44.

13. N. Cohn, *The Pursuit of the Millennium* 2nd ed. (New York: Harper Torchbooks, 1961), pp. 21–32.

14. See B. Lyon, "Medieval Real Estate Developments and Freedom," *American Historical Review* 63 (1952), 47–61. See also B. Tierney and S. Painter, *Western Europe in the Middle Ages, 300–1475* (New York: Alfred A. Knopf, 1970), p. 230.

15. N. F. Cantor, *Medieval History* 2nd ed. (London: Collier-Macmillan Ltd., 1969), p. 461.

16. See A. R. Lewis, "The Closing of the Medieval Frontier: 1250–1350," *Speculum* 33 (1958), pp. 475–83.

17. See M. M. Postan, "Medieval Agrarian Society in its Prime," in M. M. Postan and H. S. Habakkuk, eds., *Cambridge Economic History of Europe*, Vol. I., 2nd ed. (Cambridge: Cambridge University Press, 1966), pp. 546–632.

18. L. Genicot, "Crises, From Middle Ages to Modern Times," in *Cambridge Economic History of Europe*, Vol. I, pp. 660–741; and D. Herlihy, "Population and Social Change in Rural Pistoia, 1201–1430," *Economic History Review* 2nd Series XVIII: 2 (1965), pp. 225–44.

19. M. M. Postan, "Some Economic Evidence of Declining Population in the Later Middle Ages," *Economic Review, 2nd Series, II (1950), p. 221.

20. W. A. Cole and P. Deane, "Growth of National Incomes," *Cambridge Economic History of Europe*, VI, pp. 1–55.

21. See G. M. Trevelyan, *English Social History* (Harmondsworth: Pelican Books, 1967), pp. 25–33, 73–75.

22. A. R. Lewis, op. cit., pp. 475–83.

23. Fernand Braudel, *The Mediterranean and the Mediterranean World in the Age of Philip II*, 2 vols. (English translation, New York: Harper and Row, 1972).

24. R. Ergang, *Europe from the Renaissance to Waterloo* (New York: D. C. Heath, 1939), pp. 14–15.

25. Braudel, op. cit., pp. 405–407.

26. Braudel, op. cit., p. 739.

27. Braudel, op. cit., p. 735.

28. R. Herr, *The Making of Spain* (Englewood Cliffs, N.J.: Prentice-Hall, 1971).

29. Ergang, op. cit., pp. 275–79; E. G. Hamilton, "The Decline of Spain," *Economic History Review* 8 (1938), 168–79; J. B. Cortes, "The Achievement Motive in the Spanish Economy

Between the 13th and 18th Centuries," *Economic Development and Cultural Change*, 9 (1960), pp. 144–63. Cortes, analyzing Spanish literature for the period, concludes that the decline in the economy was long preceded by a decline in achievement motivation.

30. Braudel, op. cit., pp. 415, 800.

31. A. L. Sachar, *A History of the Jews* (New York: Alfred A. Knopf, 1965), pp. 204–13. See also C. Roth, *A History of the Marranos* (New York: Harper Torchbooks, 1966), pp. 14–16.

32. Braudel, op. cit., p. 795.

33. Bernardo Ward, quoted in H. A. Trevor Roper, *Men and Events* (New York: Harper, 1957), p. 263.

34. R. Linton, *The Tree of Culture* (New York: Alfred A. Knopf, 1955), p. 557.

35. H. G. Creel, *Chinese Thought from Confucius to Mao Tse Tung* (Chicago: University of Chicago Press, 1953), pp. 45–54, 122–24.

36. United Nations, *The Determinants and Consequences of Population Trends*, ST/SOA/Series A, Population Studies, No. 17 (New York: United Nations, 1953), p. 8.

37. Ping-ti Ho, *Studies on Population of China: 1368–1953* (Cambridge, Mass.: Harvard University Press, 1959), p. 270; see also Kung-chuan Hsiao, *Rural China, Imperial Control in the 19th Century* (Seattle, Wash.: University of Washington Press, 1960).

38. See W. H. Langer, ed., *An Encyclopedia of World History*, 5th ed. (Boston: Houghton Mifflin, 1972), p. 145, and sections on China.

39. Ping-ti Ho, op. cit., pp. 196–226.

40. Ibid., p. 216.

41. Ibid., p. 207.

42. Langer, *An Encyclopedia of World History*, *pp. 578–79, 909–916.*

43. O. E. Clubb, *20th Century China*, 2nd ed. (New York: Columbia University Press, 1972), p. 11.

44. Ping-ti Ho, op. cit., p. 265.

45. R. H. Stroup and R. E. Gift, "Underemployment in Rural South Vietnam," *Economic Development and Cultural Change* 19 (April 1971), pp. 414–23.

46. R. H. Stroup and R. E. Gift, "Underemployment in Rural South Vietnam: A Reply," *Economic Development and Cultural Change* 23: 1 (October 1974), pp. 161–62.

47. See F. Fitzgerald, *Fire in the Lake* (Boston: Little, Brown, 1972), pp. 150–57.

48. E. J. Mitchell, "Inequality and Insurgency: A Statistical Study of South Vietnam," *World Politics* 20 (April 1968), pp. 421–38. (Cited in Fitzgerald, op. cit., p. 152.)

49. A. Moller, "Youth as a Force in the Modern World," *Comparative Studies of Society and History* (April 1968), pp. 237–60.

50. N. Choucri, *Population Dynamics and International Violence* (Lexington, Mass.: D. C. Heath, Lexington Books, 1974).

51. W. P. Mauldin, N. Choucri, F. W. Notestein, and M. Teitlebaum, *A Report on Bucharest* (The World Population Conference and the Population Tribune 1974), *Studies in Family Planning* 5: 12 (December 1974), p. 370.

52. G. Myrdal, *Asian Drama* (New York: Pantheon Books, 1968), pp. 343–58, 431–47.

53. Q. Wright, *The Study of War*, 2 vols. (Chicago: University of Chicago Press, 1942).

4

Pestilence

Introduction

Examination of skeletal remains, gravestones, analyses of parish registers, and other often inadequate records and evidence indicates that mesolithic, neolithic, Roman, later Europeans, and other folk born prior to the eighteenth century could have expected an average lifetime of 20–40 years. The evidence, such as the bones used to determine skeletal age at death and tombstone inscriptions, is fragmentary. Children and infants whose remains were treated differently from adults may well be missing from the evidentiary record. Nonetheless, there can be little doubt that mortality was high.[1] A life expectancy of 30 years indicates a possible death rate of around 33 to 34 per 1,000 persons per year. With a birth rate of 38 to 39 per 1,000, a total fertility of about five children per woman, not high for a non-contracepting people, population could be expected to grow at a rate of one-half percent per year. That population did not grow continuously at this rate, or even at a lesser rate, in ancient times was due to periodic catastrophes in which large numbers of people died, and the possibility that people practiced birth control, at times on a large scale. The latter proposition is speculative and inferential but cannot be dismissed on that account.

Such growth rates as one half percent per year, though rare in ancient and medieval times for an appreciable period, did occur on occasion, as in western Europe from the eleventh to thirteenth centuries during which time populations increased three to four fold. This period was characterized by fairly good weather, relative peace and prosperity, and no major epidemics of note. The Black Death of the mid-fourteenth century rolled back the population of various areas of western Europe by at least a quarter and up to twice that if the mortality resulting from the plague outbreaks in the decades following the first epidemic wave of 1348 is also taken into consideration.[2]

To argue that as populations grow and press on subsistence and space, the force of mortality due to disease and pestilence will increase is as reasonable as to argue that as populations grow and press on resources, people will compete and war for them. This argument is, however, an oversimplification which obscures the relation between population and disease.

The oversimplification of the relationship between population and disease is frequently based on analogies with some animal population rather than on human history. Some species are reported to increase and approach the point where the available food or space can no longer sustain them. Periodically, they hunger. They crowd together and show the physiological and anatomical changes associated with stress: Their behavior becomes markedly aberrant; they become more susceptible to disease; and mortality increases to the point of a population crash. Often, however, the reasons for an animal population crash are not so clear.[3] Much may be learned from animal studies, but the fact is that humans are a different and unique species. Conclusions about humans are best drawn from studies in the context in which humans live. A number of mechanisms can be proposed to link population and disease on some abstract basis. These include stress due to crowding and hunger due to inadequate resources. None have been demonstrated as inevitable or even likely consequences of actual growth in human populations. Humans do not merely increase their numbers. They change the environment to accommodate the increasing numbers. In the process, they may or may not change the ecology into one favorable to diseases to which they must then in some fashion adapt. The changes may also mitigate some of the stresses of old.

Epidemics and Communication

Zinsser[4] wrote of the epidemics that periodically ravaged the world, both ancient and modern:

A concentration of large populations in cities, free communications with all parts of the world, especially Africa and the East, constant and extensive military activity involving the mobilization of armies in camps, and the movement of large forces back and forth from all corners of the world—these alone are conditions which inevitably determine the outbreak of epidemic disease.

These words evoke the image of milling masses.

There is some truth in Zinsser's statement but no perspective. Small isolated populations are not likely to act as reservoirs of infectious disease, or as sources of infection for other peoples with whom they have little contact. However, the community size needed to support many infectious diseases and to maintain reservoirs of infectious agents need not be very large. Actually, the cities and communities of the past were hardly large, at least by present standards. A city of 50,000 to 100,000 people or more was rare until relatively recent times, and towns of 5,000 to 10,000 were important centers of population. Not until the beginning of the nineteenth century did more than two percent of the world's population reside in cities of 20,000 or more.[5] Most people lived in rural areas, and epidemics had to spread into the country villages to be of significant destructiveness. Cities were, of course, focal points of communications through which diseases could be introduced and spread.

The important element was communication, whereby an infectious agent could be carried from one place to another, and particularly to a population which had no biological defense. Military campaigns were one such means. Frequently, a campaigning army fell prey during its journey to a strange pestilence and was decimated not by battle but by disease. Thus, the Carthaginian army encamped before the walls of Syracuse in the third century B.C. was struck by a disease similar to that which afflicted the Athenians at Syracuse a half century earlier. It probably had remained endemic in that area but had not affected the native population who, in all likelihood, had developed an immunity to it.

Military campaigns were not the only form of travel and communication. Those engaged in commerce also provided an effective channel for epidemics. Small ships and small caravans were sufficient. Once having reached a level of population sufficient to support commerce or other forms of communication, the effect, if any, of population size on epidemics is difficult to ascertain. A small and sparse population, with no previous exposure to a disease, can be quickly devastated as were the American Indians by measles, tuberculosis, and smallpox introduced by Europeans. A small and sparse population with frequent contact between groups can also maintain reservoirs of infection such as smallpox among the nomads of the Sahel. Instead of the virus dying out as it courses through a small group, it is transmitted by them to new susceptibles in their wanderings.

There was no necessary relationship between population pressure and the great pestilences which swept past civilizations. Of greater moment was the degree of contact between a people who may introduce an infectious agent and those whose biological defenses were weak or nonexistent. The great epidemics of the past—plague, smallpox, typhus, and others, including many which have not been identified—were marked by their virulence so that the well-fed and the ill-fed, the rich and poor alike seemed subject to attack and death.[6] The less virulent epidemics to which a people had developed some resistance, affected the poor more than the rich. Sparsely settled areas suffered as heavily as did those more densely populated.

The bubonic plague occupies a pre-eminent place among the epidemics that checked European population growth. The Black Death (a pandemic of the bubonic plague) of the middle and latter part of the fourteenth century reduced the population of western Europe by a quarter to a third; in England the reduction may have been as much as 40 to 50 percent in places, the estimates varying widely. Russel notes that the mortality during the plague of the sixth century in the Byzantine Empire was comparable to that suffered by England during the Black Death.[7]

The Black Death of the fourteenth century has been regarded by some as a Malthusian check, resulting from the population growth of the previous three centuries pressing hard on subsistence. Slicher Van Bath thought that the virulence of the Black Death was due to insufficient land resources leading, in his opinion, to widespread malnutrition.[8] Some authorities, however, felt that medieval agriculture could have been expanded to feed still more people.[9] In Tuscany, a century-long decline of 23 percent in the population did not diminish the force of the plague when it struck. The population around Pistoia in 1404 was only 40 percent of what it had been in 1344.[10] Whatever the nutritional condition of the people, the plague, as did other virulent epidemic diseases, struck down the rich as well as the poor, the critical factor being exposure. Almost half the clergy of England were estimated to have died in the first epidemic wave (1348–49) alone.[11]

Plague is essentially a disease of rats transmitted by fleas. The fleas may transmit the disease to humans, but rats and fleas are the reservoirs. As long as rats lived with humans and traveled with them, no community that traded and communicated with others was safe regardless of population size and density, or state of well-being. The great world epidemics tended to spread from port cities to the hinterlands. The more virulent plague epidemics were probably a result of the plague becoming pneumonic, infecting the lungs and capable of being spread by the effluvium of respiration, but these could not spread widely. Lesser epidemics may have been the result of rats leaving forest and field and other centers and spreading thence to cities. Such were the plague outbreaks which troubled many areas of England in the early seventeenth century.[12]

A study by Biraben is informative as to the manner of spread of the plague. Biraben found no correlation between the population size of the city or locality attacked and the virulence and violence of the plague epidemic in southern France between 1720 and 1722. However, those communities attacked by the plague tended to lie along the principal arteries of communication and transportation.[13]

This was the last great epidemic of the plague in Europe. The public measures taken against the plague were quarantine and isolation, but this had not been very effective in the past. However, the increased organization of society may have made these measures more effective. A more widely held theory is that the plague diminished as an epidemic force of mortality not because of conscious human intervention but probably because the *rattus rattus* was displaced as the dominant rat species of Europe by *rattus norveigus*, a less effective transmitter of plague to humans.[14] Other possible explanations include changes in construction materials (as wood and thatch became scarce) which made houses less hospitable to rats, and even a mutant form of *Pasteurella pestis* (the plague bacillus) which conferred immunity.[15]

Though the great pestilential epidemics and pandemics of history were dramatic and significant, they were sporadic and self-limiting. Over the long course of time, population growth was as much limited by mortality from everyday endemic infectious diseases as by periodic epidemics. Before the eighteenth century in Europe and later elsewhere, death rates from 35 to 40 per thousand and higher were common.

The Disease Process

A review of the disease process among humans is presented as background for a discussion of the change occurring in mortality from infectious disease and the impact of these changes on population.

Disease processes involve the interactions between agents (microorganisms, carcinogens, or other stressful factors), hosts, and the environment, including domiciles, communication and transportation networks, water supply, and places of work, as well as the natural habitat. Host, agent, and environment cannot be considered in isolation from each other. This classic perspective has been particularly useful to epidemiologists in studying the natural history of infectious diseases. It is also useful in examining the relationship between population and disease.

The mere presence of a pathogenic organism does not in itself cause disease. Most people infected with the agent of tuberculosis do not develop clinical disease. Disease occurs when the resistance of the host is weak due to the absence of an inborn or genetic capacity to resist the infection, or the absence of sufficient vigor to muster bodily defenses. The environment provides the conditions favorable to the spread of the agent and the debilitation of the host, as through poor sanitation and bad working and living conditions. The agent may be a necessary condition for the occurrence of an infectious or other disease, but it is not a sufficient condition, and a similar conclusion applies to the state of the host and to that of the environment.

Agents, hosts, and environments change, and diseases change with them. In time an accommodation is reached between pathogen and host. One type of accommodation is through genetic changes in host and pathogen. The more resistant hosts tend to survive and pass on to their offspring the same resistant qualities. The more virulent pathogens kill their hosts and perish with them. The less virulent pathogens survive and pass on their qualities. Thus, when myxomatosis, a virulent virus, was introduced among Australian rabbits as a form of biological warfare, the die-off among rabbits was at first tremendous: 99 percent in some warrens. As survivors and their progeny were reinfected, the die-off decreased. The virus had become less lethal and the rabbit more resistant.[16] Thus, myxomatosis is on its way to becoming, if it has not already become, a mild disease among Australian rabbits.

Similar processes operate to mitigate the impact of diseases among humans. When measles was first introduced to American Indians, it decimated villages and tribes. Tuberculosis, when first introduced among American Indians, also took an acute form. With the passage of generations, clinical measles took the mild form prevalent among Europeans, and tuberculosis took the chronic form as the Indians developed immunities. The same held for other infectious diseases introduced by the Europeans, who because of their genetic background and naturally acquired immunity were able to resist the epidemics which decimated the American Indians. In 1634, Governor Bradford gave thanks to God for protecting a settlement against a smallpox epidemic which devastated a tribe of nearby Indians, but did not affect the English.[17]

This, of course, was an unusual situation, for smallpox at that time was still one of the more important causes of European mortality. While smallpox was eventually eliminated from European populations by vaccination, the dreaded scarlet fever has been changing to the mild scarlatina in relatively recent times without intervention.

The relationship between environmental change, genetics, and disease has been well studied in the case of falciparum malaria, and sickling. A high proportion of the population of West Africa show the sickling trait in which red blood cells take on odd (sickle) shapes associated with an abnormal type of hemoglobin. The characteristic is determined by genetic makeup. An individual inheriting the sickling gene from both parents evidences a severe condition, sickle cell anemia, resulting in disability, pain, and often early death. If the individual inherits a normal gene or allele from one parent, and a sickle gene or allele from the other, only a mild form of sickling will develop, one which has little consequence for normal functioning at low and moderate altitude. However, this latter individual, the heterozygote carrier of the trait, will exhibit greater resistance to falciparum malaria. In an area where malaria is endemic, the carrier stands a better chance for surviving and begetting offspring than does the individual who inherited normal genes from each parent. The sickling trait is maintained in the population gene pool as a "balanced polymorphism." On the one hand, the population pays the price of a number of deaths from sickle cell anemia, which is small when compared to the prevailing levels of mortality; on the other hand, the population contains a fair proportion of persons with increased resistance to malaria.[18] When Africans transported to America no longer were subject to malaria, the advantages of the sickling trait were gone. The mortality and suffering of homozygote sicklers, however, remained and became of greater relative significance in view of the lower levels of mortality prevailing in the new environment. Other peoples, in adapting to other conditions, have developed genetic proclivities to other diseases.

Accommodation to infectious disease may also involve the development of a tolerance to the infecting organism. Cockburn[19] observed African populations who were heavily infected with schistosomiasis but who showed few effects other than some blood in the urine. More mildly infected Europeans were severely incapacitated. Recently, Baldwin and Weisbrod reported that a field study of West Indian plantation workers indicated no significant relationship between schistosome eggs in the stool and other tests of the degree of infection and work productivity.[20] The study did not include non-workers. Thus, if there were people who did not work because they had schistosomiasis, they would not have been identified. The range of infection among members of the work force was large and the presumption that disablement is a gradual process within the range of severity of infection was not confirmed. While more investigation is needed to interpret these observations and define the underlying mechanisms of tolerance, the observations are interesting.

Yellow fever, long endemic in Africa, runs a mild course there among its human and simian hosts. Transplanted to South America, probably by African slaves a few hundred years ago, the yellow fever virus became highly virulent and deadly to its New World human and simian hosts.

Natural accommodation may take time, and in the interim artificial methods to control a disease may be developed. The control of malaria, which was long endemic in many areas, increased the vitality of those in the affected areas. Work absenteeism due to malarial attacks was reduced considerably.[21] Fewer laborers were needed for a given task and general health improved, while morbidity and mortality declined.

Populations accommodate to disease in a variety of other ways. In a manner similar to that of artificial immunization, acquired immunity to an infectious organism may become widespread in a community if children are mildly infected without the virulent attack which brings on death or clinical disease in adults. Clinical disease is inhibited if infection occurs while infants are still protected by antibodies received from the mother during gestation or during nursing. If the infant is exposed to a mild infection while thus protected by short-term passive immunity, it may acquire an active immunity based on its own capacity to produce antibodies of long-duration. The relatively low incidence of poliomyelitis in some tropical countries in which this enteric virus is present may be due to a lack of sanitation which permits children to be mildly infected early in life and thus to become immunized before they are susceptible to the more ravaging effects of infection at a later stage.[22]

Changes in Disease Patterns

Ecological changes which affect the transmission of disease or the mainte-nance of reservoirs of infection in animal populations may also change the importance of a disease. These ecological changes may be the unintended effects of economic activity. Schistosomiasis becomes more common as irrigation canals are built to increase agricultural production. The canals provide a suitable habitat for the snail hosts of schistosomes, and humans, working and voiding in the canals, complete the chain of transmission. Other diseases, however, may decline with agricultural development. The decline of malaria in the plains of Mediterranean Europe was frequently associated with population growth. The need to drain marshy areas for cultivation or pasture destroyed the habitat of the mosquito vector. The first colonists of those areas may have suffered greatly from malaria. As the population of the plains increased, the marshes were drained and animals (from whom mosquitos preferred to obtain their blood meals) were grazed, the incidence of malaria declined. The successive peopling and depopulat-ing of the Roman and other marshes may well explain fluctuations of malaria in these areas. Thus, Braudel on reviewing the development of wet plains areas commented, "If the population of the plains falls and the peasant's hold on the land is relaxed, then malaria spreads again and paralyses everything." To the theory that the decline of the Roman Empire resulted from malaria, he notes, "This theory is perhaps somewhat exag-gerated and too categorical. Malaria progresses when man relaxes his efforts, and its dreaded return is as much a consequence as a cause."[23] In another time and place an increase in population, starting from a smaller base number of people may have resulted in an ecologic change favorable to the maintenance of malaria. The clearing of forests to support agriculture and village settlements and their attendant refuse may have provided mosquitos with more hospitable breeding places than they had before, while the increased numbers of people increased the chances that pathogens would survive.[24]

A small population living in isolation may enjoy fewer risks from acute infectious disease.[25] When an acute infectious disease-causing pathogen arises in a small isolated population, the hosts are quickly killed or immu-nized. If the pathogen has no suitable reservoir in the surrounding animals, or cannot exist for long outside the body or as a chronic infection in the body, it soon perishes and bothers the survivors and their progeny no more.

If humans had remained few, scattered and isolated from each other, protected from each other's ills but also from each other's store of knowledge, the history of disease and mortality would have been different. Though many of the chronic parasitizations would have been prevalent, acute fulminating diseases would have been rare and their source would have been largely the surrounding animals. By avoiding areas where sickness (such as that transmitted by the tsetse fly) prevailed, and by adaptation (as was apparently the case of Africans with regard to yellow fever harbored by monkeys), disease prevalence would be diminished. The mortality levels of some contemporary primitive groups—after tens of thousands of years of biological adaptation—is often lower than those found in Third World peasant societies of 50 to 100 years ago, before their death rates began to decline dramatically.[26]

This does not mean that the levels of mortality of prehistoric primitive hunters and gatherers were less than those of the peasant societies that followed. The archeologic evidence indicates that, on the whole (but with a number of exceptions), the life expectancy of prehistoric hunters and gatherers was not much different from that of the peasants of antiquity. If anything, the earlier hunters and gatherers seem to have had a shorter lifespan.[27] Why this should be so is not clear, for there must have been some change for the worse in the conditions of mortality when humans turned to cultivation and commerce. Changes in the way of life means exposure to new conditions to which adaptation has yet to occur.

The development of agriculture and its way of life changed the environment in which humans lived and the nature of the diseases which afflicted them. The agricultural community could be and was much larger than that of primitive hunter gatherers; settlements eventually became permanent, many surviving in one place for hundreds and even thousands of years. Contact and mixture with other communities was frequent. Tax collectors, soldiers, nomads, and traders carried diseases from one community to another. Sufficient susceptible people, newborns and those who lost acquired immunity, were available to keep many disease organisms circulating. New agents were likely to be brought into the community through contact with the outside world. Fixed settlement exacerbated the problem of maintaining a sanitary environment, and parasites accumulated in considerable concentration in the water supply and the ground.

The development of cities created new problems. A large city cannot exist without maintaining a water supply, a sewage and waste disposal system, without the assurance of a more or less wholesome food supply, or the disposal of cadavers (many of which may have been infected by virulent organisms), and even the disposal of slaughterhouse offal. These present tremendous problems. If only for these reasons, the cities and towns of the ancient and medieval world were few and comparatively small. Though the Byzantines, Romans, and others applied considerable engineering skills to maintain the viability of cities, these still were not healthy places in which to live. Those towns were healthiest where everyone had access to the open fields for waste disposal.

Until relatively recent times, the differences in death rates and life expectancies between persons residing in cities, towns, and villages were large. One estimate is that a child born in ancient Rome had a life expectancy of 20 years and twice that if born in the provinces.[28] In the late eighteenth century, mortality in Stockholm was twice that found in rural Sweden. Life expectancy for males in Stockholm was reported to be as low as 14 years and for females, 18 years. Mortality was greater in Berlin than in the towns of Prussia, which in turn, had a greater mortality than that of the countryside. A remarkably higher rate of urban mortality was also found in the United States and England in the nineteenth century and earlier.[29]

Sanitary conditions of domiciles, street, and other public places were execrable in the cities, and conditions at work were worse still. No wonder dirty peasant villages and hovels looked idyllic by comparison. Indeed, in many cities of the past, population could not grow by natural increase alone, so great was mortality, but needed to be replenished by immigration. Since only a very small percentage of people lived in cities in the past, there was a large reservoir outside the cities from which migrants could be drawn.

Until relatively recently, cities contributed little towards population growth. Until the nineteenth century, only 2 percent of the world's population lived in cities of more than 20,000 population. As cities and towns grew in size, number, and importance to the economy, conditions within them improved. London introduced a sand filter into its water system in 1829. Public refuse collection began there in 1848, and in 1865, a sewage network was established and the use of open ditches and cesspools was abandoned. (Previously, sewers had been built in some areas of London by local boards.) In the United States, the number of waterworks increased from 83 in 1850 to 3,196 in 1896.[30]

Rapid aggregation of large numbers of people into the cities resulted in an increase in diseases such as tuberculosis and other respiratory infections. The increase in tuberculosis in the early years of urbanization and industrialization—from, say 1800–1900—may have been in part due to debilitating conditions under which people lived as well as to the increased likelihood of exposure. Yet as the cities kept growing in size, and the proportion of the population living in urban areas increased rapidly (after 1900), the incidence and death rates from tuberculosis decreased in the United States and in Europe.[31] This was due not only to an improvement in living conditions but also to the development of biological resistance.

Declines in European Mortality

General declines in mortality had begun to occur in western Europe long before the twentieth century. The death rate for England and Wales in the decade 1841–51, shortly after the establishment of registration of vital events, was 22 to 23 deaths per 1,000 persons per year, much lower than it was during the eighteenth century. For the next two decades the death rate held steady, perhaps because of the increased tempo of urbanization. It started to decline again in 1871.

During the first half of the twentieth century, age standardized death rates in England and Wales declined by more than 50 percent, from 15.6 per 1,000 population to 7.5 per 1,000 (standardized to the age and sex distribution of the 1901 population). Death rates for infectious diseases declined somewhat more than 75 percent; death rates from other causes declined somewhat more than 30 percent; many of the deaths from noninfectious diseases (such as rheumatic heart disease, nephritis) had infectious processes as origins.[32]

In Sweden, where vital registration was initiated in 1751, death rates ranged from 26 to 29 per 1,000 for the last half of the eighteenth century, and in 1801 they started to decline almost continuously until the present. In France, where registration was introduced in 1801, the death rate for the following decade was given as around 28 per 1,000, declining to 23 to 24 per 1,000 by 1841, and after holding steady for several decades began to decline again in 1871, to present levels (with increases during World Wars I and II).[33] In the Netherlands, where reliable data are available only since 1850, death rates were estimated to be around 25 per 1,000 from 1850 to 1880; thereafter mortality began to decline steadily to the levels of modern times.[34] Of interest is the fact that in Hungary, where death rates were noted to be much higher when the collection of official statistics was instituted than they were in western Europe, the decline in mortality was much more rapid. From the decade following 1881 to the decade following 1931, death rates fell from around 33 to 34 per 1,000 population to less than 15 per 1,000.[35]

Thus, it would appear from registration statistics that the decline in western European mortality gained momentum during the nineteenth century. Such lags as appeared in this trend may have been due to the fact that urbanization was also gaining momentum during this period, and urban death rates were higher than rural death rates until the Europeans adapted to urban life by public hygiene, and perhaps through increased biological resistance to the disease agents that abounded in cities. During the twentieth century, death rates in cities declined faster than those in rural areas so that today little difference is discerned between the two.[36]

The surge of population growth in England and Wales, which started in the latter half of the eighteenth century, is attributed, at least in part, to a fall in mortality. It is also argued by some that an increase in birth rates was also responsible, perhaps entirely responsible, for the increased growth rate.[37] And, indeed, women were marrying at younger ages as the industrial revolution progressed. Nonetheless, the death rates recorded when vital registration was instituted in western European countries in the late eighteenth and nineteenth centuries, were much lower than they must have been in previous times. The death rate of almost 35 per 1,000 previously cited for Hungary in the late nineteenth century was probably close to that which prevailed in England in the early eighteenth century, a rate fairly close to the birth rate of the time. This is supported by studies of parish records and related documents.[38]

Causes of the Declines in European Mortality

McKeown, Brown, and Record presented a case for the Malthusian view that the general force of mortality depended on the prevailing level of subsistence, principally food.[39] They held that the decline in death rates in the eighteenth and nineteenth centuries was a result of the increased production and availability of food per person. The state of nutrition did not seem to matter for virulent infections such as plague, smallpox, and typhus, but in some of the less virulent infections (measles or whooping cough) nutrition may have mattered a great deal. McKeown and his colleagues arrived at their conclusion by eliminating factors other than increased nutrition as reasonable explanations for the decline in mortality.

They eliminated medical science because in those days the profession was not competent to deal with infectious diseases; such competence was not developed until the twentieth century. The sole medical tool of significant power was vaccination against smallpox, which was not widely used (according to McKeown and Record) until the latter part of the nineteenth century. Before that, variolation, inhaling an inoculum of smallpox itself, was used to prevent the disease, but McKeown and his colleagues dismissed it as an ineffective measure.

They allowed a small role to spontaneous decline in disease by a lessening of the virulence of such pathogens as scarlet fever, or an increasing genetic resistance as in tuberculosis. They held that such processes were slow and therefore of small significance. Other factors such as changes in ecology and associated disease vectors can also cause spontaneous-appearing declines in disease, the disappearance of plague being a case in point.

Improved sanitation or public hygiene was allowed a small secondary role by McKeown and his associates in the early decline of mortality, largely on the basis that there was no public water and sewerage control in England until the last quarter of the nineteenth century. They noted that deaths from diarrheas and enteritis (intestinal inflammations) did not decline until the 1870s. The data were admittedly unreliable because of poor diagnostic criteria for assigning cause of death during the nineteenth century.

And so McKeown et al. concluded that increased supplies of food were responsible for the late eighteenth century decline in mortality in England and western Europe. This conclusion and the underlying premise that the availability of food had indeed increased for the masses have been disputed. There is considerable evidence indicating that moderate fluctuations in the availability of food in preindustrial Europe had little effect on the levels of overall mortality. Actual famine will cause a marked increase in deaths due to starvation and infectious disease, but this does not necessarily mean that food shortfalls of a milder sort also increase mortality rates. Chambers reviewed a large number of studies, many of which attempted to correlate food shortages with increases in epidemics as well as endemic mortality in Scandinavia and England. In general, he found no relationship. The causes of the decline of mortality from disease are best sought in other areas.[40]

Wrigley noted that during the years 1557–59, England suffered very high mortality due to an epidemic of "sweating sickness," probably a severe type of influenza. Examination of the fluctuation of wheat prices, an index of the availability of food around this period showed no relationship to burials in 29 parishes. Indeed, burials increased at a time when food prices were low.[41] Utterstrom noted that in preindustrial Sweden mortality was generally higher in the east where harvest failures were uncommon compared to the northern and western regions where crop failures were common. The east had more large towns and different social conditions. Even in the west when the mortality associated with crop failures appeared to be excessive, it was found to have been aggravated by epidemics, such as the typhus outbreak of 1741.[42] Gille estimated in his study of eighteenth century northern Europe that in good crop years death rates were on the average two points lower and in bad crop years two points higher than the mean death rate.[43] Bad crop years included those of crop failure and famine.

Razzell[44] challenged the hypothesis of McKeown et al. that the rise of population in England and Wales, beginning in the eighteenth century, was due to improved food supplies, although he agreed that the population increase was a result of a decline in mortality. He noted that the increase in life expectancy was most dramatic among aristocrats (a class which never lacked for food), increasing from 36.3 years for females born between 1700 and 1724, to 58.4 years for those born between 1825 and 1846. Moreover, Razzell found that food per capita for the country as a whole decreased in the latter part of the eighteenth and early part of the nineteenth centuries. Salaman[45] pointed out that from 1660 to 1720, a day's wages would buy two-thirds of a peck of wheat, from 1720 to 1750, a full peck, but after 1750, a day's wages would again buy only two-thirds of a peck. The seventy-five years after 1750 were a time of war with the French, Americans, and others. Conditions for agricultural workers became so bad that riots were widespread, leading to the Speenhamland decision of 1795 (see pp. 67–68). The decline in mortality from earlier high levels to the more moderate levels recorded in the early nineteenth century must have started during this period when real wages were also decreasing (see note 38). In Europe, where mortality was also declining (starting around 1750) and population increasing, the real wage of agricultural labor decreased significantly between the middle of the eighteenth and the middle of the nineteenth centuries; workers were changing to cheaper foods, switching from grain to potatoes.[46] Although the potato was not used as widely among the lower classes of England as in Ireland, Arthur Young, an eminent eighteenth-century English agronomist, worked hard to promote its wider use, and its availability did compensate in part for low wages and high grain prices. Razzell noted that while the daily consumption of potatoes in England increased from .40 pounds per head in 1795 to .62 per head in 1838, the consumption of wheat declined from about 1.3 pounds per head in 1770s to .90 per head in the 1830, and that the per capita consumption of meat also declined.[47]

McKeown and his associates being reluctant to rely on analyses based on the fragmentary data of the seventeenth and eighteenth centuries preferred to argue from the more reliable statistics of the nineteenth century. Yet without attention to the forces which operated to keep mortality high in the seventeenth century, it is presumptuous to conclude that the lower mortality of the relatively stable late eighteenth and nineteenth centuries was due to the increments in the food supply. Nor is it appropriate to take government programs as an index of improved sanitation. From the eighteenth century in England, the conditions of housing and personal sanitation changed without reference to improvements in public sanitation.

Here are some factors not considered by McKeown and his colleagues when they eliminated possible causes other than improved nutrition to account for the decline in mortality during the eighteenth century. During the seventeenth century, the plague still figured prominently (the plague of 1666 was the subject and title of Defoe's fictional account a half century later). Revolution and civil war figured prominently as well during the seventeenth century in England. The eighteenth century was one of relative internal peace. Before the eighteenth century, most Englishmen lived in huts often made of wattle and usually with dirt floors; these were poorly ventilated and badly insulated. The stress on the body's homeostatic mechanisms must have been great, and chronicles of the time describe a race of wheezing and coughing people with runny noses. They slept on pallets of straw or just on straw, inhabited by fleas, lice, and other parasites. Clothing was generally made of homespun woolens or leather, nor readily cleaned or changed, and often worn until they fell apart. Bathing was rare. Even as late as 1830, an observer noted[48]

We wonder how men can endure the compound of crust of soot and secretions with which they are enveloped. Throughout the whole of laboring classes and indeed among the majority of the middling and upper classes, this subject is strangely neglected. Cleanliness is practiced in a very imperfect manner; the whole surface is seldom washed; and in most persons, the body, with the exception of hands and face, is cleaned only by the removal of those impurities which adhere to the linen.

The list of diseases spread by dirty hands and vermin is long, and conditions of personal sanitation, clothing, and shelter of those days facilitated infestation and infection.

Epidemics of the more virulent infectious diseases were less frequent during the latter part of the eighteenth century than during the seventeenth century. The disappearance of the plague as a major force of mortality was noted earlier. Razzell cites some supporting evidence to indicate that smallpox deaths also declined from the early eighteenth century to the nineteenth century, even before vaccination was available. Perhaps innoculation through variolation was more effective than presumed; perhaps the population was becoming more resistant. At the same time, there were changes in the ways of life which may have affected the transmission of disease even before the government undertook such public sanitation programs as the construction of sewage and water systems.

The industrial revolution, beginning in the late eighteenth century, brought not only economic changes but also changes in lifestyles, including increased personal sanitation and better shelter. The availability and use of soap probably did much to reduce the incidence of hand-spread infections. Increased bathing helped control louse-born diseases, as did manufactured cotton clothes and undergarments which made laundering and frequent changes possible, a degree of personal sanitation not possible with woolens and leather.

Similarity in styles of personal sanitation may explain the similarity of the mortality trends of the English of the home country, still pressed for subsistence in the late eighteenth century, and the English in the colonies with plentiful land and food. Even after the English colonists had sufficient time to establish viable and thriving communities, their mortality was perhaps only slightly better than that of the English who remained at home. Death rates in both sectors were around 25 to 30 per 1,000, and estimated life expectancies at birth ranged from 35 to 40 years at the end of the eighteenth century. The difference in population growth was due not to differences in mortality (Malthus take note) but to the great differences in fertility; American fertility was around 55 births per 1,000 while English birth rates were below 35 per 1,000.[49] The mortality to which a colonial Englishman, even of exceptional means, was subject is illustrated by the following examples noted by Heer.[50] George Washington, whose father died when George was eleven, married a 26-year-old widow, Martha, who had already borne four children, two of whom died in infancy, one at age 17, and the last in early adulthood. Thomas Jefferson's father died when Tom was fourteen. Thomas's wife, a 23-year-old widow (also named Martha), died eleven years after her 2nd marriage, having borne six children of whom only two lived to maturity.

In history, the rich never lacked for food. They were also considerably better sheltered and clothed than were the mass of poor people, and thus better protected against the elements. Nor were they engaged in occupations from an early age which covered them with dirt and offal, and exposed them to the breeding grounds of parasites. As was to be expected, the mortality of lower social classes was much higher than that of the upper classes. (This is still true except that the differences are not as great as they were formerly.) Though the upper classes were as fully fed in former times as they are at present, their mortality was still very high by present standards. It might be said that the prevalence of disease among the poor was a threat to the rich, but then the wealthy colonial in America was no less threatened with disease and death than the wealthy Englishman at home.

Male members of British ducal families born from 1480 to 1679 (excluding those who died from violence) had a life expectancy of 30 years; those born from 1680 to 1729, of 35 years; those born from 1780 to 1829 could expect to live 50 years.[51] Females born into aristocratic families between 1725–1749 had a life expectancy of 36.7 years, increasing steadily until those born between 1825–1849 had a life expectancy of 58.4 years.[52] This increase can hardly be attributed to increased nutrition, though better nutrition may have been important.

In 1842, Chadwick reported that the average age of death in working class families of Manchester was 17 years; in families engaged in trade the average age at death was 20 years; and in families of the gentry, the average age at death was 38 years. Over one-half the children born to working class families died before reaching the age of five; one-fifth of those born to the gentry died before that age. In the port city of Liverpool the average age at death for the gentry was 35 years, for trades people 22, and for laborers 15 years.[53] The same pattern of mortality prevailed in the industrialized areas of the Midlands.

The force of mortality was much milder in the dominant rural areas. For Rutlandshire around 1840, the average age at death was reported to be 52 years for the gentry, 41 years for tradesmen and 38 years for laborers.[54] For the whole of England and Wales, the general average length of life was estimated by William Farr to be 40.9 years during 1838–54.[55] In those days, cities were absolutely unhealthy places though the urban rich and well-to-do were relatively protected against the bad conditions of work and housing.

While the difference between the mortality of the rich and the poor may have been in part due to differences in nutrition, this could not have been true for the differences between rural and urban laborers. With the passage of the Poor Law of 1834, farm laborers who comprised the bulk of the rural population lost even the small subsistence they had been vouchsafed under the Speenhamland system, and were obliged either to go to the manufacturing and urban centers where they might find work and survive, or to the more horrible work house. The decision of the magistrates of Berkshire at Speenhamland in 1795, probably helped keep death rates in England from increasing during a time of depression. As a result of riots and civil commotion, the magistrates were summoned to set minimum wages relative to the price of bread. They established a scale whereby low wages were to be supplemented by a parish dole reflecting the number of children in the family and adjusted as the price of bread rose or fell. This formula, accepted by many English counties until its replacement by the Poor Law of 1834, in effect subsidized the employers of agricultural labor at the expense of the taxpayers, but it also assured that many of the poor would not starve as they had in the past. The laboring classes, however, were pauperized in the process, and even that small security was gone by the middle of the nineteenth century. Yet the levels of mortality in England did not increase. The slowing of the decline in mortality during the middle of the nineteenth century was very likely due to the rapid growth of towns and cities, which were very unhealthy places to live in those days.

The Twentieth Century

The decline of mortality, which started in the eighteenth and nineteenth centuries in Europe and North America, continued in the twentieth century as economies expanded and living and working conditions of the lower classes improved. An outstanding development was the diminution of mortality rates in cities due to more effective sanitation and public health measures. Though the force of mortality diminished in the rural sector as well, the mortality differences are now small, and related to differences in social composition. As deaths due to virulent infections declined, improvement in nutrition becomes more important for further declines as does the management of pollution, stress and health care.

The force of mortality was slowly diminishing in many of the non-industrialized countries as well. Arriaga and Davis, who studied the changes in mortality in Latin America, reported that before 1930, mortality declined only slowly in the more backward countries such as Guatemala, but more rapidly in the more advanced countries, which had experienced some level of economic growth (Mexico and Costa Rica, for example). Since 1930, however, mortality declined further and more rapidly without reference to economic growth. The latter period of rapid decline was attributed to the introduction of public health measures that did not depend on development levels.[56]

The death rates in most contemporary pre-industrial societies have been declining rapidly for at least two generations. Per capita food production, though keeping up with the unprecedented rates of population growth, have increased but little. Thus, many analysts have concluded that the principal factor in the recent decline of mortality in these nations was in good part the introduction of public health programs, immunization, malaria control, sanitation and the like.[57]

The notion that public health measures, particularly malaria control, were largely responsible for the decline in mortality, was challenged by Fredericksen with particular reference to the case of Sri Lanka (Ceylon).[58] There mortality fell in a single year from 20.3 deaths per 1,000 population in 1946 to 14.3 in 1947, following the initiation of an intensive malaria control program. (The death rate has continued to fall to 8 per 1,000 in 1972, in good part because the population includes a high proportion of young people whose risk of dying is low.) Fredericksen noted, however, that the decline occurred not only in the malaria endemic areas which were treated, but equally in the untreated non-malarial areas where most of the people lived. Moreover, the food supply had improved after the World War II shortages, while the malaria control program had opened up large tracts of land to settlement and cultivation.

Fredericksen's conclusions did not go unchallenged.[59] Prior to the malaria control program, the malarial areas of Ceylon suffered much higher levels of mortality than the non-malarial tracts. Afterward, mortality patterns in the two areas became equal. While World War II may have disrupted the importation of food, per capita food consumption in the following decades did not increase but remained at a fairly low level (around 1,900 calories per day) in terms of both calories and protein. Nonetheless, mortality continued to decline.

Gray, using a multivariate approach which considers the effect on mortality of malaria control and the various other public health measures that were deployed after World War II in Ceylon, concluded that malaria control was responsible for at least 23 percent of the fall in death rates, and other public health measures and economic development accounted for indeterminate portions of the remainder.[60]

Whatever the reason, the fact remains that mortality in Ceylon had been declining with some fluctuations even before World War II, from 31 deaths per 1,000 population in 1905 to 21 per 1,000 in 1940. The reported number of cases of plague, smallpox, cholera, typhoid fever, hookworm and deaths associated with these diseases diminished. A slight rise during World War II in the incidence of these diseases may have been due to a relaxation of government disease control programs, which were vigorously resumed at the war's end, and mortality continued to decline long after the establishment of malaria control.[61]

Preston examined and compared the mortality (in terms of expectation of life) of various countries in the 1930s and again in the 1960s, when per capita incomes had generally increased. But the decrease in mortality over these thirty years for most countries with low per capita income in the 1930s was much greater than would be expected on the basis of the increase which occurred in per capita incomes. For example, a country whose per capita income increased from $100 in the 1930s to $150 to $200 in the 1960s had a much lower mortality in the 1960s than countries with a comparable per capita income of $150 to $200 in the 1930s. Preston concluded that despite the relationship between income and mortality at any one time, the general changes which took place over that period were due to other factors, such as public health and sanitation measures.[62]

Increases in per capita income and importation of health measures are not the only significant changes that occurred between 1930 and 1960. In many countries, colonialism came to an end, accompanied in some measure by an end to colonial exactions. In some countries, incomes are more unevenly distributed than in others, leaving the major portion of the population with incomes considerably below the so-called per capita income. Preston noted that in Mexico, Venezuela, and Colombia, where incomes are very unevenly distributed, the mortality levels are significantly higher than one would expect considering average per capita income, but also noted that in the Eastern European socialist countries, where income is more evenly distributed, mortality is also somewhat higher than would be expected on the basis of per capita income.

As noted, the levels of mortality in many third world nations decreased and population grew even as per capita food consumption did not improve very much from customary low levels. Food consumption in Sri Lanka during the last thirty years has remained fairly constant, fewer than 2,000 calories per person. Nonetheless, death rates fell from 20.3 per 1,000 to 14.3 per 1,000 in 1947, continued to fall to about a rate of 8 per 1,000 currently, with a life expectancy of around 65 years or more. In Guatemala, a less densely populated country, death rates fell from 21.3 to 17.1 per 1,000 following a malaria control program in the late 1950s. Since then mortality has declined very slowly, the death rate being reported as 14 per 1,000 population in 1972.

Guatemala and Sri Lanka are both poor countries but differ in many respects, among which are the social and economic power structures. Though Guatemala had a per capita annual income of $260 in the early 1960s, twice that of Sri Lanka, the distribution of food among the population may be more equitable in Sri Lanka, the provision of better sanitation, higher literacy rate, and so on. Any combination of them would account for the more rapid decline in mortality in Sri Lanka, despite its lower average income.

In India, mortality declined slowly in the last fifty years, despite little change in the availability of food. Before independence, there was no improvement at all.[63] The decline in mortality seemed to be levelling off during the late 1960s and 1970s, fluctuating at a death rate of around 16 per 1,000, higher in rural areas (around 17 to 19 per 1,000) than in urban areas (around 10 to 12 per 1,000).[64] Many villages in India still do not have safe water supplies. Many children are so undernourished that they may not be able to withstand an attack of gastroenteritis and diarrhea (important causes of death), or to muster the biological, immunological defenses against the common childhood diseases. Improvements in sanitation, immunization, and nutrition may be essential if mortality is to decline further.

Each time and place had a pattern of disease and its attendant mortality peculiar to the prevailing conditions of life and to the biological condition of its people. Changes in patterns of disease mortality have had many causes: increase in incomes and nutritional status, introduction of public health measures, changes in the style of life, and autonomous biological changes in host, pathogens, and in the environment. At any period in history, any one of these factors may have been more significant than others. However, the great pestilences of the past and the generally high levels of mortality which kept populations in check were not much related to population or, for that matter, to levels of subsistence.

Notes

1. For summaries of the evidence see G. A. Harrison, J. S. Weiner, J. M. Tanner and N. A. Barnicot, *Human Biology* (New York: Oxford University Press, 1964), pp. 504--6; also *Determinants and Consequences of Population Trends*, ST/SOA/Series A, Population Studies, No. 17 (New York: United Nations, 1953), pp. 50--55. For a more extensive and evidentiary work, see G. Acsadi and J. Nemeskeri, *History of Human Life Span and Mortality* (Budapest: Akademiai Kiado, 1970). See also note 39, Chapter 2.

2. See P. Ziegler, *The Black Death* (Harmondsworth, England: Penguin Books, 1970), ch. XIV, for a discussion of the various estimates of plague deaths; all agree on a heavy depopulation.

3. See E. S. Deevey, "The Hare and the Haruspex: A Cautionary Tale," *American Scientist* 48:415--30; P. Handler, ed. *Biology and the Future of Man* (New York: Oxford University Press, 1970), pp. 384--85. The reader who is interested in the thesis that fertility is controlled among animal species to assure sustenance is referred to V. C. Wynne-Edwards, "Population Control in Animals," *Scientific American* 211:2, (August 1964), pp. 68--74.

4. H. Zinsser, *Rats, Lice, and History* (Boston: Little, Brown and Co., 1935), p. 132.

5. K. Davis, "The Origins and Growth of Urbanization in the World," *American J. of Sociology* 60 (March 1955), pp. 429--37.

6. M. Drake, ed., *Population in Industrialization* (London: Methuen, 1966), p. 5.

7. J. C. Russel, "That Earlier Plague," *Demography* 5:1 (1968), pp. 174--84.

8. B. H. Slicher Van Bath, *Agrarian History of Western Europe* (London: Edward Arnold, 1963), p. 84.

9. See R. Delatouche, "Agriculture Medievale et Population," *Etudes Sociales* (1955), pp. 13--23, cited by Ziegler, *The Black Death*, op. cit., p. 34.

10. D. Herlihy, "Population, Plague, and Social Change in Rural Pistoia, 1201--1430," *Economic History Review* 18 (1965), pp. 225--44.

11. See P. Ziegler, op. cit., pp. 86, 236. The clergy were perhaps particularly susceptible if they were conscientious in carrying out their ministries, thus exposing themselves to the direct transmission of the pneumonic form.

12. C. Bridenbaugh, *Vexed and Troubled Englishmen: 1590–1642* (New York: Oxford University Press, 1968), pp. 104--6.

13. J. N. Biraben, "Demographic Characteristics of the Plague Epidemic in France," *Daedulus* (Spring 1968), pp. 536--45.

14. R. Dubos, *Mirage of Health* (Garden City, N.Y.: Doubleday, Anchor Books, 1961), pp. 156--59; F. F. Cartwright, *Disease and History* (New York: T. Y. Crowell, 1972), pp. 52--53.

15. W. H. McNeill, *Plagues and People* (Garden City, New York: Doubleday, 1976), pp. 172--74.

16. F. Fenner, "Myxomatosis," *Brit. Med. Bull.* 15 (1959), pp. 240--45.

17. Cited in A. Cockburn, *The Evolution and Eradication of Infectious Diseases* (Baltimore: Johns Hopkins Press, 1963), p. 91.

18. See any text on human genetics, such as C. Stern, *Human Genetics*, 3rd ed., (San Francisco: W. H. Freeman, 1973).

19. A. Cockburn, op. cit., pp. 79--80.

20. R. E. Baldwin and B. A. Weisbrod, "Disease and Labor Productivity," *Economic Development and Cultural Change* 22:3 (April 1974), pp. 414--35.

21. See U.S. Public Health Service, Report of Phillipine Public Health Rehabilitation Program, July 4, 1946, June 30, 1950, Washington, D. C., noted in *Determinants and Consequences of Population Trends*, ST/SOA/Series A. Population Studies, No. 17 (New York: United Nations, 1953), p. 266.

22. Cockburn, op. cit., p. 212.

23. Fernand Braudel, *The Mediterranean and the Mediterranean World in the Age of Philip II* 2 vols. (English translation, New York: Harper and Row, 1972), pp. 64--65.

24. F. B. Livingstone, "Anthropological Implications of Sickle Cell Gene Distribution in West Africa," *American Anthropologist* 60 (1958), pp. 533--62.

25. F. L. Black, "Infectious Disease in Primitive Societies," *Science* 187 (February 1975), pp. 515--18.

26. J. V. Neel, "Lessons from a 'Primitive People'," *Science* 170 (November 1970), pp. 815--22, fig. 1.

27. See references cited earlier on expectation of life; also the comments and reservations of D. E. Dumond, "The Limitation of Human Population: A Natural History," *Science* 187 (February 1975), pp. 713--21.

28. W. R. Macdonnell, "On the Expectation of Life in Ancient Rome and the Provinces of Hispania and Lusitania and Africa," *Biometrika* 9 (1913), p. 370, cited in H. Brown, *The Challenge of Man's Future* (New York: Viking Press, 1954), pp. 75, 273.

29. *Determinants and Consequences of Population Trends*, op. cit., pp. 52--3.

30. Ibid., p. 58.

31. T. C. Doege, "Tuberculosis Mortality in the United States 1900--1960," *J. of the American Medical Assoc.*, 192 (1965), pp. 1045--8.

32. W. P. D. Logan, "Mortality in England and Wales from 1848--1947, *Population Studies*, 4 (1950--51), pp. 132--78.

33. T. McKeown, R. G. Brown and R. G. Record, "An Interpretation of the Modern Rise of Population in Europe," *Population Studies* 26: 3 (November 1972), pp. 347, 359, 362.

34. W. Petersen, *The Politics of Population* (Garden City, New York: Doubleday, 1964), p. 176. (Reprint ed., Gloucester, Mass.: Peter Smith, 1970.)

35. McKeown, Brown, and Record, op. cit., p. 370.

36. H. Dorn, "Mortality," In P. Hauser and O. D. Duncan, eds., *The Study of Population* (Chicago: University of Chicago Press, 1959), ch. 19.

37. H. S. Habakkuk, "English Population in the Eighteenth Century," *The Economic History Review*, 2nd Series, VI (1953), pp. 117--33; K. F. Helleiner, "The Vital Revolution Reconsidered," *Canadian J. of Economics and Political Science* 23 (1957), p. 1--9; J. T. Krause, "Some Neglected Factors in the English Industrial Revolution," *J. of Economic History* 19 (1959); also "English Population Movements Between 1700 and 1850," *International Population Conference* (New York: 1961), vol. 1. The articles by Krause are reprinted in *Population in Industrialization*, M. Drake, ed. (London: Methuen, 1969), pp. 103--27.

38. See J. D. Chambers, "Population Changes in a Provincial Town: Nottingham, 1700--1800," in D. V. Glass and D. E. C. Eversley, eds., *Population in History* (London: Edw. Arnold, 1965), pp. 334--53; S. Sogner, "Aspects of the Demographic Situation in 17 Parishes in Shropshire: 1711--60," *Population Studies* 17:2 (November 1963), pp. 126--46.

39. McKeown, Brown, and Record, op. cit., pp. 345--81.

40. J. D. Chambers, *Population, Economy and Society in Preindustrial England* (London: Oxford University Press, 1972), pp. 77--106.

41. E. A. Wrigley, *Population and History* (New York: McGraw-Hill, 1969), pp. 74--75.

42. G. Utterstrom, "Some Population Problems in Pre-Industrial Sweden," *Scandinavian Economic History Review* 2:1 (1954), pp. 103--65.

43. H. Gille, "The Demographic History of the Northern European Countries in the Eighteenth Century," *Population Studies* 3:1 (1949), pp. 3--65.

44. P. E. Razzell, "An Interpretation of the Modern Rise of Population in Europe—A Critique," *Population Studies* 28: 1 (March, 1974), pp. 5--17.

45. R. N. Salaman, *The History and Social Influence of the Potato* (Cambridge: Cambridge University Press, 1949), p. 470.

46. B. H. Slicher Van Bath, op. cit., pp. 225--7, 237.

47. Razzell, op. cit., p. 8.

48. C. T. Thackrah, *The Effects of Arts, Trades and Professions and of Civic States and Habits of Living on Health and Longevity* (London, 1831), pp. 123--4, cited in *Determinants and Consequences of Population Trends* op. cit., p. 52.

49. See Chambers, op. cit., p. 105, for England; W. S. Thompson and P. K. Whelpton, *Population Trends in the United States* (New York: McGraw-Hill, 1933), p. 263, for estimates of American vital trends.

50. D. M. Heer, *Society and Population* (Englewood Cliffs, N.J.: Prentice-Hall, 1968), p. 43.

51. See T. H. Hollingsworth, "A Demographic Study of the British Ducal Families," *Population Studies* 11 (1957), reprinted in M. Drake, ed. *Population and Industrialization* (London: Methuen, 1969), pp. 73--102.

52. T. H. Hollingsworth, "The Demography of British Peerage," cited in Razzell, op. cit., p. 7.

53. E. Chadwick, *Report on the Sanitary Conditions of the Labouring Population of Great Britain, 1842*, M. W. Flinn, ed. (Edinburgh: The University Press, 1965), pp. 228--31.

54. Ibid., p. 223.

55. Cited in G. A. Harrison, et al., *Human Biology* (New York and Oxford: Oxford University Press, 1964), p. 506.

56. E. E. Arriaga and K. Davis, "The Pattern of Mortality Change in Latin America," *Demography* 6:3 (August 1969), pp. 223--42.

57. See W. Petersen, *Population*, 2nd ed. (London: Collier-Macmillan, 1969), pp. 560--76.

58. H. Fredericksen, "Malaria Control and Population Pressure in Ceylon," *Public Health Reports* 75:10 (October 1960), pp. 865--68; "Determinants and Consequences of Mortality Trends in Ceylon," *Public Health Reports* 76:8 (August 1961), pp. 659--63.

59. P. Newman, "Malaria Control and Population Growth," *J. of Development Studies*, 6:2 (1970), pp. 133--58.

60. R. H. Gray, "The Decline of Mortality in Ceylon and the Demographic Effects of Malaria Control," *Population Studies* 28:2 (July 1974), pp. 205--29.

61. A. Cockburn, op. cit., pp. 233--50.

62. S. H. Preston, "The Changing Relation Between Mortality and Level of Economic Development," *Population Studies* 29:2 (July 1975), pp. 231--48.

63. G. Blyn, *Agricultural Trends in India 1891--1947* (Philadelphia: University of Pennsylvania Press, 1966).

64. See various reports of the Sample Registration System, Government of India.

5

Famine

Introduction

Between the years 1000 and 1855 A.D., 450 famines were recorded in western Europe.[1] Frequently these famines were localized, affecting a limited region while other regions had sufficient food or even enjoyed a surplus. During famine years mortality often increased three-fold and more.[2] In some, 25 percent of the population died. During famines fertility declined as marriages were delayed and as severe nutritional deprivation inhibited reproductive functions.

While dramatic episodes have been associated with densely populated countries such as India and China, they have occurred no less frequently among sparse as among dense populations. They have occurred in the same regions at different times, when these regions were sparsely settled and when they were more densely settled.

The immediate causes of famine were the vicissitudes of weather (droughts or floods), the misfortunes of war, and occasionally a blight that destroyed a major food crop. At least two preconditions were necessary. One was the absence of effective transportation and trade networks through which food from surplus areas could be sent to deficit areas. The threat of famine in western Europe diminished in the nineteenth century with the development of efficient transportation and trade networks which were of greater importance in this regard than improvements in agricultural techniques.

Another major precondition was the inability of communities to produce and store food surpluses in good years as a reserve for poor years. With the rather primitive storage technologies and facilities characteristic of non-industrial communities of the past (and much of the world today), a third or more of the cereals harvested might be spoiled by rats, insects, and micro-

74

organisms before the harvest was consumed over the year. If held longer, the rate of loss was increased considerably.[3] To produce a surplus worth storing for a long time under such circumstances required much more labor than was available or practicable even where the other necessary resources were present. Moreover, where the production and storage of surpluses were possible, this was often deterred by the imperatives of the prevailing economic structure (see next chapter).

Some observers have considered famines to be the result of the dependence of the afflicted population on a single crop, a so-called monoculture. The notion is that under population pressure the most productive crop per acre must be sown; if this crop fails, there is no other food source to fall back on. This notion is an extension of the Malthusian notion that left to their own resources, populations tend to expand to the very limits of available sustenance. Malthus held that the institution of private property and the profit motive mitigated this tendency. However, it was precisely these factors that were principally responsible for the dependence of the poor on a single crop, the cheapest, for subsistence, even as other crops were being produced for profit. This situation is here being examined with reference to famine. But it has also been examined in other contexts one being the generation of nutritional deficiency diseases. Pellagra, the highly fatal deficiency disease resulting from the lack of niacin, often appeared in epidemic proportions where agricultural workers were poor and obliged to subsist almost exclusively on a cheap, nutritionally poor, cereal such as corn. The land in such places (as the southern United States in the early twentieth century) was often tied to export and cash crops, while those who worked it could not afford to purchase or grow other than the cheapest food.[4] As shall be noted further, the dependence of people on a single crop stems not from population pressure but from the pressure of commercial interests.

Famine in France

Wrigley described the effects of the French famine of 1693–1694 on three parishes of Beauvaisis, each with a slightly different economic base.[5] Wrigley's account is based on a classic study of the demographic history from 1600–1730 of these parishes and on supplemental information provided by Goubert, the author of that study.[6] The three parishes were about 25 miles from each other, located at the vertices of a rough equilateral triangle which crossed the borders of Picardy. In one parish (Auneuil), the peasants engaged in a mixed agriculture, cultivating grain and herding cattle. Their lands included considerable pasture and woodlands as well as tillage. The second parish (Breteuil) was more densely populated; little land was left uncultivated and few cattle were grazed as pasture land was scarce. The population of the third parish (Mouy) included a large proportion of woolen cloth workers who had to buy their food in the market.

Excessive rains damaged the grain crops in many regions of France in the last decade of the seventeenth century; shortages appeared and frank famine occurred in 1693–94. The herds of Auneuil, however, still had some pasture, at least for a while, and supplied the people in that parish with animal products. Even so, the number of burials in Auneuil during those years was estimated at some 12 percent of the population in excess of the usual. In Breteuil where there was few animals, the excess of burials was twice as large. And in Mouy, whose clothworkers depended on marketed grain, mortality was higher still. Wrigley noted that the diversified agriculture of Auneuil helped to mitigate the effects of the famine. Without additional information, the monoculture of grain in Breteuil at that time might be attributed to the density of population. But other factors were more compelling determinants, both of the patterns of agriculture and of the population density of the region.

Though population growth was frequently associated with greater intensity of land use, the specific pattern of land use in seventeenth century France was more likely to be determined by those who held power over the land than by those who inhabited it. The French peasantry of that time lived under a feudal or seigneurial order. The nobility had by force and guile incorporated much of the land formerly owned by village communes into their personal demesne. These lands, once used as woodland and pasture, and which had been the principal source of livelihood for the poorer peasants, were put into marketable crops, usually grains. Many peasants were obliged to become sharecroppers or laborers on the lords' estates, or to find work in the small but developing industries. By a royal ordinance of 1669, the lords were permitted to incorporate into their personal demesne one-third of the common lands still remaining and it may be assumed that the lords chose the most productive land for themselves. One of the main concerns of the radicals of the French Revolution was the revocation of the "Ordinance of Triage." Robespierre proposed to the Constituent Assembly in 1791, in the interests of the people of Artois, that the lands appropriated under the ordinance of 1669 be restored to the towns, boroughs, and villages of that region so that the people could again graze their cattle and regain their former prosperity.[7] Artois (neighboring Picardy which contains the unfortunate Breteuil), and adjacent Flanders, contained great grain growing estates even before the Black Death. The area had long been a center of cloth manufacture and trade, and the landlords realized considerable profit from the commercial growing of food grains. The result was that in this region the peasants had access to very little land for grazing.

Goubert, the scholar on whose data Wrigley based his account of the famine of 1693, estimated that the French peasantry, which comprised 80 percent of the population in the time of Louis XIV, owned only half the land and, under seigneurial tenure with its obligations of rents, labor, and taxes, the peasants rarely kept half of what they produced. The rest of the land belonged to the lords, seigneurs, or others who passed themselves off as nobles. Bad times and exactions of money dues often resulted in indebtedness, high interest and, eventually, the loss of many small peasant holdings. Among the peasantry, land also was very unequally divided; only 10 percent of them possessed sufficient land to make a living by farming alone. In the villages, relatively few families owned most of the land. Most had so little land that they had to hire out as agricultural labor, engage in weaving or other crafts, usually in cottage industry. Yet France produced enormous wealth for the times, exporting grain, wines, cloth, and various implements, and supported the large armies and frequent wars which marked the reign of

Louis XIV. Goubert based his description of the economic conditions largely on his extensive demographic studies of the regions of Ile De France and Picardy but held that similar conditions prevailed throughout France.[8]

The pastoral economy of the parish of Auneuil located in Bray, and the grain-producing economy of the neighboring parish of Breteuil located in Picardy, may not have been determined so much by the numbers of inhabitants but by the commercial orientation of the lords of the lands. Had the common lands of Bray been enclosed and sown to grain on a commercial basis, the peasants would not have been able to run cattle. Instead, rather like the peasants of Picardy—mostly agricultural laborers, they would have been obliged to rely almost entirely on their wages to buy grain. Goubert[9] noted that the famine of 1693–1694 resulted not merely from the bad harvest, estimates of which ranged from one-third to two-thirds of normal. There would have been food for all, if equitably distributed. As noted, in normal periods half or more of the peasants' produce went to the overlords and much of it was exported. During these famine years prices were higher than peasant laborers could afford. Grain stocks had been depleted by the demands of the wars of Louis XIV and by poor crops in the years preceding the famine during which speculators and buyers moved the grain to those areas where higher prices could be obtained. The cloth industry of Picardy, on which the people depended for at least supplemental incomes, had been doing poorly because of the wars which had interfered with trade and was shut down. Whatever savings the cloth workers had were exhausted in the previous bad years; they could not buy grain, particularly at the prevailing prices, and so they starved.

The cloth producing districts were not always at a disadvantage in the times of famine. Following the famine of 1693–94, grain was fairly plentiful and prices were low, a situation helped by a short peaceful interlude in the reign of Louis XIV. The textile producing regions enjoyed a boom, especially Picardy which attracted many migrant weavers. The famine of 1709, due to an exceptionally cold winter that froze seed grain and animals throughout France, appeared to have had only a small effect on Picardy, despite its swelled population: Proof, as Goubert noted, that work and, therefore, food were to be had.[10]

The Irish Famine

The great Irish famine occurred when the potato crop, afflicted by blight, failed for two of the three crop years between 1846 and 1849. As a result, 1 to 2 million people died and another 2 million emigrated. And eventually, the population was reduced to about half the size it had reached before the famine. The dependence on the potato as practically the sole dietary staple of the Irish poor is frequently attributed to the rapid population growth in the century preceding the famine: the population had approximately tripled in size to between 8 and 9 million people.

The potato, introduced into Ireland just before the seventeenth century, is a very efficient food crop. One Irish statute acre planted to potatoes and supplemented with some milk, could provide a large family with an almost adequate diet. The availability of this bounteous subsistence crop enabled the population to increase markedly. The story goes that as the numbers of people increased, they became more and more dependent on the potato for sustenance, resulting in a potato monoculture. Thus, when the universal potato blight struck, the food supply vanished. This story is incomplete, however, and misconstrues the cause of the famine. Irish peasants under the British overlordship had little choice over their subsistence crop; this was determined not by population pressure but by the economic constraints to which the peasants were subject.[11]

The wretched and bitter living conditions of the Irish after the British established suzerainty were noted by writers (see Johathan Swift, *A Modest Proposal*) and politicians before overpopulation became an issue. The Penal Laws, enacted after the defeat of Jacobite Irish armies by William in 1690, completed the destruction of the social and economic fabric of the country, a process begun before Tudor times and accelerated by the devastation wrought by Cromwell's army. Edmund Burke described the Penal Codes of William as "a machine as well fitted for oppression, impoverishment, and degradation of a people, and the debasement in them of human nature itself, as ever proceeded from the perverted ingenuity of man."[12] Irish Catholics, excluded from the professions, trade and landholding, were obliged to emigrate or to accept the status of tenants. C. Woodham Smith noted that it was not uncommon for peasants in mud huts to make wills bequeathing estates which had been recently confiscated, and that the comic figure of an Irish beggar claiming descent from kings may have been speaking the truth.[13] Though the Penal Codes were relaxed toward the end of the eighteenth century, the Catholic subjugation and Protestant ascendancy were firmly established, and were to remain so for more than a century in the southern three provinces—and still trouble Ulster today.

Differences in language and religion, and the confiscations of former peasant holdings, isolated landlord from tenant and facilitated a ruthless exploitation untempered by traditional limitations on power or by humane considerations. Many were absentee landlords with greater interests in England. These and domestic Irish landlords, supported by British troops, were avid in the pursuit of high rents. In addition to the claims of landlords, tenants had to cope with one or more layers of middlemen who leased large acreages and sublet them as small parcels, primarily concerned in maximizing rents. The peasantry had little choice but to accept what was offered. The limit on the rent was the bare subsistence essential to keep the peasant alive and functioning.

The potato made it possible to allocate a relatively small portion of the land for the subsistence of the peasants, thus maximizing that portion devoted to the rent-producing cash crops. Introduced into Ireland towards the end of the sixteenth century, the potato became a staple during the seventeenth century and the principal—often the sole—food during the eighteenth century. During the wars of Cromwell and William in the seventeenth century, the potato saved the Irish. While grain fields could be fired and trampled by military raiders, the potato crop could not be destroyed except by digging.

As already noted, during the early part of the eighteenth century the ranks of the tenantry were swelled as Catholics were forbidden under the Penal

Codes of the 1690s to practice in professions, engage in commerce, purchase land or educate their young. Various domestic industries and trades were destroyed and suppressed under English policy, forcing those dependent on these industries to turn to the land. At the same time, the new proprietors of Ireland converted arable land to pasture (since wool and animal products could be exported to England), while the export of grain was restricted to keep the price of English grain high. The number of holdings available to tenants was limited by the extensive tracts of land put into pasture. The resulting hunger for land from which one could obtain a mean livelihood, if only as a small tenant, helped reduce the Irish to the most minimal levels of subsistence. Insecurity of tenure discouraged improvements of holdings as these would only serve to increase already exorbitant rents and revert to the landlord at the expiration of a lease. Frequently, the tenant would be obliged to pay a fee for the privilege of renewing a lease even at a higher rental, a practice which deprived the tenant of any surplus accumulated and placed him in ever increasing debt. So it was that the Irish even begrudged themselves houses that would revert to the landlord, but erected huts that took not more than a few days to throw up and that would serve not only to shelter their families but also their animals.

Most insecure was the family that depended on "conacre," a small plot of land let for a single crop season, and used to grow potatoes for the family's sustenance and perhaps also to feed a pig which would hopefully be sold to help pay the rent. Since cash was particularly scarce for the family dependent on conacre, their rent was paid off largely in labor at the lowest rate. The origin of the conacre system is not clear but it was apparently widespread in the eighteenth century before the great increase in population. Thus, the dependence on the potato did not originate so much from population growth as from social and political happenstance.

The Irish economy responded to England's needs. In the latter part of the eighteenth and the early part of the nineteenth centuries, England was engaged in a series of wars including those with France and the American rebels. This was also a period of population and industrial growth in England. Domestic grain production did not keep pace with the need, and the price of grain increased markedly in England. Laws regulating the export of grain from Ireland to England were relaxed; in 1806, the duties involved were abolished. The portion of the Irish estate that had been devoted to producing rent could now be profitably sown to grain. Since the cultivation of grain requires greater labor inputs per acre than does herding, holdings were let out in smaller parcels. They were thus more numerous and more readily available. Rents in Ireland are reported to have increased four-fold between 1760 and 1815; smaller holdings planted to grain produced more than the previously larger holdings. Though the income for landlords increased substantially, the subsistence level for most Irish tenants remained the same.

Concurrently, the population of Ireland increased dramatically. Connell, finding no evidence of a decrease in mortality sufficient to account for the increase in population, surmised that there was an increase in early marriage resulting in increased fertility. The earlier marriage age was made possible by the easier availability of holdings, permitting a greater number of family starts. Some support for this position is adduced from an examination of 1841 census data. (Censuses were first taken in Ireland in 1821.) In those rural regions where average holdings were small, population growth and mortality were estimated to have been higher than in the rest of the country and a larger proportion of young women were married. In those rural districts where holdings were larger, population growth was less though mortality was lower; a smaller proportion of young women were married. From 1830–39, following a period during which holdings were getting more difficult to obtain, there was a marked tendency for first marriages in Ireland to take place at a somewhat later age.[14]

Connell's hypothesis that the fall in marriage age led to increased fertility is inferential, there being little if any direct data relating to fertility levels. This is recognized by Connell who later noted an error in his estimate of the fertility ratio (children under five years of age per 1,000 women age 15–44) of Irish women derived from the 1841 census, the corrected ratio being 532 (not 644) and comparable to the figure of 522 for England and Wales of that time.[15] However, in view of the evidence that age at marriage in Ireland was on the increase, it is not inconceivable that fertility in 1841 had declined from higher levels which may have prevailed earlier.

In any case, whatever the reason for the increase in Ireland's population during the late eighteenth and early nineteenth centuries, the increased number of available holdings allowed an accommodation that would not have been possible otherwise. Reduced to a bare subsistence, a dreary existence was made tolerable by religion, the free flow of hospitality, and conjugal life. Moreover, with the insecurity of tenancy, the only form of social security for the Irish peasant was to have children who could work and who might secure a holding. The principal deterrent to raising a family was the lack of a small piece of land to provide the minimal subsistence that was required. The decrease in size and the increase in number of holdings, as land was turned from pasture to cultivation, provided the opportunity. The frequently used opportunity for emigration provided a safety valve.

While the output of potatoes had been increased to support the growing Irish population, so was the production of other crops which were used to pay the rent. As noted above, rents increased four-fold during the French wars, and these had to come from cash crops. From 1780 to 1819 the annual export of wheat increased nearly twenty-fold. This was in addition to increases in grain products such as spirits and brews. The export of linen, reflecting the production of flax, increased two-fold, and despite the turn to arable land from pasture, the annual export of bullocks and cows increased more than four-fold, that of butter 25 percent. The export of bacon increased twenty-fold.[16] The last probably represented the cash of crop of the conacre farmer who managed to raise a pig or two on potato leavings.

During the next twenty years, the wars with the French having ended, grain for the English market was available from other sources including increased domestic production, and the price of grain fell. Irish landlords moved to consolidate their formerly fragmented holdings and to turn them to pasture again. This involved evictions, and the Irish resisted being deprived of their minimal subsistence altogether. Acts of terrorism as well as more organized political and economic actions slowed down the proposed consolidations, while the Irish pressed for more subdivision and settlement of the wastes. English, as well as Irish political leaders, began to take serious note of the problem of the increasing population of paupers, discovering in the process that there was a "population problem." Commissions of inquiry were repeatedly appointed to explore the problem. Blame was placed on the rapacity of landlords, the imprudence and fertility of the Irish, and on the potato which made the intolerable situation possible. Some were of the opinion that had the Irish lived on grain they would not have been so prolific. Sir Randolph Routh, Chief of the Commissariat Office in Dublin during 1846, noted that three times as much land and labor would be required to produce in grain the nutritional equivalent of potatoes. In 1845, the Devon Commission reported that 2⅓ million acres fit for pasturage and almost a million and a half acres fit for tillage could be readily recovered from the waste.[17] This land was not available to the Irish since there was no profit to the landowners in its cultivation. Thus, the Irish lived on the potato in response to the constraints placed on them; it was not until these constraints were lifted that other foodstuffs became available to them and were included in their diet.

Nonetheless, during this period the export of wheat, oats, and barley (including meal and flour) from Ireland continued to increase. Annual exports to England before the Great Famine included an average of more than 3.3 million barrels of wheat, oats, and barley, plus almost 1.7 million cwts. (112 lbs.) of oatmeal and flour.[18] (A barrel of wheat weighed around 280 pounds; a barrel of oats, 196 pounds; and a barrel of barley, 224 pounds.) In addition, considerable quantities of grain found their way into exported spirits and brews as well as into the larders of the upper classes of Ireland and their retainers.

The export of grain from Ireland continued during the famine. The House of Commons was informed that from the time the failure of the potato crop was recognized to February 5, 1846—roughly three months—258,000 quarters (about 2 barrels to the quarter) of wheat, one million quarters of oats and oatmeal, and 701,000 hundredweight of barley had left Ireland, and that since then exports had been continuing at the same rate. Ship after ship laden with wheat, oats, cattle, pigs, and butter sailed to England under naval escort, the rent crops having been collected and transported to ports under military guard. This was protested by many, including highly placed English commissioners responsible for the relief of Ireland's problems, but they did not prevail.[19] Eventually the English did mount sporadic and desultory famine relief programs, too late and too little. Bureaucratic obstruction, the lack of experience, and economic policy constraints vitiated the effort. Food did appear in the commercial markets of Ireland but was unavailable to the poor.

Landlords carried on as usual and frequently to their own detriment. Some proprietors forgave or reduced rents, but for the most part tenants whose rents fell in arrears were evicted. Landlords, taking advantage of the situation, turned arable land to pasture, motivated in good part by the decline in the price of grain since the end of the French wars and the entry of American grain into world markets. The fact that many tenants actually paid or tried to pay rent, rather than consuming the grain or livestock it came from, was frequently remarked upon. Many attributed such behavior to the insecurity and submissiveness of the Irish, and to their ignorance.

An economist might argue, as did J. S. Mill, that the increase in rents received by the Irish landlord was a result of a growing population. Indeed, the increased rents were made possible by the increased production resulting from increased labor. But the portion of increased production that went to individual laboring families was likely to have remained at the same bare subsistence level regardless of their numbers. The laborer's portion was not determined by some free market that existed only in the minds of economists, but by the political institutions and power structure. Potentially cultivable land was still withheld from production. The condition of the Irish tenant did not improve perceptibly in the late eighteenth century, when the expansion of arable land increased the demand for labor; nor did the condition of the Irish tenant improve with the thinning of the labor supply by the famine, subsequent to which rents fell very little.[20] The land shortage, though not the land hunger, may have been exaggerated, as noted in the Devon Commission report cited earlier. Were Irish labor in short supply, the British would likely have brought in immigrants as they had in Ulster for political purposes.

The potato was the staple of the Irish diet by the eighteenth century, well before the dramatic increase in population which started in the latter part of that century. The dependence of the Irish on potatoes is better attributed to the social, political and economic conditions under which they were obliged to live, the demands for rent leaving only the barest portion for subsistence. Were there fewer Irish still forced, however, to depend on the potato, the potato blight would have been just as disastrous for them. Outsiders might have taken some comfort in the smaller number who would have died, but for the Irish individual the probability of dying or surviving would have remained the same.

Subsequent to the famine, the potato remained the principle staple for several decades. The average size of a holding increased, partly as a result of government policy and partly because the expansion of pasturage, earlier resisted, was now facilitated by the emigration of many Irish. The landlords, who were the principal determiners of land policy and utilization, found grain an unprofitable crop as increasing amounts of grain from America appeared in English markets. But not until the 1870s when, under various land reform acts, the Irish tenant obtained better conditions, including payments for improvements of the land and eventual ownership, did the potato begin to lose its place as the main dietary staple of the Irish.[21] The increase in age at marriage, which started before the famine, as noted earlier, continued. As they attained a measure of autonomy, the Irish chose to live on more than the potato and ordered their affairs accordingly, perhaps chastened by the experience for which the English were never forgiven.

Famine and Government

The Irish famine is not an isolated example of adventitious natural events being exacerbated by social and economic policies. The famines in China during the 1930s when millions died, were accompanied by the transfer of large acreages from food to opium production. This was in response to pressure by ruling war lords who levied taxes geared to the capacity of the land to produce opium rather than grain.[22]

Prior to the 1920s India exported large amounts of food grains. This fact is often taken to indicate that India at that time had more than sufficient food. Yet, prior to the 1920s, recorded famines were more frequent and more devastating than in subsequent years.[23] The caprices of climate had much to do with the frequency of famine. But the movement of food grains from unaffected areas to ports, storage facilities, or to famine areas was a matter of British policy. Nineteenth century British civil servants thought that the frequent famines were Malthusian checks that were best tolerated. One viceroy, Lord Mayo, uniquely believed that recurrent famines were more due to administrative than to natural causes.[24] In the late nineteenth century the institution of the Famine Code of India provided for a crop failure warning and famine relief system. The program was facilitated by the network of railroads built earlier for commercial and military purposes though its execution often may have been frustrated by the ideology and self-interest of the parties involved.

The recent famines in Bengal and particularly in Bangladesh (1974) have been attributed to the increase in population. But famines occurred in Bangladesh when populations were much smaller. Moreover, the recent history of this poor country predisposed that land to famine regardless of population size.

There are some similarities between the great famine in Bengal in 1943 and the recent one in Bangladesh, despite the considerable differences in the level of population pressure: Bengal's population in 1943 was perhaps 40 percent smaller than today. In the early 1940s grain stores and transportation were largely committed to the allied war effort; stores and transport suffered heavily during the Bangladesh-Pakistan conflict in 1971 and the dislocation that followed. The preconditions for famine were present at both times and the size of the population didn't seem to enter into into the equation. Floods in several of the districts triggered famine in 1943 as they did in 1974.

To prevent famine in the third world, the foresight, capability, and power of Joseph in Egypt is needed to generate and store a significant food surplus against bad times to come. Even Bangladesh could produce a food surplus if the will to do so were manifested (see p. 115). The problem is how to cope with the economic structures that govern production, storage, and distribution of such surpluses. In the interim one can expect famine years, interspersed with normal years, and years of bumper crops when the weather is more favorable than usual.

The Influence of Weather

Most famines occur when there is a period of unusually unfavorable weather deviating from the normal pattern. Humans also have had to face longer term shifts in the customary weather patterns to which agricultural and other economic activities are synchronized. According to some students of the subject, such shifts in weather patterns have been accompanied by an increase in the frequency of famines.

A number of climatologists, R. A. Bryson for one,[25] claim that we have entered a period of climatic deterioration characterized by a cooling down of world temperatures, a trend that has been in progress for a couple of decades in different areas and is expected to continue for some time. It is held responsible for many of the unfavorable weather patterns of a few years ago, the long drought (now ended) in the Sahel region of Africa, the irregularity of the monsoons over South Asia in 1974, and anomalous weather in other regions causing food shortfalls and frank famine.

As might be expected, others are of the opinion that such predictions are unwarranted, or that an exactly opposite trend is indicated by the facts. The imponderables determining weather are such that neither long-term nor short-term predictions can be made with any degree of confidence.[26]

Not only are the natural determinants of the weather system imperfectly understood, but the impact of human activities on the weather is not clear. On the one hand, there is the release into the atmosphere of dusts and smoke that shield the sun's rays and reinforce cooling trends, a phenomenon emphasized by Bryson. On the other hand, there is a release of carbon dioxide from the burning of fuels, forming an atmospheric layer which keeps heat in, a greenhouse effect that tends to warm things up. Recently, Broecker has speculated that the greenhouse effect is likely to overcome the cooling trend and that the world will grow warmer. This argument has been somewhat supported with inconclusive patterns in the southern hemisphere.[27]

Concern with the effect of weather changes on food production and on the economy is not new. The Victorian economist William Stanley Jevons was impressed by the apparent correspondence between the periodicity of sunspots, estimated in his time to be 10.46 years, and his estimates of 10.45 years as the average period between booms of the business cyles from 1721 to 1878. He concluded that the sunspots caused fluctuations in the weather, rainfall, and crops which in turn influenced business cycles. Later estimates of sunspot cycles indicated the period to be 11 years rather than 10.46 years, destroying the correspondence Jevons thought he had discerned between sunspots and business cycles.[28]

Eddy, in his review of historical observations of sunspots, noted that the important effects of solar activity on the weather may not be associated so much with the short-term 11-year cycles of relatively small amplitude, but with the longer term changes in solar radiation, occurring over centuries, whose greater amplitude may override the effects of short-term variations.[29]

Though climatic conditions are, for practical purposes, not controllable, their effects on human life and activity are nonetheless mediated by the capacity of humans to adapt. High civilizations based on agriculture and supporting relatively large populations have flourished in a variety of regions, terrains and climates: irrigated deserts, terraced mountain areas, diked marshes, benign subtropical and humid tropics, as well as temperate zone regions with long hard winters. The issue is not whether humans can adapt effectively over the long run to climatic change but whether they can respond quickly enough to the pace of such change to avoid significant dislocations.

What gives this issue an aura of urgency is the belief that the world is overpopulated, that the limits of resources are being fast approached and that climatic change which would diminish these resources further would be catastrophic. J. Gribbin, former geophysics editor of *Nature* and senior scientist in climatic research at Sussex University writes that the real urgency lies in the ". . . prospect that climatic influences will make it harder to grow food just at a time when the present population has increased to the point where food supplies are precarious. . . ." Gribbin views climatic deterioration only as a possibility.[30] Bryson and Murray, who are more certain about the unfavorable direction of climatic change, believe that population size must be adjusted to the worst of the weather cycle; otherwise nature will perform the adjustment in a cruel manner.[31] The presumption underlying both points of view is the Malthusian one that humans expand to the limits of resources so that a worsening of climate *must* result in calamity. The presumption is false. Humans control their numbers long before they approach these limits.

An unfavorable turn of climate certainly could cause more frequent droughts, frosts, short growing periods, and unseasonable rains resulting in crop shortfalls and famines. However, smaller populations would not necessarily be able to cope with these difficulties any better than larger ones. It would still be necessary to develop a social policy of surplus food production, storage, and distribution, as insurance against poor crop years. Droughts and floods are best managed by the construction and maintenance of waterworks; shorter agricultural seasons may require greater labor inputs to compensate for the lack of time available for plowing, sowing, and reaping. Thus, a larger population may actually be advantageous. These issues and the limits of agricultural growth are discussed in later sections (see following chapters). But first some observations of the effects of past climatic changes.

In the past there have been alternating periods of climatic deterioration and amelioration of varying lengths and sequences. Utterstrom[32] explained much of the economic troubles of Europe during the latter half of the sixteenth and much of the seventeenth centuries as resulting from a change in climate, a general cooling down accompanied by unseasonable rains. Food production decreased, particularly in Scandinavia, and the well being of peoples deteriorated. An earlier cooling period in the fourteenth century was purported to have caused the replacement of cereal growing by fishing as the main economic activity of Iceland. Utterstrom surmised that Sweden enjoyed a more clement climate during the latter part of the fifteenth century and the first half of the sixteenth century. But Eddy cites climatological evidence that the half century between 1450 and 1500 was particularly cold, at least in England and France.[33] It is obviously difficult to chart past climatic changes, as it is to predict future developments.

Emmanuel Le Roy Ladurie addressed the question of the impact of climatic shifts on human history and welfare. A significant problem in such analysis is the absence of authoritative data on the history of climate. Too often analysts first found the historical event and then sought some weather pattern to explain that event, rather than identifying climatic changes and observing their effects.[34]

Ladurie devoted considerable attention to the techniques of mapping historical trends in weather. In the course of this process he made some observations about the relation between weather changes and human history. He found that many of the disastrous economic conditions that have been attributed to climatic changes can be fully explained by social and economic developments. The decline of the wine industry in England and France in the late fourteenth and early fifteenth centuries was more a consequence of the labor shortage caused by the plague than the inclement weather. Where labor was available, the yield from grapes was still ample.

The "little ice age" of 1600 to 1850 in Europe occurred during a time when the modern economic development of western Europe was starting and accelerating. Though the Netherlands, France, and England experienced more adverse weather than did Spain and the other Mediterranean regions, the economies and populations of the latter contracted while those of the former expanded. The reasons are to be found in social and economic developments. There were many periods of economic and social distress during this expansion, but the reasons again are generally to be found in social processes, not climate. Land taken out of cultivation and put into sheep walks by enclosures in seventeenth century England affected the food supply more than weather changes could. Famines did occur all too frequently when unseasonal storms flooded fields or unseasonal freezes killed seed grains. Ladurie noted that the food scarcity of 1740–43 was the last such crisis of famine proportions in northern France. The weather did not improve or become more predictable, but the growth in the wheat trade, improved roads and the progress of agricultural technology protected against such crises. Even the sporadic disasters gave way to social developments as Europeans, ignoring the fact that their world was getting colder, kept increasing their productive capacities and transportation and communication networks.[35]

A few decades later the reduction in the marital fertility of French peasantry was under way perhaps because, among other reasons, there was no longer the need to have as many children as possible in the hopes that some would survive the periodic famines, pestilences, and other "natural" disasters.

The "little ice age" ended in the middle of the nineteenth century, marked by a receding of the alpine glaciers. The warming trend was at first erratic and temperatures fell again to a low point around 1890. Thereafter, temperatures rose fairly steadily until the middle of this century. Mitchell, on plotting this trend, found the amelioration to be largely in winter temperatures, affecting principally the Arctic areas, secondarily the cold and temperate zones of the northern hemisphere, thirdly the tropics, and in a much less perceptible way, the southern hemisphere.[36] As noted earlier, the trend appears to have reversed itself in recent years, and the world, according to some climatologists, is cooling down. A change of climate in one region may be associated with an entirely different type of change in another. The untimely rains of fourteenth-century Europe were associated with the droughts and dessication of the American Southwest, ending in the abandonment of many areas by formerly well established Indian cultivators. Even so, some scholars question whether this was entirely due to prolonged drought. As the rains returned, the abandonments continued. Some argue that the primitive cultivators, sparse as they were, had despoiled their lands through poor techniques, a problem to be discussed later.[37]

A change in weather of such magnitude as to reduce the arable portion of the earth to a fraction of its current size is possible; it has occurred in the past during the great ice ages. However, such changes are likely to be slow and will allow for human adaptation, including adjustments in population size. Radical changes of climate occurring so rapidly that adjustment is impossible have also been considered, including a cold trend so severe that winter snows would not melt in summer and would cover the temperate world with glacial ice within a few years. The catastrophe-prone imagination can always conjure up hypothetical conditions beyond the scope of human adaptive capabilities. But humans must cope with the world as they find it, and historically, human welfare has depended more on social organization than on the vicissitudes of weather.

The people of Iceland, precariously situated with regard to weather, are reported to have experienced at least 49 famines from 975 A.D. to 1804.[38] Moreover, though they turned to fishing, a lack of food was so prevalent almost from the time of settlement in the tenth century to the sixteenth century (a time noted by Icelandic historians to be one of near starvation) that the Icelanders had shrunk considerably in physical stature (according to Coon) but later regained their former size as one of the tallest peoples.[39] The Icelanders not only survived on their inhospitable island, but they developed what was to become one of the most democratic and egalitarian societies and were among the first to achieve universal literacy. The capital city of Reykjavik, a town of about 80,000, has been reported to support 40 book-stores.[40] This people preserved and developed further the heritage of their ancestors, who fled tyranny in medieval Norway, established representative government and justice, and composed great epics. These settlers, during the middle ages numbering perhaps 60,000 ill-fed people, produced a quantity of poets, historians, lawmakers, administrators, and bishops. Saxo Grammaticus, a twelfth-century Danish historian, noted "They make good their impoverishment with their wits."[41] Recurrent periods of oppressive cold, volcanic eruptions, famines, and epidemics so plagued the Icelanders that it is almost impossible to find a time when life was easy.[42] Famine, periodic disasters, and hostile physical environments which nonetheless still allow life to continue, have rarely if ever sapped the vitality of a people. This they do to themselves, by the way they relate to each other, by the way they organize their society.

The Influence of Trade

Large populations may be better able to defend themselves against the vicissitudes of climate and other calamities precisely because people are available to construct works, impound water, control floods. They can more readily support trade and transportation networks that, if other considerations do not intervene, would relieve shortages in one area by importing supplies from other areas. Cities, of course, would maintain trade relations with a variety of regions from which food may be obtained.

Dependence on external sources for part of the food supply is not an unmixed blessing. Political and economic changes, as well as weather, in food surplus areas may influence the availability of food for export. The commercial channels and markets through which food is distributed tend to be more responsive to profit than to need. So shortfalls in production are not shared equitably: Those who can pay get the food; others go hungry.

Braudel[43] described the food problems experienced by such sixteenth-century Mediterranean cities as Venice, Naples, Genoa, Ragusa (present day Dubrovnik). Large tracts of land were required for the optimum cultivation of grain under the dry Mediterranean weather conditions and in the absence of extensive irrigation works. In the commercial economy which prevailed in the sixteenth century, food production had to compete for land with crops providing higher monetary yields, such as olives, wines, sheep for wool, and mulberry leaves for silkworms. Thus, local grain was always somewhat short in supply and additional grain had to be imported from grain surplus areas. Its availability varied with weather as well as the political and economic conditions in the source countries. The grain trade was disorganized and rife with speculation and peculation. If a city experienced a shortage, many merchants might send their stocks to the short area even causing the price of grain to fall in the short area and rise elsewhere; on another occasion, the merchant might hesitate to ship grain into the short area for fear of a glut and a fall in prices, and the short area would remain short. Cities could not predict from one year to the next whether they would experience a glut or shortage.

As the cities of the Mediterranean grew in population, urban growth being in part due to the immigration of people from the agricultural sector, the problem of feeding the cities became greater, the crises more severe. These food crises were frequently resolved by the appearance of new sources of food supply. The crisis of the mid-sixteenth century was resolved by the importation of grain from Turkish dominions which were experiencing a grain boom and glut between 1548 and 1564. As that source dried up, purportedly due to poor harvests, hostilities and population growth within the Turkish dominions, other crises loomed, often exacerbated by the weather. (While some historians blame the lowered productivity in the Ottoman Empire to increased population, there is a considerable body of evidence which points to a deterioration of internal social relations, oppression of the peasantry, and corruption and venality of officials.[44] Several highly placed Turkish observers of the middle sixteenth century warned of the impending depopulation of the countryside should the tax burden become more oppressive. By the seventeenth century, the depopulation of the countryside was in full swing and abandoned villages were noted in many areas.[45]) Eventually, after a period in which grain was imported from the North Atlantic countries, the Mediterranean food crises were resolved by increasing self-sufficiency. Venice, which in 1586 had more than 50 percent of its grain brought in by sea, in 1588 obtained most of its grain from hinterland dominions. As the terms of trade for the Italian commercial cities fell, as the demand and prices for their goods and services decreased, they ceased to rely on foreign food imports. The urban population diminished and food production in the countryside expanded. Significantly the adjustment occurred without a Malthusian catastrophe. The Mediterranean, as its commerce waned, learned to live on its own food resources, and the pace of population growth slowed. In Spain, as the economy declined in the seventeenth century, a marked depopulation occurred accompanied by the withdrawal of lands from cultivation in some areas.

The developing nations today are confronted with the need for solutions to recurring food crises. Until recently, a quarter century of generally equable climate favored the efforts of these nations to expand their agriculture and feed their growing populations. At the same time, surplus grain stores accumulated by the United States, in its effort to maintain domestic prices, acted as a food reserve that helped compensate for periodic shortfalls. American exports may have also served to depress grain prices in developing nations and limited the incentives of indigenous farmers to produce for city markets. Perhaps the most significant export was that of food growing technology, symbolized by the "green revolution," based on high yield dwarf grain varieties which effectively use large quantities of fertilizer and water. Fertilizer must either be imported or manufactured, the latter requiring the importation of oil by many countries. Irrigation based on deep-well pumps driven by diesel fuel adds to the oil import bill. In effect, the "green revolution" cannot resolve the problem of self-sufficiency without an accompanying development of domestic energy and fertilizer sources.

During the last few years, the United States has divested itself of its grain reserves as a matter of policy. Large quantities of grain were sold to the Soviet Union partly in the interests of detente and partly as a quick way of depleting grain stocks. Little was left for relief of famines and shortfalls in hungry nations. The petroleum producing countries, for their own political and economic reasons, increased the price of oil. This resulted in shortages of fertilizer and energy which nullified many of the gains of the green revolution. So when nations such as India in 1971 felt that they were achieving self-sufficiency in food production, they proved to be mistaken. (In 1976, however, with an easing of the fertilizer shortage and the help of good weather, Indian farmers again produced a surplus of food grains, this time relative to a somewhat larger population.[46])

The increased capacity for the production of food provided by advanced technologies will not solve the problem of famine. Regardless of population size and productive capacity, if the social economic order does not provide for the production and storage of food surpluses or reliance cannot be placed on transport and commerce to compensate for shortfalls in local food supplies, there will be periodic famines.

Notes

1. F. A. Southard, "Famine," in *Encyclopedia of Social Sciences*, 1948, vol. VI, pp. 85--89.

2. H. Gille, "The Demographic History of the Northern European Countries in the Eighteenth Century," *Population Studies* 3:1, (June 1949), pp. 2--70.

3. G. Harrison, J. S. Weiner, J. M. Tanner, and N. A. Barnicot, *Human Biology* (New York and Oxford: Oxford University Press, 1964), p. 439; National Academy of Engineering, *The Food People Balance, Proceedings of a Symposium* (Washington, D. C., 1970), pp. 47--55.

4. D. A. Roe, *A Plague of Corn, the Social History of Pellagra* (Ithaca, N.Y.: Cornell University Press, 1973).

5. E. A. Wrigley, *Population and History* (New York: McGraw-Hill, 1969), pp. 64--70.

6. P. Goubert, *Beauvaisis et le Beauvaisis de 1600 a 1730*, 2 vols. (Paris, 1960).

7. P. Kropotkin, *The Great French Revolution* (English translation, New York: Vanguard Press, 1927), vol. 2, p. 417.

8. P. Goubert, *Louis XIV and Twenty Million Frenchmen* (English translation, New York: Pantheon Books, 1968), pp. 21--51, 149.

9. Ibid., pp. 215--20.

10. Ibid., p. 248.

11. The facts for the following account are derived principally from the following sources: C. Woodham Smith, *The Great Hunger* (New York: Harper and Row, 1962); K. H. Connell, *The Population of Ireland: 1750--1845* (Oxford: Oxford University Press, 1950); R. J. Salaman, *The History and Social Influence of the Potato* (Cambridge: Cambridge University Press, 1949).

12. "A letter from Rt. Hon. Edmund Burke M.P. on the subject of the Roman Catholics of Ireland," in *Digest of Evidence taken by H. M. Commissioners of Inquiry into the state of the Law and Practice in respect of the occupation of land in Ireland*, 2nd ed. (1792), pp. 86--88. Quoted by C. Woodham Smith, op. cit. p. 27.

13. C. Woodham Smith, op. cit., p. 26.

14. Connell, op. cit., p. 42.

15. K. H. Connell, "Some Unsettled Problems in English and Irish Population History," *Irish Historical Studies* VII:28 (1957). Reprinted in M. Drake, ed., *Population and Industrialization* (London: Methuen, 1969), pp. 30--39.

16. See Connell, *The Population of Ireland: 1750--1845*, op. cit., pp. 97, 99, 109, 268.   17. R. J. Salaman, op. cit., pp. 277, 307.

18. K. H. Connell, *The Population of Ireland: 1750--1845*, op. cit., pp. 97--99, 109, 268.

19. C. Woodham Smith, op. cit., pp. 75--77; see also R. J. Salaman, op. cit., p. 293.

20. Connell, *The Population of Ireland: 1750--1845*, op. cit., p. 70.

21. See Salaman, op. cit., pp. 321--22, 326.

22. O. E. Clubb, *Twentieth Century China* (New York: Columbia University Press, 1972), pp. 187--88.

23. See *Census of India: 1951*, vol. 1, pt. 1.

24. S. Ambirajan, "Malthusian Population Theory and Indian Famine Policy in the Nineteenth Century," *Population Studies*, 30:1 (March 1976): 5--14.

25. R. A. Bryson, "A Perspective on Climatic Change," *Science* 184 (May 1974), p. 753--60.

26. N. Wade, "Briefing—Cold Shower for Meteorologists," *Science* 197 (August 1977), p. 647; Alan Anderson, Jr., "Forecast for Forecasting: Cloudy," *New York Times Magazine*, December 29, 1974, p. 10; J. Gribbin, *Forecasts, Famines, and Freezes* (New York: Walker and Co., 1976).

27. W. S. Broecker, "Climatic Change: Are We on the Brink of a Pronounced Global Warming?" *Science* 189 (August 1975), pp. 460--63; P. E. Damon and S. M. Kunen, "Global Cooling," *Science* 193 (August 1976), pp. 447--53.

28. See R. L. Heilbroner, *The Worldly Philosophers* (New York: Simon & Schuster, 1961), pp. 228--29.

29. J. A. Eddy, "The Maunder Minimum," *Science* 192 (June 1976), pp. 1189--1201.

30. J. Gribbin, op. cit., p. 113.

31. R. A. Bryson and T. J. Murray, *Climates of Hunger* (Madison, Wisconsin; University of Wisconsin Press, 1977), pp. 116--19.

32. G. Utterstrom, "Climatic Fluctuations and Population Problems in Early Modern History," *Scandinavian Economic History Review* III (1955), pp. 3--47.

33. Eddy, op. cit., notes 75 and 76.

34. E. Le Roy Ladurie, *Times of Feast, Times of Famine: A History of Climate Since the Year 1000* (English translation, Garden City, N.Y.: Doubleday, 1971), pp. 7--22.

35. Ibid., p. 93.

36. Ibid., pp. 86--88.

37. Ibid., pp. 293--96.

38. Bryson, op. cit., p. 754.

39. Cited in G. A. Harrison, et al., op. cit., p. 434.

40. Donald S. Connery, *The Scandinavians* (New York: Simon & Schuster, 1966), p. 552.

41. See G. Jones, *A History of the Vikings* (New York: Oxford University Press, 1968), p. 289.

42. R. F. Tomasson, "A Millennium of Misery: The Demography of the Icelanders," *Population Studies* 31:3 (December 1977), pp. 405--27.

43. Fernand Braudel, *The Mediterranean and the Mediterranean World in the Age of Philip II*, 2 vols. (English translation, New York: Harper and Row, 1972), pp. 570--615.

44. N. Itzkowitz, *Ottoman Empire and Islamic Tradition* (New York: Alfred A. Knopf, 1972), pp. 93--98.

45. B. Lewis, *The Emergence of Modern Turkey*, 2nd ed. (London: Oxford University Press, 1968), pp. 32--33.

46. *New York Times*, June 27, 1976, section 4, p. 4.

6

Population and Subsistence

The Expansion of Subsistence

Malthusians and non-Malthusians alike would agree that the demands of population and levels of subsistence cannot long exceed the capacity of resources, but this truism can hide much disagreement. Population size is variable, subject to change by mortality, fertility, and migration. For pessimists, mortality is the ultimate regulator, for optimists, fertility. Levels of subsistence, the food, clothing, and shelter deemed necessary in diverse social settings may vary enormously. They range from levels barely sufficient to sustain physiological functions, reproduction, and work, to levels which can only be characterized as wastefully opulent. When economists and others talk of subsistence levels, or subsistence wages, they usually mean the bare minimum level, which is hard to define (see Chapter 7). Most people at most times (including the present) have lived close to the bare minimum subsistence level. Malthusians proposed that this is in good part due to the tendency of people to reproduce themselves to the limits of the capacity of the resources to which they have access to sustain them, their level of subsistence falling as more and more people try to make do with fewer resources per person. This was formalized by Malthus and Ricardo in the Iron Law of Wages. Wages could not for long rise above the bare subsistence level; if they did, then a surplus of labor is generated by a fall in death rates and increases in birth rates, and wages fall, perhaps even below subsistence. People die and do not reproduce themselves and wages go up, stabilizing around bare subsistence. The Malthusian thesis is based on the presumption that resources are relatively fixed for a given level of technology. But suppose that labor creates resources, or rather, converts heretofore unproductive or underproductive environments and raw materials into those capable of producing increased subsistence.

The relatively favorable material condition of various European peasantries after the Black Death had diminished their numbers is attributed to the improved people-to-resources ratio. But the plenitude of resources, farmsteads, towns, harbors, and manufactories available to the diminished populations were, in fact, built and developed by the much larger pre-Black Death population. These resources could well have deteriorated and reverted to a more natural state (as shall be noted later) had there been no recovery of population. The resources of a people are not fixed but are adjusted to its size, social structure, economic ethos and values.

Boserup presented a point of view which contrasts with that of Malthus in her examination of agricultural development and resources in pre-industrial societies.[1] In her study she did not inquire into the causes of population growth or stagnation but rather into the consequences. In her view, population growth was not usually limited by a lack of resources and the subsistence they could provide. On the contrary, population growth, whatever its cause, resulted in an expansion of resources and subsistence. The potential resources necessary to sustain a growing population were usually present and the technology needed to obtain additional subsistence was usually attainable if not already known. While Malthus proposed that population grows to the limits of resources, Boserup held that population growth leads to expanded resources, most of which are created by human labor.

The incentive to increase agricultural production was often lacking because this required more intensive labor and longer and harder work than people chose to do. At the extreme, there are well-documented instances of communities of primitive cultivators in Africa and elsewhere which did not produce sufficient food during the growing seasons to last through the entire year, although with additional efforts larger harvests could have been attained. But a goodly proportion of the potential labor force, particularly young men, were absent on contract labor or, if at home, did not work hard or regularly, thus leaving most of the field work to the older family members. The young people preferred to spend their energy and time in what may be termed ceremonial and leisure activities, visiting and raiding. As a consequence, these people regularly went hungry during the part of the year before new crops were brought in; they lost weight and showed signs of starvation, recouping their energy stores only as the new crop was harvested.[2]

One of these people, the Bemba, in former times had been raiders and slavers living off plunder and the sale of captives to Arabs. This was stopped by the British around the turn of the twentieth century. About all that remained of their former power was the shell of a complicated political system suitable for a people who relied on war.[3] These people, who had disdained the hoe, were obliged to live by the hoe, to give up the spear and gun and were, perhaps, not yet fully reconciled to this situation.

Whatever the level of subsistence and associated effort, when population increased, the resulting pressure to augment the food supply provided the incentive to work harder. Boserup developed this theme through an examination of the stages in agricultural development and growth. The stages were presented in a schematic (if not always historic) sequence to illustrate the intensification of land use under population pressure.

Swidden cultivation, also known as slash and burn agriculture, is among the more primitive forms of cultivation, and it is still practiced in many areas of the world today. Swidden cultivators need to have available to them large tracts of forest, at one time a dominant feature of the earth's surface. Larger trees in the sections to be cultivated are girdled or cut; the section is burned and various crops planted among the ashes. The labor spent in soil preparation is usually relatively small, and only simple tools, such as the axe and digging stick, are required since the land does not need to be cleared of roots, plowed, cultivated, or fertilized. Accumulated humus and ash provide an easily worked nutrient and friable bed for planting a variety of food crops. But the swidden plots either lose their fertility within two to three years or are taken over by weeds, and the cultivators are obliged to move on to a new section. This is no problem as long as there is plenty of forest available relative to the number of people, so that the swidden cultivators do not have to return to old plots until these are reforested, say in twenty years.

With the growth of population, larger sections of the forest have to be burned and plots revisited more frequently; the fallow period is thus shortened. On returning, the cultivators find not full-grown forest with limited undergrowth, but bush and grass. The burning of the bush is not sufficient to rid the soil of live grass roots or to provide a suitable bed of ashes. The ground around has to be hoed and otherwise prepared before seed and root crops can be planted and expected to grow satisfactorily. This involves additional labor.

As population continues to grow, the fallow periods become shorter still; the cultivators find that the forest and bush have become grasslands which require plowing and, therefore, still more work. Draft animals need to be reared and cared for.

As the fallow periods become shorter and shorter under the impetus of population growth, cropping and soil preparation become more intensive and frequent. If the droppings of animals pastured on fields during fallow periods are insufficient, other methods have to be employed, increasing the labor requirements. As waste or other lands used to pasture livestock become scarce, fodder has to be grown. Various rotation schemes are adopted to permit fields to recover from one crop while growing another. Thus, cultivators learn to grow legumes or "green manure" which fix nitrogen in the soil and restore the capacity of a field to yield grain while at the same time producing food or fodder. Ultimately, annual cropping becomes necessary and even cropping of the same field two or three times a year as weather permits. The shorter fallow periods require greater inputs of labor to accomplish the more intensive land preparation and fertilization, terracing, reclamation of wastes, construction and care of waterworks, diking, and irrigation. At any stage in this transition from land extensive to labor intensive cultivation, the increase in the productivity of land is purchased at the cost of a decrease in the marginal product of a labor unit. In the initial stages of intensification, people have to work harder to produce the same amount of food, and the incentive to do so comes from population pressure.

According to this scenario, if humans were not overcome by their numbers, they would have been overcome by work. But this is not the whole story. The growth of population and the concommitant growth of agriculture had other effects as well. The concentration of larger numbers of people permitted the division of labor and specialization; people became accustomed to regular and intensive work habits, thus increasing productivity. At different stages of agricultural development new tools and technologies were introduced to lighten work. The growth of population and agriculture resulted in technological developments and capital accumulation which in the end increased the productivity of labor and lightened the worker's burden. One might also add that some lands that were originally economically marginal became highly productive when brought under cultivation. This was true of lands reclaimed from the sea by the Dutch who are among the most productive farmers in the world.

Boserup's scheme is perhaps oversimplified in the interest of abstracting a principal trend in the history of agriculture. Bronson noted that Boserup's thesis appears to imply a single line of historical development from systems of extensive agriculture such as forest fallow or swidden cultivation to more intensive systems such as annual or multicropping.[4] Instead, Bronson proposed a variety of paths to agricultural development in which the type of agriculture practiced is not only a response to population and perhaps political pressures, but it is also a function of cultural preferences and practices and characteristics of the environment. Bronson noted that in some instances, at least, intensive types of agriculture are more productive per labor hour than extensive or swidden agriculture in the same region. Therefore, the people practicing swidden agriculture may not be following the "law of least effort" but rather a preferred way of life. In other instances, people accustomed to irrigation, as in wet rice cultivation, continued to irrigate when they moved to an area with lots of land in which they might have made an easier living by practicing extensive rather than intensive cultivation. The style of work may matter as much or more than the hours worked or the physical labor involved.

Bronson's argument does not, however, vitiate the principal thrust of Boserup's work. In many instances, a principal deterrent to agricultural development has been the investment of labor required in clearing, draining, levelling, terracing, and ditching, the construction of water impoundments, irrigation, drainage works, and the like. Once these works are completed (often taking many generations), and appropriate technologies and tools are developed, the productivity of the intensive system of cultivation in terms of labor inputs is likely to be as high as or higher than that of the extensive system it replaced, a possibility recognized by Boserup. Nor is the argument affected by the fact that cultivators may prefer to labor in the system of agriculture to which they are accustomed. Boserup's discussion is concerned with the reasons why people give up a system in which work is easy for one that is less congenial.

The intensification of labor occurs within a social cultural context that is only tangentially considered by Boserup. This context may be sufficient to explain agricultural growth as leaders and governing groups or the social order itself (where power is based on surpluses) force the production of sustenance beyond the felt needs of the cultivators. Many forms of agricultural expansion, such as the construction and maintenance of extensive irrigation systems, require a coordinating authority. And in a commercial economy, the expansion of agriculture occurs in response to an increase in the market demand for agricultural products, an increase which may occur without population growth. Population growth is not a necessary precursor to agricultural or other economic growth.

Nor is population growth necessarily followed by agricultural growth. When such a situation is apparent in history, it is often taken to validate the Malthusian thesis that there are insufficient resources available. Ladurie, in his historical study of the peasants of Languedoc (France) from the middle of the fifteenth century to the eighteenth century, concluded that the "Malthusian scissors," as he called them, operated only in traditional preindustrial societies. In these societies progress is slow, interest in technology is weak, and attention is diverted from material needs and problems by otherworldly concerns. Presumably, in modern societies there is sufficient drive and respect for technology to increase productivity and overcome the obduracy of nature.

The peasants of Languedoc doubled their number in the fifteenth and sixteenth centuries but increased their agricultural product very little. As a result they experienced very hard times through the seventeenth century. During the eighteenth century, after violent rebellions and changes in both the political conditions and the peasants' outlook, agricultural production took off.[5] Why did this not occur earlier?

Ladurie noted that the early phase of population growth in Languedoc was accompanied by an abortive expansion of agriculture. It was also accompanied by a surge in parasitism: rents, usurious interest, taxes, and tithes. The rentier prevailed over the enterpriser and, in Ladurie's words, "aggravated the Malthusian effects of an immemorial technical conservatism." However, might not the Malthusian effects been brought on by the wave of parasitism, by the wars which eventually bankrupted the kingdom and the many rebellions and civil disorders? Enterprising tenant farmers could accomplish very little in the face of the exactions of money, men, and materials, and the barriers to trade. In the face of such conditions "technical conservatism" and the maintenance of strong family units may well have been the prudent course for the mass of people. Despite the severe trials to which the agricultural economy was subjected, it did not collapse. Indeed, though the quality of peasant diets (e.g. amount of meat consumed) had deteriorated, the calories ingested per person had actually increased. The relative stability of agriculture in the turmoil of the times should be considered an accomplishment. As the ministers of eighteenth-century France tried, unsuccessfully, to head off the eventual political upheaval, social conditions did improve in Languedoc, as in France, and agricultural production increased. (Shortly afterwards, the French peasants began to practice birth control.)

If population expands, so eventually must the production of food, although social forces may delay the growth of agriculture. Boserup has described one schema of that growth which, while not the only one humans have followed, helps explain the observation that in many societies, often deemed poor, the full productive capacities of the available labor and land are not utilized.[6] Boserup's work (and that of others as well) has also pointed to the inadequacy of that type of economic analysis in which resources are regarded as fixed, when even the quality of the soil has been the product of human labor as in the case of highly productive mountain terraces, irrigated deserts, and reclaimed tide lands.

Dutch colonial administrators in the early eighteenth century concluded that Java was already overpopulated. Since then, the population of Java has increased greatly as has its food supply, without modern technology but through the adoption of more intensive cultivation practices. Geertz, in his study of the Javanese adaptation to population growth through intensification of agricultural production, noted that in some areas of North Central Java the population densities were as high as 5,000 persons per square mile, while Indonesia as a whole had an overall population density of 155 persons per square mile.[7] In the process of adapting to population density the Javanese exhibited considerable ingenuity in developing flexible social and economic arrangements to share crops as well as to intensify their agriculture. They thus maintained their communities and preserved their values rather than migrate to the sparsely settled outer islands where they might have had to live in a different fashion. The capacity of agricultural intensification to support an increasing population was cited by Wolf for a region in Mexico. It was estimated that in lowland Vera Cruz, 2,964 cultivable acres would be required to sustain 100 families practicing the local type of swidden cultivation. If permanent garden plots were cultivated along with swiddens, only 1,606 acres would be required by these 100 families. The same number of families could be supported by 212 acres under short term rotation and canal irrigation; by 148 to 173 acres under complete irrigation for mixed subsistence and commercial production, and by 91 completely irrigated acres devoted exclusively to commercial crops.[8]

Some observers today are making errors similar to those made by the Dutch observers of Indonesian agriculture more than a century and a half ago. On the basis of the fact that much African cultivation is swidden and the presumption that were other forms of cultivation feasible, the inhabitants would employ them, some experts have concluded that tropical forests are not suited for intensive cultivation. Analyses are also presented to support the view that tropical forest soils, being lateritic, are unsuitable for intensive cultivation.[9] Yet, former tropical forest in Africa is being intensively cultivated successfully and the practice is increasing. Agricultural soils are not merely the product of nature but include in their makeup the work and impact of humans. Static analyses concentrating on the here and now without attention to the human impact on soils may be misleading.

Recently, Sanchez and Buol examined the theses that much of the tropical soils are of a composition which tends to turn into laterite, a hard brick-like material, when exposed to wetting and drying as a result of clearing and cultivation.[10] They concluded from the evidence that laterization of tropical soils has been highly exaggerated and that most tropical soils, though poorly understood, are similar in most features to those found in temperate regions. Accordingly, they were cautiously optimistic that currently uncultivated tropical soils can make a major and sustained contribution to world food supplies if properly managed. Boserup noted that the land used for intensive cultivation in parts of Nigeria and other tropical regions is of the same type as that used for long fallow (forest) rotations. She proposed that most of the land in Africa is not cultivated intensively because war and slavery kept the population of the region down so that there was little need to give up swidden cultivation.

Though population growth may act as a stimulus to agricultural growth, the fact remains that social and economic processes may exert considerable influence. In a feudal subsistence society, where peasants produce for their own needs rather than for a market and where the lord has a claim on the peasant's labor and produce, the pressing of large numbers of people into the lord's personal service may reduce the labor available to expand agricultural production. In similar fashion, planned economies that place a high priority on military strength and industrialization may inordinately weaken the agricultural labor force, undermine its morale, and deprive the agricultural sector of capital. And in commercial economies, the response of agriculture to the food needs of a growing population depends on the translation of those needs, in the marketplace, into what is called effective demand, backed by the willingness and ability to pay.

Since production is a social enterprise, the expansion of agriculture depends not only on population but also on the effectiveness of the social and economic organization and the incentives and disincentives it provides. The levels of subsistence experienced by most people in history and third world countries today have nonetheless been low, but this has not been due so much to a lack of productive capacity as to social conditions, the subject of the next section.

Peasant Society and Low Subsistence Levels

During the early 1950s, the very low caloric intake and other nutritional deficits of the people of less developed countries began to receive widespread and anxious attention. In 1950, Lord Boyd Orr, the Director of the Food and Agricultural Organization of the United Nations, wrote in the *Scientific American* that two-thirds of mankind were malnourished or hungry, a figure which has since been revised downwards. Economists reported that there were more workers per unit of land than were necessary to produce the yields obtained, even with the primitive technology used; that the same output could be produced with fewer people, thereby increasing the per capita share. To these economists, many people of the developing nations not engaged in agriculture also seemed to be doing useless tasks and providing unnecessary services as hawkers and porters. The extra labor was deemed surplus and the situation one of hidden unemployment or underemployment. Some economists hypothesized that work sharing was part of a pre-industrial welfare system. People not otherwise needed in the economy received a share of the product even though their marginal productivity was small.[11] The implication was that the low productivity per person resulted from there being too many people for the available capital resources. The very sharp decrease in mortality resulting from mosquito control, immunization against infectious diseases, improvement of sanitation and of the general conditions of life, promised still larger increases in population. With growth rates of more than 2 and 3 percent per year, and with the potential for expanding the food supply considered to be limited, disaster was judged to be imminent.

But, as population increased in the 1950s and 1960s in the developing countries, so did the agricultural and food output, keeping a bare pace with population. If anything, per capita food production improved slightly in most places, though, of course, the growth of food output varied from year to year, depending on the vicissitudes of climate. (Africa experienced a slight decline, perhaps because of the political turmoil of those decades.) This agricultural growth occurred before the green revolution or other significant changes in agricultural technology.[12]

Since the potential of agricultural production in third world countries was presumed limited, where did the increased food production come from? Obviously, the limits had not been reached and the increased production could come principally from the increased application of labor and a more intensive use of land. Since an excess supply of labor was presumed to have existed, why was this excess not applied earlier to increasing the per capita food output above what appeared to be a bare physiological level? An examination of traditional agrarian institutions and economies in historical as well as contemporary perspective may provide some answers.

The general prevalence of low nutritional levels among peasants throughout history regardless of the size of population relative to resources is noteworthy. Braudel noted that the average per capita annual consumption of food grains, the bulk of the peasant's diet in the Mediterranean regions of the sixteenth century, was around two quintals (or 440 pounds) with some variation from region to region.[13] This was around or less than half of what the grain growing peasant produced, the principal crops of many others being grapes, olives, mulberry bushes, fiber, etc., the surpluses going to rents, taxes, and the like. A similar figure was cited for the depopulated Spain of 1799, though the potential for the expansion of Spanish agriculture was perhaps evidenced by the increase of population which almost doubled in the following century.

A 40-acre farm in fourteenth- and fifteenth-century Mecklenburg, North Germany, is estimated to have produced around 10,200 pounds of grain; of this, 6,200 pounds went into production costs, seed (3,400 pounds) and feed (2,800 pounds) for the four draft horses; 2,700 pounds went to pay dues to the lord, leaving only 1,300 pounds to feed the peasant and his family with a daily ration of about 1,600 calories per member, exclusive of the small amount of garden vegetables and meat they may have consumed on occasion but these are not noted.[14] The medieval peasant family of Mecklenburg produced more than sufficient food to enjoy a sumptuous diet had they been allowed to keep it. But the peasants in pre-industrial society rarely got to keep much more than was needed to keep them alive and producing. Why this was so may become clearer on closer examination of the conditions to which peasants were subject.

Wolf proposed that the principal distinction between primitive cultivators and peasants is that the latter were obliged to pay rent to an overlord of one sort or another. The overlord was frequently identified with the feudal lord or the landlord, and the peasant with the serf or tenant. These were not the only types of relationship involving the payment of a rent. The overlord could have been a tax collector or other official who had some right to the incomes from land as a grantee or as a prerogative for performing governmental functions such as the defense of the community and the administration of justice. In some times and places, moneylenders and religious officials took on the prerogatives of an overlord when the power of the state was available to enforce their claim on the product of the land.

Rent or dues included not only payment in kind or cash, but also the obligation to labor for the lord. The work may have involved the construction and maintenance of public works, roads, dikes, irrigation systems, as well as labor in the lord's field or house. The systems of reciprocal obligation and duties between peasant and overlord were frequently institutionalized in tradition, but this was often a frail protection for the peasant. The basic characteristic of the relationship was an asymmetry of power. The lord had armed retainers and the authority of the state at his call, while the peasant had recourse only to usually ineffectual rebellion. Villages were organized in a variety of social and economic patterns. These ranged from communal control of the land to systems approximating private ownership of plots which could be bought and sold. Within the village and other villages with which they may have had ties, peasants engaged in a system of exchanges through sponsorship and participation in feasts, festivals, marriage, funerals, and the like. These ceremonials served to maintain the integrity of the community but they also consumed a considerable portion of the peasant's labor and subsistence. In some Central American areas where food intake is at a low level, a man may expend the equivalent of a year's local wages to sponsor a community ceremonial, a high cost for the maintenance of community solidarity, but perhaps a necessary one.[15] The rent fund and the ceremonial fund, as Wolf called them, were of sufficient magnitude and their allocation sufficiently compelling to inhibit the accumulation of capital either of the monetized sort or through nonmonetized labor investments. Such social "surpluses" as peasants may have produced over subsistence were unlikely to redound to their material advantage. The peasants adapted by keeping their needs low and by trying to preserve as much of their leisure as possible.

The eighteenth-century Empress of Austria, Maria Theresa, interested as much in extending the tax base and increasing productivity as in preventing peasant unrest, laid down the principle that "the peasantry as the most numerous class of society, which constitutes the foundation of the power of the state, must be maintained in a satisfactory condition, which means that the peasant must be able to support himself and his family and in addition be able to pay his taxes in times of peace and war."[16] Specifically, the lords were to give up some of their traditional rights and not be permitted more than two days of their tenants' labor a week, a restriction more honored in the breach than in compliance. (Earlier, Frederick the Great had limited the forced labor of peasants on crown lands in Prussia to four days a week.) The Empress also reduced the number of religious holidays, in effect part of the peasants' ceremonial fund of time and resources, in the interest of increasing peasant production. (Russian peasants in Tsarist times were reported to have spent some 20 to 30 percent of their potential working time in festivals, in addition to another 20 to 30 percent in idleness; in Old Regime France, the Catholic Church was reported to have guaranteed 90 rest days a year, Sundays and holidays during which it was forbiddent to work.)[17] The

Emperor Joseph, Maria Theresa's son laid down the principle that the peasant be allowed to retain 50 percent of his gross product, thus limiting the sum total of state taxes, feudal dues, and the like. But the nobility of the Austro-Hungarian Empire and eastern Europe were resistant to giving up their feudal prerogatives, maintaining them in one form or another even after the Austro-Hungarian Empire was dissolved.

Not long ago, in the 1930s and 1940s, the peasants of eastern Europe (excluding the U.S.S.R., whose peasants faced different though no less oppressive conditions) were described in the same terms as those used to describe peasants of the less developed nations today. The countryside was overpopulated, the peasant was unproductive and living at a subsistence level, holdings were small and uneconomic, hidden unemployment and underemployment were rife. Economists held that only emigration and perhaps industrialization would prevent a breakdown of the economy and of society.[18] Incongruously, although the peasantries of eastern Europe were poor and hungry, large quantities of grain were exported to the industrialized west.

With the Russian victory in World War II and the establishment of socialist regimes, the feudal tenures in the eastern European countries were broken. And in the years since, food production in these regions has been increasing at a rapid rate.[19] The increase in agricultural production was accomplished by a decreasing proportion of the labor force in agriculture, though in all these countries a considerable part of the population remains peasant, if one can still use that term in the new context. Before World War II, there were large surpluses of labor which might have been employed to increase food production dramatically had not the social and economic order militated against it. The current governments of many eastern European countries (such as Bulgaria, Romania, Hungary) are concerned that their currently low birth rates and population growth rates will not be sufficient to provide the labor force required to meet their economic and political objectives, and they have taken various actions, including the limitation of abortion, in an attempt to increase fertility.

The Colonial Experience

The former colonial administrators of many third world nations benefited the people under their dominion in many ways, by the maintenance of public order, the abolition of barbaric practices, the promotion of public health, the building of transportation networks, and the establishment of schools. In other ways, they affected the lives of the people adversely. Colonies were not only markets and areas for investments but also sources of material and capital. These were frequently accumulated through taxation and exactions which were in many respects more harmful to the inhabitants than those of their former overlords. The colonial administrators, in the guise of introducing western concepts of property, tended to abrogate the traditional rights and immunities governing land usage much as did the enclosure movement in England. In some parts of India, zamindars, originally indigenous tax collectors, were vested by the British with proprietary rights, becoming in effect landlords while the peasant landholders became tenants. In former times land could not be seized for nonpayment of dues; the defaulted landholder, instead, was subject to imprisonment or other punishment. The Sales Law enacted by the British, however, directed that defaulted holdings be put up for auction.[20] Insistence on money taxes placed moneylenders and grain dealers in powerful positions, giving them claim on the peasant's production. The peasants, having no reason to think that they would benefit from working harder and longer, used their ancient defense and kept their economic needs at a low level.

The British, Dutch, and other colonial administrators knew of the peasants' reluctance to produce a surplus. The British set their land tax in Burma and India (over and above rent and other obligations of the peasants) not on the basis of the peasants' output, but on a percentage of some estimate of what the land could produce.[21] Extensive agricultural statistics were maintained by revenue offices to evaluate the productive capacity of the land. So much was the British colonial administration based on the collection of taxes or tribute that even today the chief administrative officers of Indian districts still are known as the "District Collectors." The Dutch in Indonesia used a variety of methods to collect their tribute, one of which required peasants to grow one or another specified cash crop, such as sugar cane or tobacco along with their subsistence crop, the specified crop being the property of the government.[22] The income thus derived was used to finance the construction and operation of trading cities and transportation networks, to introduce order and suppress brigandage, as well as to support the economies and enhance the wealth of the colonial powers. These exactions represented a method of forced savings and investments, but one which in effect kept agricultural productivity as well as food consumption low.

During the interval between the World Wars, the British relaxed their hold, perhaps because of increasing resistance to the colonial policies at home and abroad. But native intermediaries (zamindars, moneylenders, etc.) remained as rapacious as before.

Mamdani has summarized the change in the structure of land ownership and associated obligations which occurred under the British in the Punjab.[23] Before the British, village land in the Punjab was owned or controlled collectively with rights to cultivation assigned to villagers, a practice which, while not universal, was found in many peasant societies. Surpluses were appropriated by the state or overlord; these exactions were heavy enough to leave little for others such as moneylenders. The British instituted the pattern of private property. Cultivators became, in the eyes of the law, proprietors, liable for a portion of the tax assessed on a village. The tax was to be paid in cash and was due regardless of drought or rain. Thus, recourse to the moneylenders was virtually obligatory in bad crop years, and since they were also the grain buyers, they controlled prices as well. More than half the cultivators in the Punjab in 1918 had land mortgaged to moneylenders. The mortgagor was known as an owner tenant in the village; in official records he was listed as a tenant; interest payments were much the same as rent inasmuch as the rate was adjusted to the productivity of the land, leaving little but subsistence for the cultivator. Including the agricultural laborers who were also heavily in debt, three quarters of the population were beholden to the moneylenders, usually Brahmins. Earlier, Colonel Davies,

commissioner of Delhi, testified to the Famine Commission of 1878–79
"There was always before them the knowledge that they might have to pay a
higher rent if they sank a well or otherwise increased the productivity of the
land, and this knowledge essentially had the effect of permanently checking
any disposition on their part to lay out money in improvement."[24]

The purpose here is not to document in an extensive fashion the variety of
modes by which peasants, regardless of their communal organization and
land tenure arrangements, were divested of their surpluses. The purpose is to
indicate that they were often so divested. Low productivity and subsistence
were not results of resource limitations but of an adaptation to the lack of
social and political power. Early in history, both rulers and ruled had
learned the levels to which humans could be nutritionally deprived without
undermining the effectiveness of the labor force (see Chapter 7).

Contemporary Peasant Societies

The end of colonial domination relieved the peasantries of some exactions
but did not generally result in sufficient change to encourage higher levels of
productivity or subsistence. Landlords still exacted rents; the tenant received
little benefit from improvements to the land; and intermediaries, such as
moneylenders and grain buyers, absorbed the profits of the remaining
surplus. The attitude of a peasant in these circumstances is described by
Prawl, a former rural extension agent in India, as follows:

The writer, visiting a farm in India in an area which had recently been brought under
irrigation, asked, "Why aren't you growing a second crop of rice now that you have
water for irrigation?" The reply: "I would like to but if I do, the moneylender, priest,
tax collector or merchant will somehow manage to take most of it." All or nearly all
of his economic motivation was thus destroyed.[25]

Other writers attribute this lack of willingness of peasants to increase
production to the absence of interest in material aggrandizement and a high
value placed on leisure. These characteristics have been reported as common
in Southeast Asian countries such as Laos and Cambodia.[26] The successful
insurgencies in these areas, however, would indicate otherwise.

Contemporary peasants are often obliged to engage in a subsistence mode
of production and avoid the marketplace as much as possible. During the
1950s, only 20 percent of the food produced in India reached the marketplace[27] and that is probably an overestimate. Villagers, suspicious of government surveys, may be loathe to report their true output; thus, output may be
underreported while market transactions may be easier to monitor. The
amount of food imported into India during the 1950s, a decade free of serious
famine, was of a quantity sufficient to feed the larger towns and cities, a
further indication of the lack of orientation towards the production of a
surplus for market. In its day the British raj, as noted earlier, forced the
production of such a surplus through its revenue policies and assured a grain
surplus to feed the cities. But land taxes in the 1960s were reported to have
been no more in rupees than they were fifty years earlier despite the decrease
in the value of the rupee and the increased productivity of the land.[28]

By keeping food prices for city dwellers at low levels through imports and grants of cheap American grain surpluses, the policy of many governments in the third world gave little incentive for more intensive land use. Nor could such governments force the production of surpluses as did the colonial powers. Under the new regimes, landowning peasants were able to maintain, without much effort, their customary levels of subsistence. But the gradual breakdown of the traditional village structure of mutual obligations placed the landless agricultural laborer in a precarious position. The diminished pressure on the village landowners to produce a surplus lessened the need for the labor of the landless. Nonetheless, some of the old practices of work sharing survived, albeit losing their force with time. Thus, while the condition of the rural population in general was improving in India during the 1950s and early 1960s, the condition of the landless agricultural laborer was in general deteriorating.[29]

The commercialization of agriculture based on crops to be exported may result in the underproduction of food crops needed domestically. Some nations, in the interest of accumulating foreign exchange, continued the policy of their former colonial administrations directed towards encouraging export crops. In the former West African French colonies of Senegal, Mali, Upper Volta, and Niger, dependable markets and relatively attractive prices were established for cotton and peanuts, and research, extension, and credit services were made available to stimulate the production of export crops. This was a continuation of the policy initiated by the French colonial administration. With the exception of Mali, no such programs were maintained for food grains, the market and storage facilities for these crops being small and limited. As a result, farmers have been finding non-food crops more profitable, and have been growing hardly more grain than is necessary to feed their families. While the production and marketing of cotton and peanuts has been growing substantially in these areas, food production per capita has been declining a little, even though there appears to be large expanses of potentially cultivable land which might well be sown to grain if it were profitable to the owners to do so. As a result, there have been frequent food scarcities and some areas have experienced a continuing food deficit.[30]

Poor farmers face significant risks in expanding production. It takes money to make money. If farmers buy fertilizer to increase production and unfortunate weather results in a bad crop or the market price of agricultural produce that year is low, their small capital is lost. If the money for fertilizer is to be borrowed from a moneylender at a high rate of interest, the risks involved in attempting to increase production may be prohibitive. But even milder rates of interest do not overcome the risks involved.

In the Punjab, the principal deterrent to increased production in the past appears to have been the moneylenders' proclivity to absorb the value of increased land productivity. During the 1920s, in areas where agriculture was commercialized, moneylenders encouraged default so as to take over the ownership of land.[31]

Prices for agricultural produce may fluctuate sufficiently so that peasants who invest more than their labor stand a fair chance of being wiped out. The wealthier farmers with sufficient capital to survive a few poor years may, in the long run, make considerable profits from investments in fertilizer and other monetized factors to increase production. For most peasants, however, the risks attending such investment are such as to discourage enterprise. A case in point was examined by Bruce Cone.[32]

Recognizing that land alone is not enough, land reform programs in developing countries have sometimes included provisions for credit and marketing aids to mitigate the risks for the peasant of small means. But, generally, land reforms have been poorly implemented, thwarted by the connivance of the larger landholders and the timidity and corruption of officials. Such institutions as credit and marketing cooperatives often come under the control of the more powerful interests. Even where, as in Mexico from 1910 through 1930, extensive land reforms were introduced, the small peasants lost ground after the revolutionary momentum slowed. The end of President Cardenas' term of office in 1940 marked the beginning of an increase in the concentration of land ownership as the larger commercial farmers and ranchers dominated the agrarian economy. Jacoby, after much experience with and study of land reform, concludes that without basic changes in social and economic structures, the objectives of land reform are thwarted by the operation of the economic system.[33]

Technological advances and government development programs have thus generally benefited the minority of wealthy farmers who had clear title to their land and who were well capitalized. Competition in the marketplace with the wealthier farmers may well be driving the poorer farmers further into a subsistence mode of cultivation. In this mode, children become the principal savings.

The market for commercial food grains is limited by the poverty of the people who form the large bulk of consumers; thus, even the commercial farmers may lack incentives to make heavy investments to expand the productive capacities of their land. Irrigation and waterworks depend on government investment rather than, as formerly in many areas, on the coordinated labor power of communities. Government investments to increase agricultural output must compete with other governmental goals such as industrialization and military capability. Increased food production in some developing countries may be responding to population needs largely as these needs are translated into a monetized demand, a contrast with the past when markets were few, exchanges were in kind and followed a traditionally prescribed pattern.

The expansion of agriculture in past peasant societies was not limited to changes in land use and the development of more labor intensive techniques. Many of the high-yield grains developed in western laboratories, and so publicized today, actually had their beginnings in peasant agriculture. Dwarf wheat, in which increased application of manure resulted in an increased length of wheat head but not of the stalk, was used in Japan in 1873. Early maturing rice varieties were noted in China as early as 1000 A.D., and one of the ancestors of high-yield rice is thought to have reached Taiwan from China several hundred years ago.[34] That some students regard the peasant as a person of limited innovative capacity may be more a reflection of the limited perspective of the student than of the peasant's character. To argue abstractly that there would be more to eat if agricultural productivity increased at a faster rate than population growth is academic to the peasant who must live in the real world.

This brief overview cannot do justic to the economics of peasant society. The intention is to indicate briefly that the low levels of subsistence of peasant societies was not due to population size and dynamics, but to social and economic constraints on productive processes. Social and economic constraints, however, operate somewhere within the limits of physical constraints. These are considered in the following sections.

The Expansion of Agriculture and the Degradation of Land

For thousands of years the waters of the Yellow River gave life to the Chinese peasants living on its plain, and periodically death by catastrophic floods. Over these years the peasants, by continuous vigilance and labor, were usually able to confine the river to its channel by means of an expanding system of dikes. The struggle to do so was never ending for the silt deposits continuously diminished the capacity of the channel to carry flood waters. The dikes went higher and higher; eventually the channel was raised some forty to fifty feet above the plain. In 1852 and again almost seventy years later, the river broke out of its elevated channel, breaching the dikes and destroying millions as it sought new outlets to the sea.

Lowdermilk, seeking to determine the source of the silt, explored the headwaters of the river. He found it in the mountains of Shansi Province. There the farmers had been moving up the hills and had long ago denuded the land of trees and other ground cover resulting in erosion of the watershed and the silting of the river. Some of the cultivators had managed to conserve the remaining soils by terracing but much of the high land lay barren and cut by deep, wide gullies.[35]

Early in history the face of the land was being changed by humans who were then very few and increasing in numbers very slowly. In the process, the economic utility of some of the lands they exploited was lost. Lands in northern Yorkshire, England, were reported to have been farmed through the Bronze and Iron ages. As a result, the soils were acidified, and the ancient farmland is now moor where heather dominates. By present standards, the people who accomplished the early changes in the environment, burning the forests and turning them into grasslands, and then turning semiarid grass-lands into deserts, were not numerous, nor was their technology sophisticated. Fire drive hunters changed woodland into savanna even before swiddeners appeared on the scene. Very early in history humans lived in a world to a great extent of their own creation.[36] Then as people became more numerous around the Mediterranean, the hills of that region were denuded of their forests to support the civilizations which thrived there and the land was allowed to erode and wash into the sea. Plato, the product of that civilization, felt called upon to comment on this erosion in his "Critias." During Roman times the deforestation of that region was almost completed and that of Europe was well on its way.

Among the more fragile areas in the world today are the forested mountain and foothill regions. In these regions the soil and its water are held in place by trees and brush. As this cover is removed for firewood and for cultivation, water is no longer held in the soil, but runs down rapidly taking the fertile topsoil down as silt, flooding the plains below and clogging waterways.

After a while, the land becomes unsuitable for cultivation or other economic use and in the process the lowland valleys become adversely affected as well. Erik P. Eckholm notes that as much as 38 percent of the total land area in the eastern hill regions of Nepal, the most densely populated area of that country, was estimated to consist of abandoned fields presumed to be unproductive.[37]

The deforestation of mountain regions is not new. What is new is the rapidity of the settlement, deforestation, and in some cases erosion of mountain areas occurring in so many places at the same time. An increase in population may have something to do with this in some areas; but the most important factor, particularly in Latin America, is that commercial interests have taken over the better and lower lying lands for cattle ranches and plantations, forcing the peasants into the mountains. However, the despoilment of the mountain lands, though done by people, is not due to population pressure but to a lack of concern with conservation, a lack which may indeed be due to the absence of population pressure, as shall be discussed.

The capacity of almost any territory to sustain human society and at the same time maintain its ecological integrity by natural processes alone, without human intervention, is very limited. In simple economies with small numbers of people employing relatively weak technologies, the rhythm of nature may be depended on to replenish the resources extracted to maintain life. But the balance is delicate and easily disturbed; a small increase in numbers, continued carelessness in technique as in the use of fire, or a small change in climatic conditions may result in ecological change. Even pre-agricultural people, often presumed or purported to have been conservationists, have also been reported to exhaust sectors of their natural environment in pursuit of subsistence. Prehistoric hunters, in small bands and with simple weapons, may well have caused the extinction of many of the large mammals of the Pleistocene. Ancient Aleuts are likely to have overhunted the otter, a key predator in the ecological community from which the Aleuts drew their sustenance. The ecology changed as a consequence and, of necessity, so did the subsistence base of the early Aleuts.[38]

It would appear that humans tended to deplete their resources, and seek alternatives early in their history. Large populations, growing at relatively rapid rates and using more powerful technologies, may ruin an environment in relatively shorter periods, within a few generations, and thus destroy the basis of their existence. But the power inherent in numbers and technology could also be turned to conservation and reclamation were the social and economic structure and motivation conducive to such development. The motivation frequently arises out of necessity, often a result of population growth which also provides the labor force needed for reclamation work.

Some few peoples, the primitive Eskimo and Australian aborigines among them, have depended on unaided nature to provide them with a source of subsistence, at least in the past, and have received the plaudits of many who would not change places with them. Most peoples, out of compulsion or choice, have attempted to work towards a less limiting relationship with their environment. This required a relatively large work force to assist nature in maintaining the productive potential of the land. The key to such enterprise was appropriate social coordination, the willingness to work harder—frequently related to necessity and to the absence of easier ways of making a living.

Nepal, in which Eckholm noted so much deterioration and abandonment, is one of the few Asian countries which has been producing food surpluses in recent times. And as Eckholm notes, the Nepalese have not had to face a serious historical problem of land shortage. Many of the hill people of Nepal have migrated to the Terai, a forested plain formerly infested with malaria. While terracing was necessary to cultivate hillsides, conservation practices common among other terrace cultivators were not apparently essential to their survival.[39] The Nepalese, who are profligate in their use of land, would likely have been more conserving were the need to be so more apparent, as would be the case if they could not migrate. The pre-Columbian Andean Indians, living in fairly densely populated communities, managed through a system of terracing and irrigation to cultivate the same type of terrain as in Nepal without destroying it. The invading Spaniards destroyed the irrigation system along with the economy and government, and decimated the population of the region. Some students report, however, that there were signs of overpopulation and environmental deterioration before the Spaniard arrived on the scene.[40]

Ecological change often accompanies economic activity and signs of environmental deterioration are frequently associated with the human presence. But that is only one aspect of the relationship between humans and their environment. The other involves restoration, not to the pristine state of original nature, but to a state more compatible with human needs. Often however, it was easier to abandon land than to restore it to a productive state.

The abandonment of the urban center of the old Mayan civilization of 600 A.D. and the rise of the new Mayan cities some 250 miles to the north provides an illustration. The agricultural economy of the Mayans was based considerably on swidden cultivation. Sufficient surpluses were garnered to support urban centers and the upper classes, priests, and nobles. In time, as swidden cultivation became more intense, the areas around the urban centers became grassland, no longer suitable for swidden cultivation. Ceram, following a theory formulated by Morley, noted that at this point there was a clear need for the invention of the plow, but the invention did not occur despite the technical competence of the Maya in other areas. The distance between the upper classes and the mass of the people was held responsible for this failure. (A more reasonable explanation may lie in the absence of animals which might have been domesticated to draw the plow. This need not, however, have precluded the development of other suitable devices or even population control.) The peasants cultivated forest plots further and further removed from the old cities. There came a time when it was impractical for the peasants to return to the cities which were abandoned and reestablished 250 miles to the north.[41]

Whether the plow would have been invented or other solution found had there been no virgin territory available is, of course, a speculative issue. While population growth resulted in the destruction of the original forest (which has since recovered), one can also speculate that a greater population pressure might well have resulted in a more permanently settled economy.*

The process of environmental destruction and reconstruction involves population but as part of social historical development. War, civil disorder, competition between groups, disregard for the welfare of others, phenomena which more often than not have little relation to population pressure, have resulted in the destruction of considerably more natural resources than has population.

Ancient Mesopotamia, though receiving little rain (except for occasional devastating, flooding torrents) sustained relatively large populations for millennia before reverting to desert. The Mesopotamian cities held back the desert by developing and maintaining irrigation systems which gradually failed only after thousands of years. And this failure was due not to pressure on resources, as is sometimes argued, but to the inability to live in peace.

In some instances lands suffered from salinization. To prevent this, over-irrigation must be avoided; the land must be well drained, and the water table kept low. At other times silt clogged the irrigation canals. The desertification of these lands has been sometimes attributed to overpopulation.

Jacobsen and Adams discussed the history of salinization and siltification of canals in Ancient Mosopotamia as revealed by archeological findings.[42] In some areas of what is now Southern Iraq, the soil became more and more saline between the years 2400 and 1700 B.C., after the land had been farmed for millennia. The farmers adapted by shifting from wheat to barley cultivation, barley being a more salt-resistant crop. But as salinization progressed, the yields of barley decreased and eventually the area was abandoned.

They traced the beginning of the process of salinization in these areas to the frequent wars between the various cities of that area, the sites of the ancient Sumerian culture. These cities drew water for irrigation from the Euphrates River. One of the warring cities had cut the canal which provided a rival city with water. The rival responded by digging a canal to the relatively distant Tigris River, providing themselves a water source less vulnerable to attack. With time, this canal was almost a river, so that the area was being fed water by the Tigris as well as the Euphrates. The land watered by both the Euphrates and the large canal from the Tigris was incapable of draining both sources without an increase in the level of the water table. Seven centuries of salinization and eventual abandonment of the area followed as a result of people not learning to live in peace. The waters of the Euphrates were by themselves sufficient to supply the needs of that area, were these waters not subjected to the strategy of war.

The center of political power and civilization shifted to the north, in what is now central Iraq. Jacobsen and Adams' study of the deposition of silt is concerned with a defunct former irrigation system, the Nahrwan canal system which served that area in antiquity, taking water from the Diyala River. The population and associated irrigation systems of the Diyala River area of central Iraq waxed and waned several times before the twelfth century

*Since this was written, significant evidence has been adduced to indicate that the Mayans had indeed developed and used agricultural techniques other than swidden in pre-Hispanic times. (See P. D. Harrison and B. L. Turner, eds. *Pre Hispanic Maya Agriculture* (Albuquerque, N.M.: University of New Mexico Press, 1978.)

A.D. The basic technical problem with this irrigation system appeared to be the cumulative deposition of silt which had to be removed from the canals and deposited on the fields. The efficiency with which this problem was managed was often related to political developments and associated population size.

The archeological finds reported by Jacobsen and Adams indicated a resurgence of population growth in that area beginning between 539–531 B.C., following a millennium of population decline and stagnation. From 150 B.C. to 226 A.D., population density attained the level reached more than 1,000 years earlier and kept increasing to a maximum density sometime during the Sassanian Dynasty (226–637 A.D.). The irrigation system in the interim had become a remarkable and complex piece of hydraulic engineering that required a strong central authority to coordinate its operation and a large labor force for maintenance.

The central authority was frequently undermined by social unrest and military ventures. Wars and the cutting of canals resulted in abandonment of towns and fields. The system was thus often deprived of the labor force and coordinating authority needed to maintain it and, as a result, the watercourses were periodically clogged with silt deposits beyond the capacity of the remaining population to manage. As people returned, the system was restored. The irrigation system of the Diyala basin was never restored, however, after the breaching of the Nahrwan Canal in military actions of the eleventh and twelfth centuries, nor did there appear to be signs of deterioration before that time. Thus, Jacobsen and Adams viewed many of the detrimental changes as having been consequences of both social and natural factors. They concluded that the Mongol invaders were unjustly blamed for destroying the civilization that was based there. The fact remains, though, that the further depopulation of the area by the Mongols helped to assure that the former prosperity based on irrigation would not return for some time.

Toynbee found support in such events for his thesis that civilizations do not fail because their technology fails them, but rather that techniques fail because the civilizations they support fail. Without the benefit of Jacobsen's and Adams' archeological finds, he traced the waxing and waning of irrigation systems and populations in Mesopotamia through the times of the Persian-Roman wars, the Arab invasions, and internal conflicts to the coup de grace inflicted by the Mongols. He noted a similar trend in Sri Lanka. There, a highly organized irrigation system, in what is now the arid area of the country, helped to support a larger population up to the twelfth century than lived on the island in the mid-twentieth century. This system was destroyed by invasions and war. Depopulation indicated to Toynbee that the inhabitants had not the heart or vigor to restore their former works. Without care, the area became unproductive and malarial.[43]

The failures of central governments and civilizations had different impacts in different regions. In Egypt, the dependability of the Nile floods allowed interrupted, though diminished, cultivation when dynasties fell and population declined. The coordinating hand of central government may have been missed, but it was not essential to the continuance of life. In Mesopotamia, the undependability of rains and floods necessitated a highly developed waterworks system. This required the coordination of a central government and civilization. Without this government the land returned to desert, suitable only for nomadic pastoralists.

North Africa, where deserts now predominate, was once a principal granary for ancient Rome, able to support a large and thriving population. When Scipio destroyed Carthage in 146 B.C., he saved 24 volumes written by Mago, a Carthaginian who was considered the foremost authority on Mediterranean agriculture in those days. The disappearance of the high civilizations in this area and the failure of its agriculture is often blamed on a change in the prevailing weather patterns. Many students of the subject find no evidence that such a change occurred, while archeological evidence and the books of Mago reveal an agricultural technology that included sophisticated waterworks and soil and water conservation techniques quite suited to intensive agriculture in that terrain and climate. Lowdermilk noted that what had changed in that region was not the weather but the people. In the sixth century A.D., nomad invaders destroyed the cities and the civilizations which had flourished there. Herding was substituted for agriculture as the dominant economic activity.[44] A substantially reduced population denuded much of the ground cover through overgrazing, leaving the land subject to erosion. But they had plenty of room to roam in and could always raid the few remaining farmers and cities if they required something from those sources.

While pastoralism appears to some to be a suitable way to exploit the little moisture and scattered oases of semi-arid and desert lands, the population-resources balance among pastoral nomads can be easily disturbed. Unlike cultivators, pastoralists have developed few methods for intensifying the production of animal stock. Irrigation of pasture, the cultivation of animal fodder and green manure, and other approaches to growing livestock on limited ranges are methods associated with settled peoples and a labor force sufficient for the task. Expansion of the nomad pastoral economies is by extension of ranges or greater exploitation without increasing the productivity of the range. This may be one of the reasons that the lands used by pastoralists are often semiarid or grasslands which appear unsuitable for agriculture. Were more human labor invested in these lands, they might appear as different today as do the Israeli kibbutzim from the range of the Bedouin.

Many pastoral peoples are aware of the productive capacity of cultivation and maintain either symbiotic or predatory relations with settled peoples from whom they obtain grain and artifacts. Some pastoralists engage in agriculture of one form or another if only to harvest wild cereals and grasses. But, in general, they consider cultivation a demeaning occupation. The Mongols of old despised settled communities and farmlands, destroying the one and turning the other into grazing land with little provocation. Ghengiz Khan, after the taking of Kansu (1226–1227 A.D.), was advised by one of his counselors to destroy a population of as many as 10 million peasants, useless for the war plans of the Mongols, and to turn their lands into horse pasture for the cavalry. He was dissuaded by another more humane counselor who pointed out the vast tribute and taxes which could be extracted were the peasants permitted to live and work.[45] Other cities and lands which fell to the Mongols were not so fortunate.

Pastoral nomads must find this life satisfying in comparison with the settled life of cultivators. Governments interested in increasing productivity and decreasing the predation of nomads have found it difficult to induce them to settle down, though under population pressure many, indeed most, nomad groups in history have turned to cultivation or have been otherwise absorbed into peasant societies.

N. Wade, reporting in *Science* on the long drought of the first few years of the 1970s and the resultant famine in the Sahel region of Africa, attributed the suffering of the indigenous nomadic herdsmen in part to overpopulation and overgrazing of the frail semiarid regions. At one time death rates among these people were sufficiently high to keep population from growing. Water was sufficiently scarce so that the herds which provided sustenance were necessarily limited and the peoples lived in balance with the ecology. An increase in population and a series of good weather years, control of animal diseases, and lusher pastures permitted an increase in the size of herds. Through international aid programs, many deep wells were installed which added to the water supply so that in some areas the limiting factor was not water, as formerly, but grazing land. But the Sahelian drought was so severe that the shores of Lake Chad had receded in places some fifteen miles from their former line and the lake itself had split into three. Timbuktu, a trading center and a river port, was cut off from the Niger as its harbor dried up. Wade argued that were the nomads and herds fewer, the long drought would have had a lesser impact on their grazing lands.[46]

Under drought conditions, fewer herdsmen and livestock may indeed have had a better chance of finding some remaining pasture. Pastoral nomads have one advantage over cultivators in that they can more readily move their economic base as necessity dictates and opportunity allows. However, to use this advantage, the Sahelian pastures would need to have been considerably more sparsely populated than they were. Population densities in the Sahel, including the agricultural areas, are less than five persons per square kilometer, and in the semiarid regions of the nomadic sector the densities are even lower than that. Indeed, the principal problem in providing famine relief was the absence of a transportation network, in good part due to the sparseness of population.

Paradoxically, the problem of the Sahel may well be too few rather than too many people. The reported failure of the wells bored (by donor nations) in semiarid regions of the Sahel may have been due to the absence of enough people to exploit them effectively. These boreholes are reported to have become the center of little deserts. As other pastures dried, large herds converged on the wells denuding the surrounding pastures of grass and churning them into quagmires in which nothing would grow and into a desert when they dried out.[47] The fault lay not in the wells but in the absence of water management and distribution systems, a formidable task for small bands of nomads. The construction of waterworks in the absence of a population infrastructure and appropriate social organization to manage them leads to the same end as did the social breakdown and depopulation of the ancient Mesopotamian towns. The security of the nomad may hinge on their turning to a more settled way of life, akin to that of the cultivator, using land more intensively and with greater care.

Population growth has intensified the demands humans have placed on land for sustenance. It has also provided the incentive to increase the productivity of the land, to maintain its quality, and to conserve it while supplying the labor to accomplish these ends. A people with unexploited resources tend to be prodigal, but they become conservators when they need to. Areas abandoned because the land lost its productivity can be matched by areas which have been under continuous and increasingly intensive cultivation for thousands of years, as in Europe, China, India, Egypt, and Japan, the land appearing none the worse for wear. These lands may have been less fragile than those which gave out, providing people with more time to learn how to manage them, but there was also the incentive to learn. If a society wills it, ruined lands—like the dustbowls of the American depression and the desert areas of Israel—may be restored. The productivity of land is bound to the labor and attention expended on it, and population growth may contribute much more to land reclamation than it does to its destruction.

The Physical Limits to Agricultural Growth

Lester Brown, a well-known analyst of the world food situation, discerned some trends which he took to indicate that scarcity and food shortages were likely to become chronic rather than temporary episodic occurrences. He noted that surplus grain stocks, largely North American, which helped cushion world food shortfalls in past years had been depleted and grain lands in the United States and Canada which had been withheld from production had been brought back into production by 1974–1975 to meet the increasing dependence of large parts of the world on the importation of grain from North America. The fact that many regions in Africa, Asia, Latin America and Eastern Europe which were grain exporters prior to World War II, had since become grain importers, was taken by Brown to indicate that the potential of these areas to sustain their own populations was diminishing. Demand for food had increased as a result of increased affluence in developed nations and increased population in the developing nations. Under the pressures of population growth some lands were being degraded while the grain productivity of land which increased worldwide from an average 1.4 metric tons per hectare in 1962–1963 to 1.9 metric tons in 1972–1973 had in the following two to three years fallen slightly to a little more than 1.8 metric tons per hectare. This slight fall in productivity was in good part attributed to the tightening supply of energy and fertilizer, the inferior quality of lands brought into recent production, and the vicissitudes of weather. Brown felt that it may have also signalled more permanent limitations of the conditions of land quality and energy, water, and fertilizer availability, and a long-term span of unfavorable weather.[48]

The changes noted by Brown in the direction of the grain trade, countries which formerly exported grain now importing grain, may be more reflective of social change than of agricultural potential. Food exports produced in Eastern Europe prior to World War II were not the product of a favorable resources-to-people ratio. Indeed, Eastern Europe appeared to be overpopulated at the time. Food produced on great landed estates was exported to the profit of the large landholders though people at home were hungry. During the same pre-World War II period, famine ridden China was the principal exporter of soybeans. In Russia under Stalin, food was appropriated by force and used to support industrialization, even as peasants were allowed to starve at home. Nor did the colonial countries such as India, Burma, and those in Africa export food because their populations had plenty to eat; indeed, they probably had less to eat than they do today. The exports were, in effect, taxes exacted by and used largely for the benefit of the colonialists even when famine threatened.

It is doubtful that the declining productivity discerned by Brown over a short period presages the future more accurately than the longer term trend of increasing productivity which preceded it. The short term downturn in food production may only reflect a fluctuation in the longer term trend. Few trends are monotonic or stable in direction, and it would be unrealistic to expect world food production to be so. Indeed, in the few years since Brown wrote his pessimistic prognostication, the situation has been quite different. Despite continued population growth, the immediate problem seems to be one of food surpluses rather than shortages and the possibility that lower farm prices will result in curtailed production. Should the weather take a turn for the worse for a year or two, as it likely will, and if food policies do not take that possibility into account, then concern will again be with food shortages. For the poor who cannot pay for it, however, food is always short.

Not all observers are as pessimistic as Brown. The eminent agricultural economist Colin Clark estimated in 1967 that the earth could feed 47 billion at an American standard of consumption and 157 billion at a Japanese standard without recourse to what he called science fiction technologies.[49] Other observers, though not as sanguine as Clark about the carrying capacity of the earth, are nonetheless cautiously optimistic.[50] Even the United Nations Food and Agriculture Organization, which in 1952 was described in *The Economist*[51] as "a permanent institution . . . devoted to proving that there is not enough food in the world to go round," sees hopeful prospects, though with various caveats and qualifications.

Estimates of the world's food producing capacity can be based on current technologies and knowledge, or they can include consideration of prospective and feasible technological developments. The discussion here is limited to current capabilities. Nonetheless, the possibility exists that lands not now considered cultivable will become so, that the seas can be cultivated to provide more food, and that other sources of food will be developed through technologies not yet developed.[52] But a discussion of the potential levels of food production is better based on the current experience.

Estimates of resource potential, even without the intervention of technological forecasts, are often conjectural and experts disagree with each other. Moreover, the capability of humans to realize the productive potential is even more difficult to assess with confidence. The capital investments required may appear excessive, the energy requirements prohibitive, and the political and social priorities assigned to increasing food availability may often conflict with other objectives. Nonetheless, it may be helpful to review some of the estimates of land available for food production.

A number of studies indicate that less than half the land which could be used for crop production under current conditions is cultivated world wide; only one-third of the potentially arable land is cultivated at any one time.

These studies include such considerations as topography, water availability, the absence of serious problems such as alkalinity, types of crops and forages, transportation, location, possibilities for multiple cropping, and costs of bringing land into production.[53]

It was estimated in 1962 that only 45 percent of cultivable land in developing countries was under cultivation; in North America only 50 percent of arable land was being used; and in Australia and New Zealand only 10 percent of arable land was being cultivated. More recent estimates, perhaps based on better data, give an even more optimistic view of the potential land available for food production world wide, though in some areas unused new land is not readily available. In many parts of the world, the dependence of food production on land area is declining as it becomes easier and more profitable to intensify land use. Thus, in developing countries, grain areas expanded 1.1 percent annually between 1960 and 1971 while grain production rose twice as rapidly; in the developed countries, grain production rose 2.5 percent annually while the land planted to grain was decreasing.[54]

In India food production keeps increasing at a faster rate now than earlier. Despite dire predictions for a hundred years, Indian agriculture has more than kept pace with population, attesting to the productive power of intensification of land use.[55]

There is still considerable room in the developing countries for increasing the yield for individual crops and increasing the number of crops which can be obtained per year from the same fields. In the densely populated areas of Asia, where uncultivated potentially arable land is limited, food production per hectare is still only a fraction of that of comparable land in developed countries. In 1972, cereal yield per hectare in India, whose land is in no way inferior, was one-fifth that of Japan; in 1961 the fraction was slightly larger.[56] The difference is due in large part to the additional inputs, fertilizers, pesticides, water, and related care used by the Japanese in their agriculture. The production, delivery and application of these inputs are heavily dependent on energy sources such as oil. The limiting factor in agricultural production may not be land but the availability of these additional inputs or substitutes for them. Nonetheless, even countries whose access to these additional inputs is limited, vary considerably in the productivity of their lands, and this may well reflect intensity of labor inputs.

In India, a hectare of cultivated land produced 1.1 metric tons of grain in 1972, a hectare in Bangladesh produced 1.5 metric tons, and in Indonesia 2.1 metric tons. Some of the highest population densities for agricultural regions are found in Java where increases in food production depended on increasing yields per unit of land. In Indonesia, yield per hectare was increased 40 percent from 1961 to 1972.

On the other hand, the yield per hectare of grain land in densely populated Bangladesh did not increase during this period despite the considerable increase in population. This may have been due in large part to the political and economic disorganization during this decade, as discussed earlier, while during the 1960s when Bangladesh was East Pakistan, much of the government investments in growth were allocated to West Pakistan. The climate of Bangladesh is ideally suited for multiple cropping; three crops a year could be readily grown if water was controlled and the labor force employed. Yet the intensity of multiple cropping patterns in Bangladesh is significantly less than that of Taiwan, Korea, and China, where the weather is harsher and less suitable. Its fields yielded only one-fifth the output per acre of some other less well endowed lands. In the 1960s, only 5 percent of its agricultural land was irrigated and its fields yielded from one-and-a-third to less than one-and-a-half crops a year out of a potential three.[57] The foregoing estimates are subject to considerable reservation but there is no question about the potential for increased food production in Bangladesh. Moreover, the construction of waterworks would help to control the periodic flooding, a major cause of famine in that part of the world. Bangladesh is poor in capital but its large labor force could be gainfully employed in this construction, were the incentives and social and economic channels for such employment present. (Since this was written, the outlook for Bangladesh has improved considerably.)

Not only is a small portion of the earth's potentially cultivable land being used but it is not being used to full capacity. Revelle, extrapolating from the productivity of the American Midwest, estimated that with high quality farmland worked at a comparable level of technology, only 170 million hectares would be needed to feed the world's 4 billion people, compared to the 1.4 billion hectares currently in cultivation, and 3.2 billion hectares (24 percent of the land surface) which are deemed potentially arable. (An additional 3.6 billion hectares are deemed suitable for grazing.) Revelle further estimated that the potential cropped area can be increased by irrigation and multiple cropping to 4.2 billion hectares within a generation.[58]

The possibility of bringing all agricultural lands to the productive capacity of those in highly efficient enterprises is small. And, as Revelle noted, the highly efficient agricultural enterprises now depend on nonrenewable resources for energy and other inputs, and these resources will eventually run out. The issue is whether substitutes can be found, preferably renewable ones. This is not out of the range of possibility or probability. As was noted by Revelle, plants store more energy (from the sun) than humans invest in their production, and most of this energy is stored in inedible crop residues (straw, chaff, etc.) which are often discarded. Recapturing half of this energy through fermentation to methane or alcohol, for example, would satisfy the mechanical energy requirements of agriculture and that required for the synthesis of chemical fertilizers. While recycling of energy used in agriculture may be within the realm of possibility, technological probability will depend (among other considerations not yet known) to some degree on the need. As in the case of conservation and reclamation discussed earlier, humans expend energy and substance on new technologies in proportion to the urgency of need and rewards in view. Most people respond to what impinges on their lives, and do not yet see the need with the same urgency as do the prophets of doom.

In the interim, and for some generations to come, there appears to be considerable room for expansion on the basis of currently conventional technologies. The potential for land reclamation in semiarid countries is large. The semiarid Sahelian regions of Africa now largely desert and recently plagued by drought, lie over ground water reservoirs which could, if the water were brought up (a plan to do so over 75 years is being considered), add 2.5 million irrigated hectares to agricultural production. The Sudan contains vast areas of marsh which, if drained and the water resources harnessed, could provide new farmlands of a productive capacity sufficient to perhaps double the amount of food the world now produces.[59] Large amounts of capital, well beyond the capacity of developing countries, would be needed to effect these projects using modern technologies. The same objectives could probably be accomplished more slowly by using older methods and a large labor force. The issue is not whether there is or is not room for expansion—there is—but whether humans can be expected to control population growth in good time, a subject for later discussion.

Social Limits to Agricultural Growth

The amount of additional food needed to assure adequate subsistence levels for all, without detracting from anyone's even excessive diet, is small. The number of people (excluding those in Asian planned economies) with insufficient protein/energy supplies in 1970 was estimated to have been around 462 million, including 28 million in developed countries.[60] An additional 500 calories in grain supplied to each of these people each day would alleviate their protein calorie deficiency. An additional 25 million tons of grain, about 2 percent of the world's grain production, could fill that gap. With proper incentives, this amount could have been easily supplied.[61] But this would not have solved the problem of malnutrition; the problem is not one of production but of distribution, the inability of the poor to buy food or obtain access to land. This has been discussed somewhat in the context of developing countries. The problem also exists in developed countries.

The principal deterrent to feeding the world's population is not physical, but social. Yet the principal response of officials to the problem of feeding this growing population has been to support the "green revolution," the development of high yield food grains effectively using more water, fertilizer, and labor than the traditional varieties. Some observers argue that the lack of an evolutionary history and adaptation to local disease conditions, dependence on irrigation and fertilizer, and other such physical factors makes the adoption of high yield varieties hazardous. Even if these problems are resolved, the social deterrents limiting the levels of production in traditional agriculture still operate and are more resistant to change than technological factors. The capital requirements of the new technology make it more difficult for small farmers to compete, and the incentives for producing food remain the same. The poor are thus not likely to be any better fed. Two books, recently published, present detailed analyses of the operation of current social deterrents to food production and distribution that are only touched upon here.[62]

The objective of commercial food producers is to make money, not to feed a hungry populace. Food production may also be limited by this objective. Governmental food policies are directed toward the national interest as perceived by those with money. Thus, during the depression years, while many went hungry, the United States government authorized the destruction of foodstuff and the idling of cropland to maintain prices of farm produce. The policy was defended on the ground that only by such incentives would the farmer continue to produce. Food production was thus limited by government policy.

World War II, the subsequent reconstruction of Western Europe, and the Korean War provided markets for American agricultural expansion, but not for long. In 1954, the Agricultural Trade Development Assistance Act (Public Law 480) was passed, described by its subtitle as "An act to increase the consumption of United States agricultural commodities in foreign countries, to improve the foreign relations of the United States and for other purposes." The principal objective of the law was to get rid of United States agricultural surpluses and by doing so, to obtain clients. Though altruistic objectives such as relief of malnutrition and promotion of economic development were part of the law's expressed policy, there can be little doubt as to the priority of the United States national interest in trade, as well as support of political allies and economic associates. Whatever the effectiveness of United States aid policies (and they have been severely criticized by many), significant amounts of food were exported to third world countries. However, the presence of cheap American grain in third world markets may have removed some incentives to production and thus inhibited agricultural expansion in those countries.

American agricultural growth was stimulated to a large extent by the expansion of domestic and European economies. During the 1950s and 1960s, the demand for food increased partly because of population growth, but also because the increased income of North Americans and Western Europeans increased demand for meat and other animal products. Many times more grain is required to produce the same nutritional equivalent in animal products as may be obtained directly from the grain. Thus, while Americans consumed four to five times as much grain per capita (almost a ton a year per head), much of it in animal products, as did Indians, they obtained only half again as many calories from that level of consumption. Increased domestic consumption and foreign exports during the 1950s and 1960s still did not prevent surpluses from accumulating, so large were the increases in United States agricultural productivity. During the late 1950s and early 1960s, acreages planted to wheat in the United States were often less than 60 percent the acreage planted in 1952–1953. From 1963 to 1968 the acreage planted to wheat in the United States increased to some 80 percent of the acreage planted in 1952–1953. Shortly thereafter, major export countries found it advisable to cut back grain production. Between 1968 and 1970, areas sown to wheat declined in the United States, Canada, Australia, and Argentina from 50 million hectares to 33 million hectares, while production declined from more than 80 million to less than 60 million tons per year.[63] Since 1973, with the dissipation of surpluses, idled land was brought back into production. In the interim, around 90 million tons of wheat alone could have been produced had production not been cut back. In 1976 and 1977, grain surpluses were again accumulating.

The depletion of grain surpluses and increases in grain production by the major exporting countries resulted from a number of circumstances little related to population growth. Bad weather, drought in some regions, floods in others, resulted in famine in many third world nations and crop shortfalls in some of the developed nations. The Soviet Union experienced poor crops in 1972-1973 and chose to maintain its recently increased level of consumption by importing tremendous quantities of grain obtained on favorable terms from the United States. During the same period, the OPEC countries significantly increased the price of the oil they exported, resulting in increased foreign exchange with which they could import additional grain and even take steps to upgrade the diets of their people by feeding livestock. At the same time, increases in the price of petroleum limited the amount of fertilizer and energy which could be applied to agricultural production in other third world countries.

Despite continuing high petroleum prices, grain production recovered and advanced with the help of fair weather; the year 1977 saw bumper crops all over the world. American farmers suffered grievously from low farm prices and protested vigorously for higher price supports. If these are forthcoming it can only be with increased government intervention and reductions in agricultural production until the next round of shortfalls.

Current reports of the world food situation concentrate on grain, the principal food of the third world, and give the impression that grain exports to these lands are a sort of gift. While some small amount of grain exports from the United States are grants for famine relief and the like, such grants have become a very small part of the total exports. Most of the grain is paid for by products, largely agricultural, from the third world. Thus, in 1974 the value of India's agricultural exports exceeded the value of its grain imports; this occurring in a year when poor weather adversely affected agricultural output in India.[64] Agricultural exports (largely sugar, coffee and bananas) from Latin America to the United States for the first six months of 1975 were valued at $2.2 billion; agricultural exports from the United States to Latin America during this period were valued at $1.3 billion.[65] In Central America, a region of intense land hunger, great tracts of fertile land are cultivated or ranched to supply American markets. While the poor of Honduras go hungry, the country exports 1,000 pounds of bananas per Honduran every year, and its large cattle ranches supply American fast food restaurants with beef. The exchange of food and other agricultural products between grain surplus countries and the rest of the world is not a one-way affair. In many countries agricultural land is used to grow exportable crops, these being more profitable than food grown for the indigenous poor.

The planned economies, whose stated objectives include the growing of food to feed people rather than make a profit, also experience difficulties in making the maximum use of their resources. Political considerations, military priorities, and the like, often intervene. The forced collectivization of the Soviet peasantry, the greater emphasis on military and industrial enterprise, and the destruction by Lysenko (with the support of Stalin) of the scientific infrastructure in agricultural genetics in the late 1940s and early 1950s is reflected in the current inefficiency of Soviet agriculture. And the Chinese, who are purported to be currently making considerable progress in agricultural development, for the time being at least, not long ago experienced considerable disruption because of political turbulence.

Regardless of the availability of resources, humans have been largely limited by their own social organization. Increases in the levels of subsistence have been restricted not so much by the levels of resources relative to population and population growth rates as by social constraints. This is evidenced by the prevalence of low subsistence levels in most third world countries regardless of resource levels and population growth rates. This is no less apparent in Latin America and Africa where large tracts of potentially cultivable land are available than in Asia where there remains little unoccupied, potentially arable land, and where increased food production depends on the intensification of agriculture.

Notes

1. E. Boserup, *The Conditions of Agricultural Growth* (Chicago: Aldine, 1965).

2. A. I. Richards, *Land, Labour and Diet in Northern Rhodesia*, 2nd ed. (London: Oxford University Press, 1961); P. De Schlippe, *Shifting Cultivation in Africa* (London: Routledge and Kegan Paul, 1956); M. Sahlins, *Stone Age Economics* (Chicago: Aldine Atherton, 1972), pp. 51--69.

3. See R. F. Stevenson, *Population and Political Systems in Tropical Africa* (New York: Columbia University Press, 1968), pp. 88--114.

4. B. Bronson, "Farm Labor and the Evolution of Food Production," B. Spooner, ed., in *Population Growth: Anthropological Implications* (Cambridge, Mass.: Massachusetts Institute of Technology Press, 1972), pp. 190--218.

5. E. Le Roy Ladurie, *The Peasants of Languedoc*, trans. J. Day (Urbana, Ill.: The University of Illinois Press, 1974).

6. C. Clark and M. Haswell, *The Economics of Subsistence Agriculture*, 4th ed. (London: Macmillan, 1970); C. Clark, *Population Growth and Land Use* (New York: St. Martin's Press, 1967); M. Sahlins, op. cit.

7. Geertz, C., *Agricultural Involution: The Processes of Ecological Change in Indonesia* (Berkeley: University of California Press, 1963), pp. 13, 33.

8. E. R. Wolf, *Peasants* (Englewood Cliffs, N.J.: Prentice-Hall, 1966), p. 29, based on Angel Palerm, "The Agricultural Bases of Urban Civilization in Mesoamerica," in *Irrigation Civilizations: A Comparative Study*, J. H. Steward, ed., Social Science Monographs I, Social Science Section, Dept. of Cultural Affairs (Washington, D. C.: Pan American Union, 1955), pp. 29--30.

9. M. McNeil, "Lateritic Soils," *Scientific American* 211:5 (November 1964), p. 86.

10. P. A. Sanchez, and S. W. Buol, "Soils of the Tropics and the World Food Crisis," *Science* 188 (May 1975), pp. 598--603.

11. A. Mather, "The Anatomy of Disguised Unemployment," *Oxford Economic Papers* 16:2 (July 1964): 161--93; A. Lewis, "Economic Development with Unlimited Supplies of Labor," in A. N. Agarwala and S. P. Singh, eds., *The Economics of Underdevelopment* (London: Oxford University Press, 1958), pp. 400-49. Much has been written pro and con on this subject. For a critical overview of the theory and facts see G. Myrdal, *Asian Drama* (New York: Pantheon Books, 1968), II, pp. 959--1069; III, Appendix 6, pp. 2041--61. The subject will be discussed in greater detail in another chapter.

12. See U.S. Department of Agriculture Economic Research Service, *The World Food Situation and Prospects to 1985*, Foreign Agricultural Economic Report No. 98, Washington, D.C., 1974, pp. 12--18; 58--62; see also Food and Agricultural Organization of the United Nations, *The State of Food and Agriculture* (Rome, 1967); and preceding and subsequent reports.

13. F. Braudel, *The Mediterranean and the Mediterranean World in the Age of Philip II* 2 vols. (English translation, New York: Harper and Row, 1972), pp. 420--23.

14. E. R. Wolf, op. cit., pp. 5, 6, 9. Based on W. Abel, *Geschichte der deutschen Landwirtschaft vom frühen Mittelalten bis zum 19 Jahrhundert, Deutsche Agrargeschichte II* (Stuttgart: Eugen Ulmer, 1962).

15. Ibid., p. 7.

16. Quoted by Ernst Wangerman, *The Austrian Achievement: 1700--1800* (New York: Harcourt Brace Jovanovich, 1973), p. 70.

17. M. Sahlins, op. cit., p. 91, based on A. V. Chayanov, *The Theory of Peasant Economy* (Homewood, Ill.: Richard D. Irwin for the American Economic Association, 1966), p. 74; P. Lafargue, *The Right to Be Lazy* (English translation, Chicago: Kerr, 1909). First French ed., 1883.

18. H. Seton-Watson, *Eastern Europe Between the Wars: 1918–1941*, 3rd ed. (New York: Harper and Row, 1962), p. 97.

19. *The World Food Situation and Prospects to 1985*, p. 15.

20. P. Spear, *India: A Modern History* (Ann Arbor: University of Michigan Press, 1972), p. 263; S. Wolpert, *India* (Englewood Cliffs, N.J.: Prentice-Hall, 1965), p. 81.

21. J. S. Furnivall, *Colonial Theory and Practice* (Cambridge: Cambridge University Press, 1948); N. Keyfitz, "Political-Economic Aspects of Urbanization in South and Southeast Asia," in P. M. Hauser and L. F. Schnore, eds., *The Study of Urbanization* (New York: Wiley, 1965), pp. 265–309.

22. C. Geertz, op. cit.

23. M. Mamdani, *The Myth of Population Control* (New York: Monthly Review Press, 1972), pp. 51–59.

24. *Punjab Report in Reply to the Enquiries Issued by the Famine Commission 2 (1978–1979)*, p. 592, quoted in Mamdani, op. cit., p. 58.

25. W. L. Prawl, "Its the Agents of Change Who Don't Like Change," *Ceres (F.A.O. Review)*, 2:4 (July–August 1969), p. 57.

26. D. Bloodworth, *An Eye for the Dragon: Southeast Asia Observed* (New York: Farrar, Straus & Giroux, 1970), pp. 301–2.

27. Ministry of Food and Agriculture, India, *Report on India's Food Crisis and Steps to Meet It* (prepared by the Ford Foundation, 1959).

28. Gilbert Etienne, *Indian Agriculture: The Science of the Possible* (Berkeley: University of California Press, 1968); N. Keyfitz, op. cit., pp. 265–309.

29. Ministry of Labour and Employment, India, *Agricultural Labour in India*, 1964.

30. See N. Pritchard, "Initiating a New Grain Marketing Program in West Africa," in *The Marketing Challenge*, Economic Research Service, U.S.D.A., Foreign Agricultural Economic Report No. 96, 1970, pp. 33–37.

31. M. Darling, *The Punjab Peasant in Prosperity and Debt* (Bombay: Oxford University Press, 1957), chapter 12, cited in Myrdal, *Asian Drama*, op. cit., p. 1042.

32. B. W. Cone, "Some Brazilian Farmers Don't Use Fertilizer—Why?" in *War on Hunger* (September 1971); "Why Farmers Would Not Use Fertilizer, A Brazilian Example," Mimeograph, Battelle Pacific Northwest Laboratories, Article 3885; submitted to Technical Front, War on Hunger, U.S. State Dept., Washington, D. C.

33. E. H. Jacoby and C. H. Jacoby, *Man and Land: The Essential Revolution* (New York: Alfred Knopf, 1971). See also R. Stavenhagen, "Social Aspects of Agrarian Structure in Mexico," in R. Stavenhagen, ed., *Agrarian Problems and Peasant Movements in Latin America*, (New York: Doubleday Anchor, 1970).

34. D. G. Dalrymple, *Development and Spread of High Yield Varieties of Wheat and Rice in the Less Developed Nations*, Economic Research Service, U.S.D.A., Foreign Agriculture Economic Report No. 95 (July 1974), p. vii.

35. W. C. Lowdermilk, *Conquest of the Land Through Seven Thousand Years*, U.S. Department of Agriculture, Agriculture Information Bulletin No. 99, 1953, rev. 1975.

36. G. W. Dimbleby, "The Impact of Early Man on His Environment," in J. P. Cox and J. Peel, eds., *Population and Pollution* (London and New York: Academic Press, 1972), pp. 7–13.

37. E. P. Eckholm, "The Deterioration of Mountain Environments," *Science* 189 (September 1975), pp. 764–70.

38. P. S. Martin and H. E. Wright, Jr., eds., *Pleistocene Extinctions: The Search for a Cause* (New Haven: Yale University Press, 1967); see also C. A. Simenstad, J. A. Estes, and K. W. Kenyon, "Aleuts, Sea Otters, and Alternate Stable-State Communities," *Science* 200 (April 1978), pp. 403–11.

39. *The World Food Situation and Prospects to 1985*, p. 83; Eckholm, op. cit., p. 765.

40. Eckholm, op. cit., p. 766.

41. C. W. Ceram, *Gods, Graves and Scholars; The Study of Archeology* (First published, 1949. Reprint ed., Harmondsworth, England: Penguin Books, 1974), chapter 29.

42. T. Jacobsen and R. M. Adams, "Salt and Silt in Ancient Mesopotamia," *Science* 128 (1958), pp. 1251–58.

43. A. J. Toynbee, *A Study of History*, vols. I--VI, abridged by D. C. Somervell (London: Oxford University Press, 1946), chapter XV, pp. 255--74.

44. Lowdermilk, op. cit.

45. R. Grousset, *The Empire of the Steppes* (English translation, New Brunswick, N.J.: Rutgers University Press, 1970), pp. xxvi--xxvii, 251.

46. N. Wade, "Sahelian Drought: No Victory for Western Aid," *Science* 185 (July 1974), pp. 234--37.

47. Ibid., p. 236.

48. L. R. Brown, "The World Food Prospect," *Science* 190 (December 1975), pp. 1053--59.

49. C. Clark, op. cit., p. 153.

50. *The World Food Situation and Prospects to 1985;* U.N. Food and Agriculture Organization, *Assessment of the World Food Situation, Present and Future* (prepared for the World Food Conference, Rome, 1974). The issue of *Science* 188 (May 1975) is devoted to the food situation and contains a number of balanced assessments by observers of various aspects of the food situation; see also *Scientific American* 235:3, (September 1976).

51. *The Economist,* August 23, 1952, p. 456.

52. See P. Low, "Prospects for Abundance: The Food Supply Question," in H. M. Bahr, B. A. Chadwick, and D. L. Thomas, eds., *Population, Resources, and the Future: Non-Malthusian Perspectives* (Provo, Utah: Brigham Young University Press, 1972), pp. 59--86.

53. L. L. Bladeslee, E. O. Heady, and C. F. Framingham, *World Food Production, Demand and Trade* (Ames, Iowa: Iowa State University Center for Agricultural and Rural Development, 1973); *The World Food Situation and Prospects to 1985;* President's Science Advisory Committee, *The World Food Problem*, Report of the Panel on the World Food Supply, Washington, D.C., 1967, vol. 2, pp. 405--69.

54. *The World Food Situation and Prospects to 1985*, p. 59.

55. See J. W. Mellor, "The Agriculture of India," *Scientific American* 235:3, (September 1976), pp. 154--63.

56. *The World Food Situation and Prospects to 1985*, p. 65, Table 30.

57. See D. G. Dalrymple, *Survey of Multiple Cropping in Less Developed Nations*, Foreign Agriculture Economic Report No. 91 (October 1971) Economic Research Service, U.S.D.A., Washington, D.C.

58. R. Revelle, "The Resources Available for Agriculture," *Scientific American* 235:3 (September 1976), pp. 164--78.

59. W. D. Harper, "The Development of Agriculture in Developing Countries," *Scientific American* 235:3 (September 1976), pp. 196--205.

60. U.N. Food and Agriculture Organization, *Preliminary Assessment of the World Food Situation*, Rome, 1974, cited in *The World Food Situation and Prospects to 1985*, p. 50.

61. See *The World Food Situation and Prospects to 1985*, p. 50--51.

62. See S. George, *How the Other Half Dies: The Real Reasons for World Hunger* (Montclair N.J.: Allanheld, Osmun and Co., 1977); and F. Lappe Moore and J. Collins, *Food First* (Boston: Houghton Mifflin, 1977).

63. *The World Food Situation and Prospects to 1985*, pp. 21-23.

64. U.S. Department of Agriculture, Economic Research Service, *World Agricultural Situation*, WAS-8, October 1975, Washington, D.C., p. 12.

65. Ibid., p. 14.

7

The Social Impact of
Low Levels of Subsistence

Introduction

The low levels of subsistence prevalent in much of the world today are obviously no check on population growth, even among the most poorly fed people. Though Malthusians perennially expect death rates to increase, such increases occur largely in extraordinary times of famine and severe food shortage. Reliable data about deaths from famine and food shortage today are rare. But a study of a limited rural area of Bangladesh showed that the death rate for 1971 increased 40 percent over the normal from about 15 per 1,000 population to 21 per 1,000. This was the year of the war for independence, which resulted in severe food shortages and in other breakdowns as well. (The death rate for 1974–75, another famine year, this time due to floods, was again reported to have increased from 15 per 1,000 to 20 per 1,000 in this area.) The study of 1971 indicated that a large proportion of the excess deaths was due to intestinal infections, diarrheal diseases, shigellosis, cholera, etc.[1] The following year the death rate was only slightly in excess of normal and the birth rate in that area was estimated to have dropped eight percent from somewhat more than 45 births per 1,000 to almost 42 births per 1,000. The combination of excess deaths one year and fewer births the next had little affected population growth: the temporarily increased death rate was not high, nor was the temporarily decreased birth rate low.

Mortality was particularly high among preschool children under age five. Over 8,000 children from one to ten years of age in a district of Bangladesh were examined for nutritional status in December, 1970, and were then followed to June, 1972, through the war for independence and its associated food shortages. (The ratio of arm circumference to height was used as an index of nutritional status.)[2] Somewhat more than two percent (2.3 percent)

122

of these children under ten had died during the eighteen month period; most of them were of children under five, 4 percent of whom died. Of these under five, death occurred twice as frequently among the 50 percent who scored below the median of the nutritional status scale as among those who scored above the median. Deaths were most frequent in the first few months following the examination, indicating that many of the children judged to be malnourished may have been already ill and on the way to dying. Overall, the death rate for children during this period was about 30 times the United States rate, yet there was considerable population growth in Bangladesh. The levels of subsistence would have to decline to much lower levels than normally prevail in this poorest of nations before mortality would increase to a level controlling population growth.

The chances of surviving very low subsistence conditions improves markedly after early childhood. This is somewhat anomalous. Though meeting nutritional requirements during infancy and early childhood is highly critical, the actual food needed is not much, compared to older children and adults. Yet undernutrition (lack of sufficient food to maintain weight or support growth), and malnutrition (lack of essential food elements) afflict, at one time or another during their first five years of life, the majority of children in the developing countries[3] resulting in decreased resistance to infections and high fatality rates for illnesses such as measles and other childhood diseases which run a mild course in developed countries. So a child, not affected directly by low nutritional status, may be devastated by the stress of an infection which would be of little danger to a well-fed child. An undernourished child who escapes infection may appear to be unscathed. In the instance of kwashiorkor, a nutritional disease, Barnes and Gyorgy noted that the affected children are not necessarily those receiving the poorest basic diet, but more often those in whom an added stress has occurred, infection being the most important stress factor.[4]

Nutrition experts have been successful in identifying many gross pathologies and defects of individual development and functioning associated with very specific severe nutritional deficiencies such as vitamin, iodine and iron deficiencies. The number of such diseases is large. Pellagra, a vitamin (niacin) deficiency disease, may be prevented by including leafy vegatables in the diet. Kwashiorkor, a severe form of protein malnutrition often resulting in death or mental retardation, affects infants and children. Anemia, due to iron deficiency, frequently affects persons who are heavily parasitized and lose considerable blood; supplemental feeding of iron can increase the vitality of afflicted work forces although it would be better to get rid of the parasites. Cretinism and goiter, prevalent in iodine deficient areas, are readily prevented by iodizing the salt supply. The incidence of gross nutritional deficiency resulting in clear clinical disease is much more prevalent in the developing than in the developed countries (where they were also quite prevalent not many years ago). But concern with the effects of nutritional deprivation goes beyond those resulting in clinical pathology and includes those in which the pathology is not as clear.

Nutritional experts, however, have not been so successful in defining the minimal food requirements (calories, protein, etc.) for normal or, as some would have it, optimal functioning. The criteria often set forth were based more on judgment and inference than on clear-cut experience in which specific nutritional deficiencies result in specific pathologies that can be prevented or cured by correcting the deficiency. Part of the difficulty was in defining normal functioning and related food needs in view of the wide differences among peoples in body size and weight, parasite infestations, energy requirements for work, and the other demands on the body. At the same time, judgments have had to be revised as experiences of different peoples with different diets were accumulated. The early criteria were based on experience in European and American settings, adjusted somewhat for height, weight, and climate in the area studied. The first World Food Survey[5] estimated that an average of 2,600 calories per person per day was required to assure adequate nutrition. This was only 100 calories fewer than the present Food and Nutrition Board's recommendation for a moderately active American adult weighing 70 kg (about 155 lbs.)[6] although a larger proportion—30 percent—of the people in developing countries were under ten years old and required less food. In addition the people in developing countries are in general smaller than Americans. F.A.O. estimates of individual food needs were revised downwards on a number of subsequent occasions, those for South Asia to about 1,900 calories per person on the average.[7]

This is close to the almost 2,000 calories per head estimated by Weiner to be needed by a simple agriculturalist family of five, father, mother, and three children, all of whom but the youngest child engage in some work such as food getting, building, etc. The calories were not distributed equally among the family members but according to basal physiological needs, work needs and other activities including strenuous recreation and ceremonials.[8] The presumption was that the combination of foods supplying this energy will also include appropriate amounts of other essential nutrients.

Obviously, there is a basic nutritional level required if humans are to thrive, but this level is not necessarily known and varies depending on the demands placed on individuals.[9] The best diet for humans may well prove to be one close to some minimal level, provided it is balanced and contains the requisite nutrients. A series of experiments performed in the 1930s by McCay showed that rats, whose caloric intake was restricted early in life (but supplied with essential protein), enough to delay growth and maturation, enjoyed a considerable increase in longevity with no discernible ill effects other than that they were smaller.[10] More recently, Ross reported that marginal undernutrition (low calorie diets) in rats, such that they were smaller through life than controls fed *ad libitum*, resulted not only in longer-lived animals but also in the prolonged maintenance of liver enzymes patterns characteristic of youth.[11] Sinex concluded that most investigators working with caloric restricted animals felt that these remained younger, more alert, and active.[12]

If rats are starved or nearly so during the period of most rapid growth, various bodily functions will be impaired, some permanently. R. K. Chandra reported that three-week old rats who for six weeks afterwards (almost to the time of attaining full growth) were fed only 25 percent of the optimal amount fed to control animals were, in addition to being stunted, much poorer in immunoglobulin antibody forming cells. The deficiency was passed on to offspring by female rats.[13]

The application of conclusions drawn from animal experiments to the human condition is hazardous; not only are physiological requirements and mechanisms different but the requirements and conditions of life are different also. Nonetheless, the experiments cited indicate that though close to starvation diets are bad, rapid maturation is not necessarily good, nor are low levels of nutritional intake and small size bad in themselves.

The problem is that many people do not receive even a minimal level of subsistence, even at the lowered standards. Estimates of the proportions of the world's people suffering from calorie and protein deficiencies have been revised downward from about 66 percent to 20 to 25 percent,[14] and these estimates may still be high. These lowered estimates do not indicate an improvement in world nutrition as much as a decrease in the level of subsistence deemed necessary.

Growth and Maturation

The most clearly marked changes which accompany an increase in the general levels of food consumption are an increase in size (height and weight) and, to a lesser degree, an increase in the rate of maturation; puberty and attainment of adult height occur at an earlier age. The height of Europeans and Americans has been increasing from generation to generation, the average person today being about three inches taller than 100 years ago. Less well-to-do people have always been, on the average, shorter than those better off, in large part because they were not as well fed. The size of those less well-to-do has been increasing at a faster pace this past century than the size of those better off and thus the difference between them is less now than it was in the past.[15]

Other factors besides nutrition, such as outbreeding and fewer infections, may also be responsible for the increase in height. Constant infections may consume nutritional intake, thus leaving less for growth processes. If dominant genes for tallness (height) are found in greater frequencies among specific groups, then outbreeding would result in the wider dissemination of such genes. But the principal reason for the increase in stature appears to be increased nutritional intake. During years of war and food shortage in Europe (for example, World Wars I and II), the trend towards increased size was slowed and even reversed.[16] Large increases in height and maturation rate may occur within a single generation. In 1957, 13-year-old Japanese boys were reported to be some 13.9 cm. shorter than 13-year-old Americans of Japanese descent. Among the older males (18 years), the differences diminished to 6.4 cm.: still appreciable. This was attributed to the difference between Japanese and American diets.[17]

Not only has there been an increase in height among Americans and Europeans in the past century, but they also reach full adult stature and sexual maturation at an earlier age. The age of menarche decreased in Sweden from around 15.7 years in 1885 to around 13.8 years in 1950; in Norway from a little more than 17 years in 1840, to around 13 years in 1950; and in the United States, from a little over 14 years in 1950 to less than 13 years in 1955.[18] Poorer women experienced menarche at a later age than those well off. This difference disappeared as nutritional levels equalized in European countries.

Douglas reported in 1966 that he found no sigificant difference in age at menarche for girls of different social economic classes in Britain (if anything, lower-class girls matured earlier) though considerable differentials were still found in height.[19] In many contemporary developing countries, where nutritional levels are low, the average age at menarche is relatively young, though still influenced to a small degree by nutritional factors. Gopalan and Naidu [20] cite a survey by Prabhakar et al. of 24,000 Indian girls. Among girls from families with per capita annual incomes of more than Rs. 100, the age of menarche averaged 13.2 years; from those with incomes of less than Rs. 100, which is poor indeed, even for India, the mean age at menarche was 14.56 years.

Size as an Index of Nutrition

The people of the third world are on the average shorter and lighter than westerners, and their children mature at a somewhat slower pace. These differences are in good part due to differences in food intake, and short stature or low weight is often taken to be a sign of malnutrition. The greater the deviation from some standard of height and weight for age, the greater the presumed degree of malnutrition.[21]

Wray[22] explored the effect of family size on nutrition in his study of the prevalence of malnutrition in preschool children in rural Candelaria, Colombia. Growth status relative to age was the index used to identify malnutrition. Among preschoolers from one and two child families (a small minority of the families surveyed), 32 and 34 percent respectively were deemed malnourished; but among preschoolers from families with three or more children the proportion of malnourished preschool children increased somewhat inconsistently with increasing family size. Among families with 3, 4, 5, 6, 7, 8, and more children, 41.0, 40.7, 41.9, 46.7, 40.3, and 46.2 percent, respectively, were deemed to be malnourished.

Since families with one or two children may include a greater proportion of those with higher social status, and since the differences among families with three and more children were not consistent, while one-third of the children from one and two child families were deemed to be malnourished in any case, it is difficult to know how to interpret Wray's data. Wray notes that of 1,094 children under six years of age, 284 (28 percent) were classified as having first degree malnutrition, 148 (14 percent) as having second degree malnutrition, and 14 (1.3 percent) as having third degree malnutrition. The implications of third degree malnutrition are of much greater significance than those of first or second degree malnutrition. It is of little help to lump all these degrees under the category of malnutrition, particularly when the measure of malnutrition is size.

Behar reported that in Guatemala where malnutrition is reported to be widespread, a national sample of 800 rural families showed that while 13 percent of children under five were clinically malnourished (only 1.5 percent severely so), 70 percent of Guatemalan children under five would be considered malnourished if only body weight for age was used as a criterion of nutritional status.[23] Cravioto, Delicardie and Birch cited a survey of 4,000 rural Indian children under five years of age in which only one percent were considered to be suffering from severe protein calorie malnutrition.[24] They noted that this estimate was based on a single point in time and that it was not unlikely that 5 to 10 percent of children were at one time or another affected.

If size alone were the criterion, anywhere up to 50 percent of the people in many third world countries can be said to be suffering from malnutrition, or have suffered it at some time during their lives. The implications of such estimates are not always clear. If small size were the only outcome of low levels of nutrition, there would be little professional concern.

Mentation

A chilling prospect held out by some observers is that the low levels of nutrition in many countries result in widespread mental deficiency which leads to a vicious circle in which poverty leads to deficiencies which lead back to poverty. Several issues need to be explored in evaluating this. The first problem which presents itself is the definition of mental deficiency, an issue beyond the scope of this book, but one which cannot be ignored. The usual measures of intellectual ability and deficiency are tests commonly called intelligence tests, but frequently designed to predict academic aptitude. For infants and very young children who may be difficult to examine by verbal and other symbolic methods, developmental tests and scales may be used which essentially measure motor behavior and neurologic functioning appropriate for age. What the results of such tests, particularly when administered in early childhood, mean for future performance is not always clear.

In a group of children studied longitudinally, IQ's between six and eighteen yeas of age were reported to have changed 15 or more points for 60 percent, 20 or more points for 37 percent, and 30 or more points for 9 percent of the group. Correlations between tests administered at two to five years of age and those administered later were particularly low.[25] Part of these discrepancies may be due to the fact, discussed later, that individuals mature at different rates and paces while IQ's are standardized for age, implicitly assuming that individuals are at the same stage of development at the same age. A more recent report on I.Q. constancy noted that among 80 normal middle class children, the average change in IQ between ages 2½ years and 17 years was 28.5 points; one in three changed more than 30 points and one in seven, more than 40 points. These were not random changes but consistent directional trends over time; those who scored higher (or lower) at age 17 than at age 2½, increased (or decreased) their relative score periodically as they were tested at intermediate ages.[26] The observation is consistent with the notion that individuals mature at different rates but the slow maturers eventually catch up.

A recent study of the effects of birth order and family size (number of siblings) on intelligence is informative on the significance of IQ, though this was not the purpose of the study. The IQ scores of 400,000 men born between 1944 and 1947 in the Netherlands, and processed through the induction procedure for military service, were examined for their relationship with the birth order and the size of family.[27] The test used to measure IQ was the Raven Progressive Matrices, presumably a culture-free test. The findings were consistent with those of many other studies of the same phenomenon; men from small families and within families, those of lower birth order, that is, first, second, third, children, tend to score higher than those from large families and higher birth order.

Zajonc proposed that the reason children of small families and early birth order score higher on intelligence tests is that they are exposed to more adult parental contact, to mature verbal and abstract reasoning, than are the later born children and children of large families who interact more with children, their siblings.[28] While Zajonc's theory does not, of course, account for all the factors that enter into determining intelligence, it does identify an important element, the intellectual climate of orientation. This comes not only from family size, which itself is influenced by that climate, but also from the broader cultural milieu and the life and life's work for which individuals are being prepared.

This is illustrated by some of the findings in the study of the Dutch military inductees. When the inductees were divided into classes based on father's occupation, nonmanual worker, manual worker, or farmer, the children in the largest family size category (nine or more children) in the nonmanual worker class had, on the average, a significantly higher IQ than the first or second child in the smaller size families of the manual worker and/or farmer classes, not a remarkable finding inasmuch as social class background is the strongest correlate of IQ. Those of farmer backgrounds scored very low on IQ, considerably below those from nonmanual and manual worker families. What makes this extraordinary is that Dutch farmers have been among the most productive agriculturalists, the most energetic and most ingenious, particularly in view of the challenges they met and overcame. Indeed, the productivity of the Dutch agricultural worker relative to that of the non-agricultural worker is among the highest in the world.[29] No one would infer that this was so because they ranked very low among their countrymen in IQ. But had they been among the least productive and more sluggish agriculturalists, the inference might well have been made.

Another problem with using IQ scores is that they are standardized on chronological age. Some individuals develop physically and mentally at a slower pace than others, and as noted earlier, the pace of physical development may be strongly influenced by nutrition. Anastasi noted that anatomical and physiological characteristics related to developmental status (such as head size, body size, skeletal age based on X-rays of bone structure, etc.) do correlate with intelligence among children but the correlations between these physical characteristics and IQ diminish with age as individuals approach maturity, and practically vanish when full adult status is reached. Of particular interest is a reported high correlation (almost .80) between basal metabolic rate (BMR) and IQ among 200 children, the higher the BMR, the higher the IQ.[30] During periods of rapid growth the basic metabolic rate tends to be higher. Yet children of the same chronological age are tested and treated often as if they were of the same developmental age and their adult potential is judged accordingly.

Tanner examined the relationship between the tempo of growth and intellectual ability reported for large samples of children. IQ scores of early maturing children (boys with a peak height-increase velocity before age 14½ years of age, girls before age 12) are consistently higher at all ages between 7 and 17 years in a longitudinal study than those of late maturing children (boys with a peak height-increase velocity after age 15½, girls after age 13). The difference was small and as far as was known, was thought to almost vanish as each group completed their growth. A study of a random sample of over 7,000 Scottish school children aged 11 years, indicated that the average IQ of children increased one to two points per increase of one inch in stature, when age was controlled. Since the relationship between IQ and stature becomes very weak as children mature into adulthood, the use of age bound tests (IQ and developmental tests) that depend on chronological age for standardization to predict adult performance is not only inadequate but also unfair.[31] Children whose growth is slower and who reach full growth later whether because of nutritional or other factors are likely to be penalized by judgments of their eventual intellectual capacities or developmental status. Such children may be denied entrance to academic curricula on the basis of an age-standardized IQ score taken at age 11 as was common practice in the United Kingdom. Age 11 was a particularly poor choice for an age-graded examination since it is a time of transitional development for many. The debasement of one's self image resulting from the low opinions and expectations of others[32] as well as the denial of opportunity, may well be doing more damage than a slower rate of maturation.

Since poor people tend to be both smaller and less advantaged with regard to intellectual stimulation than those better off, part of the relationship between stature and IQ is due to difference in social class. Part is also due to the fact that smaller children are growing at a slower rate, intellectually as well as physically. The children of the poor are also heavily exposed to infections which may slow the pace of physical and neurological development. Many children's diseases which generally run a mild course in developed countries, tend to be very severe in less developed countries, resulting in deaths, growth retardation, and possibly neurologic damage. The increased severity of such diseases is generally attributed to the poorer nutritional status of children. This, and the damage done by common infections, may be aggravated by poor and mistaken child care and health practices. Latham and Cobos reported that a survey of a Colombian community, where malnutrition was prevalent, showed that 53 percent of the children were weaned before they were six months of age; that 54 percent of the mothers withheld food when their children had diarrhea, and 39 percent withheld food when their children had fever, both common occurrences in preschool children.[33]

The clearest link between intellectual development and nutrition comes from studies of children suffering severe malnutrition. Winick and Rosso found a lower number of brain cells in nine Chilean infants who had died from severe nutritional marasmus, compared to the brain cells of 10 control children who had died of accidents or poisonings.[34] A large number of animal experiments and human autopsy findings have demonstated that severe undernutrition during the late fetal and early postnatal periods results in defective brain development and structure, smaller brains, fewer and smaller brain cells, fewer neuronal interconnections, and deficient glial cell formation, and the like. Clearly the brain needs nourishment to grow and develop so that the individual can function normally, but how much nutrition will suffice? Studies demonstrating a direct relationship between mental retardation and nutrition involve largely clinical cases.[35] As such, the subjects were very sick children and some were practically moribund. These were children who had suffered from kwashiorkor, marasmus, or other severe nutritional disease; they required medical attention, including hospitalization, in areas where such action is a last resort. In one such study, malnourished infants had not been breast fed during their infancy but had subsisted entirely on a diet of flour and water.

Families in which children are so severely undernourished as to require clinical attention may be different from other families even in communities living at subsistence levels. Comparison with an appropriate control is necessary if the effects of being reared in a poor family environment are not to be confounded with the effects of poor nutrition. In one study, controls of the same age and sex were selected from lower socio-economic class families living in urban poverty as were the families of the index cases. But while the home environments of the control group were fairly stable, the home environments of the identified grossly undernourished children included alcoholism, illegitimacy, unemployment and broken homes.[36] More adequately nourished siblings reared in the same family at about the same time may provide better controls. But the lack of appropriate controls is not the only deficit to be taken into account.

Follow-up of infant cases of malnutrition do not often extend beyond late childhood. Thus, there is little knowledge of how they develop in later years and perform as adults.

Hertzig and his coworkers reported on an examination of 71 Jamaican boys, who had been hospitalized for severe malnutrition (e.g., kwashiorkor and marasmus) during the first two years of age, received an average of almost two months of in-patient care, and whose intelligence was tested from three to seven years afterwords. The formerly hospitalized children were compared with their brother or half-brother closest to them in age and also with unrelated male classmates and neighbors close to them in age. On the Wechsler Intelligence Scale for Children (WISC), the subjects scored 57.72 with a standard deviation of 10.75; the sibs scored 61.84 with a standard deviation of 10.82, and the unrelated controls scored 65.99 with a standard deviation of 13.59. Thus while, on the average, the subjects scored less than their sibs and the sibs less than unrelated controls, there was considerable overlap in scores among the three groups. Whether hospitalization for malnutrition occurred in early infancy (0 to 7 months), in late infancy (7 to 12 months), or during the second year of life had no effect on the score.[37]

Birch (1972) proposed that these results supported the notion that even moderate malnutrition had a detrimental effect on mentation. A family that included a child so severely malnourished as to require hospitalization also would have been likely to underfeed the other children; hence, the lower scores of the sibs relative to the controls. The argument is, however, very tenuous since children of such families are likely to experience other deprivations and cultural handicaps as well.

Nor can the possibility be excluded that the lower average performance of the subject cases relative to their sibs was due to a lag in development rather than to a permanent condition. A comparison of South African children, who had been hospitalized for kwashiorkor when they were 10 to 48 months old, with nonhospitalized siblings (and also with a control group of a previous study) nine to ten years later, showed no difference in scores between the formerly hospitalized malnourished children and controls on a WISC-type IQ test.[38]

Also to the point is a study by Winick and his coworkers of the development of Korean orphans adopted into American families.[39] The orphans selected for study were female; they were less than two years old when first admitted to the adoption service (between 1958 and 1967), and less than three years old when adopted. They were reported to have been full term at birth and evidenced no physical defect or chronic illness when first examined by a physician. But they differed widely in nutritional status when they were first observed. One group (42 children) was considered malnourished since they were below the third percentile of normal Korean children of the same age in height and weight. A second group (52 children) falling between the third and twenty-fourth percentile in height and weight were considered to be moderately undernourished, and the third group (47 children) above the twenty-fifth percentile in height and weight were considered to be well nourished. Records of school achievement and intelligence test scores were obtained from schools these children were currently attending (grades one to eight). The differences in original size between the three groups diminished considerably though the group which had been severely malnourished was still somewhat shorter and lighter than the moderately malnourished, who were shorter and lighter than the well-nourished group. All three groups were larger on the average than Korean children of the same ages, though smaller than American children. The first group which had earlier suffered, or was presumed to have suffered, extreme deprivation had a mean IQ of 102; the second group, 106; and the third group, 112: all above the average for Americans, perhaps reflecting the stimulation received from their adoptive families. While the small difference between the mean IQ's of the three groups may reflect the initial differences in nutritional status and slowing of development, the children were still quite young, and these differences may still vanish as they approach maturity. Winick and his coworkers argued that recovery from a bout of severe malnutrition may be contingent on a long period spent in a more stimulating environment.

Monckeberg discussed the difficulty in separating out the effects of undernutrition and cultural deprivation on mentation, both of these being so closely involved. He studied 60 poor schoolchildren aged seven to nine years, selected because they were small for their age, who were fed three nutritionally adequate meals a day at school for nine months. The students made good gains in height (an average of 4.1 cm.) and in weight (an average of 2.7 kg.) but not in IQ. The possible explanations were that either these children had suffered irreparable brain damage early in life; that nine months of good nutrition was not long enough to show improved IQ's; that socio-cultural deprivations to which the children were still subject were the significant determinants of IQ. Monckeberg cited another experiment in Colombia. Three-year-old undernourished slum children were provided an adequate diet plus a program of physical and cognitive stimulation for a year. A comparable control group with similar nutritional and cultural background received only an adequate diet. While both groups made good physical gains, the group receiving only the adequate diet did not improve in intellectual development; the group receiving both an adequate diet and stimulation achieved mental development levels similar to those of middle class children.[40] This demonstrated that the effects of earlier low nutritional levels were likely to be reversible, but that school is not by itself necessarily a stimulating environment.

Pertinent to this discussion are the findings of Jerome Kagan, a Harvard psychologist, who since 1971 has been studying the mental development of rural Guatemalan children in two remote villages, one Spanish speaking and the other, a still more isolated village, Indian speaking. These findings were discussed by Gloria Levitas in the context of some new interpretations of the pace of mental development in different cultural settings.[41] Kagan found that while village infants appeared to be undernourished, listless, and retarded, the older children appeared more normal, the more so as their age increased. At age three, the children lost what was described as a ghostlike quality. On a series of tests designed to measure mental development in terms of such general capabilities as recall and recognition memory, perceptual ability, inference, etc., the very young children performed considerably behind middle class Cambridge (Mass.) children of the same age. But the difference in performance diminished at five to eight years of age and the performance of Guatemalan children eleven years of age or older was comparable to that of middle class American children of the same age. This did not mean that the Guatemalan children would have performed as well as American children on academeic aptitude tests and the like; the attempt was to measure intellectual qualities commonly needed in all cultures. Kagan attributed the lag in the development of these qualities among the younger Guatemalan children to a lack of stimulation characteristic of the manner in which they were reared. As the children grew older and were more exposed to the experiences of village life, the effects of their early deprivation were overcome. While Kagan's research was not specifically concerned with the effects of undernutrition in early childhood, it and other related research brings into question, as Levitas suggested, several widely held notions about intellectual development. These include the usefulness of age-graded intelligence tests to predict future performance and the notion that retardation early in life necéssarily affects later attainments. These notions have prejudiced evaluations of the potential competence of people of cultures different from our own, and of those in our own culture who for one reason or another develop more slowly than others.

The most vulnerable period for brain damage from malnutrition is when the brain is developing and growing most rapidly, at which time relative nutritional requirements are high. Among humans, this critical period includes the latter part of gestation and early infancy.[42] An indication of how children subject to early nutritional deprivation, during their gestation as well as in infancy, fare as adults is the subject of a study reported by Zena Stein and her colleagues. The study involves the mental performance of males at age 19 who were carried *in utero*, born, or passed their infancy during the Dutch famine of 1944–1945.[43] During World War II, food rations in Holland provided individuals with about 1,500 to 1,600 calories per day, and often less, fewer calories per person than is normally consumed in less developed countries today. From September 1944 to May 1945, the Nazis had imposed a transport embargo on Western Holland, cutting off its food supplies in retaliation for a railway strike. In the cities of Western Holland, daily food rations fell to an average of 700 calories, including less than 20 grams of protein per person from December 1944 through May 1945, and rations reached a low of 450 calories per day. As might be expected, mortality increased and clinical studies noted frequent hunger edema and weight losses of around 25 percent among patients.

The birth rate, which had started to fall in July, nine months after the famine started, fell to one-half to one-third of expectation. Nutritional levels were so low that many women were likely to have become infecund. In the embargoed region, half the women were reported to have become amenor-rheic and many others had irregular menstrual cycles.[44]

The subjects studied by Stein and her colleagues were 125,000 males born in selected famine and control cities during the three years, 1944 to 1946; these included 20,000 who were presumed from birthdate and place to have been exposed to the famine *in utero* or as infants. Routinely, all males in the Netherlands are called up for induction between ages 18 and 19 and receive physical and psychological examinations if they are capable of appearing. For residents of institutions who cannot appear, reports, including clinical records, are reviewed to justify exemption from military service by the medical officer in charge of the induction center. Thus, those who had been institutionalized were represented in the study.

Briefly, the findings indicated no difference betwen controls and famine-exposed individuals in the incidence of severe or mild mental retardation or in IQ's as determined by the Raven Progressive Matrices Test. The best predictor of IQ was the father's occupation. The usual relation of IQ to class held to the same degree in both famine and non-famine areas.

The families of pregnant women would have been expected to protect them by sharing their little food, but the evidence is that whatever the adjustment, pregnant women were still very much undernourished. The average birth weight had declined from a normal 3,500 grams to 3,000 grams during the famine; maternal weight after delivery had declined on an average to four standard deviations below the weight of parturient mothers after the famine, an impressive loss. Evidently the mothers' physiology continued to be highly protective of the fetus despite the unusual stresses. Another point made clear by the data presented is that the children who must have passed through their early infancy during the famine period did not appear to be severely affected intellectually though their risk of mortality as infants had increased significantly.

After the *hongerwinter*, nutrition returned to normal, but remained at low levels. The period of hunger was about six to seven months duration, so that the findings may have limited significance. However, rations in the Netherlands were short during the entire occupation of four to five years, less than 2,000 calories with little more than 40 grams of protein per person per day, no more than that available in many third world countries. Investigations indicated that even pregnant women were consuming only around 1,925 calories, long before the *hongerwinter*. As a result of the famine, mortality increased and births decline, but the children who were produced and survived were not mentally damaged.

The findings of Stein and her coworkers are in contrast with those of others who have tied mental retardation to deficiencies in the mother's diet. Knobloch and Pasamanick[45] reported that children born in the winter months (January through March) ran a greater risk of being admitted to the Columbus (Ohio) State School for the mentally retarded. (The author had an opportunity to analyze data on admissions to a California state institution for the mentally retarded and found a similar relationship.) Originally, Knobloch and Pasamanick had anticipated finding an increased risk among summer births on the hypothesis that increased viral infections during the winter, in the eighth to twelfth weeks of gestation, would affect the brain of the fetus during this critical period of development when the anlage of the nervous system is being laid down. The eighth to twelfth week of gestation was probably selected as the critical period by analogy with the pathogenesis of rubella-induced malformations of the fetus which are associated with infection during the period when the fetal brain and nervous system are formed. Finding quite the opposite, they sought another explanation and hypothesized that maternal dietary deficiencies were involved. The same authors observed that a similar relationship existed between winter births and increased risk of pregnancy complications reported in New York City for 1956. They concluded:

On the basis of data thus far accumulated it appears highly likely that inadequate maternal diet, particularly during the early months of pregnancy as a result of summer heat might result in cerebral-anoxia producing complications of pregnancy that in turn might account for significant increase in mental deficiency and possibly other constituents of a continuum of reproductive casualty.[46]

That is a highly inferential statement from the evidence that there is an increase in pregnancy complications among winter births as compared to summer births (9.5 percent compared to 6.9 percent), and a much smaller relative increase in mental retardation. No attempt was made to consider possible causes other than nutrition. No attempt was made to assess nutritional intake of mothers giving birth to retardates; the relationship between nutrition and pathology was speculative. Today, the critical effects of maternal malnutrition on brain development are deemed more likely to occur during the latter phases of pregnancy, the period of most rapid fetal and brain growth, rather than during the first trimester, as hypothesized by Knobloch and Pasamanick.[47]

Researchers such as Birch, Knobloch, and Pasamanick, and others, have regarded nutritionally deprived mothers to be subject to significantly increased risks of pregnancy complications and of bearing low birth weight babies. Low birth weight babies, defined as weighing less than 2,500 grams (and often considered to be premature) show higher death rates in early infancy and increased risk of disability in later life than do babies of "normal" birth weight. The disabilities associated with low birth weight include neurological and intellectual defects. These children are more frequently born to poor families, and to smaller mothers regardless of social class. Some researchers traced the small size of mothers to nutritional deprivation of grandmothers.

That low nutritional levels result in low birth weight babies and also in smaller people has been amply demonstrated. However, as Abramowicz and Kass have pointed out in their extensive review of research into prematurity, this does not mean that the deficits associated with low birth weight babies are due to their small size.[48] Since low birth weight infants are born more frequently into poor families, it is difficult to separate the biological from the environmental effects. In studies where social class was controlled, the association between low birth weight and neurological deficits became attenuated. Then only a small minority of low birth weight children show neurological, motor, and intellectual defects later in life, and this minority is concentrated among the small proportion of infants with birth weights below 1,500 grams; about 10 to 15 percent of this minority of very small infants show deficits. Low birth weight can be caused not only by low levels of nutrition but also by various pathologies about many of which little is known. But not all low birth weight babies are associated with pathology. Thus Abramowicz and Kass concluded:

. . . the effect of low birth weight on child development is not established. Low birth weight is of concern because perinatal death is more common in smaller infants and because children with cerebral palsy, mental retardation and other neurologic difficulties often begin life weighing less than 2,500 grs. Death and disability must have biologic causes but the relation of low birth weight to them may be irrelevant. Available evidence suggests that many factors can be responsible for low birth weight. Some of these may contribute to infant morbidity and mortality, others may not.[49]

Low birth weights do not of themselves lead to neurologic deficits. Indeed, some brilliant and effective people (Newton, Darwin, Voltaire, Napoleon, Renoir, Hugo, Churchill and others) were reported to have been premature.[50] The association between low birth weights and increased risk of mortality and morbidity is more likely due to the many instances in which both result from causes still unknown. In industrialized countries, the incidence of prematurity and the death rates among prematures have declined slowly compared to infant mortality in general, despite increased nutritional and health levels.

Indeed, in some respects, low birth weights may be an adaptation. In California during 1959, 13.5 percent of black births were considered premature (2,500 grams or less birth weight) compared to 7.3 percent of white births. Among these births the optimal neonatal one-year survival rates for whites (99.4 percent) were at birth weights between 3,501–4,000 grams. Above and below these weights, mortality increased. For blacks, the optimal survival rates (99.1 percent) were between 3,000–3,500 grams and for other non-whites, largely Orientals, the optimal neonatal survival rate (99.6 percent) was in the same range as that for blacks. Despite the fact that the neonatal mortality rate of black infants was considerably higher than that of white infants (26 neonatal deaths per 1,000 live births for blacks, compared to 17 for whites), the neonatal death rates of black infants under 2,500 grams birth weight was less than that of white infants of low birth weight (161 per

1,000 live births for blacks to 179 for whites). Orientals, who had a slightly higher prematurity rate (8.7 percent) than whites, had much lower neonatal mortality.[51] Abramowicz and Kass cite similar findings from other regions.

That malnutrition is a serious problem among poor children is evident from the number who require hospitalization and who die needlessly from infections. But statements such as "Today 70 percent of the world's population seriously risk permanent [brain] damage," made in a popular magazine,[52] obscure the issue. This statement is not justified on the basis of the clinical cases studied, much less on the basis of the prevailing low levels of subsistence in much of the world. For the majority of people living at low levels of subsistence, the problem is not with constraints of inadequate mental or physical capability but with the constraints of their social and economic milieu.

The Vigor of the Work Force

The philosopher, Feuerbach, blamed the failure of the revolution of 1848 in Europe on the poor diet of the lower classes. According to him, the debilitated potato eating lower classes were no match for the more vigorous meat eating ruling classes and their retainers. Unless a cheap substitute for meat was adopted (Feuerbach recommended beans) the potato eating Irish, the vegetarian Hindus, the salad eating Italians were doomed to oppression because of their inability to muster the energy to resist effectively.[53]

Economists such as Leibenstein and Belli inferred that the vigor and enterprise of the work force of developing nations may be significantly impaired by their poor diets.[54] Other contemporary observers went almost as far as Feuerbach and anticipated political upheaval if the apathetic masses were better fed.[55]

Alphonse Gintzburger[56] traced the backwardness of the highland Maya peasants of Guatemala to the repression of oral sadistic aggressive tendencies developed in the course of a hungry childhood and competition within the family for the limited supply of food. The attainment of wealth (food) was seen as occurring only at the expense of others, an undertaking that invited retaliation. This evoked anxiety and repression of aggressive sadistic tendencies. The end was neurotic fatigue, loss of enterprise, lethargy, apathy and indifference or stolidity in the face of deprivation. Gintzburger concluded his analysis by advocating not only the improvement and supplementation of nutritional intake as part of development programs, but also some approach to group psychotherapy to help break the vicious circle.

Gintzburger's proposed psychodynamic connection between food scarcity and stagnation cannot be readily validated empirically and is noted here only to illustrate the variety of theories available. Most observers are concerned with the more direct physiological effects of nutritional deprivation on prenatal, infant and child development and on the capacity of workers to produce.

P. Belli[57] argued that the evidence from IQ studies of severely malnourished clinical cases, effects of diet on development and the like, indicate that the work force of developing nations is debilitated by undernutrition. Leibenstein sought more direct evidence in the reported nutritional experience of German workers and their output during World War II.[58] Though the evidence of that experience indicated that nutritional deprivation, particularly if it is severe, does significantly reduce the output of workers engaged in strenuous industrial occupations, the implications for the productivity of workers in low subsistence societies are not clear.

During World War II, food rations, including calorie allowances, of German industrial workers were significantly decreased, as were those of the general population. This reduction was accompanied by a reduction in the productivity of coal miners and steelworkers among others. Part of this association can be attributed to the deficits in food energy. But one should be cautious in drawing conclusions, for the same war which resulted in food shortages also resulted in dislocations in the work force and work processes.

More informative are some observations and experiments performed by German scientists during that period. When food allotments of groups of steelworkers, coal miners, and other workers engaged in strenuous activities were increased 400 calories over the restricted wartime levels, their productivity also increased. However, a further increase of 400 calories per day allotted to coal miners whose intake had previously been increased to 3,100 calories per day (of which 1,500 calories were considered to be expended in the maintenance of basic metabolic functions and 1,600 were work calories), was not matched so much with increases in work output (the increases were small), as with increases in body weight.[59]

While nutritional levels in third world countries include an average of around 2,000 calories per person, the average includes children who comprise a large proportion of the total and whose consumption is less than half the consumption of working adults. The latter are not usually engaged in the kind of strenuous activity performed by coal hewers or steamhammer operators; those working in modern sector enterprises can generally afford a higher level of nutrition than their compatriots in traditional occupations. Smaller stature, a consequence of lower levels of nutrition, also serves to diminish food requirements relative to Europeans.

The German workers of World War II were reared under dietary conditions characteristic of the West before being subjected to nutritional deprivation. The effects of such deprivation on their productivity may not be analogous to that of smaller sized people who are reared and work in low subsistence conditions. The work efficiency of Guatemalan peasants in an area where malnutrition was common was reported to have been no less than that of workers in well-nourished regions.[60] Even so, Keller and Kraut noted that the Germans subjected to a long period of nutritional deprivation had adapted to these levels and did not appear to be as debilitated by this as were a group of Americans subjected to similar levels of undernutrition for a short period of time in an experiment conducted by Keys in Minnesota (see note 59).

The accomplishments of small peoples, undernourished by Western standards, cannot be ignored. Japanese soldiers during World War II performed as effectively as did their larger American counterparts; and after the war, these same Japanese went on to spark a record in economic growth and enterprise. The Kikuyu of Kenya, on a diet of cereals, tubers and legumes, have been transforming their economy while their Masai countrymen, taller, heavier, and living on animal products, keep to the old ways. A number of observers concluded that small size may be regarded in some respects as an adaptation to food shortage, of little importance unless accompanied by diminished health and productivity.

In contrast to the illustrative approach taken above, Franke and Barrett[61] examined the argument of Belli in more systematic fashion. As noted earlier, Belli argued that malnutrition retards the physical and mental development of the work force, decreases its vigor, and is thus likely to inhibit economic growth. Belli noted that countries with high per capita protein supplies also had high per capita incomes; this relationship also holds if the per capita income of countries is compared with the protein supplies available ten years earlier. This, of course, does not demonstrate that the higher per capita incomes were due to the greater protein supply since high income countries could be expected to have had a greater protein supply—particularly meat and dairy products—and a high income a decade earlier. Belli did not claim that his correlation analysis demonstrated cause and effect, but that it supported his hypothesis that undernutrition retards the development of a productive labor force.

Franke and Barrett employed a more empirical and rigorous statistical analysis based on cross lagged correlations to examine the relation between protein supply and growth in per capita income. In one analysis, growth in per capita income of a country at one time is correlated with the protein supply at a later time; in another analysis, income growth and protein supply are examined concurrently; and finally, per capita protein supply is correlated with per capita income growth at a later date. Also for purposes of analysis, they divided the countries of the world for which appropriate data were available into two groups based on the availability of per capita protein supplies of more than 75 grams and less than 75 grams per day. By this division, separate analysis of the effects of nutrition in rich and poor countries could be made. Among the poor countries, those with less than 50 grams of protein per capita could be said to have had an inadequate protein supply; those with more could be said to have had an adequate supply. Furthermore, since the adequate development and performance of adult workers was presumed to depend on their nutritional experience in childhood, consideration was given to the protein supplies available as much as 20 to 30 years prior to the time at which income growth is reviewed.

The results of the Franke and Barrett analyses showed that differences in the availability of proteins did not affect subsequent economic growth but rather the converse; as income increases, proteins become more available. Thus, economic development is not hindered by a vicious cycle of poverty begetting malnutrition which begets poverty. Other factors are more pertinent. They concluded that the justification of nutrition programs is to assist the malnourished poor, a humanitarian objective which is worthy in itself and needs no economic justification.

Reproductive Capacity

Low levels of nutrition may increase the age of menarche by a few years and thus shorten the span of a woman's reproductive capability. Full reproductive capability or fecundity, marked by regular ovulation, does not generally follow immediately upon menarche, but is usualy delayed. This is the period of adolescent sub-fecundity.[62]

In 1960, Garn and Haskell observed that fat children attained puberty at an earlier age than lean children.[63] Recent research by Frisch and MacArthur[64] on age of menarche and menstruation among American women suggests that menarche is initiated with the attainment of a certain minimum body fat content associated with a certain critical weight for height. As a young woman approaches maturity and attains this critical weight (along with the other physiological changes required), she begins to have menstrual cycles. A well-nourished young woman will reach this critical weight earlier than a poorly nourished one and will thus experience menarche at an earlier age. Frisch has carried the research further to hypothesize that lowered fertility among the poor of past societies may have been due not to efforts to control fertility as much as to low nutritional levels operating through a variety of channels including early onset of secondary sterility.[65] Frisch's theory is subject to considerable reservation as discussed below.

Depletion of body fat below a certain level results in amenorrhea, but deprivation must be extreme. Thus, amenorrhea not related to pregnancy among women of reproductive age has been noted on a significant scale only among starving women such as concentration camp victims or during a famine. Menstruation also ceases in clinically anorexic women.[66] These are women who barely eat, suffer severe weight loss and psychological stress, suffering from a pathological condition which can lead to death, hardly a group from which such generalizations should be made. Such women resume menstruation as the condition of starvation ends.

While frank starvation results in a temporary loss of reproductive capacity, the effects of undernutrition are not so clear. One mechanism linking nutrition and reproduction is lactation, the production of milk which places significant demands on fat reserves. After delivery, women are temporarily sterile for an average period of two to three months due to post-partum amenorrhea. The period of post-partum amenorrhea can be extended another six to nine months if the infant is breast fed by the mother, and longer in societies where women nurse with considerable intensity. Frisch and others have suggested that nutritional status, through its effects on menarche, lactation amenorrhea, and other reproductive processes may thus have significant implications for the fertility levels of developing societies, keeping the birth rates of some of these societies below what they might otherwise be.

It has been suggested that the change from a hunting and gathering economy to agriculture was accompanied by an increase in women's body fat reserves and a decrease in the intensity of lactation, assisted by the increased availability of alternate foods suitable for infant feeding. The result was a shorter period of lactation amenorrhea and a higher birth rate. This thesis appears to be supported by recent observations of the Dobe !Kung, hunter-gatherers of the Kalahari (Botswana). Many of these people have in recent times turned to cultivation and keeping goats, becoming sedentary consumers of grain and milk. The women were no longer subject as they would have been in the nomadic life to the energy demands of carrying heavy burdens, including children, as they migrated on foot and performed other tasks. Among the nomadic !Kung, menarche occured between the ages of 15 and 17; the first child was born when the mother was between 18 and 22 years old; children were breast fed for three to four years; and the lactation and energy demands on body fat presumably led to a long interval between births of three to five years. The !Kung are also known to have practiced occasional infanticide when one birth followed too soon upon another; it would have been exceedingly difficult for a mother to carry more than one child on the march. Those !Kung who have become sedentary and turned cultivator have also become larger and heavier. The interval between births has decreased some thirty percent, on the average, and fertility is thus increased.[67] This may have been due to changes in intensity of lactation as well as body fat. It is also possible that a discontinuation of the occasional practice of infanticide may have led to an apparent increase in fertility. (A soon to be published definitive work by N. Howell on the demography of the Dobe !Kung may be informative in these regards. The work was not available at the time of this writing. The writer depended on other sources for material relating to the !Kung and Howell's projected work.)

The proposed mechanism whereby lactation prolongs the period of post-partum amenorrhea is based on the depletion of the mother's fat reserves below the levels required to maintain menstruation and ovulation. A full term pregnancy is estimated to require 50,000 calories, and lactation 1,000 per day over those normally required.[68] However, other mechanisms such as neural hormonal interactions also regulate menstruation and ovulation, and these mechanisms may be inhibited by intensive suckling.[69] Thus, if the required fat reserves are in fact small and the neural hormonal processes are of greater importance, nutritional deprivation, except when very severe, may have but small impact on the resumption of menstruation and ovulation.

Examination of the relationship between nutrition and post-partum amenorrhea may be informative. Since few mothers in industrialized countries intensively nurse their infants for appreciable periods of time, much of our information on lactation amenorrhea comes from studies in developing nations. Data from the rural Punjab and from Taiwan show similar findings.[70] In both Taiwan and the Punjab, the most important factor influencing the length of post-partum amenorrhea following a live birth among lactating women was age. In the Punjab (1955–1961), the duration of post-partum amenorrhea ranged from an average of 7.4 months for women age 15 to 19 years, to 13.5 months for women of more than 40 years. In Taiwan (1965 interviews), the range was from a mean of 7.8 months for women 18 to 24 years old, to 13.4 months for women 40 to 44 years old who had nursed their children. This is a remarkable concordance considering the difference in conditions of health, nutrition, and the like, in these two areas and times. Jain and his coworkers[71] reported that among Taiwanese women who breast fed, those with higher education (and presumably better nutrition), had shorter periods of amenorrhea than did those with lesser education; but they noted also that those with higher education tended to breast feed for a shorter period of time, so that when the differences in lactation were taken into account, there was little difference in amenorrhea related to education or urban-rural residence. In any case, the average length of post-partum amenorrhea for Taiwanese women of all ages who had breast fed was 10.6 months; for Punjabi women who breast fed, it was around 11 months.

Berman and his coworkers reported similar findings among Eskimos. N. L. Solien de Gonzalez reported that among Guatemalan women, post-partum amenorrhea averaged around 12 months. A study of English women (probably of lower class) reported that of those who lactated for eight months or more, 59 percent were amenorrheic at the time of weaning, a result consistent with those cited for developing nations. Solien de Gonzalez cited a 1960 study of lactating Italian women in which 69 percent did not resume menstruation until the end of the lactating period.[72]

The intensity of lactation is important since partial breast feeding at infrequent intervals shortens the duration of post-partum amenorrhea.[73] While nursing women of peasant societies or the poorer classes cannot be expected to exclusively breast feed children for an extended period of time beyond early infancy, they may be expected to breast feed exclusively as long as possible with as little other food as feasible. In communities where infant foods are readily available, relatively few women nurse; those who do, nurse for short periods and with considerable supplementation of infant feedings with prepared foods.

In most modern communities the minority of women who breast feed their children do not do so intensively or for long. Some researchers did not hesitate to take the experience of such short term partially nursing mothers to indicate that lactation amenorrhea is considerably shortened by ample nutrition. Salber, Feinleib and MacMahon credit nutritional status (better for American than for Indian mothers) for the short average period (five months) of lactational amenorrhea among their study group of Boston mothers who partially breast fed their infants for six months or more.[74] Potter comes to the same conclusion about a group of urban (Santiago) Chilean women who breast fed their infants fully for 61 days on the average and continued partial nursing for another 51 days on the average before stopping altogether. Though post-partum amenorrhea lasted 112 days on the average, Potter cites an abstract stochastic model which predicted that had full nursing lasted six months and partial nursing continued thereafter, post-partum lactation amenorrhea would have lasted only six months.[75]

The notion that the lactational amenorrhea is prolonged by maternal undernutrition appeared to be supported by the longest reported duration (18 months) of lactation amenorrhea coming from a study of around 200 women in Matlab Thana, Bangladesh.[76] The Bangla people have very low nutritional levels. Bangla women, however, are also very avid breast feeders, nursing their children intensively and long. But more extensive studies in Bangladesh and elsewhere, which permit comparisons of both nutritional status and nursing habits, indicate that the latter is the important element in prolonging lactation amenorrhea.

A large survey of more than 2,000 nursing women, including mothers of children 13 to 21 months old, in the same region provided similar findings, a median duration of lactation amenorrhea of 18 months. The duration was shorter for younger women and for those supplementing their nursing with a higher quality supplement, and only slightly longer for those suffering maternal malnutrition.[77] The conclusion was that the pattern of breast feeding played the primary role in determining the length of post-partum amenorrhea in this culture. Long average durations (18 months) of post-partum amenorrhea were also reported for lactating women in Zaire and

Somalia. Research reports from Guatemala and Bangladesh cited by Knodel indicated that the difference in length of post-partum amenorrhea among women of different nutritional status in the same cultures are not large.[78] The important factor in prolonging the duration of post-partum amenorrhea is the intensity of nursing and the hormonal processes this engenders.

Recent reports based on observations rather than abstract models indicate that undernutrition does not significantly slow reproduction. One would imagine that the differences in the duration of post-partum amenorrhea—18 months in Bangladesh and 11 months in the Punjab—would be reflected in related differences in fertility. But this did not occur.

Although both the Khanna and Matlab populations were considered to be non-contracepting, there were indications that this may not have been so. In the Khanna study, the average age of mothers giving birth to their last child was 37 years and 36 years for the wives of the relatively well-off landowning farmers, though the women were not yet close to menopause. This pattern has been observed in several areas of India, some where the last child is born when the mothers were younger still—around 35 years old, on the average, and at least ten years from menopause.[79]

Fertility rates among the older Matlab women over 30 appeared to be declining also. Ten percent of the Matlab women interviewed admitted to some form of contraceptive practice, mostly coitus interruptus. Five women (one using the pill, three with IUD, and one with husband sterilized) were excluded from the study. However, previous studies in the area had shown that about a third of the small number of women known to have accepted birth control services in public clinics did not admit on a later interview to ever practicing family planning.[80] Thus, even women who made some effort to obtain services were loathe to admit to the practice of birth control, if indeed they did use it. Others not so bold may have been more reluctant to admit its use. Forty-seven (or 24 percent) of the small sample of 197 Matlab village wives studied, did not conceive though they were menstruating during the entire two-year period of the study.

If the Matlab study was representative of Matlab women in general, the birth rates of that poorly nourished region should have been lower than that of Khanna, provided that contraception was not practiced in either area and that such characteristics as population age structure and age of marriage were similar. However, the birth rate in the Matlab area was estimated to be around 47 births per 1,000 population per year for 1968 and 1969; that of the Khanna villages was estimated to be 38 per 1,000 per year from 1957 to 1959, the years of the Khanna study. The difference is further reflected in the percentage of children less than ten years old in the respective populations, 36 percent in Matlab, 28 percent in Khanna.[81]

The high fertility of other peoples whose health and nutritional status may not have been very good on the whole is also impressive. If stature and rate of maturation are any indicators of nutritional status, Europeans were relatively undernourished in the nineteenth century. Eighteen-year-old Dutch civil militia conscripts had an average height of 63 inches in 1870 and 64 inches in 1890, compared to 68.5 inches in 1960.[82] But Dutch Catholic women, married before age 25 in 1891 and remaining married for at least twenty years, had almost nine live births per woman on the average; wives of agricultural workers and other wage earners (the poorer classes) produced an average of eight children each.[83] In the mid-nineteenth century, where age of menarche was advanced and nutritional status presumably poor, marital fertility rates of 350 live births per 1,000 married women of reproductive age per year were reported for many regions in the northern Swedish agricultural areas and in some German communities.[84] These people may or may not have practiced prolonged nursing. Many undernourished societies whose women practice prolonged breast feeding are reported to have birth rates of close to 50 per 1,000 with married women bearing an average of eight children and more if they remained married over their reproductive years. Even if the natural birth interval of a cohabiting, non-contracepting, and lactating woman were, on the average, as long as three years (longer than generally observed) and her period of fecundity as short as 25 years (shorter than generally observed), the woman could easily give birth to more than eight children even if none of them died in infancy. If infant mortality were high so that nursing ended prematurely, she could have borne more. In a society where nutritional levels are so low that they do indeed significantly lengthen the duration of lactation amenorrhea, infant mortality is likely to be quite high. As a consequence, lactation will frequently end after a short period, and menstruation resume. The depressing effects of lactational amenorrhea on fertility are likely to be compensated to a high degree by high infant mortality, and lactating women would be enabled to maintain high levels of fertility.

The effect of decreased nutrition through an increase in age of menarche would obviously shorten the period of time during which women would be fertile. Yet there may be compensations which lessen this effect. Cowgill suggests that part of the reason for the increase in age at marriage during the seventeenth century in England may have been an increase in the age at menarche resulting from a deterioration in nutritional status. Average age at marriage for women, however, had increased from 24 years to more than 28 years during the period she studied. Age at menarche, high as it might have been, was not likely to have approached either age, but Cowgill notes further that 30 percent of the married women over 40 years old were still having babies.[85] In England birth rates were around 35 per 1,000 despite the high age of marriage and the fact that up to 20 percent of women over 50 had never married (see Chapter 9). Had practically all women married, even at the late age they did, birth rates would have been well over 40 per 1,000. In India, in 1961, practically all women were married at an average age of 15. The birth rate during that year was around 42 per 1,000 population.

In India in the 1950s and early 1960s, when birth control was reported to have been rarely practiced, only small differences in birth rates were noted between the upper and lower classes. In some areas the women of the lower castes were reported to have given birth to an average of 8 children or more, 8.8 children in one instance, while women of the upper castes gave birth to 7 children or more. In other areas fertility was lower, and the upper class women 45 years of age or older reported having given birth to slightly more children than the lower classes, averaging 4.9 and 4.6 children, respectively.[86] Since infant and child mortality was considerably greater among the poor, and women tended to forget or at least not report children who had died, the estimates for the number of children born to poorer women were lower than actuality.[87] The poorer classes in India were and are generally underfed, yet their fertility appears no lower because of it.

The people of Bangladesh, poorer than those if India, have very high fertility: an estimated total fertility rate of 7.1 children and a birth rate of 49 per 1,000 based on a 1974 national survey.[88]

Although menarche is delayed by low levels of nutrition, these must be low indeed to have a significant effect, sufficient to delay menarche several years. Other factors may also be involved. The people of Matlab Thana, Bangladesh, appear to be among the more undernourished in the modern world. Whatever their age at menarche, the women are practically all married by age 20 and the marital fertility rates of these women between ages 15 to 19 are high, more than 250 births per 1,000 per year,[89] indicating that even the effect of adolescent subfecundity is limited.

Lactation amenorrhea extends the sterile period and thus limits potential fertility. Yet no people has been observed to attain the maximum conceivable level of potential fertility. Assume that the biologically feasible minimum interval between births for a non-lactating woman is 18 months: 4 months on the average to get pregnant, 9 months of pregnancy, 2 months of post-partum amenorrhea, 2 months to compensate for fetal deaths, and another month for good measure. If a woman married at age 15 and continued to reproduce until she was 45, she could have as many as 20 children; if she married at 20, she could have more than 16. Few women have borne so many children. The Hutterites, a religious sect living on communal farms on the American plains exhibited one of the highest fertility rates observed, averaging 10.4 births per completed family, though the average age of Hutterite women at marriage was 22 years.[90] The average length of post-partum amenorrhea among Hutterite women has been estimated to be six months.[91] Despite the nearly universal practice of breast feeding among the Hutterites, they do not nurse intensely; infants receive supplements of baby foods as early as six weeks and by six months infants have access to all adult foods. Pacifiers are widely used to satisfy infants sucking needs and some infants are totally weaned by four months; those that continue to nurse do so sparingly.[92] The average interval between live births among Hutterite women was estimated to be around 26 months,[93] compared to 31 months for Punjabi women. Had the Hutterite women married at age 15, they might have had on the average 12.5 instead of 10.4 children, assuming that other factors did not intervene.

Few other populations have been reported to have such high fertility as the Hutterites, but many have come close with an average of eight children or more per couple even under conditions of prolonged lactation and low levels of nutrition. This may require earlier marriage and a longer period of exposure to pregnancy than experienced by the Hutterites. There is little to indicate that, were the natural controls on fertility removed, an increase in the number of children would be long tolerated before a change in fertility related behavior occurs. Thus, while improved health conditions and the decline in mortality over the past thirty years in the third world resulted in more women living through the reproductive years, fewer widows, and perhaps increased fecundity, the associated increases in fertility were not generally very large and, as will be discussed later, fertility rates are decreasing rapidly.

Humans are omnivorous and capable of faring under a variety of dietary regimens, from the almost exclusive dependence on flesh as among the Eskimos to the exclusive vegetarian diet of the orthodox Brahmin. Among those poor whose diets lack variety and are limited to inferior foods, one is likely to find a relatively high incidence of nutritional deficiency diseases, pellagra among maize eaters, beriberi among (polished) rice eaters, and the more general conditions of marasmus and kwashiorkior among their infants and children. But the generally low levels of subsistence which are the lot of most people in the world today, as they were in the past, are not likely to result in such levels of high mortality (say a death rate of more than 30 per 1,000), or of low fertility (say a birth rate of less than 35 per 1,000), as to automatically reduce population growth. Nor do such low nutritional levels seriously diminish the vigor and productive capacities of a people within the patterns of their society. Whatever impact low levels of subsistence may have on the capacities of people, these are difficult to separate from the overwhelming effects of the general condition of their society.

The levels of subsistence required by humans to function effectively may well be lower than is often presumed. But the tragedy is that many people are denied even this minimum level by the manner in which food is produced and distributed. The frequent hunger and constant insecurity of a significant portion of the world's population will not be overcome by blaming overpopulation.

Population size and growth were unlikely to have been kept in check in the manner proposed by Malthus. On the contrary, low levels of subsistence are likely to be associated with high fertility. Not because, as De Castro erroneously thought, malnutrition increases fecundity, nor because poor people are indifferent to the arrival of children (though this may be true of some of the personally disorganized poor), but because under the conditions prevailing in most low subsistence societies, children and family are the only guarantors of security, personal integrity, and survival.

Notes

1. See G. T. Curlin, L. C. Chen and B. Hossain, "Demographic Crisis: The Impact of the Bangladesh Independence War (1971) on Births and Deaths in a Rural Area of Bangladesh," *Population Studies* 30, (March 1976), pp. 87–105.

2. A. Summer and M. S. Loewenstein, "Nutritional Status and Mortality: A Prospective Validation of the QUAC Stick," *American Journal of Clinical Nutrition* 28:3 (March 1975), 287--92.

3. See M. C. Latham, "Nutrition and Infection in National Development," *Science* 188 (May 1975), pp. 561–65.

4. L. H. Barnes and P. Gyorgy, "Recent Advances in Infant Nutrition," in C. H. Bourne, ed., *World Review of Nutrition and Dietetics* (New York: Hafner, 1962), p. 10.

5. Food and Agriculture Organization, *World Food Survey*, United Nations, Washington, D.C., 1946.

6. Food and Nutrition Board, National Research Council, *Recommended Dietary Allowances*, National Academy of Science, Washington, D.C., rev. 1974, pp. 26--29.

7. United Nations World Food Conference, "Assessment of the World Food Situation"

(Rome, 1974), p. 66; cited in T. S. Poleman, "World Food: A Perspective," *Science* 188 (May 1975), pp. 510--18.

8. G. A. Harrison, J. S. Weiner, J. M. Tanner, and N. A. Barnicot, *Human Biology* (Oxford: Oxford University Press, 1964), chapter 26, Table 8, p. 414.

9. See letter by J. V. G. A. Durnham, O. G. Edholm, D. S. Miller, and J. C. Waterlow, "How Much Food Does Man Require?" *Nature* 242 (April 6, 1973)p. 418.

10. C. M. McCay, "Chemical Aspects of Aging and the Effect of Diet on Aging," in A. I. Lansing, ed., *Cowdry's Problems of Aging*, 3rd ed. (Baltimore: Williams and Wilkins, 1952), pp. 139--202.

11. M. H. Ross, "Aging, Nutrition and Hepatic Enzyme Activity Patterns in the Rat," *J. Nutrition*, 97:4 sup. 1, part. II (April 1969), pp. 565--601.

12. F. M. Sinex, "Biochemistry of Aging" *Perspectives in Biology and Medicine* (Winter 1966), pp. 208--24.

13. R. K. Chandra, "Antibody Formation in First and Second Generation Offspring of Nutritionally Deprived Rats," *Science* 190 (October 1975), pp. 289--90.

14. See Poleman, op. cit., pp. 510--18, Table 1.

15. Harrison et al., op. cit., p. 352.

16. J. M. Tanner, "Earlier Maturation in Man," *Scientific American* 218:1 (January 1968), pp. 21--27; see also Harrison et al., op. cit., pp. 348--57.

17. W. W. Greulich, "A Comparison of the Physical Growth and Development of American Born and Native Japanese Children," *Am. J. of Physical Anthropology* 15 (December 1957), pp. 489--515.

18. Tanner, op. cit.

19. J. W. B. Douglas, *The Home and the School* (London: MacGibbon & Kee, 1966), p. 78.

20. C. Gopalan and A. N. Naidu, "Nutrition and Fertility," *Lancet* (November 1972), pp. 1077--79.

21. See N. S. Scrimshaw and J. E. Gordon, eds., *Malnutrition, Learning, and Behavior* (Cambridge, Mass.: Massachusetts Institute of Technology Press, 1967), pt. 2, "Malnutrition and Retarded Growth in Man" for several discussions of various criteria of growth in the evaluation of malnutrition.

22. J. D. Wray, "Population Pressure on Families: Family Size and Spacing," in R. Revelle, ed., *Rapid Population Growth*, vol. 2, (Baltimore: Johns Hopkins Press, 1971), pp. 2103--46.

23. M. Behar, "Prevalence of Malnutrition Among Preschool Children of Developing Countries," in N. S. Scrimshaw and J. E. Gordon, eds., *Malnutrition, Learning and Behavior* (Cambridge: Massachusetts Institute of Technology Press, 1968), pp. 30--41.

24. K. S. Rao, et. al., *Bulletin WHO* 20 (1967); cited in J. Cravioto, E. R. Delicardie, and H. G. Birch, "Nutrition, Growth and Neurointegrative Development: An Experimental and Ecologic Study," *Pediatrics* 38:2, Part II Sup. (1966), pp. 319--72.

25. M. P. Honzik, J. W. Macfarlane and L. Allen, "The Stability of Mental Test Performance Between Two and Eighteen Years of Age," in R. G. Kuhlen and G. G. Thompson, eds., *Psychological Studies of Human Development* (New York: Appleton Century Crofts, 1952), pp. 149--57.

26. R. B. McCall, M. I. Appelbaum, and P. W. Hogarty, *Developmental Changes in Mental Performance*, Monographs of the Society for Research in Child Development 38, 150 (1973).

27. L. Belmont and F. A. Marolla, "Birth Order, Family Size and Intelligence," *Science* 182 (December 1973), pp. 1097--1101.

28. R. B. Zajonc, "Family Configuration and Intelligence," *Science* 192 (April 1976), pp. 227--36.

29. C. A. Breitenlohner, *Structural Changes in West European Agriculture, 1950--1970*, U.S. Dept. of Agriculture Economic Research Service, Foreign Agricultural Economic Report No. 114, Washington, D.C. (November 1975), Table 5, pp. 11--13.

30. A. Anastasi, *Differential Psychology*, 3rd ed. (New York: Macmillan, 1958), pp. 151--55.

31. Harrison et al., op. cit., pp. 363--65; J. W. B. Douglas, op. cit.

32. See R. Rosenthal, "The Pygmalion Effect Lives," *Psychology Today* 7:4 (September 1973), pp. 56--93.

33. See M. C. Latham and F. Cobos, "The Effects of Malnutrition on Intellectual Development and Learning," *American Journal of Public Health* 61:7 (July 1971), pp. 1307--24.

34. M. Winick and P. Rosso, "The Effect of Severe Early Malnutrition on Cellular Growth of the Human Brain," *Pediatric Research* 3 (1969), p. 181.

35. Z. A. Stein and H. Kassab, "Nutrition," in J. Wortis, ed., *Mental Retardation: An Annual Review*, vol. 1 (New York: Grune & Stratton, 1970), pp. 92--116; H. G. Birch, "Malnutrition, Learning and Intelligence," *American Journal of Public Health* 62:6 (June 1972), pp. 773--84.

36. Studies of infant undernutrition and subsequent intellectual development by M. B. Stoch and P. M. Smythe in South Africa and by S. Champakam, S. G. Srikantia and C. Gopalam in India, cited and discussed in J. C. Loehlin, G. Lindzey and J. N. Spuhler, *Race Differences in Intelligence* (San Francisco: W. H. Freeman and Company, 1975) p. 315.

37. M. E. Hertzig, H. G. Birch, S. A. Richardson and J. Tizard, "Intellectual Levels of School Children Severely Malnourished During the First Two Years of Life," *Pediatrics* 49 (1972), pp. 814--24.

38. D. E. Evans, A. D. Moodie and J. D. L. Hansen, "Kwashiorkor and Intellectual Development," *South African Medical Journal*, 45 (1971), pp. 1413--26; J. D. L. Hansen, C. Freesemann, A. D. Moodie, and D. E. Evans, "What Does Nutritional Growth Retardation Imply?" *Pediatrics* 47 (1971), pp. 299--313.

39. M. Winick, K. K. Meyer and R. C. Harris, "Malnutrition and Environmental Enrichment by Early Adoption," *Science* 190 (December 1975), pp. 1173--75.

40. Fernando Monckeberg, "Nutrition and Mental Capacity," *Boletin de la Oficina Sanitaria Panamericana*, English ed. 7:1 (1973), pp. 87--93.

41. G. Levitas, "Second Start," *New York Times Magazine*, June 6, 1976, pp. 42--48.

42. See H. G. Birch, "Malnutrition, Intelligence and Learning," *American Journal of Public Health* 62:6 (June 1972), p. 777.

43. Z. Stein, M. Susser, G. Saenger and F. Marolla, "Nutrition and Mental Performance," *Science* 178 (November 1972), pp. 708--13; see also Z. Stein et al., letter in response to criticism of Bradley, *Science* 180 (April 1973), 134--5; Z. Stein, M. Susser, G. Saenger, and F. Marolla, *Famine and Human Development: The Dutch Hunger Winter of 1944--45* (New York: Oxford University Press, 1975).

44. C. A. Smith, "The Effect of Wartime Starvation in Holland on Pregnancy and its Product," *American Journal of Obstetrics and Gynecology* 53 (1947): 599--608.

45. H. Knobloch and B. Pasamanick, "Seasonal Variations in the Birth of the Mentally Deficient," *American Journal of Public Health* 48 (1958), pp. 1201--08.

46. B. Pasamanick and H. Knobloch, "Seasonal Variations in Complications of Pregnancy," *Journal of Obstetrics and Gynecology* 12:1 (July 1958), pp. 110--112.

47. Birch, "Malnutrition, Learning and Intelligence," op. cit.; J. Dobbing, "The Later Development of the Brain and its Vulnerability," in J. A. Davis and J. Dobbing, eds., *Scientific Foundations of Paediatrics* (Philadelphia: Saunders, 1974), pp. 565--77.

48. M. Abramowicz and E. H. Kass, "Pathogenesis and Prognosis of Prematurity," *New England Journal of Medicine* 275:16 (October 1966), pp. 878--85; 275:17 (October 1966), pp. 938--43; 275:18 (November 1966), pp. 1001--7; 275:19 (November 1966), pp. 1053--59, and conclusion.

49. Abramowicz and Kass, op. cit., p. 1058.

50. Abramowicz and Kass, op. cit.

51. California State Department of Public Health, Bureau of Maternal and Child Health, *Perinatal Mortality and Survival—California, 1949--1959: A Decade of Experience*, rev. ed. (1963), p. 26, Table 10; p. 36, Table 14; and p. 44, Table 18.

52. R. Lewin, "Starved Brains," *Psychology Today* 9:4 (September 1975), p. 29.

53. Quoted in Sidney Hook, *From Hegel to Marx* (Ann Arbor: University of Michigan Press, 1962), pp. 271--72.

54. P. Belli, "The Economic Implications of Malnutrition: The Dismal Science Revisited," *Economic Development and Cultural Change* 20:1 (October 1971), pp. 1--23; H. Leibenstein, "The Impact of Population Growth on Economic Welfare—Non Traditional Elements," in R. Revelle, ed., *Rapid Population Growth*, vol. II (Baltimore: Johns Hopkins Press, 1971), pp. 175--97.

55. See H. E. Eichenwald and P. C. Frye, "Nutrition and Learning," *Science* 163 (February 1969), p. 648.

56. A. A. Gintzburger, "Psychoanalysis of a Case of Stagnation," *Economic Development and Cultural Change* 21:2 (January 1973), pp. 227--46.

57. Belli, op. cit.

58. Leibenstein, op. cit.

59. W. B. Keller and H. A. Kraut, "Work and Nutrition," in G. H. Bourne, ed., *World Review*

of Nutrition and Dietetics (New York: Hafner Dahl, 1962), vol. VIII, p. 69--81; see also H. A. Kraut and E. A. Muller, "Calorie Intake and Industrial Output," *Science* 104 (November 1946), pp. 495--97.

60. J. C. Waterlow and G. A. O. Alleyne, "Protein Malnutrition in Children: Advances in Knowledge in the Last Ten Years," in C. B. A. Anfinsen, Jr., J. T. Edsall and F. M. Richards, eds., *Advances in Protein Chemistry*, vol. 25 (New York: Academic Press, 1971), pp. 117--241 (on the basis of a personal communication from F. Viteri, who measured the work efficiency of Guatemalan peasants in malnutrition endemic areas).

61. R. H. Franke and G. V. Barrett, "The Economic Implications of Malnutrition: Comment," *Economic Development and Cultural Change* 23:2 (January 1975), pp. 341--50.

62. Solomon H. Katz, "Biological Factors in Population Control," in B. Spooner, ed., *Population Growth: Anthropological Implications* (Cambridge: Massachusetts Institute of Technology Press, 1972), pp. 351–69.

63. S. H. Garn and J. A. Haskell, "Fat Thickness and Developmental Status in Childhood and Adolescence," *American Journal of Diseases of Children* 99:19: 746–51.

64. See R. E. Frisch and J. W. MacArthur, "Menstrual Cycles: Fatness as a Determinant of Minimum Weight for Height Necessary for Their Maintenance or Onset," *Science* 185 (September 1974), pp. 949–51.

65. R. E. Frisch, "Demographic Implications of the Biological Determinants of Female Fecundity," *Social Biology* 22:1 (Spring 1975), pp. 17–22.

66. A. H. Crisp and E. Stonehill, "Relation Between Aspects of Nutritional Disturbance and Menstrual Activity in Primary Anorexia Nervosa," *British Medical Journal* 3 (July 1971), pp. 149–51.

67. See R. B. Lee, "Population Growth and the Beginnings of Sedentary Life among the !Kung Bushmen," in *Brian Spooner, ed., Population Growth: Anthropological Implications*, op. cit., pp. 329--42; see also G. B. Kolata, "!Kung Hunter Gatherers: Feminism, Diet and Birth Control," *Science* 185 (September 1974), pp. 932–34.

68. World Health Organization, "Nutrition in Pregnancy and Lactation," WHO Technical Reports Series No. 302, 1965.

69. For a brief review of these processes and appropriate references, see S. Katz, op. cit.

70. See R. G. Potter, M. L. New, J. B. Wyon and J. E. Gordon, "A Case Study in Birth Interval Dynamics," *Population Studies* 19: 1 (July 1965), pp. 81--96; R. G. Potter, M. L. New, J. B. Wyon and J. E. Gordon, "Applications of Field Studies to Research on the Physiology of Human Reproduction: Lactation and its Effects Upon Birth Intervals in Eleven Punjab Villages, India," in M. Sheps and C. Ridley, eds., *Public Health and Population Change* (University of Pittsburgh, 1965), pp. 377–99; A. K. Jain, T. C. Hsu, R. Freedman and M. C. Chang, "Demographic Aspects of Lactation and Postpartum Amenorrhea," *Demography* 7: 2 (May 1970), pp. 255–71.

71. Jain et al., op. cit.

72. M. L. Berman, K. Hanson and I. L. Hellman, "Effect of Breastfeeding on Postpartum Menstruation, Ovulation and Pregnancy in Alaskan Eskimos," *American Journal of Obstetrics and Gynecology* 114 (October 1972), pp. 524--34; N. L. Solien de Gonzalez, "Lactation and Pregnancy: A Hypothesis," *American Anthropologist* 66 (1964), pp. 873–78; M. Robinson, "Failing Lactation: A Study of 1,100 Cases," *Lancet* (January 16, 1943, pp. 66--68.

73. T. McKeown and J. R. Gibson, "A Note on Menstruation and Conception During Lactation," *Journal of Obstetrics and Gynecology of the British Empire* 61 (1954), pp. 824--26; A. Sharman, "Menstruation After Childbirth," *Journal of Obstetrics and Gynecology of the British Empire* 58 (1951), pp. 440--45.

74. E. J. Salber, M. Feinleib, and B. MacMahon, "The Duration of Post-Partum Amenorrhea," *American Journal of Epidemiology* 82:3 (1966), pp. 347--58.

75. R. Potter, "Changes of Natural Fertility and Contraceptive Equivalents," *Social Forces* 54:1 (September 1975), pp. 36--51; and A. Perez, P. Vela, R. Potter and G. S. Masnick, "Timing and Sequence of Resuming Ovulation and Menstruation after Childbirth," *Population Studies* 25:3 (November 1971), pp. 491--503.

76. L. C. Chen, S. Ahmed, M. Gesche and W. H. Mosely, "A Prospective Study of Birth Interval Dynamics-Rural Bangladesh *Population Studies* 28 (July 1974), pp. 272--97.

77. S. L. Huffman, J. Chakraborty and W. H. Moseley, "Nutrition and Post Partum Amenorrhea in Rural Bangladesh," presentation at the 1977 meeting of the Population Association of America, St. Louis, Mo., abstracted in *Population Index* 43:3 (July 1977), p. 411.

78. J. Knodel, "Breast Feeding and Population Growth," *Science* 198 (December 1977), pp. 1111--15.

79. R. G. Potter, J. B. Wyon, M. Parker, and J. E. Gordon, "A Case Study of Birth Interval Dynamics," *Population Studies* 19:1 (July 1965), pp. 81--96; R. G. Potter, M. L. New, J. B. Wyon, and J. E. Gordon, "A Fertility Differential in Eleven Punjab Villages," *Milbank Memorial Fund Quarterly* 53 (April 1965), pp. 185--201; see also D. G. Mandelbaum, *Human Fertility in India* (Berkeley: University of California Press, 1974), pp. 32--33.

80. J. Stoeckel and M. A. Chowdhury, "Pakistan, Response Validity in a KAP Survey," *Studies in Family Planning* 47 (1969), pp. 5--9; L. Green, "East Pakistan: Knowledge and Use of Contraceptives," *Studies in Family Planning* 39 (1969), pp. 9--14.

81. For the data base for these comparisons, see W. H. Mosely, A. K. M. A. Chowdhury and K. M. A. Aziz, "Demographic Characteristics of a Population Laboratory in Rural East Pakistan," Center for Population Research (NICHD) Research Report, September 1970; and J. B. Wyon and J. E. Gordon, *The Khanna Study* (Cambridge: Harvard University Press, 1971).

82. Tanner, op. cit.

83. G. Z. Johnson, "Differential Fertility in European Countries," in National Bureau for Economic Research, *Demographic and Economic Change in Developed Countries* (Princeton: Princeton University Press, 1960), pp. 36--76.

84. G. Carlson, "The Decline of Fertility: Innovation or Adjustment Process," *Population Studies* 20:2 (November 1966) (pp. 149--74); see also Tanner, op. cit.

85. U. Cowgill, "The People of York, 1538--1812," *Scientific American* 222:1 (January 1970), pp. 104--12.

86. Mandelbaum, op. cit., pp. 42--44.

87. National Sample Survey, "A Note on Recall Lapse," *Report No. 110, Fifteenth Round, July 1959--June 1960* (Delhi: Gov't of India, 1966).

88. See W. B. Watson, ed., *Family Planning in the Developing World* (New York: Population Council, 1977), p. 32.

89. See W. H. Mosely et al., "Demographic Characteristics of a Population Laboratory in Rural East Pakistan," op. cit.

90. J. W. Eaton and A. J. Mayer, "The Social Biology of Very High Fertility among the Hutterites: The Demography of a Unique Population," *Human Biology* 25:3 (September 1953), pp. 256--62; *Man's Capacity to Reproduce* (Glencoe, Ill.: Free Press, 1954), p. 20.

91. M. Sheps, "An Analysis of Reproductive Patterns in an American Isolate," *Population Studies* 19 (1965), pp. 65--80.

92. G. E. Huntington and J. A. Hostetler, "A Note on Nursing Practices in an American Isolate with A High Birth Rate," *Population Studies* 19 (1966), pp. 321--24.

93. C. Tietze, "Reproduction Span and Rate of Reproduction among Hutterite Women," *Fertility and Sterility* 8 (1957), pp. 89--97.

8

Fertility Behavior
and Modern Society

The Demographic Transition and Social Analyses

The discussion of changes in fertility behavior is conveniently begun with those which accompanied the industrialization and modernization of several western European countries and countries of western European settlement. The experience of these countries is well documented and the conditions associated with declining death rates beginning at the end of the eighteenth century, and followed by declining birth rates beginning at the end of the nineteenth century, have been extensively studied. The pattern of these changes is called the demographic transition. Some observers have regarded the demographic transition in western Europe as a prototype for others. But different patterns of demographic transition are being found in different cultures, and even the European pattern was not uniform.

Western Europe entered the demographic transition with lower birth rates than are found in less developed countries today. The fertility of western Europeans had declined before the industrial revolution to a moderate level, about 35 births per 1,000 population per year. This earlier reduction was a result of women marrying at older ages and many not marrying at all (see Chapter 9). Paradoxically, the initial effects of the early phases of the industrial revolution was to increase birth rates in many areas as the traditional controls on marriage and fertility broke down and as new job opportunities made it easier for people to marry and start families.[1] But as industrialization advanced and the conditions of work and life improved, children lost much of their economic value and fertility declined, eventually to reach low levels.

In France, exceptional among European countries, birth rates began to decline in many regions in the late eighteenth century as a result of birth control within marriage. This occurred while the French people were still largely peasant and death rates were still relatively high. This development is discussed later in the chapter on fertility in preindustrial Europe.

During the eighteenth century, death rates began to decline in western Europe, particularly in the United Kingdom and Sweden, from levels of about 30 or more deaths per 1,000 population per year to the current death rates of 9 to 10 per 1,000 population. The expectation of life increased from 30 to 40 years during the eighteenth century, and to 70 years and more in recent times. This increase in longevity was attributed to improvement in the economic conditions of life, improved sanitation and nutrition, changes in disease organisms and host resistance, public health, and other reasons some of which may still be unknown.

For a hundred years after the death rates began to fall, birth rates in western Europe remained stable or increased somewhat in many areas; births exceeded deaths, leading to an extended period of population growth. As a result, the numbers of people of European descent grew at a rate never before experienced, though not as high as among many third world countries today. Europeans increased their proportion of world population from 20 percent in the early eighteenth century to 33 percent in the early twentieth century.[2] This is known as the period of transitional growth for it was not a permanent state. Around 1875, birth rates in many western European countries (United Kingdom, Netherlands, Sweden, etc.) started to decline, a trend which is still continuing.

The general explanation for this decline in fertility in the later nineteenth and in the twentieth centuries can be summarized as follows: With industrialization, urbanization, and modernization, the family lost its centrality in economic and social life. Children lost their economic value as factors of production and sources of future security. Increased wealth and the proliferation of a wide variety of sources of satisfaction (including fuller participation of women in the social, economic, and cultural life of the community), provided alternatives which competed with childbearing and family life. The lower death rates provided assurance to parents that their children would survive. Indeed, parents had to control their fertility if they wished to partake of the other available satisfactions. Increased educational levels expanded the horizons of parents, as well as their capacity to make effective use of contraception. At the same time, changes occurred in the gratifications or values many parents obtained from children. Parents might reasonably aspire to a better life for their children in the present and in the future, particularly if children were well prepared to take advantage of opportunity. Parents with such aspirations could choose to have fewer children, each of whom could thus have more of the family's time and resources.

In the early days of industrialization, the family was still an important source of economic security and satisfaction. The humanization of work and increase in real wages had hardly begun, and child labor provided families with economic benefits. Towards the end of the nineteenth century, conditions for the masses began to improve and a change in lifestyles was underway. In the interim, population growth helped provide the labor force for the growing industries and a market for their goods.

Studies showed considerable differences between the rich and the poor, between the educated and the uneducated, and between urban and rural populations in the rate at which births began to decline. The fertility of the rich, the educated, and the urban declined first and more rapidly, so that a considerable differential in fertility appeared between socio-economic groups. With time, the differentials between these groups became smaller as rural residents and those with less education and income also reduced their fertility.[3] The benefits of industrialization and the change to modern life styles had first accrued to the rich and the urban residents and later to others. Differences in fertility and the rate of fertility decline were also noted between religious groups such as Catholics, Protestants, and Jews, and were attributed to differences in associated values and lifestyles. With time, these differences in fertility have decreased also.

Even before the dramatic decline in fertility had begun, some nineteenth century observers[4] proposed that as incomes and productivity increased through economic development, so would the level of subsistence and the standard of living to which people would aspire. As a result, couples would limit the number of their children to achieve and maintain these higher standards. Malthus, as noted earlier, also entertained this possibility in his later years.

During the 1930s, fertility declines in the United States and western Europe had reached replacement levels or less. Many young women bore no children at all, and many bore only one. Population still continued to grow slowly, because while women were having fewer children than were needed to replace their generation, there was a higher proportion of younger women and men in the population as a result of the higher fertility of their parents than there would be in the future at prevailing levels of fertility. If this low fertility had continued for some time, population would have started to decline. This decline in birth rates had been accomplished with rather primitive contraceptive techniques compared to those in use today and frequently in the face of laws against the sale, advertisement, instruction, and even use of contraceptives. That a good portion of women were able to practice effective birth control is indicated by the fact that 44 percent of American women who were born between July 1, 1905 and June 30, 1910, and passed their prime reproductive years during the depression, had fewer than two children. Twenty-two percent had only one child and another 22 percent had none, though half of the women with no children were married. The net reproduction rate, measuring the degree to which this cohort of women replaced themselves in the next generation, was 874 per 1,000 women, presaging a decline of 13 percent from one generation to the next.[5] The last stage of the demographic transition was thus seen as leading to a decline in population.

The demographic transition has been summarized by Notestein as involving three stages: (1) the stage of high growth potential characterized by high mortality and high fertility but with little or no population growth (This is known as the period of high growth potential because growth will occur as mortality declines.); (2) the stage of transitional growth due to a decline in mortality with a lag in the decline of fertility (Growth is considered transitional because as the decline in fertility catches up with the decline in mortality, growth will cease.); and (3) the stage of incipient population decline occurring when fertility declines below the replacement level so that population will diminish after a time.[6] Other observers of demographic history have proposed a five-stage transition which is a little more finely drawn than the three-stage transition, but basically not different.[7]

The details of the demographic transition were elucidated by social analysis, the examination of fertility behavior in the different social, occupational (including female employments), educational, religious, residential (along an urban-rural continuum), and other groups, of which a population is composed. Differences in fertility were related to differences in the lifestyles of these groups, and changes in fertility were related to changes in population composition and lifestyles which accompanied industrialization and modernization. Demographers applied these analyses, based on western European experience, to developing countries in an attempt to discern differentials in fertility that might indicate trends.[8] Often, as in studies of Indian fertility in the 1950s and 1960s, few consistent differentials in fertility were found except among the small westernized segment of the population. The implication appeared to be that without modernization at least at some minimal level, there was likely to be little reduction in fertility. Studies of fertility differences between countries related various indicators of modernization (literacy, school enrollment, urbanization, newspaper circulation, telephones, non-agricultural employment, per capita income, etc.) to changes in fertility and mortality.[9]

While fertility in the developing countries was being viewed in the perspectives of demographic transition and modernization theories, the value of these perspectives in understanding developments in fertility trends in post-World War II societies were brought into question.

The Post World War II Baby Boom

Demographers in the 1930s and the early 1940s regarded the population of the western world as being in a state of incipient decline. Economists felt that the absence of population growth to stimulate the economy was helping to prolong the depression and that steps needed to be taken to compensate for the loss of this stimulus.[10] World War II provided the stimulus needed to end the economic depression of the 1930s. In the United States, the period which followed the war was one of unprecedented economic growth abetted in part by large investments in the military and by the growth in government services. These in turn helped support the expansion of the private sector of the economy. The need to restore the shattered economy of western Europe stimulated economic growth there as well as in the United States. The increase in income and per capita income was accompanied by an increase in fertility, the "baby boom," which caught demographers by surprise. Birth rates increased in all social classes and all former predictions as to future population size were invalidated. The presumption of demographic theory that fertility would decrease as income and modernization increased appeared to be mistaken.

While many of the older generation of American women (up to 12 percent of women born from 1905–09) had never married, almost all (95 percent) of the younger generation of women, coming into their reproductive years during the 1950s, married. They married younger and bore children at an earlier age than did their mothers. While many of the older generation of married women had no children or only one child, few of the younger women of the 1940s and the 1950s had fewer than two children. At the same time that young married women were bearing children at earlier ages than expected, some of the older women who had postponed childbearing because of the depression and World War II bore children at older ages; thus, part of the increase in the birth rate could be called an accordion effect, due to the difference in the timing of births among two generations.

The increase in American fertility from 1946 to 1957 did not mean an increase in the proportion of large families of five or more children; indeed the proportion of such families was decreasing. The increase in birth rates was due in good part to fewer families having less than two children and most families having two to four children; childless or single child women, more common among the upper and middle classes than among the lower classes before World War II, were few and inconsequential after the war. The increase in birth rates was due in good part to an increase in the fertility of the middle and upper classes.[11]

Some demographers concluded that while the timing of births may be variable and affected by external conditions, the average number of children born per women was likely to remain constant and could be obtained from surveys of the number of births women intended or expected to have. Cohort fertility measures, reflecting anticipated as well as actual completed family size, were presumed to be better predictors of future trends than the extrapolation of period fertility measures reflecting behavior in a given interval of time such as a year. If women delayed or hastened the building of families in some years, they were expected to compensate in subsequent years to achieve the intended family size. Cohort measures replaced period measures for use in making population projections.[12] (A population projection, not necessarily a prediction, is a mathematical extrapolation from present to future populations based on assumptions regarding fertility behavior, mortality, and migration in the interim.) Surveys from the 1940s to the early 1960s indicated that intended and actual American family size would be relatively constant, including a fraction more than three children on the average. This implied considerable future population growth. The surveys, however, were not successful in anticipating changes in fertility behavior and the more sophisticated methods of projection were thus of little help.

Assumptions about future fertility behavior in the United States, even when expressed with broad upper and lower limits, have not been able to include the magnitude of the changes that actually occurred. As recently as 1967, the United States Bureau of the Census published a series of high to low population projections based on a completed fertility of 3.35 children per woman for the high projections (derived from the experience of the baby boom) to a low projection of 2.5 children. By 1970, fertility and fertility expectations reported in surveys had dropped so fast that the Bureau dropped the high projection of 3.35 children for completed family size and changed the lower bound to a completed family size of 2.11 children, or replacement level fertility. By 1972 fertility had reached the lower bound or replacement level, and the Bureau again dropped the high projection based on a fertility of 3.1 children, and added a new lower bound based on a completed fertility of 1.8 children, well below the replacement level.[13] In 1974, the total fertility rate in the United States reached 1.8 children. In 1975 the Bureau introduced a new lower bound of 1.7 children per woman into the calculation of projections of future populations.[14]

The downward trend in United States fertility cannot be expected to continue indefinitely. Birth rates may reflect fluctuations in economic conditions as well as lifestyles. At times, some women or couples will delay having children, in effect reducing the birth rate, and later have children, thereby raising the birth rate somewhat, as occurred in 1976–77. Out-of-wedlock births may increase as a result of changes in social mores or the relaxation of social controls. This may present a problem, but it will not be a population problem as the impact on total fertility is not likely to be large. In the context of modern lifestyles and economics, children are so often a burden with few benefits that one or two may eventually prove to be sufficient for the needs of most.[15] Birth rates may even decline further as they have in Germany where the birth rates from 1970–75 were less than the death rates and falling.

Economic Analyses of Fertility Behavior

The earlier analyses of the decline in western fertility were made largely by sociologists in terms of changes in lifestyle and family function. Following their analyses, birth rates might have been expected to fall further with increased incomes and modernity. Yet, the baby boom occurred during a period of increased incomes and urbanization.

Along with the general increase in fertility, new relationships were discerned. D. S. Freedman[16] reported that among a national sample of wives surveyed in 1955, those whose husbands had a higher relative income (that is, higher than might be expected on the basis of age, education, and occupation) tended to have higher fertility. Her analysis was limited to families in which all children were wanted and which had practiced family planning or intended to do so.

Perhaps the clearest indication of the relationship between income and fertility came from special tabulations of the 1960 U.S. census for white wives aged 35–44 and 45–54, married once and classified by wife's age at marriage, and husband's education, occupation, and income. Many of these women completed their families during the baby boom. On the whole, the fertility of the women, in terms of children ever born, showed the expected inverse relationship with income. However, women who had married at age 22 years or older, and whose husbands' income was higher than the average of their occupation and education counterparts, also had higher fertility. (Women who had married at a younger age did not show this relationship.)[17] The standard of living a family aspired to is to some degree determined by education and occupational status. A higher income than is usual for a particular status permits a couple to have more children and still maintain the living standards deemed appropriate for that group. Why this should apply only to women who married after age 22 is not clear. Perhaps couples can better evaluate their needs and potential resources at a later age.

Freedman and Coombs[18] reported findings with similar implications. In their study of a sample of Detroit wives, those women who regarded their family income as adequate expected more children than those who regarded their incomes as inadequate; wives who anticipated large increases in income expected and had more children than did those who did not anticipate a large increase in income.

In Sweden[19] couples with annual incomes over 40,000 Swedish crowns, and married 9 to 13 years by 1967, had more children on the average than similar couples with incomes of 20,000 to 40,000 crowns, but fewer children than those with incomes below 20,000 crowns. The differences in fertility, however, were not very large; the very high income couples had about 2,250 children per 1,000 couples, those with moderate to high incomes (20,000–40,000 crowns) had a little more than 2,000 children per 1,000 couples, while middle income couples (15,000–20,000 crowns) had 2,300 per 1,000 couples. Those with low incomes (under 15,000 crowns) many of which were rural couples, had a little more than 2,600 children per 1,000 couples. It was presumed that the latter, although practicing birth control to the same degree, were not as effective as the others. Even so, in contemporary low fertility societies, the absolute differences in the fertility of the various classes are not large, though fertility differentials between classes persist.

Becker, an economist, introduced a new dimension in fertility analysis to explain the unexpected new relationships between income and fertility.[20] He argued that since children lost their value as an economic resource they became largely consumption items, consumer durable goods which give pleasure and satisfy other values and needs. The consumption of durables increases as income increases, and so does the number of children.

Becker held that the reason poor people have more children is not because they want them but because they do not do very well at contracepting; when the poor have better access to and use contraception more effectively, the relationship between fertility and income will become clearly positive. Some support for this position is derived from the findings of the Indianapolis study[21] of fertility which occurred largely before the "baby boom." Among families who planned the number of their children, those with higher incomes had more children. Family sizes even during the baby boom were relatively small (3–4 children on the average) and the differences in average family size of the different social classes were diminishing.

Duesenberry[22], in a comment, and Blake[23], in more detailed discussion, argued that the style of life including the expected number of children per family, and expenditures on them are heavily determined by social class.

With a higher income, a couple may support more children, but other factors associated with having a higher income tend to discourage large families. Children of higher income families cost more, they are more expensively cared for, clothed, and educated than are children from lower income families. The increased expenditure on the "quality" of children limits the number of children. In effect, wealthy people are not really free to spend their money in any way. Unless they are eccentric, they spend their money in prescribed ways characteristic of their class. Therefore, the sociological variable of "class" is more important to fertility decisions than the economic variable of "income." Income may be used as part of an index of social class. Though income would appear to be limiting factor on the number of children, the imperatives of lifestyle for the rich result in their having fewer children than the poor. The well-off also buy more expensive automobiles and other consumption items than do those who are less well off. But they do not buy fewer automobilies; they buy more.

Freedman and Coombs, in their study of Detroit area white married women, found that family income and material aspirations for chidren were not as highly correlated as might be expected. These aspirations were measured by ascertaining how important parents felt it to be that children have separate bedrooms, private lessons, good allowances, summer camp experiences, and memberships in clubs or scouts. These cost money and parents who wanted to spend more on each child expected to have fewer. However, income was correlated with the expectation that children would go on to college, but this was the expectation of 75 percent of the women interviewed. Some 40 percent of the interviewed women with one or two children had already set money aside for this purpose and expected to have fewer children.[24]

Time and psychic energy may be more limiting factors on fertility than direct monetary costs. Unlike other consumption items which can be stored when not in use, the bearing, nurturing, and rearing of children requires the time of parents, particularly that of the mother, in a servantless society. Once born, a child represents a large commitment, not readily avoided. The more educated the mother and the higher her earning potential the greater are the alternative uses she can make of her time. Her time is more valuable in monetary and psychological terms. If she does not work, she may wish to spend her time in activities other than child care, cooking, and housework. Giving up these other alternatives to raise children is the opportunity cost. (See also Chapter 10 for a discussion of the compatability between female labor force participation and having children in different societies.) Economists[25] have formalized these conceptions in multiple regression equations in which fertility depends on the husband's income and opportunity cost to the mother as reflected by wife's income or education. While these equations help explain some—up to 50 percent—of the variation in fertility between individuals of a cohort or generation, or at a given time, they do not explain the changes which take place between generations and times. Thus, despite the limited utility of these equations in explaining variation in past fertility, they are, for all practical purposes, useless for predicting future fertility.

Microeconomic models purporting to explain the factors that influence a couple's decision to have children can become very complicated mathematical formulations as attempts are made to compensate for the considerable oversimplification of reality involved in modeling. In retrospect, it is easy, though deceptive, to assume that couples who started out to build a family had some idea of the number of children they wanted and what their income would be. In reality, couples starting out to build a family may or may not have some preconceived notion as to how much money they will make and how they would like to spend their money and time, including the amount on children. But as they progress through life, grow older, face different conditions, accumulate information and experiences, the basis for their decisions and preferences change. Some critics have faulted economic fertility theory for not considering the complexities of the decision-making process.[26]

Simon has examined the effect of husband's income on a couple's decision to have an additional child when they already had a given number from zero to five children, that is at different stages of family building. He found that an increase in income increased the likelihood that parents with one child or none would go on to have an additional child but decreased the likelihood that parents with three or four children would go on to have more. This mixed effect could not be explained by appealing to economic theory though it is consistent with the decrease in the magnitude of fertility differentials which has occurred.[27]

A principal problem with economic analysis is that many of the variables are "economic" only by definition. Family income, the most "economic" variable used, is a poor predictor of fertility when plugged into economic equations by itself, acting more as an index of social class and lifestyle associated with low fertility than as an index of resources available to rear children. Only when other factors are brought into the equation does income begin to behave in a positive though hardly powerful fashion. These other factors may be couched in economic terms such as "income elasticity of quality demand (for children)" or "opportunity cost of wife's time." In fact, they may reflect lifestyles whose development is not readily explained by economic theory. Using wife's education as a surrogate for earning capacity may be a particularly deceptive ploy since her education may represent an influence on the formation of tastes and preferences as well as an index of earning capacity. To say that an educated woman places a high premium on her time is merely to say that she has many options; these options are available in part because her family's income is generally larger than that of an uneducated woman. With appropriate and ingeniously conceived variables, explanatory econometric models of fertility behavior may be constructed, but the explanatory power of such models often depends on the social and cultural factors which are also reflected by the economic variables. When the social and cultural, as well as the economic milieu changes, studies based on these variables give conflicting results.

Thus, while income and consumption of goods continued to increase in Europe and America during the 1960s, fertility fell, attesting to a change in the preference system, the hierarchy of things people would like to possess and the activities they would like to engage in. Children and family life may have become intrinsically less attractive than other values as income continued to increase during the 1960s, in contrast to the trend of the 1950s, a phenomenon which may not be subject to economic analysis.

Though economic analysis of fertility behavior has sometimes been presented as conflicting with the sociological analysis, attempts have been made to reconcile the two. Economic analysis takes the lifestyle and associated preferences of people as given. Easterlin[28] proposed that fertility is a function of preferences or tastes, income and relative costs. He noted that economists are frequently loathe to analyze preferences. This may be justified in times when preference systems or lifestyles are stable, uniform, and unchanging, but they cannot be ignored when value systems are changing rapidly.

Easterlin proposed that young people in the late 1940s and the 1950s had higher fertility than their parents because their tastes were formed during the depression; in the straitened homes of their parents, they grew up accustomed to modest living standards. During the late 1940s and the 1950s, these young people found themselves in rather good economic circumstances (relative to those in which they were reared) and with modest living standards; they were thus in a position to have more children than their parents. On the other hand, the children and the adolescents of the 1950s were brought up in relative prosperous circumstances. The reference living standards and consumption habits of young people of, say, age 20–24 were not those experienced by their parents at that age, but rather those experienced when their parents were 35 to 44 years old. The material aspirations of the younger generation thus came into conflict with their fertility aspirations since young people entering the labor market as new employees in the 1960s could not be expected to earn enough to support a standard of living equal to that seen in their parents' homes. To maintain their high reference standard of consumption, lower fertility levels would be required at least in the earlier period of marriage. Postponing births is the first step to not having as many children.

Easterlin's proposed explanation of the decline in fertility during the 1960s (contrasted with the rise of fertility in the 1950s) is tied to aspirations for higher standards of living associated with more constricted employment opportunities. Part of the reason young people were well off during the 1950s was that there were proportionately fewer of them in the work force because of the low fertility of the 1930s. In the 1960s the proportion of young people increased and so did competition for jobs. By the 1980s, the proportion of young people in the work force will be low again and Easterlin noted the possibility or probability that fertility would increase at that time.[29]

The proportion of young people in the work force is significant to their fortunes only relative to the employment opportunities open to them. A sluggish economy, perhaps in part due to low population growth, could decrease such opportunities. As noted earlier, this was a common view of experts during the depression that ended with World War II. But other issues related to changing values and lifestyles may well be more important to future fertility than those raised by the Easterlin hypothesis.

While the increase in per capita expenditures on consumer durables lagged somewhat behind the increase in per capita disposable income (in constant dollars) during the 1950s, a period of increasing fertility in the United States, the increase in per capita expenditures on consumer durables during the 1960s, a period of decreasing fertility, was double the 30 percent increase in per capita disposable income.[30] Some portion of the income, which in the 1950s had gone into having children, may have gone into the purchase of consumer durables in the 1960s. Some indication that this trade-off between consumer goods and children occurred in households is provided by findings from Freedman's and Coombs's study of Detroit wives interviewed in early 1961 and again in late 1962. Couples owning one car expected more children than did couples with two or more cars, even when income and religion were controlled. But only 34 percent of the couples with more than one car and 43 percent of the couples with only one car gave economic reasons for not wanting more children. The researchers interpreted this as indicating that having more cars and less children did not reflect alternative ways of spending income but rather the selection of a lifestyle which included more activities and interests outside the home.[31] The fact remains that the lifestyle selected did involve different patterns of consumption of time and material resources.

Economic analyses of fertility behavior in a society where children provide little in the way of economic benefit to parents do not explain why children are valued more or less than other uses of time and money. One might be tempted to label children and family life as "inferior goods" to be given up when more attractive goods can be obtained; this is not an explanation nor does the label add to understanding of fertility behavior. The contribution of economic analyses lies in their indication that whatever the value of children, economic constraints, as well as the presence of other available sources of satisfaction, do operate to limit the number of children people have, another facet of the adaptive quality of human fertility behavior. This has been evidenced more clearly and directly in the effect of business cycles on marriage and fertility.[32]

Family Size Intentions and Fertility

Researchers have assumed that, regardless of the reasons, people have some idea of the number of children that they would like to and expect to have; if asked properly, individuals give a meaningful response to the number of children thought to be ideal, desired, and intended. Such questions were, therefore, included in the numerous surveys of fertility behavior conducted in the United States and abroad. In developing countries such inquiries were incorporated in surveys of knowledge, attitudes, and practice of family planning (KAP surveys). During the 1950s and early 1960s in the United States, the patterns of response to questions relating to the number of births expected by married women showed a remarkable consistency despite differences in survey questionnaires and other study variations. Over that time period women expected somewhat more than three births per woman on the average, and average performance came close to expectations. During the 1960s, American demographers talked about the 2–4 child family norm.[33]

This did not mean that each woman interviewed maintained the same expectations over a long period of time; for some, the expectation of the number of children they would have went up with time; for others it went down. Some women found that they could not have the number of children expected because they were infertile; others were not good at birth control and so had more; and for others the conditions of life had changed. Perhaps many women were not very sure about their exact intentions and had only a rough idea. But while the correlations between anticipated and actual eventual family size were low for individual couples, individual changes balanced each other so that the average anticipated and the average size eventually attained were close.[34]

Thus it was with some justification that the authors of the report on the first "Growth of American Families Study," a national survey of fertility and fertility expectations of American married women in 1955, had hoped that the information obtained would provide the basis for charting future fertility and population growth.[35] However, neither this survey nor subsequent ones presaged the course of fertility and expectations of the later 1960s and early 1970s.

According to results in the Current Population Survey of the U.S. Bureau of the Census, wives age 18–24 years in 1967 were expecting to have 2.9 children on the average; in 1973, wives 18–24 years old were expecting to have 2.3 children, while wives 25–29 years old, many of whom were 18–24 years old and married in 1967, were expecting only 2.4 children on the average. In 1976, just three years later, wives aged 18–24 were expecting an average of 2.1 children which is replacement level fertility.[36] Single women expected to have 1.9 children on the average.

The total fertility rates over this period declined to a low of 1.8 children in 1974. Both the changed fertility expectations of women and actual changes in fertility prompted the downward revision of the series of population growth projections of the Bureau of the Census.

As mentioned, pre-1965 studies showed that while individual women changed their expectations up or down, the average number of children expected by a cohort of women remained constant. After 1967, the average number of children expected by the same (or similar) group of women changed over a period of five years or so. In the United Kingdom, Peel[37] noted that one-third of married women in his study had revised the number of their birth expectations significantly downward, after being married five years. Among these women, economics was the reason given by 52 percent; physical or mental health and stress was the reason given by 19 percent; and another 11 percent gave as the reason the hard work involved in caring for a family. "I didn't realize they [children] were such hard work; they stop you doing everything, don't they?" (The mothers and grandmothers of these women probably did not have as much to do outside of home and children.) Ten percent of the women in the study revised their birth expectations upward, almost half of these because of unintended pregnancies; the net result in the number of children expected by the same group of women was a decline from an average of 2.61 in 1965 to 2.23 in 1970. In the United States, a sample of white married women who had been interviewed in the 1970 National Fertility Survey and had remained married continuously since, were reinterviewed in 1975. More than a third of those who, in 1970, intended to have more children, did not have any more; of these, 70 percent stated that they had changed their minds.[38]

The failure of studies to anticipate changes in fertility behavior and intentions which occurred only a short time after the surveys, reinforced the doubts some researchers had about the usefulness of surveys about desired family size, expected number of children, etc. Ryder[39], one of the directors of the National Fertility Surveys, discussed the technical and substantive pitfalls of this approach in his presidential address to the Population Association of America. Hawthorne[40] also commented on this approach raising the basic issue of whether humans have such clear and lasting notions of what their intentions or wants are with regard to the number of children, that they can meaningfully respond to the question. The fact that respondents, when interviewed, say that they want or intend to have three children may be an artifact of the questionnaire, which asks for a definite answer from obliging people. As is often likely, while respondents answer truthfully to the best of their knowledge, they have little idea of what the future holds in store for them nor, for that matter, how they will react to the situations which may arise. When asked about intentions relative to past fertility, the respondents' answers may be strongly affected by current attitudes and adjustments. Thus, the interpretation of expressed intentions and wants is more difficult (if not hopeless) than is often assumed, particularly when the behavior involved is far in the future.

Even as the techniques of ascertaining fertility intentions and their usefulness in predicting fertility behavior were being questioned, some psychologists focused on the study of how fertility and related intentions are determined, on presumptions that these intentions are forerunners of behavior. Fishbein and Jaccard[41] (and A. Davidson as well) proposed that behavior and the intent to behave in a certain way depends on a set of attitudinal and normative beliefs about the performance of the behavior involved, and the strength with which these beliefs are held. This is a very straightforward approach, though somewhat sophisticated in its formulation. The attitudes towards an act include beliefs about the consequences of the act (for example, taking contraceptive pills can lead to illness). Normative beliefs include the individual's perceptions of the opinions of relevant others; the motivation to conform to the expectations of these others is an important factor also. Information about attitudes, beliefs, perception, and motivation to comply may be obtained from responses to questionnaires, scaled, and combined in a multiple regression equation that indicates which factor is important and which not so important in predicting intention. Thus, if a belief that the pill causes cancer (negative attitude) is associated with intentions not to use the pill, then propaganda (or education, if you will) needs to be directed at disabusing women of this belief.

The thesis proposed by Fishbein and Jaccard is that volitional intentions and behavior are mediated by attitudinal and normative beliefs. External forces are presumed to affect behavioral intentions through determining or changing attitudes and norms. Yet, as Fishbein and Jaccard recognized, there is often a discrepancy between behavioral intent and actual behavior. Among other reasons, they proposed that this discrepancy is due to a lack of specificity in defining exactly what behavioral act is intended (to contracept in general as contrasted with taking the pill), and to the time lag between the expression of the intention and the performance of the associated behavior. Thus, when students were asked whether they intended to have premarital sexual intercourse in general, there was only a moderate correlation ($r = .28$) between the expression of intention to engage in premarital sex and the actual engagement in such behavior by the end of the semester. When asked about the intention to have premarital sexual relations during the current semester, the correlation was much higher ($r = .68$). The fact is that a yes or no response to a query about a specific intention may be influenced by plans well on the way to fruition or even behavior currently in progress. If a person, intending to make a purchase, is on the way to the store or even in the store, the likelihood that a purchase will be made is greater than if that person expressed the intention to make a purchase in the future. The intention in that case may reflect only a vague notion.

The erosion, with the passage of time, of the predictive power of an expression of intention is in part due to the development of new circumstances requiring a different response from that intended originally, or to experiences which indicated that the intended response was not appropriate. According to Fishbein and Jaccard, these cause attitude changes which are followed by behavioral change.

The consistency of attitudes and expressed intention (which is also an attitudinal variable) reported by Fishbein and Jaccard is not surprising; nor is the frequent discrepancy between expressed intentions and subsequent behavior during time of change. The former condition results from the tendency of people to maintain a consistent set of beliefs to reduce psychological dissonance if nothing else; the latter from adaptation to conditions.

As students of cognitive dissonance have noted, changes in behavior may precede changes in attitudes as people do what they feel they need to do, and adjust their attitudes to minimize dissonance or internal conflict.[42] Attitudes may be little more than a rationalization of one's behavior and circumstance. The formulation of the "cognitive dissonance" theorists is one of many which focus on the need of individuals to maintain some psychological semblance of consistency among their behaviors, attitudes, beliefs, and the like.[43] If behavior is in conflict with attitudes, a way is found to adjust either the behavior or the attitudes to achieve what may be termed a sense of psychological consistency. One of the experimental findings of researchers in cognitive dissonance is that when an individual is induced to change a behavior pattern for a perceived small reward or reason, the latter results in dissonance which is resolved by changing attitudes; when the reason or reward is large or compelling, it provides sufficient psychological justification in itself such that the individual exhibits little need to change attitudes.[44] Thus if people want and have fewer children for what they feel are good and compelling reasons, they may have no need to change their attitudes towards high fertility. These considerations do not preclude circumstances in which attitudinal changes precede behavioral changes or where both are concordant.

Blake felt that the tolerance for large families expressed by respondents in a poll she commissioned indicated that the low birth expectations expressed by women in fertility surveys were not firm and that birth rates may rise again.[45] In Blake's 1972 survey, half of the respondents, including 57 percent of those less than 25 years old, considered two children as being the ideal family size. A few favored fewer than two children, and a sizeable minority thought three or more children to be the ideal family size. In response to a question as to what size family would be considered too large, a sizable majority did not consider a four-child family as too large, and 35 percent did not consider a five-child family as too large. By way of contrast, 81 percent of respondents considered a one-child or childless family as being too small. This tolerance for large families meant, in Blake's view, that there was little "normative" restriction on large families and considerable "normative" restriction on small families.

But as Bumpass[46] has noted, the tolerance for large families expressed by respondents does not necessarily mean that they want to have large families. The relative number of large families has been steadily diminishing over the long term, even during the "baby boom," which was due to fewer people having fewer than two children, not to more people having more than five children. Since then, the number and proportion of single-child and childless families has been increasing, as has the proportion, though still small, of married women expressing their intention to either remain childless or have only one child.

As predictors of future fertility, the surveys of intentions have not been very useful in predicting a change in the trend. Even if a change of intentions preceded a change in behavior, it was not by long, while changes in attitudes are often likely to follow or coincide with behavioral change. Fertility intentions are not the only predictors that have become suspect these past years. In 1973 the U.S. Bureau of the Census announced the discontinuation of Surveys of Consumer Buying Expectations because the data collected were only marginally useful:

"In simple demand models which relate the level of new car purchases to a set of variables with potential explanatory power (e.g., buying plans, consumer sentiment, the level of income and the level of employment), the Census Bureau measure of expected purchases is significant by the usual statistical tests for the period 1959–1966, but not for the period 1967 to the present."

A similar statement is made for the non-auto durables. Indices of expected new car purchases did not correlate with purchases even in the short range of six months. Though the Bureau of the Census eliminated the survey on expectation or attitude, it will continue to collect data on ownership and purchases (behavior) of large durables.[47]

The temptation to conclude that people do not know what they want is strong. But the discrepancy between responses taken as an expression of attitude, and subsequent behavior, may be an artifact of asking the wrong questions. The respondent may answer truthfully, but underlying the answer are a set of implicit, though perhaps unconscious assumptions about the future and even the present which are not expressed in the response. If things change or the assumptions prove incorrect, then the respondent adapts and behavior may change even before attitudes.

Since two people are involved in generating children, any discrepancy in the interests between them are obscured in regarding the product, a child, as the result of a joint decision or non-decision. In his review, as Goldberg[48] noted, at various stages of family building the interests of one or the other of the pair may become dominant but little is known as to how the process works. Other observers have noted the need for information in this area; the discussion has often been abstract, adding little empirical knowledge to our fund of information.[49] A reasonable supposition would be that while family size expectations in the early stages of family building may be influenced by preconceived orientations and values, in the later stages revisions of family size expectations are conditioned by experience and pragmatic considerations.

Personality and Fertility Behavior

While studies of social and economic factors have provided many significant insights into the determinants of fertility in the past, studies of psychological factors have as yet contributed very little. This is a strange state of affairs, since the bearing and rearing of children are associated with motivations and feelings, some of them rather strong and pervasive. These feelings and motivations may be related to a need for a sense of identity and self image, a need for security, a need to nurture, anxiety about having children, and a host of other needs and feelings which have been inventoried by psychologists in one context or another.[50] Thus far, the inventoried motivations and feelings and the personality traits with which these may be associated, have been connected with fertility only abstractly through psychological reasoning. There is little or no evidence that in fact these needs make for much difference in fertility. Early studies of the relationship between fertility and such personality characteristics as manifest anxiety, nurturance needs, need for achievement, alienation, tolerance of ambiguity, and many others have shown few significant results or some which appear to conflict with each other.[51] One of the conclusions of the "Indianapolis Study," an early survey of fertility in the United States, was that fertility is more closely related to "broad social factors . . . the observed relation of fertility behavior to most of the psychological characteristics considered was generally much less pronounced or less regular. . . ." when socioeconomic status was held constant.[52] Subsequent studies provide no basis for changing this conclusion.

The absence of any apparent connection between personality traits, as measured by psychological variables, with the number of children a person has or with contraceptive behavior was not easy to accept. The lack of consistent relationships found in the studies of personality traits and fertility was often attributed to the immaturity of our knowledge and methodology of personality research, to the inadequacy of the definitions of the personality traits involved, the way they are conceptualized or thought about, and the way they are measured. The authors of the Indianapolis Study expressed reservations about the adequacy of their psychological approaches. So did the authors of the Princeton study[53], who used more sophisticated social psychological measures and found little relationship between psychological variables and fertility. Fawcett[54], noting the paucity of findings relating psychological variables and fertility in a significant fashion stressed the need for more sophisticated research methodologies.

The Hoffmans[55] noted that the social context in which a personality trait occurs must be considered in evaluating the trait's relationship to fertility behavior. They noted that during the 1930s Kelly had found that "anxious dependent" women had fewer children while the Princeton study in the 1950s showed no relationship between anxiety and fertility.[56] The 1930s were, of course, more difficult times economically than the 1950s. During the 1950s, times were not only better, but medical care, washing machines, and other appliances made child rearing easier. Thus, anxious people may have been more cautious in undertaking commitments to children during the 1930s than in the 1950s. In any case, the needs and motives emanating from a specific personality structure may be differently expressed in different situations. The Hoffmans suggested that studies of homogeneous groups in specific contexts may provide better indications of the effects of personality traits on fertility than have been thus far found. If rigid controls of the social context are required to discern the effects of personality traits on fertility, then the context, situation, or circumstances may be a more significant determinant of fertility than personality. As differences in fertility between socio-economic groups diminish or vanish, psychological traits may appear to become more important in explaining the remaining differences in fertility between people. Significant as this may be for family planning programs interested in identifying those prone to unwanted pregnancies, the prevention of teen-age pregnancies and the provision of heath services, the fertility differentials associated with psychological characteristics are likely to be of little demographic significance compared to the fertility differences induced by changing circumstances. In the end. the social economic context is thus likely to be the most important determinant of fertility behavior.

Modernity and Fertility

Poor husband-wife communication, misconstruction and lack of awareness of the motives of the marital partner were reported to inhibit effective birth control.[57] The more restrictive the family structure on the wife's freedom and activities, the less the practice and effectiveness of birth control. In Puerto Rico where these observations were made, birth rates were dropping rapidly even as the study was being published. Undoubtedly, birth rates would have fallen more rapidly had husbands and wives communicated their mutual interest in limiting fertility. The drop in fertility was accomplished by a large proportion of fertile women accepting sterilization (rather than trying to communicate with their husbands?).

Machismo, aggressive maleness purported to be common among Latin American men, could be taken at face value as influencing fertility, as men try to demonstrate their virility by siring children. Yet in Puerto Rico at least, empirical evidence showed little or no relationship between measures of machismo and birth control practice or fertility.[58]

Nonetheless, the difference between fertilities of third world peoples and those of the west are thought by some to be in some significant way related to differences in personality traits.[59] These differences in personality traits are derived from the distinctions made by some social analysts between "traditional" and "modern" societies, with their respective personality types, a distinction which has not gone without criticism.[60] A significant criticism concerns the notion that the traditional personality type is resistant to change. That personality, typified by the peasant, is reported to be not only conservative but suspicious, fatalistic, and possessed of other backward characteristics. The lack of progress in many of the developing countries is blamed in some part on the traditional orientation of its inhabitants.[61] In constrast, the modern personality type is implicitly presumed to be innovative, in control, rational, and enterprising, a proposition which may not bear critical scrutiny.

Williamson[62] attempted to discern the relationship between two indicators of modernity and favorable attitude to birth control in samples of factory workers from five nations: India, Pakistan, Nigeria, Chile, and Israel. One of the indices of modernity used was the expressed "ideal family size" based on the rationale that modern people want small families. The relationship between "ideal family size" and favorable attitude to birth control was in the expected direction, but the correlations were small to moderate. (r = −.23, .−.09, −.11, −.36, −.14, for Nigeria, Chile, Pakistan, India, and Israel, respectively.) The second indicator of modernity was the index of subjective efficacy defined as "the respondent's feeling that he is in a position to control his own fate, that he can cope with his present environment and that it is possible for a man to have an impact on his environment." This was measured by questionnaires. The correlations between the index of "subjective efficacy" and favorable attitudes to birth control were also small to moderate (r = .28, .08, .18, .14, and .15, for Nigeria, Chile, Pakistan, India, and Israel, respectively). A high "subjective efficacy" and a low expressed "ideal family size" would appear to logically lead to a favorable attitude towards birth control; yet neither variable had a very strong relationship to favorable attitudes to birth control. More significant is the fact that the number of children which respondents had was not related to their attitudes to birth control (even when age was controlled) and only minimally and inconsistently related to the index of subjective efficacy. The apparent discrepancy between attitudes and behavior might bear examination could we be sure of the credibility of respondents who in their own way may try to provide interviewers with correct answers as noted later. (see Chapter 10, 11).

Goldberg[63] called attention to an aspect of modernization that would appear to be particularly pertinent to a decline in fertility, the aspect being the changed position of women, their increased access to activities and enterprises outside the family independent of male supervision and overview. Nonetheless, the effect on fertility may depend on the particular context or circumstances. As women in modern societies achieve still greater independence and access to opportunity, there will be fewer deterrents for single women, having no wish for marital or other comparable relationships, to beget and rear children. (They are not likely to exceed the fertility of their more conventional sisters.) And, as shall be discussed later (see Chapter 10) there are traditional societies in which women are relatively independent, economically and otherwise, and still find it advantageous and prefer to have many children. Nor, as shall become apparent later, does male dominance preclude adjustments in fertility.

There are, of course, differences in lifestyle and work organization between modernized and industrial societies and, for want of a better term, more traditional old-fashioned societies whether agrarian or urban. These make for differences in the cultural and intrinsic values children represent to parents, in the cost and ease of rearing them, and in the returns parents can expect from the effort. In contemporary traditional societies, some people live more than others in the modern sector with regard to occupation or leisure activities or some combination of the two and these differences should be correlated with fertility behavior. With increased adoption of lifestyles characteristic of contemporary industrial societies, where goods, services and even less tangible values are obtained in the market place, where relations with others—employers, employees, friends, colleagues and relatives—tend to become casual and uniform and lacking strong personal commitments, and where children can do little productive work, they tend to become a burden and of little economic benefit. But the varieties of beliefs, attitudes and motivations which characterize the personality structures of the peoples of less industrialized, commercialized societies or even of subsistence societies are not so rigidly fixed that they can not recognize when children and family building become burdens to be avoided, even in the absence of modernization.

As the Rudolphs noted, the forms of traditional societies were not fixed in the past and are changing in the present, responding to circumstances.[64] While the distinction between modern and traditional ways is often useful (as a heuristic device) the distinction may lead to erroneous conclusions. Both ways contain rational and irrational elements and both ways are dynamic or changing. They are the results of past social change and developments and the point of departure for future developments. The notion that the path of future development of traditional societies must lead through the ways of contemporary modernized society fails to recognize the variety of alternative courses open to humans and reflects the ethnocentricity of many western observers. Modernity need not be a precondition for a decline in fertility.

Notes

1. E. A. Wrigley, *Population in History* (New York: McGraw-Hill, 1969), pp. 145--202.

2. D. B. Bogue, *Principles of Demography* (New York: Wiley, 1969), p. 48.

3. G. Z. Johnson, "Differential Fertility in European Countries," in National Bureau of Economic Research, *Demographic and Economic Change in Developed Countries* (Princeton, N.J.: Princeton University Press, 1960), pp. 36--70; C. V. Kiser, "Differential Fertility in the United States," (same volume), pp. 77--116.

4. United Nations, *The Determinants and Consequences of Population Trends* (ST/SOA/Series A Population Studies No. 17) (New York: 1953), pp. 32--33.

5. W. H. Grabill, C. V. Kiser and P. K. Whelpton, *The Fertility of American Women* (New York: John Wiley, 1958), p. 331; A. A. Campbell, "Three Generations of Parents," *Family Planning Perspectives* 5:2 (Spring 1973), pp. 106--12.

6. For one of the many classic statements of the demographic transition, see F. W. Notestein, "Population—The Long View," in T. W. Schultz, ed. (Chicago: University of Chicago Press, 1945), pp. 36--57.

7. C. P. Blacker, "Stages in Population Growth," *Eugenics Review*, 39:3 (October 1947), pp. 88--102.

8. E. Driver, *Differential Fertility in Central India* (Princeton, N.J.: Princeton University Press, 1963); D. Yaukey, *Fertility Differentials in a Modernizing Country* (Princeton, N.J.: Princeton University Press, 1961).

9. F. W. Oechsli and D. Kirk, "Modernization and the Demographic Transition in Latin America and the Caribbean," *Economic Development and Cultural Change* 23:3 (April 1975), pp. 391--419.

10. See, for example, G. Myrdal, *Population: A Problem for Democracy* (Cambridge, Mass.: Harvard University Press, 1940); also A. H. Hansen, "Economic Progress and Declining Population Growth," *American Economic Review* 29 (March 1939), pp. 1--15 (Presidential Address, Meeting of American Economic Association, Detroit, Mich., Dec. 28, 1938).

11. Campbell, op. cit.

12. J. S. Siegal and D. S. Akers, "Some Aspects of the Use of Birth Expectations Data From Sample Surveys for Population Projections," *Demography* 6:2 (May 1969), pp. 101--16; H. S. Shryock, J. S. Siegal and associates, *The Methods and Materials of Demography*, Bureau of the Census, vol. 2 (May 1973), pp. 785--91.

13. U.S. Bureau of the Census, *Current Population Reports Series P-25* No. 493 (1972), "Projections of the Population of the United States by Age and Sex: 1972 to 2020," Washington, D.C.

14. U.S. Bureau of the Census, *Current Population Reports Series P-25*, No. 601 (1975), "Projections of the Population of the United States: 1975--2050," Washington, D.C.

15. See C. Gibson, "The Elusive Rise in the American Birthrate," *Science* 196 (April 1977), pp. 500--503 for a considered analysis of the short run trend in fertility.

16. D. S. Freedman, "The Relation of Economic Status to Fertility," *American Economic Review* 53:3 (June 1963), pp. 414--36.

17. C. V. Kiser, W. H. Grabill, and A. A. Campbell, *Trends and Variations in Fertility in the United States* (Cambridge: Harvard University Press, 1968), Tables 11.2, 11.3, pp. 211--15.

18. R. Freedman and L. Coombs, "Economic Considerations in Family Growth Decisions," *Population Studies* 20:2 (November 1966), pp. 197--222.

19. E. M. Bernhardt, "Fertility and Economic Status—Some Recent Findings on Differentials in Sweden," *Population Studies* 26:2 (July 1972), pp. 175--84.

20. G. Becker, "An Economic Analysis of Fertility," in National Bureau of Economic Research, *Demographic and Economic Change in Developed Countries* (Princeton, N.J.: Princeton University Press, 1960), pp. 209--31.

21. P. K. Whelpton and C. V. Kiser, eds., *Social and Psychological Factors Affecting Fertility* (New York: Millbank Memorial Fund, 1951), vol. 2, pt. 9, Fig. 8.

22. J. S. Duesenberry, "Comment" (on Becker's paper), Nationasl Bureau of Economic Research, op. cit., pp. 231--34.

23. J. Blake, "Income and Reproductive motivation," *Population Studies* 21:3 (November 1967), pp. 185--206; also J. Blake, "Are Babies Consumer Durables? A Critique of the Economic Theory of Reproductive Motivation," *Population Studies* 21:1 (March 1968), pp. 5--25.

24. Freedman and Coombs, op. cit.

25. J. Mincer, "Market Prices, Opportunity Costs and Income Effects," in *Measurements in Economics—Studies in Mathematical Economics and Econometrics*, in memory of Yehuda Grunfeld (Standford, Cal.: Stanford University Press, 1963), pp. 67--82; W. Sanderson and R. J. Willis, "Economic Models of Fertility: Some Examples and Implications," in National Bureau of Economic Research, *New Directions in Economic Research*, 51st Annual Report, (September 1971), pp. 32--42.

26. B. A. Turchi, "Microeconomic Theories of Fertility: A Critique," *Social Forces* 54:1 (September 1975), pp. 107--25; N. K. Namboodiri, "Some Observations on the Economic Framework for Fertility Analysis, *Population Studies* 26:2 (July 1972), pp. 185--206.

27. J. L. Simon, "The Mixed Effects of Income Upon Successive Births May Explain the Convergence Phenomenon," *Population Studies* 29:1 (March 1975), pp. 109--22.

28. R. A. Easterlin, "Towards a Socioeconomic Theory of Fertility: A Survey of Recent Research on Economic Factors in American Fertility," in S. Behrman, L. Corsa, and R. Freedman, eds., *Fertility and Family Planning, A World View* (Ann Arbor: University of Michigan Press, 1969), pp. 127--56; also R. A. Easterlin, "On the Relation of Economic Factors to Recent and Projected Fertility Changes," *Demography* 3:1 (1966), pp. 131--53.

29. For a review and criticism of the Easterlin hypothesis see also "Fertility, Aspirations and Resources: A Symposium on the Easterlin Hypothesis"; D. Freedman, "Introduction"; R. Easterlin, "The Conflict Between Aspirations and Resources"; H. Leibenstein, "The Problem of Characterizing Aspirations"; V. K. Oppenheimer, "The Easterlin Hypothesis: Another Aspect of the Echo to Consider"; R. D. Lee, "Demographic Forecasting and the Easterlin Hypothesis"; W. C. Sanderson, "On Two Schools of the Economics of Fertility", in *Population and Development Review* 2, Nos. 3 and 4 (September/December 1976), pp. 411--77.

30. *U.S. Statistical Abstract, 1971*, Table 489, p. 308.

31. Freedman and Coombs, op. cit.

32. See V. L. Galbraith and D. S. Thomas, "Birth Rates and the Interwar Business Cycles," *Journal of American Statistical Association*, 36 (December 1941), pp. 465–76; R. A. Easterlin, "The American Baby Boom in Historical Perspective," *American Economic Review*, 51:5 (december 1961), pp. 869–911. For a contrasting view see also D. Kirk, "The Influence of Business Cycles on Marriage and Birth Rates," in National Bureau of Economic Research, *Demographic and Economic Change in Developed Countries* (Princeton, N.J.: Princeton University Press, 1960), pp. 241–57. Kirk holds that the effects of business cycles on fertility are not very significant in view of other social developments (e.g., modernization) which in the long run excercise considerably more influence on fertility.

33. See R. Freedman, "American Studies of Family Planning and Fertility: A Review of Major Trends and Issues," in C. V. Kiser, ed., *Research in Family Planning* (Princeton, N.J.: Princeton University Press, 1962), pp. 211–27.

34. See C. F. Westoff, E. G. Mishler and E. D. Kelly, "Preferences in Size of Family and Eventual Fertility Twenty Years After," *American Journal fo Sociology* 62:5 (March 1957), pp. 491–97; also D. Goldberg, H. Sharp and R. Freedman, "The Stability and Reliability of Expected Family Size Data," *Milbank Memorial Fund Quarterly* 37:4 (October 1959), pp. 369–85.

35. R. Freedman, P. K. Whelpton and A. Campbell, *Family Planning, Sterility, and Population Growth* (New York: McGraw-Hill, 1959).

36. U.S. Bureau of the Census, *Current Population Reports, Series P-20*, various issues, (Birth Expectations and Fertility; Prospects for American Fertility; Fertility Expectations of American Women, 1968–1977).

37. J. Peel, "The Hull Family Survey II—Family Planning in the First Five Years of Marriage," *Journal Biosocial Science* 4 (1972), pp. 333–46.

38. C. F. Westoff and N. B. Ryder, "The Predictive Validity of Reproductive Intentions," *Demography* 14:4 (November 1977), pp. 431–54.

39. N. B. Ryder, "A Critique of the National Fertility Survey," *Demography* 10:4 (November 1973), pp. 495–506.

40. G. Hawthorne, "Review Symposium—Psychological Perspectives on Population," J. Fawcett, ed., *Demography* 11:3 (August 1974), pp. 537–43.

41. M. Fishbein and J. J. Jaccard, "Theoretical and Methodological Considerations in the Prediction of Family Planning Intentions and Behavior," *Representative Research in Social Psychology* 4 (1973), pp. 37–51.

42. L. Festinger, "Cognitive Dissonance," *Scientific American* 207:4 (October 1962), pp. 93–102; D. J. Bem, "Self-Perception: An Alternative Interpretation of Cognitive Dissonance Phenomena," *Psychological Review* 74 (1967), pp. 183–200.

43. See R. Brown, *Social Psychology* (New York: Free Press, 1965), pp. 549–609.

44. L. Festinger and J. M. Carlsmith, "Cognitive Consequences of Forced Compliance," *Journal Abnormal and Social Psychology* 58 (1959), pp. 203–10.

45. J. Blake, "Can We Believe Recent Indications of Birth Expectations in the United States?" *Demography* 11:1 (February 1974), pp. 25–44.

46. L. Bumpass, "Comment on J. Blake's 'Can We Believe Recent Indications of Birth Expectations in the United States?' " *Demography* 12:1 (February 1975), pp. 155–56.

47. U.S. Bureau of the Census, *Current Population Reports, Series P-65*, No. 46, Consumer Buying Indicators July 1973.

48. D. Goldberg, "Some Recent Developments in American Fertility Research," in National Bureau of Economic Research, *Demographic and Economic Change in Developed Countries* (Princeton, N.J.: Princeton University Press, 1960), pp. 137–51.

49. Namboodiri, op. cit., pp. 185–206.

50. E. H. Pohlman, *The Psychology of Birth Planning* (Cambridge, Mass.: Schenkman, 1969); L. W. Hoffman and M. L. Hoffman, "The Value of Children to Parents." in J. T. Fawcett, ed., *Psychological Perspectives on Population* (New York: Basic Books, 1973), pp. 19–76.

51. See for instance, P. K. Whelpton and C. V. Kiser, eds., *Social and Psychological Factors Affecting Fertility*, 5 vols. (New York: Milbank Memorial Fund, 1946, 1950, 1952, 1954, 1958); C. F. Westoff, R. G. Potter, P. C. Sagi, and E. G. Mishler, *Family Growth in Metropolitan America* (Princeton, N.J.: Princeton University Press, 1961); C. F. Westoff, H. G. Potter, and P. C. Sagi, *The Third Child* (Princeton, N.J.: Princeton University Press, 1963).

52. C. V. Kiser and P. K. Whelpton, "Summary of Chief Findings and Implications for Future Studies," (from *Social and Psychological Factors Affecting Fertility* op. cit.), *Milbank Memorial Fund Quarterly* 36 (1958), pp. 282–329 (esp. 318–319).

53. Westoff et. al., *Family Growth in Metropolitan America,* op. cit.

54. J. T. Fawcett, *Psychology and Population* (New York: The Population Council, 1970).

55. Hoffman and Hoffman, op. cit.

56. Ibid., p. 40.

57. J. M. Stycos, "Husband-Wife Communication and Fertility," in J. M. Stycos, *Family and Fertility in Puerto Rico* (New York: Columbia University Press, 1955), pp. 166–80. Reprinted in C. B. Nam, ed., *Population and Society* (Boston: Houghton Mifflin, 1968), pp. 438–46.

58. R. Hill, J. M. Stycos and K. Back, *The Family and Population Control: A Puerto Rican Experiment in Social Change* (Chapel Hill: University of North Carolina Press, 1959).

59. J. T. Fawcett and M. H. Bornstein, "Modernization, Individual Modernity and Fertility," in J. T. Fawcett, ed., *Psychological Perspectives on Population* (New York: Basic Books, 1973), pp. 106–31.

60. Dean C. Tipps, "Modernization Theory and the Comparative Study of Societies: A Critical Perspective," *Comparative Studies in Society and History* 12:2 (March 1973), pp. 199–26.

61. See E. Rogers, *Modernization Among Peasants, The Impact of Communication* (New York: Holt, Rinehart and Winston, 1969).

62. J. B. Williamson, "Subjective Efficacy and the Ideal Family Size as Predictors of Favorability Towards Birth Control," *Demography* 7:3 (August 1970), pp. 329–39.

63. D. Goldberg, "Socioeconomic Theory and Differential Fertility; The Case of the LDCs," *Social Forces* 54:1 (September 1975), pp. 84–106.

64. L. I. Rudolph and S. H. Rudolph, *The Modernity of Tradition* (Chicago: University of Chicago Press, 1967). See Introduction, pp. 3–14.

9

Fertility Declines in Pre-Industrial Europe

Introduction

The demographic transition was first posed as a description of the pattern of mortality and fertility declines in some western European countries. Some have regarded it as the basis for a theory of demographic change in general. The theory hinges on modernization and industrialization whose first demographic effect is a decline in mortality, followed by a decrease in fertility, also occurring under the impetus of modernization. This is only one of the ways in which fertility rates have declined but not the only way. Even among the countries of European descent which have undergone the classically described transition to low birth rates, the details of the process were quite varied.

Though no modern society today exhibits the relatively high fertility characteristic of traditional agrarian societies, the first people in modern western European history to show sustained signs of birth control and movement toward small families were the French, while France was still largely an agrarian nation. The English, though experiencing rapid industrialization in the eighteenth and nineteenth centuries, did not appear to begin controlling family size until the latter part of the nineteenth century, almost a century after the French who began to practice birth control when mortality was still high, above 30 per 1,000. The mortality of the Hungarians was also high when their fertility rates began to decline and practically at the same pace as the decline in mortality starting around the turn of the twentieth century, while Hungary was largely agrarian.

Coale[1] discussed the lack of generality or universality in the principles frequently associated with the notion of the demographic transition. He noted that general and marital fertility rates were quite variable and not

172

uniformly high in the different regions of pre-industrial Europe. And although all modernized countries now have low fertility rates, there was no consistency in the level of modernity (in terms of literacy, urbanization, proportions of the labor force in agriculture, and the like) which determined when and how fast the fertility of different countries declined. Factors other than those usually associated with the demographic transition were thus heavily involved in declines in fertility.

While people in different areas may have been responding with different intensities to the various facets of modernization, they were at the same time subject to various forms of population pressure. Friedlander[2] wrote, "The adjustment in reproductive behavior made by a community in response to a rising strain, such as that resulting from higher natural increase, is likely to differ, depending on the ease with which the community can relieve the strain through outmigration." To illustrate this thesis, he compared the changes in English and Swedish fertility, mortality, migration and growth in the nineteenth century and in the first two decades of the twentieth century. In England and Wales, industrialization and urbanization proceeded at a rapid pace, the increase in the urban population having been in good part a result of rural to urban migration. Though the population of England increased rapidly during the nineteenth century, the rural population remained fairly stable and despite high birth rates because of rural to urban migration. By 1850, half the population was urban and by 1900 almost three-quarters. Rural birth rates did not begin to decline from levels approaching 40 per 1,000 until the last half of the nineteenth century (reaching 30 per 1,000 in 1900) when the pace of rural to urban migration slowed down. In Sweden the pace of industrialization was much slower; by about 1850, only 10 percent of the population was urban, increasing to only 22 percent by 1900. Opportunities for rural to urban migration were small. Rural fertility was moderately low in Sweden, 30 to 35 per 1,000 population throughout most of the nineteenth century, levels not reached in rural England and Wales until the end of that century. The surge in Swedish emigration to America towards the end of the century, a still difficult venture, is further evidence of the buildup of population pressure in rural Sweden and the absence of opportunities for the easier and perhaps less stressful internal migration.

Demeny[3] noted that while the decline in fertility in the more urbanized and industrialized Austrian section of the Austro-Hungarian Empire appeared to fit the conventional picture of the demographic transition, fertility declines in the more rural and less advanced regions of Hungary did not. Indeed, in one of the more backward provinces (Krasso Szoreny), marital fertility in 1880 was as low as that reached in Vienna two decades later. This province was the easternmost of a contiguous group of seven in which villages with what might be considered natural fertility levels were rare. By 1910 many of these villages had birth rates below 20 per 1,000 population and an increasing proportion of families were raising only a single child despite a general backwardness, including a high level of infant mortality. In different regions of this area, which contained a multiplicity of intermingled national and religious groups, different ethnic communities took the lead in reducing fertility. Demeny concluded that common forces must have been at work, the paramount ones being economic, limiting access to land and employment. Diffusion of attitudes towards small families and receptivity of particular cultures to the idea probably affected the timing of the decline in fertility. As shall be noted later, the economic constraints on fertility were still operating in the 1920s and 1930s in these areas.

Most of our information on the fertility behavior of historic pre-industrial peoples pertains to the sixteenth through nineteenth centuries and largely to the European experience, though China and Japan have also been examined by researchers in population. Undoubtedly, people practiced birth control before these times. Prehistoric people likely practiced various forms of birth control, including abortion as well as infanticide, as do contemporary primitive people, and as the ancient Greeks and Romans are known to have done. The extent and demographic effects of such practices and the correlates can hardly be known with confidence for early times, but the historic record permits more reliable surmises and inferences for later periods.

There is some evidence that medieval European peasants, in some areas at least, controlled their fertility sufficiently to reverse a population growth trend which had resulted in very dense agricultural settlement. For over a century before the plague struck in 1348, the population of rural Pistoia in Tuscany had been falling; the number of rural communes and hearths had decreased. The population in 1344 was estimated to be almost a quarter less than it was in 1244. There is some evidence that even in 1244 population had been declining for some time. Thus, when the plague struck, it was not against a population increasing blindly against subsistence. Indeed, though mortality was high, it was difficult to tell how much of the decrease in population up to 1404 (when population was 30 percent that of 1244) had been due to the plague and how much to the fall in fertility. As population recovered subsequent to 1404, an enumeration of 1427 showed that poor households with tax assessments of less than 50 florins contained an average of fewer than one-and-a-half children under fifteen years of age per household, while households with tax assessments of over 250 florins contained an average of more than three children per household; households intermediate between the poor (more than half the households) and the rich (almost 5 percent of the households) had intermediate numbers of children. The children of the poor were more likely to die than the children of the rich, and the poor were more likely to send their children to the homes of the rich as servants and the like. But Herlihy,[4] who analyzed this data, thought that these doings were not sufficient to explain the differences in the numbers of children in the households of the rich and the poor. Chroniclers of the time had noted that poor girls had little hope of marriage and even those of intermediate wealth had to wait some time before a sufficient dowry could be accumulated for them. Thus, delayed marriage helped limit the number of children. Also, hard economic times may have obliged married couples to refrain from having children. One Pistoiese chronicler noted that for a long time before 1399, the Florentine women appeared to be barren, but after the plague of that year which enhanced the economic opportunities, inheritances, and the wealth of survivors, many women became pregnant. These and other observations led Herlihy to conclude that reproductive rates were very sensitive to adverse social and economic conditions in medieval rural Pistoia.

Increase in Age of Marriage

In the decline of birth rates associated with modernization, the upper classes were first to control their fertility. This was not necessarily the pattern when fertility declined in pre-industrial societies. In these instances, fertility declined more directly in response to constraining economic circumstances, and the poor as a class had lower fertility, with some exceptions, than the rich.

Stys[5] conducted a retrospective study of the fertility of a large group of peasant women who resided in 20 villages of southern Poland and who were born between 1855 and 1929. In each cohort (group of women born in the same period), the wives of larger landholders had born more children than wives of the smaller landholders. Among the wives born between 1855 and 1880 (average birth year was 1875), those with farms less than a single hectare in size gave birth to 5.35 children on the average; those with farms of 5 to 10 hectares (only two wives had farms of more than 10 hectares) gave birth to 8.35 children on the average. (Wives with intermediate size farms had comparable numbers of births relative to the size of the holding.) The wives with smaller farms had married at an average age of 25 years and had their last child at an average age of 40. Those with larger farms had married at an average of 21 years and had their last child at an average of 42½ years. Thus, much of the difference in the number of births was due to the extended period of active childbearing of the wives of larger landholders, almost 44 percent longer than that of the wives of small holders.

The richer women had not only the reproductive advantage of a longer period of exposure to pregnancy but also the advantage of exposure to pregnancy during the more fertile years under age 25 when the duration of lactation amenorrhea and postpartum sterility is the shortest. By age 21, most rural Polish peasant women would have been out of the period of adolescent sub-fecundity as the average age of menarche for rural Polish girls, the great majority of whom were poor, was estimted to be slightly more than 17 years in 1890.[6] Thus, the principal factor in the lower fertility of poorer women was their later age of marriage.

During the period studied by Stys, the average size of the farms in the area (and in Poland generally) decreased with time, as they were subdivided to provide children with property. Subdivision of the larger farms occurred more rapidly as there were more children to provide with land while among the smaller farms, a higher proportion of children left agriculture altogether. In 1850 slightly less than 50 percent of the farms were smaller than five hectares; in 1931, 85 percent of farms were smaller than five hectares though the proportion of extremely small farms had diminished considerably; farms were not subdivided indefinitely.

The conditions which determined the age of menarche improved, for the age of menarche for women of rural Poland decreased slowly to about 16½ years in 1910 and less than 16 years by 1930.[7] This would indicate increasing fecundity or capacity of women to bear children. Nonetheless, Stys traced a steady decline in the fertility of the succeeding cohorts of women which followed those born between 1855-1881. This decline took place among all classes. Though birth control of some sort within marriage was apparently being used first among the richer peasants, it was rapidly taken up by the poorer peasants whose fertility remained lower throughout this transition. The average number of live births per peasant women declined steadily from 6.48 for women born between 1855–1880 to 2.22 for those women born between 1915 and 1918.

Fertility may be controlled in many ways. Malthus advocated that people delay marriage or not marry at all. In western Europe, this approach was largely responsible for the decline in fertility during the seventeenth and early eighteenth centuries. During those centuries, women married late in life and many never married so that the proportion of marrieds among women of reproductive age (15–50 years) was less than 40 to 50 percent depending on the area. In some areas of England and Sweden, the average age at marriage rose to 30 years while some 20 percent of women never married. Hajna[18] found this European marriage pattern characteristic of many late pre-industrial societies of the seventeenth and eighteenth centuries west of a line drawn roughly from Leningrad to Trieste. In eastern Europe, the proportion of marrieds among women of reproductive ages at any one time often exceeded 70 percent. Fertility declines in eastern Europe were to a great extent mediated by birth control within marriage. Along with the increase in age of marriage, people in some areas of western Europe began to practice birth control within marriage, early in the eighteenth century. By the nineteenth century, if not earlier, women had begun to marry at younger ages and the western European pattern of late marriage became a thing of the past except in Ireland.

Cowgill[9] reported that in the city of York (England), the mean age of first marriage for women increased steadily from 23.5 years in 1560 to 28.5 in 1720. The average family size shrank from 4.86 in the sixteenth century to 3.32 in the eighteenth century. Cowgill hypothesized that the reason for the change in marriage patterns was that the age of menarche for women was increasing. She noted that the age at which women gave birth to illegitimate children had also increased. However, other studies of the same period have indicated that premarital conception was common and that betrothal may have been regarded as sufficient license for intercourse as Laslett suggested, or more generally, as a courting convention, as Hair believed.[10] Thus, it was not unlikely that much of the illegitimacy was due to marriages not being formalized as intended. In any case, as was discussed earlier, there is no direct evidence of menarche occurring on the average so late in any population.[11] The reason for the increase in age at marriage is better sought elsewhere.

There was no improvement in English mortality during the seventeenth century. If anything, the levels of mortality increased somewhat, as epidemics and local famines exacerbated the conditions wrought by the economic and political dislocations of the time. Thus, a decline in mortality need not be a prerequisite for a decline in fertility.

The reason for the increase in age at marriage may be found in economic developments. Towards the end of the sixteenth century and the beginning of the seventeenth century, changes in the structure of the economy of England started to gain momentum; enclosures dislocated many peasants; land was withdrawn from cultivation and put into sheepwalks to supply the growing textile industries; the price of food rose and real wages fell, and

craftsmen were being displaced by commercial enterprises. Thus the economy did not provide the population with the employments necessary to
maintain customary levels of living.[12]

The large number of spinsters and the increase in age at marriage may be
considered an adaptive response to economic constraints. Birth rates declined
from a level which sustained growth, to between 30 and 35 births per 1,000,
not much higher than the death rates.[13] Population growth ceased.

The principle that marriage should await the availability of an independent livelihood to support the new family may explain why many people did
not marry in the areas where this principle was extant. It does not explain
why women married later, however, since the livelihood was largely in the
hands of men. Though the man may have had to wait until a relatively
advanced age, he could have selected a young wife rather than an older one.
Additional factors are the matters of dowry and the family as an economic
unit. A girl from a poor family, who in any case was likely to marry a poor
boy, might have to wait a considerable time before even a meager dowry of
household goods as well as cash could be accumulated, an accumulation to
which she might contribute by her own efforts, perhaps as a spinster, a word
which originally designated an occupation, later an unmarried woman, and
finally a never married woman with no prospect of marriage. Since the
family was an economic unit, a prospective bridegroom or his family, aside
from the dowry, may well have favored a bride who was competent in an
economic sense, capable of contributing significantly to the economic
viability of the family, a consideration which was the more important
during hard times and among the poor. In such circumstances the groom (or
his family when marriages were arranged) might well have favored older
brides who were possibly more skilled and resourceful. In societies where the
household economy is more extended, as in joint families, this consideration
may not be as important as that of obtaining a more compliant younger bride
who could more easily be integrated into the new family. In western Europe,
where the nuclear family prevailed as the basic economic unit, the differences
in age between brides and grooms was small though husbands were usually
older than their wives. In Hedmark (Norway) of 1801, while the wives of
farmers (the wealthier group) were, on the average, almost four-and-a-half
years younger than their husbands, those of the poorer crofters were only
one-fifth of a year younger, and 47.5 percent of wives of crofters were one or
more years older than their husbands. In Colyton, England of 1647–1769, the
average age of brides was one to two years older than grooms in first
marriages; the average age of brides at first marriage was 30 years.[14]

The principle that a man should not marry until he was in possession of a
livelihood, a holding, or some craft,[15] helped to control fertility in pre-
industrial Europe. Unmarried sons and daughters who could not find a
living elsewhere may have been obliged to remain in the parents' or, if they
were dead, in the eldest brother's home in the undesirable status of a sort of
relative-servant, at least in some parts of the Netherlands[16] or, as was likely in
England and elsewhere, to enter the household of some other family as an
inservant with little opportunity to marry.[17]

This was a hard adjustment under which a portion of the population was
denied, or obliged to delay, entrance into a full life in order to preserve the

patrimony of others. Perhaps there were some compensations if the servant was accepted as a member of the master's household and provided the security and support pertaining thereto. More likely, the position of the servant was very onerous, more so even than that of a full family member subservient to the often arbitrary whims of the head of the household. Nonetheless, the moral and institutional delays and inhibitions of marriage were effective in slowing population growth given the mortality which prevailed in the seventeenth and early eighteenth centuries, as it has been in Ireland in more recent times under moderately low levels of mortality.

The system broke down under the impact of the industrial revolution and commercialization of agriculture. Laborers were no longer tied to a master's enterprise or as servants in the proprietor's household; indeed, they may not have been welcome as such. They became proletarians, a precarious position perhaps made easier by having children to help support the family. The growth of a large number of cottage industries supplying commercial entrepreneurs with finished goods, as in the "put out" system, facilitated the formation of independent households. The result was an increase in fertility which some observers felt was as important or more important than the decline in death rates in causing the surge in population growth at the end of the eighteenth century.[18] Petersen[19] noted that the number of landless proletarians in the province of Groningsen in the Netherlands quadrupled in the century beginning with 1775, following their conversion from farm laborers of the inservant type.

Wrigley[20] cited an example from the demographic history of the parishes of Le Vieuxbourg in Belgian Flanders, in the late eighteenth and early nineteenth centuries. The quality of soil could not support an expansion of agriculture, and the system which made marriage contingent on the availability of a holding had maintained the population resources balance. After a period of population decline and stability from the middle of the seventeenth century to the middle of the eighteenth century, the population of Le Vieuxbourg began a period of growth sparked by an apparent increase in fertility. The growth was made possible by an expansion in linen manufacture operating, as did so many pre-industrial enterprises, on the put-out or homework system. More and more people turned to the poor living afforded by cottage industry. But in the 1840s conditions became particularly miserable for the Flemish cottage industry workers as cheaper products from English and French factories came into the market. By that time, the bulk of the labor force was employed in the linen industry and the resulting depression affected most of the population. Deprez,[21] from whom Wrigley derived the data for his account, noted that by the end of the eighteenth century, 75 percent of the working population of Le Vieuxbourg was dependent on the linen industry. Deprez noted also that in other sandy soil districts with poor agricultural potential, such as Overysel and Twente in the Netherlands, industry also supported a marked increase in population.

The situation in Le Vieuxbourg was compared by Wrigley with that of the neighboring Pays d' Alost, a richer, more fertile area. This region experienced a spurt of population growth starting in 1720, twenty years before that of Le Vieuxbourg. This growth ended in about fifty years as the ratio of births to marriages became smaller than that of Le Vieuxbourg. The implication was that as the prosperity of the Pays d'Alost region was preserved by population control, so was the poverty of Le Vieuxbourg increased by population growth.

Yet the people of Le Vieuxbourg had, in the earlier absence of the linen industry, maintained control over their numbers; probably this did not lead to a satisfying economic or social life. Encouraged by the opportunity afforded by the linen entrepreneurs, they sought a more satisfying life in cottage industry, though still a poor one. Setbacks and unemployment occurred largely as a result of changes in the economy not related to population. By contrast, the linen industry after a small start in the Pays d'Alost did not take hold.[22] This was due possibly to the greater fertility of the soil in the Pays d'Alost which provided a better living for its inhabitants. In the long run, the people of Flanders and the Netherlands, still densely populated, did succeed in making a better life for themselves, an enterprise which may have been assisted or stimulated by their numbers.

Thus Wrigley[23] concluded that it is difficult to predict the ultimate impact of population growth pressing on resources. At the same time he argued that the response of the fertility behavior governing population growth in pre-industrial societies was not very sensitive to the constraints of resources. He used the term "lurch" to characterize what appeared to be maladaptive or unreasoning changes in fertility. But what appeared to be a lurch, as in the increase in fertility in Le Vieuxbourg, may reflect the possibility that the observer was not aware of all the pertinent factors. This may well be the case in Wrigley's study of fertility in pre-industrial Colyton, England, in which he also observed lurches in fertility behavior.[24]

He noted that female age at marriage, though varying significantly, did not seem to follow economic trends closely. From 1560 to 1646, mean female age at first marriage in Colyton was 27 years; from 1647 to 1719, 30 years; from 1720 to 1769, 27; and from 1770 to 1837, it was 25 years of age. Since real wages in England declined during the first period but stabilized during the second period, Wrigley felt that the increase in age at marriage was not responsive to the economic situation and he used the term "lurch" to describe the change.

The change in age of marriage should have been related to the economic condition of Colyton, not England. Wrigley did not have the appropriate data and assumed that conditions in Colyton in Devonshire were not different from those in England as a whole. But as Bridenbaugh[25] noted, England did not have a national economy in the latter part of the sixteenth and early seventeenth centuries; different regions and localities experienced different economic conditions. He noted that in the second half of the sixteenth century and the first half of the seventeenth, the townsmen of Devonshire, particularly those of Exeter, the country seat and close to Colyton, enjoyed a general prosperity and unusual economic expansion. While in other areas of England arable lands were being enclosed for sheep walks and tenant cultivators were evicted, in Devonshire the farmers, because of the unsuitability of the land for tillage, were already in the business of supplying wool for the textile trade.[26] Thus, while much of England experienced hard times during this period, the townspeople of Devon enjoyed a relative prosperity. Afterwards the centers of textile and other industries moved to the north; Colyton and Devon may have suffered hard times during this transition until their economy stabilized.

Of particular interest is Wrigley's finding that the women of Colyton during the years 1647–1719 not only married later but that their marital fertility declined sufficiently to indicate that some sort of birth control was being practiced within marriage. This finding cannot be generalized to England, but does indicate at least that birth control may have been practiced even at that early date.

While the English at home during the sixteenth and early seventeenth centuries found themselves constrained to reduce their fertility, those English who migrated to the colonies found themselves no longer so constrained. During the colonial period, American fertility was very high (about 55 births per 1,000 population). After 1800 the Americans also began to control their fertility, initially through later marriage. Yasuba,[27] who studied the decline in the fertility of white women in the United States from 1800 to 1860, showed that the areas in which the most rapid declines occurred were those in which the availability of cultivable land was most limited. He discounted the effects of urbanization and industrialization since urban and industrial growth in these areas was slow at the time and did not involve a significant part of the population. When labor was needed by farm families opening land, it was forthcoming. When the need for labor declined, so did fertility.

Birth Control Within Marriage

The practice of birth control within marriage was noted in France as early as the eighteenth century. In France, the agrarian economy predominated for a much longer time than in England; industrialization and urbanization started later and progressed more slowly. Yet the French began to lower their birth rates through birth control on a large scale a century before other western European nations.

By the end of the seventeenth century, birth control had taken a firm hold among the nobility and though they married much earlier than the rest of the population, their fertility was much lower. Within the aristocracy, a woman marrying before age 20 and staying married until age 45–50, had on the average 6.15 children for marriages occurring between 1650 and 1699, 2.79 children for marriages occurring between 1700 and 1749, and 2 children for marriages occurring between 1750 and 1799.[28] The average age at which these wives gave birth to their youngest child declined from 31 years to 25 years over this period.

The peasantry of France also reduced their fertility, at first by delaying the age of marriage and later by birth control within marriage. Between 1675 and 1760 in the village of Crulai (1,000 inhabitants) in Normandy, the birth rate was about 36 per 1,000 (with a death rate of 31 per 1,000), and declined slowly until the French Revolution in 1789, largely through a decrease in the proportion of women married. (The birth rate was estimated to be 31 per 1,000 between 1760 and 1789 and the death rate 23 per 1,000 population.) Thereafter, the decline in birth rates was quite rapid, reaching 20 per 1,000 in 1810, this time through a decrease in marital fertility, indicating the use of some sort of birth control. Ganiage noted a sharp decline in marital fertility between women married before and after 1780 in his study of parish records of three villages of Beauvaises. Studies from various other areas of France reveal similar findings.[29] In Valmary's study of an area in southwest France, fertility within marriage appeared to have declined earlier in the eighteenth century than in the locales of the other French studies cited.

Birth rates in France continued to decline from the eighteenth century through the nineteenth and well into the twentieth centuries so that despite a decline in mortality, population growth was slowed considerably. While Britain's population more than quadrupled from the beginning of the nineteenth century to the beginning of the twentieth, the population of France did not even come close to doubling in the same period.

Not all regions of France relied on birth control within marriage to lower fertility. In many regions delayed marriage served to control fertility well into the nineteenth century. Van der Walle examined age at marriage and marital fertility of the various departments (administrative regions) of France for the year 1866. In those departments where women married late (at an average age for first marriage of 27.5 years), fertility within marriage was 70 percent higher than in those districts in which women married at an earlier age (22.1 years) though the numbers of children were not that much different.[30] Those who married young and were exposed to pregnancy for a longer time were obliged to use contraception if they wished to avoid having large families.

The circumstances which induced the French peasantry to begin the practice of birth control at the end of the eighteenth century are not fully explained. Death rates were not low; parents were not assured of surviving sons with a high level of probability. While French peasants were poor, they were still better off than other European peasantries of the eighteenth century. They improved their status without the intervention of industrialization or urbanization. The historical events in this period were those leading to and surrounding the French Revolution of 1789 which profoundly altered the life of the peasantry. A review of these events indicates that certain parallel developments in English and French social history were accompanied by parallel developments in fertility behavior. When developments in socio-economic history diverged so did the patterns of fertility behavior.

In the early feudal history of France, much of the woods, wastes, and pastures belonged to the village communities, or communes, as among many other peasantries. The feudal lords held the prerogatives and obligations of administering justice, maintaining order and defending the realm, in return for which they had the right to various taxes and dues including payments in kind and a goodly portion of the peasants' labor. The lords also used their power to bring some of the land under their immediate control as personal demesne. Some of the wealthier peasants also managed to accumulate land as permanent lease-holders of the lords or even as proprietors but still with feudal obligations to the lord. The wealthier peasants, frequently claiming descent from the original founders of the commune, had the greater voice in village councils. The poorer often worked as agricultural laborers and in domestic industry, and supplemented their incomes with the use, permitted by commune councils, of the woods and commons. Conflict existed between these groups of peasants but they were united in their opposition to the encroachments of the nobles on their common resources as well as to the oppressive taxation in money, kind, and labor.

The "Edict of Triage" of 1669 in the reign of Louis XIV was particularly oppressive. This law authorized the nobles to select and incorporate into their personal demesnes one-third of the remaining communal lands in their areas of jurisdiction and did nothing to prevent them from taking more. In the succeeding years the aristocracy, as they found it profitable to do so, enclosed the most productive parts of these lands, leaving for the commoners the less productive segments. This worked to the particular detriment of the poorer peasants who depended largely on the access they were permitted to the commons.

This act was similar in some respects to the enclosures in England except for their ultimate result. The English commercial and landlord classes improved the productivity of agriculture, contributing to the base which supported the development of commerce and industry. The French aristocracy were largely consumers, and prodigious consumers at that. They invested little or nothing in the land whose product they appropriated. They taxed even grain from other areas which might cross their toll stations on the way to relieve a famine stricken district. Louis XIV deliberately encouraged the nobles to become parasites living at the court in Versailles, thus losing their former independence and rebelliousness. Triage helped provide the income necessary. The drain on the national income of Louis' interminable wars and the high living aristocrats put the Ancien Regime on the road to bankruptcy. The burdens of national and local taxes and feudal dues were being increased at the same time as the resources and opportunities on which the peasant depended—the common lands, commerce, and domestic industry, and agricultural labor—were diminishing. Fertility levels of 30 to 35 per 1,000 resulting from an increased age of marriage appeared to be extant in the seventeenth century in France as in England. In England, the misery of the seventeenth and early eighteenth centuries were resolved by embarking on a period of economic growth through the Industrial Revolution. In France they were resolved through a political and social revolution, and for a century the patterns of fertility behavior in the two countries diverged, with stable or increasing fertility in England and decreasing fertility in France.

The French Revolution was a complex affair in which the various social and economic interests opposed to the old order vied to establish a system consistent with their particular interests. One of the outcomes was a redistribution of land and change in land tenures over much of France. A high water mark was the Law of June 11, 1792 passed by the Convention. The law provided that communal land appropriated by the aristocracy in the previous two centuries, including those taken under the 1669 Edict of Triage, be restored to the village communes; and that the village communes could by one-third vote of all inhabitants choose to divide this land equitably and proportionately among the families according to the number of family members; this land was to be free from seizure for debt for a period of ten years, giving the peasant time to improve and develop it. The lands confiscated from emigre nobles and clergy were first sold in large parcels, and were thus unavailable to poor peasants. Later, the Convention by its order of November 22, 1793, directed that this land be subdivided to the degree feasible and sold with low long-term payments. During the Thermidorean reaction, the decrees of 1796 and 1797 suspended further land distribution under the land reform laws; however, many of the French peasantry had already become independent smallholders.

The foregoing account was based largely on the work of Kropotkin who, though critical of the compromises effected by the greater power of the rich and enterprising to take advantage of the revolutionary developments, nonetheless concluded that although the revolution had appeared to fail in many respects, it created a free and secure peasantry, unique in history.[31] In England the peasantry was destroyed by enclosure (see Chapter 14).

The occurrence of two series of events in history, the decline of French birth rates and the French Revolution, does not demonstrate in any conclusive fashion that these are connected. France at that time was among the most densely populated countries. As a result of the French Revolution, the peasantry became essentially small proprietors, secure in their tenure for a while at least. The abolition of internal tariffs and tolls, which had inhibited the movement of food, effectively eliminated famines. These had threatened not only life but had resulted in indebtedness which took the efforts of many family members to work off. The feudal dues, requiring large peasant families to produce both surplus and subsistence, were gone. The new laws of inheritance required a division of property among all heirs and the family holding would soon come to naught were there too many heirs. As long as tenure was secure, a couple with no heirs could find security in their later years by renting or crop sharing. The decline in family size, even though mortality rates were still moderately high (20 to 25 deaths per 1,000 population), was at least consistent with these developments. Admittedly, a causal connection between the fertility decline and the change in land tenure has yet to be demonstrated, but the concurrence of these events together with the possibility of population pressure is suggestive.

Land reform did not occur uniformly throughout France; in some of the more conservative areas it hardly occurred at all. Nor can it be assumed that the subsequent history of agrarian relations remained stable or benevolent. The relationship between fertility decline and the changes in patterns of land holding might thus be studied in greater detail. In any case, the French peasantry has demonstrated that modernization, industrialization and urbanization are not requisites for the development of the small family norm among rural folk. (By way of contrast, the French who had migrated to Canada in the sixteenth and seventeenth centuries had very large families. Land and other resources were plentiful while labor was scarce, in contrast to the situation in densely populated France.)

Withdrawal (*coitus interruptus*) was the method thought to be used by French peasants to control births.[32] Wrigley[33] thought that withdrawal was probably employed to control fertility in Colyton, Devon. Withdrawal is a simple method requiring no device or special knowledge but considerable discipline and self-denial on the part of the male. Nonetheless, the French managed to control their fertility so effectively that politicians and others were concerned about the low birth rates for more than a century and a half following the Revolution.

Some Further Observations

People have rarely continued to reproduce so as to increase their numbers for long in the face of worsening economic conditions. During the sixteenth century, starting perhaps earlier, the population of Spain increased as did those of other Mediterranean areas. Whether the growth resulted from a diminution of the force of mortality or an increase in fertility does not appear to be documented. This growth was accompanied by economic expansion and provided the labor and to some extent the market which made such expansion possible. (See discussion of Spain in Chapter 3.)

The period of economic growth ended towards the end of the sixteenth century, and a severe decline set in. Of the 16,000 silk and wool textile looms in Seville only 400 remained by 1620; of the 50 woolen manufactories of Toledo, only 13 remained by 1665. Only a few of these 13 survived the century. Shipbuilding practically ceased, though in the sixteenth century, Spain had the second largest merchant marine. Except for trade with the colonies, Spanish commerce of the seventeenth century was largely in the hands of foreigners. Agriculture, particularly the commercial cultivation of olive, grape, and mulberry, also declined. A report in 1619 of the number of livestock in the bishopric of Salamanca noted a decrease of 60 percent since 1600. Contemporary reporters complained that large tracts of land were going out of production and the level of brigandage and vagabondage was intolerable. Land was available for cultivation but the proprietors and tax collectors, by their exactions, discouraged the peasants from working it.[34]

The decline in the economy was accompanied by and in part due to a decline in population from perhaps as high as ten million in the sixteenth century Spain to perhaps as low as six million by the beginning of the eighteenth century.[35] Many people emigrated, many others did not marry, and mortality may have increased as well. The state of the nation was not helped by depopulation. A council appointed by Philip III in 1618 reported that "The depopulation and want of the people in Spain is at present much greater than was ever seen or heard of before. . . ." The Cortes of Castile stated in 1621 that "There will soon be no peasants to work on the land, no pilots on the sea, none to marry." As early as 1603, Philip III and leading theologians met to devise ways of containing the increase in celibate clerics.[36]

The Black Death of the fourteenth century in Europe which in a shorter time resulted in a comparable loss of population was not associated with an economic decline of such magnitude as was the depopulation of Spain in the seventeenth century, a depopulation which hindered that country in commercial competition with the Atlantic nations. The agricultural economy changed from one orientated to commerce to one oriented to self-sufficiency and subsistence. Braudel[37] referred to this as a reversal and refeudalization of agriculture. Though operating at a lower level in terms of producing wealth, the economy was more self-sufficient and was probably less subject to the effects of economic fluctuation elsewhere. Relieved of the vicissitudes of a commercial economy which operated ineffectively, population growth resumed in the eighteenth century.

Spain remained largely rural and backward until recent times. Yet fertility declines lagged only a few decades behind those of more advanced European countries. Spanish fertility may have started to decline from very high levels as early as the nineteenth century, quite possibly due to a reduction in marital fertility through the practice of coitus interruptus.[38] From 1900 to 1950, while annual per capita income rose only some 11 percent to a level of $250, birth rates fell from 40 births per 1,000 population to 20 births per

1,000.[39] Only 16 percent of this decline could be attributed to an increase in the age of marriage, the rest being due to a decline in marital fertility. This despite the strong Catholic tradition opposing birth control. Moreover, the pace of decline in birth rates in different regions was not associated with urbanization, literacy levels, proportion of the labor force in agriculture, or other factors which characterized the demographic transition in western Europe. Leasure, on whose study of Spanish fertility of this period the above description is based, did discern a pattern. Fertility appeared to be similar in provinces located in the same cultural linguistic region, though the levels of literacy and occupational structure of these provinces were different. However, though provinces within ethnic regions may have had differing economic bases (agriculture, mining, manufacture, etc.), each ethnic region may have had a common socio-economic history which was reflected in fertility. As noted earlier, Demeny found that in 19th century Austro-Hungary, the same ethnic groups located in different areas had different fertility patterns. He postulated the possibility of economic factors being involved.

Thirty years ago, Hugh Seton-Watson[40] wrote that overpopulation was the fundamental problem of the eastern European peasantry. The problems of eastern European countries of that time seemed to resemble those of the less developed nations today, predominately peasant, underfed, underemployed, and overpopulated. Eighty percent of Bulgaria's population and 78 percent of Romania's in 1918 were reported to have been peasants, predominantly smallholders. Rosenstein-Rodan estimated that up to 25 percent of the agrarian population of eastern and southeastern Europe was redundant.[41] Underemployment, even if hidden and not characterized by outright unemployment, appeared to be a permanent feature. Seton-Watson reported that prior to World War II in Romania, 62 percent of the manpower employed on holdings of less than three hectares, more than half the total number of holdings, was estimated to be wasted; in Poland at least one-third the available manpower was wasted, and so on. Moreover, the outlook for a rapid decline in birth rates was dim. For Romania of 1937, more than 46 percent of the total population and more than 48 percent of the peasant population were estimated as less than 20 years old. This presaged considerable momentum of population growth unless there was a sharp decline in fertility. Migration (as well as industrialization) was seen by observers as one of the principal outlets for excess population, and that channel had been effectively closed by changes in United States immigration policy.

(For all the hunger and misery in eastern Europe, great stores of grain were produced which were exported to the west. Rosenstein-Rodan, in his discussion of the process of industrialization in eastern Europe, remarks that one result of industrialization would be the cessation of raw cereal exports from that area and their replacement by exports of processed foods.)

Yet, close observation revealed indigenous efforts to control births. As discussed earlier, Demeny[42] noted that even before the turn of the twentieth century, several Hungarian provinces had evidenced declines of marital fertility despite high infant mortality. An examination of Hungarian vital statistics revealed that the trend became more universal with time.

The relatively precipitous decline in the Hungarian death rate from 33–34 per 1,000 in the decade following 1881 to 15 per 1,000 in the decade following 1931, was paralleled by a sharper decline in birth rates, from 45 per 1,000 in the decade following 1881, to 21 per 1,000 in the decade following 1931.

By the 1930s Hungary was the slowest growing of eastern European nations, with a population growth rate of .007 per year compared to .013 for Romania and Yugoslavia. Hungary was also the most urbanized of these countries, but fertility limitation was also characteristic of the peasantry, many of whom were not much affected by modernization. Low fertility was observed in areas inhabited by relatively prosperous peasants but also in more typical areas inhabited by poor peasants. Seton-Watson[43] noted that the findings of the "Village Explorers" (researchers into village life of the 1930s) indicated that the "one child system" was widespread in the country-side. The peasants were reported to have said that they did not want to bring children into the world to live in such poverty as they had to endure. There was no doubt among these observers that fertility control was spreading and economists were concerned about the future of the nation if the trend were to continue. While Hungary was not considered to be quite as overpopulated as the other eastern European countries, its land ownership was the most highly concentrated. In 1935, 73 percent of holdings included only 10 percent of the land, while 0.7 percent included almost half the land. Thus, while the land was not as densely settled as in other eastern European areas, it was nonetheless unavailable to the peasants.

In the early 1920s the Romanian birth rate was estimated to be close to 40 per 1,000. In 1930 the Romanian birth rate was 34.1 per 1,000, though only 21.4 percent of its population resided in urban areas. Urbanization did not proceed rapidly (in 1963 somewhat more than 30 percent of the population was reported to be residing in urban areas), yet the Romanian birth rate had dropped to 29.5 per 1,000 by 1938 and to 24.2 per 1,000 in 1953. The decline in birth rate of Romania is often attributed to the industrialization and urbanization of the country following World War II. It is apparent that the decline started earlier, when Romania was predominantly peasant as are many of the contemporary developing countries. In 1972, 52 percent of the Romanian labor force was still engaged in agriculture.

Population growth rates in early twentieth century Bulgaria were probably close to 2 percent per year with a birth rate exceeding 40 per 1,000 population per year before 1920. From 1924 to 1936, the Bulgarian birth rate declined from 40 per 1,000 to 26 per 1,000; the death rate during this time was moderate, reported as about 16 per 1,000 population in 1930–1931.[44] Thus, even without access to birth control services, the people of eastern Europe were responding to population pressure while students of the situation despaired.

In the post World War II period, fertility declined so markedly in the eastern European nations that declines in population appeared imminent. In 1967, Romania placed severe restrictions on abortions (which had previously been easy to obtain) in order to avoid a population decline, and abortion is being restricted in other eastern European countries as well for similar reasons. The social changes in levels of aspiration occurring in eastern Europe since the war may have accelerated the decline of fertility. In any case, within little more than a generation, what appeared to be a problem of overpopulation turned into a fear of underpopulation.

The socialist countries of eastern Europe were well served by birth control services, at least until recent times. Greece, a non-socialist country with a large rural population of traditional orientation, was not served by government services, and contraceptives were not widely available. But birth rates declined to comparable levels nonetheless, being 16 per 1,000 in 1972, and birth rates in rural areas were not much different from those in urban areas. Valaoras and his colleagues[45] found that condoms, withdrawal, and abortion (illegal) as a backup, were the methods used in Greece. The European experience would indicate that a high level of modernization is not a prerequisite for a decline in fertility.

Notes

1. A. J. Coale, "The Demographic Transition," in Proceedings of the IUSSP (International Union for the Scientific Study of Population), International Population Conference, Liege, Belgium, 1973, pp. 53--71.

2. D. Friedlander, "Demographic Responses and Population Change," *Demography* 6:4 (November 1969), pp. 359--81.

3. P. Demeny, "Early Fertility Decline in Austria-Hungary: A Lesson in Demographic Transition," in D. V. Glass and R. Revelle, eds., *Population and Social Change* (London: Edward Arnold, 1972), pp. 153--72.

4. D. Herlihy, "Population, Plague and Social Change in Rural Pistoia," *Economic History Review* 18 (1965), pp. 225--44.

5. W. Stys, "The Influence of Economic Conditions on the Fertility of Peasant Women," *Population Studies* 11:2 (November 1957), pp. 136--48.

6. J. M. Tanner, "Earlier Maturation in Man," *Scientific American* 218:1 (January 1968), pp. 21--27.

7. Tanner, op. cit.

8. J. Hajnal, "European Marriage Patterns in Perspective," in D. V. Glass and D. E. C. Eversley, eds., *Population in History* (London: Edward Arnold, 1965), pp. 101--43.

9. U. M. Cowgill, "The People of York: 1538--1812," *Scientific American*, 222:1 (January 1970), pp. 104--112.

10. P. E. H. Hair, "Bridal Pregnancy in Earlier Rural England Further Examined," *Population Studies* 24:1 (March 1970), pp. 59--70; also P. Laslett, *The World We Have Lost* (New York: Scribners, 1965), pp. 139--45.

11. Tanner, op. cit.

12. J. D. Chambers, *Population, Economy and Society in Pre-Industrial England* (London: Oxford University Press, 1972), pp. 128--51.

13. S. Sogner, "Aspects of the Demographic Situation in 17 Parishes in Shropshire: 1711--1760," *Population Studies*, 17:2 (November 1963), pp. 126--46; J. D. Chambers, "Population Changes in a Provincial Town, Nottingham: 1700--1800," in Glass and Eversley, eds., in *Population in History* op. cit.

14. K. M. Drake, "Marriage and Population Growth in Norway, 1735--1865," unpublished Ph.D. Thesis, Cambridge, 1964, cited by E. A. Wrigley, *Population and History* (New York: McGraw-Hill, 1969), p. 103; see also Wrigley, op. cit., p. 87.

15. W. Peterson, *The Politics of Population* (New York: Doubleday, 1965), pp. 181--85.

16. Ibid, pp. 183--84.

17. P. Laslett, "Introduction," pp. 16--23, on the stem family; pp. 56--58, on kin, servants and composition of households; "Mean Household Size in England Since the Sixteenth Century," pp. 125--58; M. Anderson, "Household Structure and the Industrial Revolution; Mid-Nineteenth Century Preston in Comparative Perspective," pp. 215--36, in P. Laslett, ed., with the assistance of H. Wall, *Household and Family in Past Time* (Cambridge: Cambridge University Press, 1972).

18. H. S. Habakkuk, "English Population in the Eighteenth Century," *Economic History Review*, 2nd Series, VI (1953), pp. 117--33; K. F. Helleiner, "The Vital Revolution Reconsidered," *Canadian Journal of Economics and Political Science* 23 (1957), pp. 1--9; J. T. Krause, "Some Neglected Factors in the English Industrial Revolution," and "English Population

Movements Between 1700 and 1850," reprinted in M. Drake, ed., *Population in Industrialization* (London: Methuen, 1969), pp. 103--27.

19. Petersen, op. cit., p. 185.

20. Wrigley, op. cit., pp. 137--39.

21. P. Deprez, "The Demographic Development of Flanders in the Eighteenth Century," in Glass and Eversley, *Population in History*, op. cit.

22. Deprez, op. cit.

23. Wrigley, op. cit., p. 140.

24. Wrigley, op. cit., pp. 141--2; E. A. Wrigley, "Family Limitation in Pre-Industrial England," *Economic History Review*, 19 (1966), reprinted in M. Drake, ed., *Population in Industrialization* op. cit., pp. 157--94.

25. C. Bridenbaugh, *Vexed and Troubled Englishmen: 1590-1642* (New York: Oxford University Press, 1968), p. 202.

26. Ibid. pp. 130, 206.

27. Y. Yasuba, "Birth Rates of the White Population of the U.S., 1800--1860," *Studies in Historical and Political Science*, Johns Hopkins University Series LXXIX, No. 2 (1961).

28. L. Henry and G. Levy, "Ducs et Pairs sous l'Ancien Regime: Characteristiques Demographiques d'une caste," *Population* 15 (1960), pp. 807–30, cited in J. Sutter, "The Effect of Birth Limitation on Genetic Composition of Populations," in S. Behrman, L. Corsa, and R. Freedman, eds., *Fertility and Family Planning: A World View* (Ann Arbor: University of Michigan Press, 1969).

29. E. Gautier and L. Henry, *La Population de Crulai, Paroisse Normande, Etude historique* (Paris: Presses Universitaires de France, Institut National d'Etudes Démographique, 1958) cited in Sutter, op. cit.; also cited by Hajnal, op. cit.; J. Ganiage, *Trois Villages de l'Ile de France, Etude démographique* (Paris: P.U.F., I.N.E.D., 1963) cited by Sutter, op. cit.; P. Girard, "Apercus de la démographie de Sotteville—les-Rouen vers la fin du XVIIIeme Siècle," *Population* 14 (1959): 485–508; E. Deniel and L. Henry, "La population d'un village du Nord de La France, Sainghin en—Melantois de 1665--1851," *Population* 20:4 (1965), pp. 563--602; P. Valmary, *Familles paysannes au XVIIIeme siècle en Bas-Quercy, Etude démographique* (Paris, P.U.F., I.N.E.D., 1965). Cited in Wrigley, *Population and History*, op. cit. Note: P.U.F. is Presses Universitaires de France; I.N.E.D. is Institut National d'Etudes Démographique.

30. E. Van der Walle, "Marriage and Marital Fertility," in D. V. Glass and R. Revelle, eds., *Population and Social Change*, op. cit., pp. 137--51.

31. P. Kropotkin, *The Great French Revolution, 1789--1793*, 2 vols., translated from the French by N. F. Dryhurst (London: Wm. Heinemann, 1909) Vanguard Press printing, 1927, vol. 2, chs. 48--51.

32. H. Bergues et al., *La prevention des naissances dans la famille. Ses origines dans les temps moderns*, (Paris, P.U.F., I.N.E.D., 1969) cited in Wrigley, *Population in History*, op. cit.

33. E. A. Wrigley, "Family Limitation in Pre-Industrial England," op. cit., pp. 82--109.

34. R. Ergang, *Europe From the Renaissance to Waterloo* (New York: D. C. Heath, 1939), pp. 275--80.

35. See J. A. Vandellos, "La Evolución Demográfica de España," *Bulletin d l'Institut internationale de statistique*, (Netherlands) 27, No. 2 (1934), pp. 180--90 cited in *Determinants and Consequences of Population Trends* (New York: United Nations, 1953), p. 19; see also R. Ergang, op. cit., pp. 275--80 .

36. Ergang, op. cit., pp. 277--78.

37. F. Braudel, *The Mediterranean and the Mediterranean World in the Age of Philip II* (Eng. trans, New York: Harper and Row, 1972), pp. 593--4.

38. M. Livi-Bacci, "Fertility and Population Growth in Spain in the 18th and 19th Centuries," *Daedalus* (Spring 1968), pp. 523--35; also "Fertility and Nuptiality in Spain from the Late 18th to the Early 20th Century, Part 2," *Population Studies* 22:2 (1968), pp. 211--34.

39. S. W. Leasure, "Factors Involved in the Decline of Fertility in Spain, 1900--1950," *Population Studies* 16:3 (March 1963), pp. 271--85.

40. Hugh Seton-Watson, *Eastern Europe Between the Wars, 1918--1945*, 3rd ed. (New York: Harper & Row, 1962), p. 97 (originally published, Cambridge: Cambridge University Press, 1941).

41. P. N. Rosenstein-Rodan, "Problems of Industrialization of Eastern and South-Eastern Europe," *The Economic Journal* (June--September 1943). Reprinted in A. N. Agarwala and S.

P. Singh , eds., *The Economics of Underdevelopment* (Bombay: Oxford University Press, 1958), pp. 245--55.

42. Demeny, op. cit., pp. 154--72.

43. Seton-Watson, op. cit., p. 108.

44. United Nations, *The Determinants and Consequences of Population Trends*, (ST/SOA/ Series A. Population Studies No. 17), pp. 61, 72.

45. V. G. Valaoras, A. Polychronopoulou and D. Trichopoulos, "Greece: Post War Abortion Experience," *Studies in Family Planning* 46 (October 1969), pp. 10--16.

10

Fertility Declines in Contemporary Non-Industrial Nations

Introduction and General Assessment

In 1970 almost three-quarters of the world's population lived in economically less developed countries. The populations of these countries have been growing at rates of 2 to 3 percent per year and more. While for most developing countries population growth of more than one percent a year dates back little more than one or two generations, some countries—Egypt and Indonesia, for example—experienced considerable growth even in the nineteenth century. The high growth rates were largely a result of declines in mortality in the face of very high fertility, considerably higher than prevailed in the west before it entered the demographic transition. The decline in mortality accelerated after World War II giving rise to the unprecendented high population growth rates experienced by third world countries this past quarter century. The future size of the world's population will depend on the course of events in the developing nations where the overwhelming majority of people live.

To those who view population growth with alarm, the traditional patterns of high fertility appear to be yielding slowly at best. But examined in the context of historical experience, fertility rates in many developing areas appear to be falling very rapidly at a much faster rate than that experienced by western Europe during the demographic transition. There are reasons to believe that those countries not now evidencing rapid fertility declines will in time do so as conditions give rise to the need.

Excluding China where radical social changes have occurred about which we know little, the third world countries whose birth rates declined earliest and most rapidly generally have been islands, city-states, or densely populated countries with circumscribed areas and few opportunities for emigration. The third world countries whose birth rates were less than 30 per 1,000 population in 1975 were Fiji, Trinidad and Tobago, Barbados, Cuba, Taiwan, Hong Kong, Sri Lanka, Singapore, Puerto Rico, Mauritius, Reunion, Costa Rica, South Korea, and Chile. The birth rates of Jamaica, Panama, and possibly Colombia were just a few tenths more than 30 per 1,000. The decline in birth rates was often rapid; in Singapore from over 40 per 1,000 to less than 18 per 1,000 in less than two decades; in Mauritius from over 40 per 1,000 to 25 per 1,000 in twelve years; in Costa Rica from 48 per 1,000 to 28 per 1,000 in fourteen years. All these countries have relatively low death rates. While changes in age of marriage played some part in the reduction of fertility, the increasing use of contraception and the consequent decline of marital fertility was the most important factor involved. Often the decline in birth rates occurred in the context of an increasing proportion of women being in the reproductive ages due to a formerly high fertility and rapidly decreasing mortality.

In many of these countries and others, declines in fertility over a decade were equivalent to those which occurred in western Europe and the United States over a period of a century or more, and over a half century in some eastern European countries. The times were, of course, different; mortality levels are much lower today than formerly, and the societies are differently structured with birth control methods easier to obtain and use.

A significant feature of recent declines in birth rates is the relative rapidity of declines once they start. In eastern Europe, fertility, starting at much higher levels than those of the west before the demographic transition, declined more rapidly than in the west once birth rates began to fall. The same is true of developing countries in which birth rates begin to fall. This is supported by a compilation made by Kirk more than a decade ago of the time it took various countries to reach a birth rate of 20 per 1,000, once it had attained a birth rate of 35 per 1,000.[1] A national birth rate of 35 or less per 1,000 is likely to indicate that people are attempting to control their fertility unless there is another reason (inordinate sterility from venereal disease, for example) for this intermediate level of fertility. A country with a birth rate of less than 35 per 1,000 population before 1830 took 131 years to reach a birth rate of 20 per 1,000; for each succeeding period since 1830, a smaller and smaller number of years were required for a nation to go from a birth rate of 35 per 1,000 population to one of 20 per 1,000. Countries which had attained a birth rate of 35 or less per 1,000 between 1921 and 1950 required only 34 years on the average to reach a birth rate of 20 per 1,000. Kirk estimated that those countries which attained a birth rate of 35 or less since 1951 would require only 21 years, on the average, to reach a rate of 20 per 1,000. He emphasized the spread of modernization (increasing income per head, energy consumption, non-agricultural economic activities, female literacy, newspaper circulation, etc.) as an important factor in the more rapid adoption of birth control. These developments are occurring more rapidly today than they did a century ago.

The experience of fertility declines in pre-industrial Europe should alert us that external modernization is not necessarily the only force behind the decline of fertility in developing countries. The geographically circumscribed countries listed as among the first to reduce their fertility vary considerably in per capita income and types of prevailing economies though, in general, their populations are fairly literate and may be characterized as more modern than other developing countries. However, the same could be said of some countries whose birth rates were not falling so rapidly, such as Mexico, Surinam, and others. The fact that most of the countries listed are islands or relatively small circumscribed areas and are densely populated would indicate that population pressure is part of the force motivating fertility control.

Taiwan, Korea, and Mauritius are not only among the more densely populated but are also among the most intensively cultivated countries. (In the case of Sri Lanka, where fertility rates have been declining more slowly than in the other countries cited, a large part of the island, formerly less habitable because of malaria, was opened to internal colonization after World War II by malaria control programs.) While family planning programs may have helped many women to control their fertility, fertility began to decline markedly in these countries before the programs gained momentum. Many patrons of such programs would have eventually found ways to limit their fertility without these programs though possibly not as effectively or rapidly.

Emigration opportunities are limited for the peoples of the developing countries today. As population pressure increases, and no other acceptable alternative is available, birth rates, as will be shown, may be expected to decrease. Population pressure is not uniformly perceived. The island of Java in Indonesia includes some of the most densely populated agricultural regions in the world, more than 5,000 people per square mile in some areas. The island was considered to be heavily overpopulated by a Dutch colonial administrator more than a century and a half ago when the population was a fraction of what it is today.[2] Nearby Bali is another densely populated agricultural island. The outer islands of Indonesia are sparsely populated and suitable for colonization. Despite the encouragement of the Dutch and, more recently, the Indonesian governments, the people of Java have been loathe to emigrate from their island. In the past they preferred to stay, intensify their agricultural practices, and hold fast to their cultural, familial and social ties. More recently, they migrated no farther than Djakarta, which has been growing very rapidly, and to other cities on the island. Now recent reports indicate that the high Javanese and Balinese fertility rates have started to move rapidly downwards. (See p. 207.)

Bangladesh remains one of the few very densely populated areas which has not shown signs of a move towards lowered fertility and this despite long standing and extensive efforts to promote family planning services. Sub-Saharan African nations, mostly sparsely populated, have not in general shown signs of a decline in fertility. Egypt and Tunisia, both heavily populated relative to their economic base have been experiencing a recently accelerated decline in fertility.

In addition to modernization and population pressure (that is, difficulty in accomodating increasing numbers), a third group of factors should be considered. These revolve around the relation between economic equity and security to fertility; presumably the greater the economic equity and security, the less the need for children to help the family in the economic struggle.

Equity—equality in economic power, in access to resources, and in distribution of incomes—assures that the benefits of economic and income growth are more widely distributed and limits the possibility of invidious aspirations. In view of the fact that the levels of inequality are relatively high everywhere, a finding that a country shows relative income equality compared with other countries may not indicate very much. Nonetheless, some researchers have reported a relationship between declines in fertility and the degree of equality in the distribution of national income. Moreover two of the low fertility countries, South Korea and Taiwan have both experienced apparently successful land reform movements. Although the research has not been very extensive nor the concept of equity well defined, the notion that economic equity would facilitate a decline in fertility appears to be plausible and worth consideration.[3]

Several problems are posed by research on equality and fertility beyond the basic one of defining equality and its measurement. The countries in the non-socialist world which show greater equality of income distribution are also densely populated, relatively modernized, and economically developed, with development pervading all sectors of the economy. Taiwan and South Korea, with successful land reform programs and industrialization, are among the examples cited by equality researchers. Countries with unequal income distribution—The Philippines, Mexico, Brazil, India, and Thailand, often cited as examples—are often larger, less densely populated, and characterized by economic development which is limited to specific areas and economic sectors with much of the economy and large areas of the country still operating with little cash and in the traditional manner. Thus, it is difficult to separate out the effects of equality from those of density and levels of development. Moreover, while equality may facilitate a decline in fertility, it is not a necessary cause or condition of a decline in fertility.

In Brazil, Thailand, and India, birth rates are beginning to decline. In Panama, where the poorest 40 percent of the population received a much smaller share of the total income in 1969 than 1959, fertility declined rapidly during that period and after. Colombia, whose income distribution is among the most unequal in the world, although it may be slowly improving, also has experienced rapid fertility declines, as noted by Potter et al.[4]

Potter and his colleagues related the drop in Colombian fertility to the increasing pace of modernization, levels of education, and changes in the types of occupations engaged in by Colombians. Based on their analyses of contraceptive practice in Colombia, they dismiss the effects of equality and the claims of A.I.D. population division officers that the introduction of family planning services was important in effecting the decline in Colombian fertility. Other analysts have argued that family planning service programs have been responsible for about one-fourth of the fertility decline of around 12 to 13 percent between 1969 and 1973.[5]

The latter conclusion was based on the association between woman years protection against pregnancy based on the amount of contraceptive services provided by family planning programs in various areas and fertility changes. Obviously, if fertility is controlled some method must be involved and programs may be convenient sources of that control method. Were there no family planning program in operation, it is not unlikely that other sources of birth control would have been found and used. The fertility of the different regions of Colombia varied with their levels of education, urbanization, and occupational characteristics. (Teachman and his associates did not discern much of a relationship between the levels of urbanization and education, and changes in fertility; had they tried to relate changes in fertility to *changes* in urbanization and educational levels, as did Potter and his associates, they might have come to different conclusions.)

The issue of the impact of family planning programs on fertility is an important one. Whatever else may be moving people to control their fertility these days, there have also been tremendous efforts by large foundations and by governments to promote birth control and provide the required services. People all over the world have been subjected to propaganda and information as they never have been before. The effects are the subject of a later chapter.

Many of the developing countries with strong fertility declines had been subjected to some combination of the forces of modernization, increased economic equality, and population pressure. Given the character of political and economic systems, the degree of economc equality and security is likely to be limited, and in some instances extremely limited. There are also considerable forces—social, economic, and environmental—which may limit the pace of economic growth and modernization. The fertility experience of Europe indicates that pre-industrial socieites can find ways to control fertility in response to population pressure nonetheless.

The Case of India

Many studies of fertility behavior in less developed countries showed few consistent indications of those differentials in fertility which characterized the demographic transition in western countries such as England, the Netherlands, Sweden and the United States. The earlier decline in fertility among the upper classes and urban residents of the western countries presaged a more general decline as modernization and associated values diffused through the society. Similar patterns were sought in the study of differential fertility in developing countries, including India.[6] Discerning little or no general declines in fertility nor consistent differentials in the fertility behavior of different classes, except among the small highly educated Europeanized groups, many analysts concluded in the 1950s and early 1960s that the fertility behavior of pre-industrial peoples is relatively intractable and determined by traditional values and practices. The small differences discerned between groups, often inconsistent from one study to another, were attributed to varying cultural norms rather than to deliberate control of fertility. Such norms may be institutionalized in traditional age of marriage, proscription of widow remarriage, sexual taboos, and other customs affecting fertility. In 1951, Davis wrote that: "It [Indian fertility] is controlled to a considerable degree by indirect institutional and nondeliberate customs such as the taboos on widow remarriage. The presence of such institutional controls does not suggest that fertility will decline soon in India and Pakistan."[7] Robinson argued that the small differences sometimes discerned in urban-rural fertility in India and other third world countries before 1960 was often due to unreported higher urban infant mortality and the failure to account for this in the measurement and reporting of fertility.[8] (Since then, mortality in urban areas has decreased markedly, and in many less developed countries urban mortality is lower than rural mortality; the same may be said of urban fertility.)

Analysts often held out little hope for a fertility decline in the less developed countries unless the social and economic structure and associated value systems were modernized.[9] Davis, in a classic paper, stated that populations which restrain their growth in response to decreased mortality are those with rising incomes.[10] Control of fertility is exercised by families to conserve their relative standing in an increasingly prosperous society, and to maintain the benefits of economic development. He doubted that people control their fertility because of poverty except in unusual circumstances. Since the peoples of the less developed countries are poor and have limited capacity for economic growth, the outlook appeared dim, particularly as larger and larger populations continued to press on resources.

Such conclusions may be premature. For many of the less developed countries, experience with high population growth rates is relatively recent. Such categories or variables as rural-urban residence, occupation, education, economy, and social class, used in analyzing the demographic transition in industrializing nations may not be suitable for examining the fertility of pre-industrial peoples unless they have experienced significant modernization. The developing countries today are faced with a different set of circumstances than were the industrializing western societies in their transition to the contemporary state. There is no reason to expect that the transition of the developing nations will follow the same timetable or pattern to reach low fertility levels.

It may be futile in the context of India, for instance, to seek the type of fertility diferentials found in the west. Indian society is largely rural and traditional; 80 percent of the population resides in villages, and many of the town dwellers, of rural origin, derive their lifestyle and values from these origins and expect to return to their native villages.

There are, however, several patterns in Indian fertility, each of which may be of different significance. Such findings as those reported by Saxena[11] that the Uttar Pradesh village woman over 45 who belonged to the lowest social classes had an average of 8.8 live births compared to 7.6 live births for the highest class category, can be explained without recourse to fertility control. Higher infant mortality among the poorer categories may shorten lactation amenorrhea and decrease the average birth interval so as to permit the birth of an additional child. A difference in the age at which childbearing ceased may partly explain the Khanna Study finding that Jat caste women over 45 years of age who had been continuously married had 7 live births compared to 8.2 live births for the low caste Chamar women. (The relatively small number of women in the Brahmin and commercial classifications had an average of 8.1 live births.)[12] The Jat women had their last child at an average age of 36, the poorer Chamar women at an average age of 38. In a study of urban Brahmin women, it was reported that while the average age of menopause was almost 45.8 years, the mean maternal age at birth of the last child was 33.4 years; other studies of a variety of Indian communities of different types show similar findings.[13] Moreover, a variety of traditional methods of birth control, including primitive abortion techniques, are known but the degree to which they are practiced is unknown.[14]

The virtual cessation of childbearing by relatively young women would indicate that birth control is being practiced to some degree; and while poorer women may give birth to more children than do those who are better off, they are likely to end up with fewer surviving children because of the higher mortality among them. But even among poorer women, reproduction tends to end long before the capacity to produce children ends.

While observers of Indian fertility have spent much time and energy in examining the differences between social classes and the like, they have noted but paid little attention to the wide differences in fertility between regions; for example, the average of 8 children born to women of the northern regions in the studies noted above, and the fewer than 5 children born to the women of the south (as in rural Mysore).[15] S. P. Jain, a dean among Indian demographers, noted the wide variation in fertility between states and attributed these to differences in social cultural tradition.[16] The different regions of this large and geographically diverse country differ more in resource and demographic characteristics and consequent population pressure in the context of a subsistence economy than they do in social cultural ways. Whether these economic differences may be related to the differences in fertility is a question which deserves much more attention.

In most developing nations, the population growth of recent years has been generally accompanied by agricultural and economic growth. In some areas people have had little difficulty increasing production to meet the needs of a growing population whose standard of subsistence has been historically low, while elsewhere—even in the same country—there have been difficulties. The author attempted to ascertain a relationship between the availability of resources and fertility in areas where modernization has had little impact. Rural India of 1961 was the subject for the investigation summarized in the following section.

Fertility Variation and Resources in Rural India

For the decade 1954–1964, the United Nations Food and Agricultural Organization reported that Indian agricultural production kept pace with population increases and that caloric intake might even have improved despite population growth of around 2 percent per year.[17] Per capita food production had not increased markedly but, nonetheless, the condition of most peasants generally improved. Since Independence and perhaps earlier, the easing of land taxes relieved the peasants of much of the exactions by the government and its intermediaries of up to 50 percent of land output. During the 1960s, Indian peasants paid the same land taxes in rupees as they had some forty to fifty years before despite inflation and the increased productivity of the land. As a result, in the 1960s taxes on the land were in effect a small fraction of what they had been when they were used to capitalize trading centers and other colonial ventures.[18] While India was a food-exporting nation before 1921, those exports were savings forced by the British raj to finance the colonial enterprise. During the same period that India was a food-exporting nation, the incidence of famine was high.[19]

Within their own frame of reference, Indian peasant families on the average were not likely to have seen deterioration in their condition since Independence. While food production kept pace with population growth for all India, this was, of course, an average trend. Some areas must have been in a better resource position than others to increase output; other areas must have found that their capacity to increase output was limited. Some peasant groups (landholders) fared well; others (agricultural laborers) fared poorly. The effects of modernization and new technologies on agricultural output in the years preceding 1961 were minor. Using data obtained from the 1961 Indian census, the author investigated whether the rural people of resource-poor districts in India tended to have lower fertilty compared to those in relatively resource-rich districts.

The Indian census of 1961 provides information about the size of population by age, sex and marital status, and rural-urban residence for various geographical subdivisions such as states, districts, and smaller units. It also provides information on acreages cultivated by households, family structure, size and composition of the labor force, and other data. These data permit construction and comparison of direct and indirect measures or indices of the resources available to rural populations, their fertility, their growth, mortality, age at marriage, family and household structure, and a number of other pertinent variables. The comparisons were limited to the rural populations since these were more likely to be what is considered traditional in their behavior and response to resource limitations. Moreover, their principal natural resource, land, was more readily ascertained from the census than the more complex resources involving commerce and manufacture which urban dwellers depend upon.[20]

The principal indicator of resources was the amount of land cultivated per household (including those of agricultural laborers) dependent on cultivation. The productivity of land varies, of course, according to its intrisic qualities and the labor expended on it. While it was not feasible to obtain estimates of district agricultural output, data were available on crop outputs per acre for the 16 states of India in 1960–1961. The output per acre (expressed in rupees) for Kerala, where the average acreage cultivated per rural household was estimated to be 1.4 acres, was six times as large as the output per acre in Rajasthan where the average acreage cultivated per rural household was around 15.7 acres. For all India, the average productivity of land per acre varies inversely with the amount of acreage cultivated per household,[21] but the output per household varied directly with the acreage.[22] Thus, areas with larger acreages per household were at an advantage, though the areas with small acreages tended to compensate by more intensive cultivation, and the areas of greater intensity of settlement could be expected to be more fertile. In some of the rural areas with small acreages, the rural population also had access to other resources such as employments in modern sector occupations—manufacturing, transportation, etc.—and in primary occupations other than cultivation, such as plantations, lumbering, mining, and fishing. Some of these employments may be considered as signs of modernization. In any case, their net effect in India, 1961, appeared to be that of making high fertility possible in areas with limited land resources.

Analyses were performed to explore the relationships among fertility (as indicated by child-woman ratios), household composition, marital age, sex ratio, and resources, including the acreage cultivated per household in rural areas and the proportion of workers involved in presumably modern employments. (The net effect of differences in child mortality on the child-woman ratios were taken into consideration in further analyses but these do not affect the findings.)

The findings showed that there was a wide range of fertility between the rural populations of the districts of India. Although the indices of fertility used in the study were child-women ratios, their range reflected birth rates from around 30 births per 1,000 population to 55-60 per 1,000 population. Much of the variation observed was strongly related to the resources, principally cultivated land; the greater the resource base, the higher the fertility. In many of the districts where the holdings of rural families were small but fertility remained high, the people had access to employment in modern sector enterprises, which in effect gave them additional resources. Moreover, much of the association between indices of fertility and resources was independent of institutional factors such as age of marriage, widow-hood, and family structure, though in some few districts one or another of these factors appeared important. The child-women ratios were not much related to an index of child mortality. If anything, the greater the index of child mortality, the greater the fertility. Though this relationship was weak, it is consistent with the notion that as infant and child mortality decrease, so does fertility. Also, the apparent mortality levels were not much related to the size of the average holding. Finally, these differences in fertility were not related to such indices of modernization as the proportion of literates or educated or the degree of urbanization of the district, perhaps because modernization had not cut deeply into the population.

That age at marriage made little difference in fertility within the Indian context is not surprising. Most Indian women married young, around 15 to 16 years of age on the average. Only 12 percent of the districts showed a mean female age at marriage of 18 years or over, and many of these showed rather high fertility. In addition to the possibility of adolescent sub-fercundity depressing the fertility of youthful couples, marriage in India does not necessarily signify the beginning of a conjugal relationship. The latter begins after a second ceremony when the parents decide that the couple is ready for sexual union and the begetting of children. Even a consummated marriage before 18 years of age may have little effect on fertility, considering adolescent sub-fecundity, and the customary long visits of younger married women to their parents who generally reside in a village other than the one into which their daughter's marriage is arranged. Thus, many of the districts in which women married young did not show an increased fertility. In one of the lower fertility districts (that of Lahaul and Spiti) the average female age of marriage was around 24 years. This was an isolated and poor mountain area with little in the way of economic resources and such an advanced age of marriage was unique.

In another low fertility district (Ratnagiri), many husbands spent long periods of time away from their wives earning a living in cities and returning to their villages only occasionally.[23] But urban opportunities are limited, and the rural population is so much larger than the urban population, that only in a few villages do an appreciable portion of men earn their livelihoods in the cities. While some proportion of the variation between districts may be explained by delay in starting a conjugal relationship or lack of opportunity for sexual union within the conjugal relationship, much of the variation cannot be so explained.

In view of some current discussions about the depressing effect of poor nutrition on fertility, there may be a temptation to attribute the low fertility of resource-poor districts to low nutritional levels if the differences in nutritional levels are indeed related to resources. This has not been established, and in any case (as noted in Chapter 7), the relationship between nutrition and fertility is not so apparent except in extreme cases of deprivation. More significant is the fact that in the large number of studies of Indian fertility conducted before 1960, little or no differences in fertility were found between most social and economic classes despite large differences in the nutritional statuses of these classes. In his introduction to an early Indian National Sample Survey report which found higher fertility among the poor than among those better off, Mahalanobis noted, "It is possible that the number of children born (or surviving) is very small in the case of couples who are almost destitute." But the fact established by the survey was that the poorest groups of couples, those with per capita monthly expenditures of less than Rs.10 per month (around $1.20 to $1.50 at that time) had the highest fertility.[24]

Marital fertility in India during the 1960s was much lower for all age groups than that of non-contracepting European married women during the eighteenth century. General fertility levels in India were high because almost all women were married by age 20. (As noted earlier, towards the end of the pre-industrial period in western Europe, marriage was delayed considerably and a goodly proportion of women never married.) For Indian women aged 20–29, marital fertility has been estimated as being around 300 births per 1,000 women per year; for women aged 30–39 it has been estimated to be around 200 births. For women married before 1780 in several French villages, the annual marital fertility of those aged 20–29 was more than 500 births and for those aged 30–39, more than 400 births per 1,000 women per year.[25] Fertility differences between Indian women and non-contracepting western women of more than 200 years ago may be difficult to explain in terms of differences in institutional practices related to frequency of intercourse, length of lactation, or to differences in nutritional status. The Indian fertility rates are based on all-India data, and there is apparently wide variation in marital fertility between districts. Therefore, the differences in marital fertility of women in many of the low fertility areas of India and the non-contracepting European women must be greater still, while in some areas married Indian women have fertility almost as high as the European women of the past.

The mechanisms underlying the fertility rates among Indian women of low fertility districts are in general not apparent, and such mechanisms would need to be elucidated before the findings noted above could be considered as deliberate efforts to control fertility. Moreover, the relationships are taken at a single point in time, reflecting changes which occurred in the past as well as those which may be occurring in the present. Since adaptation takes place over time, longitudinal studies are needed to fully validate the findings. The possibility that birth control, even of a primitive sort, may have been practiced when custom and lactation were not sufficient to constrain births cannot be excluded.

The 1971 Indian census showed that population had grown less than expected in the previous ten years. This may have been due to the possibility that decreases in mortality were not as large as expected as well as to decreases in birth rates. There is, of course, the possibility of an undercount in the 1971 census. If the undercount was not more than that of 1961, the birth rate in India may have fallen 10 percent or more. Estimating birth rates in countries without accurate population and vital statistics data is hazardous. The U.S. Bureau of the Census estimated India's birth rate to be 37 per 1,000 in 1972.[26] A more recent estimate is a birth rate of 35 per 1,000 in 1974. Since this drop was probably not uniform over the country, the decrease in fertility in some areas may have been dramatic.

Although the author did not anaylze the returns from the 1971 census to see whether the relationship between resources and fertility still held, occasional studies by others, though not directed to this question, are informative. Mukherjee[27] described the results of a survey conducted in 1971–1972, of a large sample of almost 17,000 married men and women in Haryana and Tamil Nadu. In the author's study of the Indian census of 1961, the rural areas of the districts of Haryana, formerly part of Punjab, were relatively resource rich, with comparatively large holdings per household, while those of Tamil Nadu (formerly Madras) were resource poor. This was still true in 1972. The rural Haryana women reported a median monthly household expenditure of 247 rupees while those of Tamil Nadu reported a median monthly household expenditure of 130 rupees. Of the men canvassed in rural Haryana, 62 percent were classified as cultivators, which in the Indian context is understood as being one who works his or her own land or rented land. Only 37 percent of the rural men canvassed in Tamil Nadu were so classified; many of the others were presumably employed as agricultural laborers or in other low paid employment. (The differences between reported monthly expenditures of urban Haryana and Tamil Nadu households were not so marked.) Though the median age at marriage for the rural women of Haryana was 12.6 years compared to 16.5 years for those of Tamil Nadu, the median age at consummation of the marriage was reported as being 16.4 and 16.6 years respectively. Yet the rural married women of Haryana (the more prosperous state) reported a mean number of pregnancies of 5.6 while those of Tamil Nadu reported a mean number of 3.5 pregnancies. Many of the women in these samples had not completed childbearing; the likelihood is that there may be greater differences in the size of completed families.

The relationship between higher household expenditures and higher fertility is not, of course, evidence of cause and effect, but it is consistent with the findings of the author's study based on the 1961 census. The higher level of literacy in Tamil Nadu may be proposed as a reason for lower fertility. Within Tamil Nadu the fact that the urban population is much more literate than the rural is not followed by a differential in reported urban-rural fertility.

Indeed, in less literate Haryana (with higher fertility), respondents were reported to be more aware and more likely to be users of birth control methods than were the respondents in Tamil Nadu. The results of Mukherjee's survey are to be taken with reservations. For although a smaller proportion of respondents in Tamil Nadu report being protected by sterilization, official family planning program statistics would indicate that a much greater proportion of eligible couples in Tamil Nadu are protected by sterilization than are so protected in Haryana. Whether greater reliance can be placed on the respondents or on the official statistics is difficult to evaluate.

The situation in Kerala, poor and most densely populated, but most literate and in many other respects most advanced of the Indian states in terms of health and other social indicators, will be discussed in a later chapter.

Family Structure and Fertility

As noted earlier (see Chapter 2), conflicting findings about the effect of family structure (such as joint family or nuclear family) on fertility have been presented by various researchers. The author's study provides some indication that family structure may not be as important in the determination of fertility as the economic context in which it occurs.

The relationship between the prevalence of joint family arrangements in the districts and district fertility was also examined, though not fully reported in the reference article. Two types of joint household arrangements were distinguished. The first is referred to as "lineal joint family" and was defined as the ratio of the number of married sons reported as residing with the head of the household to the number of households.

The second type is referred to as "collateral joint family" and was defined as the ratio of the number of married male relatives (other than sons) residing with heads of households to the number of households. They may include married brothers sharing a household in which one is listed as head, or other combinations. There were, on the average, 24.4 married sons and 14.4 married male collateral relatives living with household heads per 100 households.

The relative number of couples living in lineal joint family arrangements showed a small positive correlation with the general fertility and a slightly larger correlation with the number of cultivated acres per household. When the number of cultivated acres was controlled, the small positive correlation between lineal joint family and fertility vanished. (In fact, it became negative but negligible.) The mean age at marriage for males was very highly correlated (negatively) with the prevalence of lineal joint households ($r = -.84$). The lower the age at marriage, the greater the tendency to live with parents. Males would hardly be in a position to marry as early as they do in some areas of India, were it not that the married couple could live with the husband's parents at least for a few years. Thus the lineal joint family is a necessary arrangement, at least temporarily, when marriage is undertaken at a relatively young age. Moreover, it may even help start family units on the way to independence; the young family unit, when it leaves the joint household, is likely to have a child or two old enough to help out.

Taken over all India, there was no correlation between the prevalence of collateral joint family living arrangements and general fertility, nor was there a correlation with size of cultivated holding. This was due to the statistical cancelling effects of opposite trends in the northern region and in the southern region, as designated by the census. In the northern zone, the districts with increased prevalence of collateral joint family arrangements tended to be those with decreased size of landholdings,[28] and in this area the increased prevalence of collateral joint families was associated with decreased general fertility.[29] In the Southern zone, the prevalence of collateral joint family arrangements was associated with increased size of landholdings,[30] and with increased general fertility.[31]

The above analyses are based on so called "ecological correlations." These tell something about the districts in which the subject family structures occur, but they do not tell anything about the families themselves. However, the findings suggest the impact of such family arrangements on the general fertility are more a function of the economic circumstances in which they are found than of the intrinsic family structure itself.

Female Labor Force Participation and Fertility in Pre-Industrial Society

The hazards of examining behavior elsewhere from the vantage point of western society is illustrated by the relation between the employment of women and fertility. In western societies employed women have fewer children than those who stay home, at least in the middle classes. This is due to the proclivity of infecund women to enter the labor force as well as the control of fertility by women who work.[32] But in peasant and traditional societies where female labor force participation is in agriculture or cottage industry, employed women show little or no difference in fertility compared to women not employed. This is supported by studies performed in Puerto Rico and rural Japan, Turkey, India, and elsewhere. Stycos and Weller proposed that an important consideration of the effect of female labor force participation on fertility relates to whether the type and place of work is compatible with having and rearing children.[33]

A paper by Dr. Helen Ware[34] of the Australian National University in Canberra reported some pertinent findings. In Western Nigeria, most adult women are in the labor force as cultivators, traders, and artisans. Fertility is very high and only a minority of women want fewer than five children. Ware noted that working Nigerian women are fairly independent and are frequently in control of the incomes they earn. Yet the non-working wives often have the fewest children, and the working wives not only have many but want them. She concluded that models of fertility behavior developed in the context of western industrialized societies are inappropriate for an understanding of fertility in the context of African societies. Fertility rates among the West African nations, at this writing, are among the highest in the world, estimated to be around 55 births per 1,000 per year in many areas and studies in addition to Ware's indicate that many African people aspire to large families.[35] Perhaps this is due in part to the high infant mortality levels, though these are not as high as formerly, when there was little population growth in Africa. A variety of reasons may be adduced to explain the absence of a relationship between female work force participation and fertility in "traditional" societies. Work does not conflict with family life; the assistance of neighbors and relatives ease the problem of child care, a frequent problem in the west. Children appear to be highly valued. Yet if they were a heavy burden and returned little in economic gain to their parents, they would probably lose much of their intrinsic value.

In West Africa, women frequently have an independent economic role in sustaining the household, forming associations to protect their interests and in some areas dominating markets and retail trade.[36] In India, women have a subordinate role in the peasant economy at least in the formal sense, the cultural ideal being that women remain in the home in purdah. But economic circumstances may dictate otherwise. The relationship between womens' participation in the agricultural labor force and fertility in these circumstances was part of the author's study of Indian fertility cited earlier. In this study, female participation in the agricultural labor force was measured by the ratio of the proportion of females in the agricultural work force to that of males. In the rural areas of India, the rate of female agricultural labor force participation in 1961 was 59 percent that of males; among the districts the ratio ranged from 20 percent to a proportion larger than that of males. Women worked largely as agricultural laborers, the distinction being made in the census between agricultural laborers and cultivators. A presumption in the study was that women in this context work not to enhance their sense of status or achieve and maintain their independence but because of necessity. Where land is poor, or where the agricultural work seasons are so short that men cannot provide all of the labor required, increased labor is needed to provide subsistence. Women must then join the agricultural work force at least during peak season.

This formulation is supported by the following findings. Among the districts there was a small negative correlation[37] between the female-male literacy ratios and the female-male agricultural labor force participation ratio, indicating that if anything, in districts where females were less literate than males, they tended to show a relatively higher participation rate in agricultural work. Among the states, the correlation between output per acre and the female-male agricultural labor force participation ratio was negative.[38] The correlation indicated that females participated in the agricultural labor force to a greater extent in the less productive regions, and that their participation did not increase productivity levels over the regions where they were not employed. There was only a small positive relationship between the average size of holding in the district and the female-male agricultural labor participation ratio.[39]

In district rural areas where higher proportions of females were employed in agriculture, fertility tended to be lower.[40] This does not necessarily mean that the women who worked had lesser fertility, though this may indeed have been the case. The data showed only that the districts in which relatively greater proportions of rural women worked in agriculture showed lesser fertility, however this came about. Since female participation in the agricultural work force occurs to a greater degree in areas of less productive land, the findings support the notion that general fertility adapts to the pressure on resources.

In different social contexts, women work for different reasons and thus their fertility behavior is subject to different constraints of costs and benefits. Fertility responds not to an abstract variable but to what that variable represents in the context of the situation in which it occurs.

The Bias of Western Observers

The perceptions of some observers of the effects of population growth and fertility behavior are distorted by their class and ethnocentric bias. Patterns of fertility behavior in some societies appear irrational from the perspective of another society. However, closer examination may reveal that this behavior is appropriate under the conditions in which the observed population lives.

Mahmoud Mamdani critically examined one of the larger controlled field studies of family planning in India.[41] The purposes of the field study were to describe the demographic behavior (fertility, mortality, migration, etc.) of Punjabi villagers and to assess the effects of family planning education and services on such behavior. The demographic behavior of these test villages over a period of ten years was compared with a number of comparable control villages which did not receive family planning education services. Mamdani's review concluded that the class bias of the researchers distorted their perceptions of the villagers' needs and the basis of their fertility motivations and therefore the program failed. Perhaps a more apt description of the bias would be "ethnocentric." The principal study directors were highly trained professionals with experience in public health programming and research. The field staff was supervised by well trained Indians, native to the region in which the study was conducted and presumably well versed in the indigenous culture. Still they were of a different class and culture.

The results of the project were disappointing. The advantages of family planning were explained to and discussed with the villagers. The advantages presented included the possibility of better education for children if there were fewer of them, larger inheritances, less fractionation of land, better health, relief from the stresses of overpopulation, and so on. Many villagers appeared to agree and said that they would accept family planning services if such became available. When these services were offered, however, only a small proportion of the people actually accepted contraceptives (only foam tablets were made available) and even among those who accepted contraceptives, only a few actually used them. More than ten years later, in 1968, the birth rates in the test villages which received the services were no different from those of the control villages. If anything, the control villages had slightly lower birth rates. The project staff concluded that the villagers would require considerable education before they would become aware of the consequences of their fertility behavior. The research directors noted, "Westerners have strong feelings about the values of persons and human life not necessarily shared by Punjabi villagers. Some readers may feel that the pressures arising from growing numbers of people were self-evident. The villagers did not always hold that view." Some of the villagers had similarly uncomplimentary views about the foreigners.

In addition to a review of study protocols and findings, and interviews with the project staff both in the United States and India, Mamdani included a visit to one of the test villages. There he interviewed a number of the village residents to ascertain their perceptions of their condition and of the study group. Some villagers thought the study project foolish; others thought that it had an ulterior purpose, such as spying for the government revenue service. By and large, the villagers did not think they had a population problem and could not believe that the project staff believed this either. Therefore, the project must have had other objectives. Nonetheless, many villagers reported that they had expressed agreement and willingness to practice family planning and to cooperate with the project staff though they did not follow through with action. They had expressed agreement with the project staff out of politeness. When Mamdani queried why they had agreed and not voiced their misgivings, one of the villagers responded, "But they were so nice, you know. And they came from distant lands to be with us. Couldn't we even do this much for them. Just take a few tablets? Ah! even the gods would have been angry with us. They wanted no money for the tablets. All they wanted was that we accept the tablets. I lost nothing and probably received their prayers. And they, they must have gotten some promotion." Another answered, "Babuji, someday you'll understand. It is sometimes better to lie. It stops you from hurting people, does you no harm and might even help them."

Few of the villagers were in a position to educate a son even if they had a small family. But a large family, even if poor, could hope to support the education of at least one or two of its members if the others were gainfully employed. While land was scarce and dear, many sons working together and taking advantage of a variety of available employment opportunities in towns and elsewhere could hope to enlarge family earnings. A small family might be hard pressed to do so or to afford the hired labor necessary to operate a larger holding. Through a number of interviews, the manner in which families were benefited by large numbers of children as perceived by the villagers was explored by Mamdani. The villagers were ready to experiment with and try new technologies in agriculture (tube wells, high-yield seeds, etc.), to purchase domestic conveniences (sewing machines, bicycles), to try new jobs in towns, to obtain education for their children; but they saw no benefits in family planning.

Mamdani felt that the researchers approached population control from a middle class perspective appropriate to the context from which they came but inappropriate to the circumstances with which the villagers had to cope. He concluded that only social change would result in circumstances where people would no longer have to rely on large families to assure their welfare. Then the villagers might take to contraception in a conscious attempt to limit their fertility.

But social change or no, and despite the high fertility ethic espoused by villagers to Mamdani, the fertility of both the test villages which received birth control services and the control villages which did not, had declined during the period between the initiation of the study and Mamdani's review. Birth rates were reported to have fallen almost 20 percent, from 38 per 1,000 during 1957–1959 to 31 per 1,000 during 1966–1968. Both the Khanna study staff and Mamdani attributed this to the increase in the age at which marital sexual unions began for village wives, from almost 18 years of age in 1956 to almost 20 years in 1969. Mamdani claimed that the need for labor at home, even female labor, was such that families delayed sending their daughters to the husbands' villages. Nonetheless, this two-year change in the age at marriage was not likely to have been responsible for much of the marked fertility decline. (As noted earlier, in western Europe, birth rates of about 35 per 1,000 were common when women were marrying at about 28, while 20 percent never married at all. In the Punjab, women were still marrying young and practically all women married.) Moreover, from the data presented by the Khanna study it is apparent that the largest part (practically all) of the decline in birth rates between 1957 and 1968 occurred before 1962—before the prosperity of the green revolution—while the increase in age at which brides arrived in husbands' villages for consummation of their marriages began after 1962.

The decline in birth rates probably began much earlier than 1960. Wyon and Gordon reported that in 1959, 28 percent of the study population were children less than ten years old. This is consistent with the proportion of children reported in the 1961 census for rural Ludhiana district (which included the Khanna villages). This is also less than the proportion of children in the population of the Punjab (31 percent) or India (30 percent) in 1961. Furthermore, the Khanna study reported that by 1969, the proportion of children less than ten years old in the villages had declined further to 24 percent from the 28 percent reported for 1959. A decrease of that magnitude in the proportion of children under ten years of age would indicate that birth rates had declined considerably earlier in the decade than did the increase in the age of marital cohabitation.

(The Khanna study, whatever its biases regarding attitudes of villagers, is a rich source of demographic data about birth intervals, effects of lactation, migration, initiation of sexual unions, as well as births and deaths.)

Mamdani, perhaps because of his own bias, failed to consider the possibility that social change or no, even a pre-industrial people may feel a need to limit their fertility if population presses on available resources. And, as Mamdani noted himself, a behavior change may occur before it is reflected in a change in attitudes. While focusing on the attitudes which appeared consistent with a high fertility ethic, he passed over that behavior which was not.

Nonetheless, Mamdani's work, along with too few others, is a welcome contrast to the dominant themes in the literature of population growth and associated policy. This literature is replete with characterizations of peasants as being rigid, fatalistic, suspicious, mean, tradition oriented, irrational, and conservative, in short, maladaptive and generating their own misery. Even when the peasant exhibits beneficence to his fellow, the process is deemed detrimental. Work sharing practices are characterized as hidden unemployment and unproductive, though several economists have presented evidence that the marginal peasant laborer still produces a respectable product. But perhaps the most salient agrument is that western appraisals of "hidden unemployment" are based on parochial middle class notions which ignore cultural differences in the value placed on work, work sharing, and the distribution of its product, a subject which is discussed in more detail later.

If the bias of research is hidden within the technical jargon of scientific works, it is blatantly obvious in polemics. One of Mamdani's many critics contrasts the "parents who, like the English during the Industrial Revolution, breed them [children] for the money they can earn and work them in degrading and menial occupations from 5:00 a.m. to 9:00 p.m." with "those who come thousands of miles from the comforts of the West with the message of responsible parenthood."[42] This without reference, on the one hand, to the terrible conditions attending the Industrial Revolution, the role of the industrialists who were the principal beneficiaries of child labor, the difficulties of families in subsisting on the wages of a single member nor, on the other hand, to the tangible rewards which accrued to many latter day missionaries sponsored by wealthy foundations and a wealthier government.

Some Further Observations

The estimated birth rate for India has declined to 35 per 1,000 population, a drop of 16 percent in the ten years between 1965 and 1975. Such estimates are only approximate since there are few developing nations with good vital registration systems and estimates are extrapolated from survey and census data which are themselves often inadequate. They are, however, the best we have and meaningful when a number of differently arrived at estimates are consistent. Moreover, India is not the only developing country which has experienced a significant decline of fertility in the last ten years, though short of attaining a birth rate below 30 per 1,000. Egypt, Thailand, Turkey, Colombia, Malaysia, The Dominican Republic, Tunisia and a number of countries noted earlier in this chapter have experienced more rapid fertility declines while Brazil, Mexico, El Salvador, and Venezuela, have shown significant though lesser declines in fertility within this decade. Recently the decline in birth rates in Indonesia has accelerated.

In eastern Java and Bali, the birth rate has dropped 17 percent over the five year period 1971–1976. The indications are that the fall in birth rates is gaining momentum. Contrary to what many experts expected, surveys showed that the decline in fertility occurred not among those who were educated or modernized nor in regions which were better off, but in the poorest, most densely populated parts of Indonesia.[43] Birth rates in East Java dropped from an estimated 37 per 1,000 in 1965 to 30 per 1,000 in 1975, and in Bali from 45 per 1,000 to 30 per 1,000 over the same period. Birth rates in West Java were still high (44 per 1,000) though moving downwards slowly.[44] Fertility in the outer islands is also high. Apparently, the people of Indonesia, or at least of East Java and Bali, long considered overpopulated, responded to population pressure without any basic social change and before any apparent population induced holocaust or otherwise induced increase in mortality.

In general, the countries of South and East Asia have been showing the most rapid declines in fertility, followed by those of Latin America. Except for Egypt, Tunisia, Mauritius and Reunion, all heavily populated in their economically productive areas, the countries of Africa, generally sparsely populated, have not shown much sign of a downward trend in fertility. The pattern of decline can be reasonably attributed to either modernization or population pressure or to social reform and change.

There are exceptions, notably Bangladesh, among the most densely populated areas of the world, in which there has been little sign up to 1975 of a significant decline in fertility. This despite intensive and long-term family planning efforts. A decade or two ago, the same could have been noted for East Java and for Kerala in India; both more densely populated than Bangladesh and both now experiencing a rapid reduction of fertility.

As noted in the preceding chapter, the relative timing and rate of declines in the fertility of European countries could not have been predicted by comparing indicators of modernization, urbanization, industrialization, education, and the like, even among countries which served as models for demographic transition theory. In some instances the early stages of industrialization was accompanied by increased fertility, as old controls broke down and increasing urban job opportunities relieved population pressure in the countryside. In some of the currently developing countries the early effects of development on fertility behavior appeared to be consistent with demographic transition theory; in others the effects appeared to be inconsistent.[45] Other factors may intervene, but the direction of fertility is clear in both those societies which modernize and those which do not.

The development of a highly intensive agriculture and a system of indigenous social and economic relations, which in effect made room for almost all, enabled the Javanese to cope very effectively with high density while opportunities to emigrate were ignored. The Javanese preferred not to emigrate from their island to the outer islands where land was open. In time, the limitations of geography and commercialization of agriculture made themselves felt, and Indonesian fertility has begun to fall without any preceding calamity or deterioration. Many analysts, with anthropologists prominently among them, make much of the need to know the local conditions and the local culture in order to understand the demographic behavior of a particular group of people. This argument cannot be disputed in principle and is implicit in many excellent study and program ventures. There is a basic need, however, to develop generalizations to help determine what in a particular culture is salient to the issue at hand and what is peripheral.

Mary Douglas[46] proposed that the source of motivation for fertility control is similar for most peoples. Population control is, according to her, ". . . more often inspired by concern for scarce social resources, for objects giving status and prestige, than by concern for dwindling basic resources." Often the concern with scarce social resources served to protect basic resources. The Tikopian islanders were reported to have controlled their fertility, through contraception, abortion, and infanticide, not to keep a balance with land for the basic subsistence crops (yams and taro) which was plentiful and available for the asking, but with the rarer coconut palms which provided flavoring for foods and important elements for ceremonial feasts. On the other hand, as Douglas also noted, communities that were heavily engaged in political competition with other communities eagerly recruited new members even though their lands are eroding. (This point is based on observations from Africa. How far the competing groups would have accepted the erosion of soils and despoilment of resources were they living in areas of greater population density is another question.) Douglas concluded that if people had access to the objects providing prestige, status and security, in short a higher standard of living, they would be more likely to reduce their fertility.

Few primitive people press against the resources available to sustain them.[47] So it is not surprising that Douglas did not discern resource limitations as a cause of fertility control. Under the pressure of competition, possibly with survival at stake, pre-industrial communities do expand their number, but rarely if ever to the point where they need to expend almost their entire effort in making a living—except under the compulsion of other humans. People are indeed responsive to dwindling basic resources, but resources used to satisfy non-subsistence values tend to become scarce before subsistence resources do. Thus, these other values protect subsistence if they are not associated with destructive behavior like war.

In any locale and time, particular conditions and circumstances, perhaps unique, may facilitate, inhibit, or even reverse the fertility trends usually associated with modernization; and modernization is not a necessary prerequisite for a decline in fertility. That economic development and modernization have resulted in fertility declines are facts of history. But the notion that economic development and modernization are prerequisites for such declines is an outcome of the bias which is prevalent about the workings of the pre-industrial mind and personality, a bias which does not take into consideration the social and physical circumstances with which such peoples must cope. Demographic transition theory may be called into question on many grounds and lately it has been done frequently by persons who are nonetheless troubled by population.[48]

Nonetheless, modernization is eventually accompanied by low fertility though the pace of fertility decline may vary from place to place. In similar fashion, the forces of population pressure which induce lowered fertility in traditional societies may be leavened by other factors but in the end these factors give way to the ultimate determinants. Resources, technology, the manner in which work is organized and its product distributed, and the lifestyles to which people can realistically aspire are the characteristics which matter most in determining levels of fertility. Family and household structure, relations with mothers-in-law, religious attitudes and other characteristics cannot be ignored. They are important considerations in the development of health, welfare, family planning and other services personal and otherwise. Customs and institutions governing marriage, sexual intercourse, nursing and a host of other practices can be directly related to fertility. Indeed, the expression of these institutions and customs can form a sequence of acts and conditions resulting in the birth of babies.[49] But customs and institutions and attitudes change, and even without change there is considerable latitude within them for fertility control. A great variety of cultures and peoples know of some form of contraception or abortion, and infanticide is not rare either (see Chapter 11).

The ultimate determinant of fertility change is not family structure, religion, or mothers-in-law, but socio-economic circumstances. Culture may influence but in the end conforms to economic imperatives and human needs. A significant deterrent to lower rates of population growth are those conflicts and competitions which constrain families and communities to maintain large forces.

The indications are that fertility behavior in developing nations is responsive to the effects it generates, and it changes accordingly. If fertility appears to be changing too slowly or not radically enough, it may be only because the urgency of the need for change is overestimated by observers, and the costs of rapid fertility change are underestimated. Humans have never before experienced the rapid growth rates of currently developing nations but, again, they never before were equipped with the technical capacity to cope with such growth. This rapid growth is largely a result of a rapid decline in death rates. At the same time, the lag between recent declines in death rates and those of birth rates is generally shorter, and the fall in birth rates is more rapid, than that of the classical demographic transition in western Europe. This is so, regardless of the motivating forces, modernization, population pressure, or otherwise. Whether and to what degree the decline in fertility has been helped by the promotion of family planning and the implementation of other population policies is another issue and another chapter.

Notes

1. D. Kirk, "Natality in the Developing Countries: Recent Trends and Prospects," in S. Behrman, L. Corsa and R. Freedman, eds., *Fertility and Family Planning: A World View* (Ann Arbor: University of Michigan Press, 1969).

2. J. M. van der Kroef, *Indonesia in the Modern World*, vol. II, (Bandung, 1956), p. 7, cited in E. Boserup, *The Conditions of Agricultural Growth* (Chicago: Aldine, 1965), p. 59.

3. See W. Rich, "Smaller Families Through Social and Economic Progress" (Washington, D. C.: Overseas Development Council, 1973); N. Birdsall, "Analytical Approaches to the Relationship of Population Growth and Development," *Population and Development Review*, 3: Nos. 1 and 2 (March and June 1977), pp. 63–102 (Birdsall's article includes a brief criticism of the notion and associated research.); R. Repetto, "Income Distribution and Fertility Change: A Comment," (on N. Birdsall's argument, above); and N. Birdsall, "Reply," *Population and Development Review*, 3:4 (December 1977).

4. See M. P. Todaro, "Development Policy and Population Growth," *Population and Development Review* 3:1/2 (March/June 1977), Table 2, p. 29; see also A. Berry and M. Urratia, *Income Distribution in Colombia* (New Haven: Yale University Press, 1976), pp. 27–46; I Adelman and C. T. Morris, *Economic Growth and Social Equity in Developing Countries* (Stanford, Cal.: Stanford University Press, 1973), cited in J. E. Potter, M. Ordonez G., A. R. Measham, "The Rapid Decline in Colombian Fertility," *Population and Development Review* 2:3/4 (September/December 1976), pp. 509–28. Potter et al. is discussed in the text.

5. J. D. Teachman, D. P. Hogan and D. J. Bogue, "A Components Method for Measuring the Impact of a Family Planning Program on Birth Rates," *Demography* 15:1 (February 1978), pp. 113–29.

6. See E. D. Driver, *Differential Fertility in Central India* (Princeton, N.J.: Princeton University Press, 1963).

7. K. Davis, *the Population of India and Pakistan* (Princeton, N.J.: Princeton University Press, 1951), p. 82.

8. W. C. Robinson, "Urban Rural Differences in Indian Fertility," *Population Studies* 14:3 (March 1961), pp. 218–34; also "Urbanization and Fertility, the Non-Western Experience," *Milbank Memorial Fund Quarterly* (July 1963), pp. 291–308.

9. See G. W. Roberts, "Reproductive Capacity and Reproductive Performance in Less Industrialized Societies," *Annals of the American Academy of Political and Social Science: World Population* (January 1967), pp. 37–47.

10. K. Davis, "The Theory of Change and Response in Modern Demographic History," *Population Index* 29:4 (October 1963), pp. 345–66.

11. B. B. Saxena, "Differential Fertility in a Rural Hindu Community: A Sample Survey of the Rural Uttar Pradesh India," *Eugenics Quarterly* 12:3 (1965), pp. 137–45.

12. J. B. Wyon and J. E. Gordon, *The Khanna Study: Population Problems in the Rural Punjab* (Cambridge, Mass.: Harvard University Press, 1971).

13. See D. G. Mandelbaum, *Human Fertility in India* (Berkeley: University of California Press, 1974), pp. 31–33.

14. Ibid., ch. 4.

15. United Nations, *The Mysore Population Study*, Population Study No. 34, U.N. Dept. of Economic and Social Affairs (New York, 1961), p. 125.

16. S. P. Jain, "State Growth Rates and Their Components," in A. Bose, ed., *Patterns of Population Change in India 1951–61* (Bombay: Allied Publishers, 1967), pp. 13–32.

17. United Nations, *The State of Food and Agriculture 1967* (Rome: Food and Agricultural Organization, 1967).

18. Gilbert Etienne, *Indian Agriculture, The Science of the Possible* (Berkeley: University of California Press, 1968); N. Keyfitz, "Political-Economic Aspects of Urbanization in South and Southeast Asia," in P. Hauser and L. F. Schnore, eds., *The Study of Urbanization* (New York: John Wiley, 1967), pp. 265–309.

19. *Census of India, 1951*, vol. I, pts. 1A, 1B.

20. For a formal report of this study, see D. S. Kleinman, "Fertility Variation and Resources in Rural India (1961)," *Economic Development and Cultural Change* 21:4, pt. 1 (July 1973), pp. 679–96.

21. The correlation coefficient r = –.79.

22. r = .75.

23. P. Visaria, "Urbanization, Migration and Fertility in India," in A. Campbell et al., eds., *The Family in Transition*, National Institutes of Health (Washington D.C.: U.S. Government Printing Office, 1971), pp. 257–84.

24. A. D. Gupta, R. K. Som, M. Majumdar, and N. S. Mitra (with an introduction by P. C. Mahalanobis), *Couple Fertility, The National Sample Survey No. 7*, Gov't of India (Indian Statistical Institute, 1955), pp. ii, 42.

25. Based on data from G. Narain, "India, The Family Planning Program Since 1965," *Studies in Family Planning*, No. 35 (New York: Population Council, 1968), p. 3; J. Ganiage, *Trois villages de l'Ile de France, Etude démographique* (Paris: P.U.F., I.N.E.D., vol. 1 (1963): p. 148, cited by J. Sutter, "The Effect of Birth Limitation on Genetic Composition of Population," in S. Behrman, L. Corsa, and R. Freedman, eds., *Fertility and Family Planning: A World View* (Ann Arbor: University of Michigan Press, 1969, p. 214. These are consistent with other reports which may be cited.
Note: P.U.F. is Presses Universitaires de France; I.N.E.D. is Institute Nationale d'Etudes Démographique.

26. U.S. Bureau of the Census, *World Population 1973*, International Statistics Program Center (Washington, D. C.: U.S. Government Printing Office, 1974)).

27. B. N. Mukherjee, "A Comparison of the Results of Family Planning KAP Surveys in Haryana and Tamil Nadu, India," *Studies in Family Planning* 5:7 (July 1974), pp. 224–31.

28. r = –.34

29. r = —.32

30. r = .50

31. r = .52

32. R. Freedman, P. K. Whelpton, and A. Campbell, *Family Planning, Sterilization and Population Control* (New York: McGraw-Hill, 1959); R. Freedman, G. Baumert, and M. Bolte, "Expected Family Size and Family Values in West Germany," *Population Studies* 13 (1959–1960), pp. 136–50.

33. A. J. Jaffe and K. Azumi, "The Birth Rate and Cottage Industries in Underdeveloped Countries," *Economic Development and Cultural Change* 9:1 (October 1960), pp. 52–63; M. Gendell, "The Influence of Family Building Activity on Woman's Rate of Economic Activity," United Nations 1965 World Population Conference (New York: United Nations, 1967), pp. 283-87; N. V. Sovani and K. Dandekar, "Fertility Survey of Nasik, Kolaba and Satara (North) Districts," Gokhale Institute of Politics and Economics Publication No. 31 (Poona, 1955); J. M. Stycos and R. H. Weller, "Female Working Roles and Fertility," *Demography* 4:1 (1967), pp. 210–17.

34. H. Ware, "The Relevance of Changes in Women's Roles to Fertility Behavior: The African Evidence," (paper, 1975 meeting of the Population Association of America, April 17–19, 1795, Seattle, Washington). See also J. Wolverton *Seattle Times*, April 20, 1975, H-6, "Do Jobs Really Cut Birth Rates? African Study Disputes Women's Status Theory," *Seattle Times*, April 20, 1975, H-6.

35. G. M. K. Kpedekpo, "Attitudes Toward Family Planning and Limitation in Ghana," *Population Review* 14: Nos. 1 and 2 (December 1970), pp. 52--58.

36. N. B. Leis, "Women in Groups: Ijaw Women's Associations," in M. Z. Rosaldo and L. Lamphere, eds., Women, Culture and Society (Stanford, Cal.: Stanford University Press, 1974), pp. 223--42.

37. $r = -.17$

38. $r = -.45$

39. $r = .11$

40. $r = -.33$

41. M. Mamdani, *The Myth of Population Control* (New York: Monthly Review Press, 1972). The study reviewed and criticized by Mamdani was J. B. Wyon and J. E. Gordon, *The Khanna Study*, op. cit.

42. D. Wolfers, "Population Adventures and Misadventures in the Subcontinent," *Family Planning Perspectives* 5:3 (Summer 1973), p. 189.

43. D. Andelman, "Indonesian Census Shows New Trends," *New York Times*, June 28, 1977.

44. W. B. Watson, ed., *Family Planning in the Developing World* (New York: Population Council, 1977), p. 13, Table 1.

45. M. Gendell, "Fertility and Development in Brazil," *Demography* 4:1 (1967), pp. 143--58; A. O. Zarate, "Fertility in Urban Areas of Mexico: Implications for the Theory of Demographic Transition," *Demography* 4:1, (1967), pp. 363--73.

46. M. Douglas, "Population Control in Primitive Groups," *British Journal of Sociology* 17 (1966), pp. 263--73.

47. M. Sahlins, *Stone Age Economics* (Chicago: Aldine Atherton, 1972).

48. M. E. Teitelbaum, "Relevance of Demographic Transition Theory for Developing Countries," *Science* 188 (May 1975), pp. 420--25; I. Tinker et al., *Culture and Population Change* (Washington, D.C., American Association for the Advancement of Science, 1976) (rev. ed.).

49. For a detailed discussion of the sequence of events which affect fertility, see K. Davis and J. Blake, "Social Structure and Fertility: An Analytic Examination," *Economic Development and Cultural Change* 4:3 (1956), pp. 211--35.

11

Fertility and Birth Control Programs

Introduction

Fertility behavior is adaptive to the degree that people exercise sufficient control over the number and, in some societies, spacing of their offspring to assure themselves not only of survival but also of the attainment and preservation of desired values and lifestyles. This implies that fertility behavior is fairly rational. Rationality does not require that behavior be completely planned. It is sufficient that at critical junctures the appropriate choice or deliberate act ensues.

Couples in different societies might expect a certain fertility pattern to result from customary behavior. Penile subincision may reduce the fertility of Australian aborigines; menstrual taboos may have no impact on fertility or may even increase fertility by confining the frequency of intercourse to the more fertile period of the ovulatory cycle. Among orthodox Jews, intercourse is proscribed from the time menstruation starts until the wife experiences the purification of a ritual bath generally around seven days after menstruation ends.[1] Thus, intercourse is effectively concentrated in the period surrounding ovulation. For all the variation in nutritional status, sterility, nursing, and sexual practices, only a very few presumably noncontracepting societies are reported to have had a completed fertility of ten or more children per married woman, on the average. Most have a completed fertility of around eight children.[2] A number of presumably noncontracepting societies are reported to have had an average completed family size of less than seven children when the mother married young and survived to age 45. One cannot be sure that birth control of one sort or another, including abstinence, was not practiced to some limited degree in reportedly noncontracepting societies, particularly where the fertility of women declines abruptly in the latter part of the reproductive period, as when married women of 35 or less stop bearing children as was noted earlier for many areas of India.

Many people in contemporary preindustrial society have been reluctant to admit to the practice of contraception, even when, as in studies of a high fertility community, they were known to have patronized a family planning clinic or to have used contraceptives.[3]

The oft cited statement of traditional folk, that they accept the number of children God wills, is not significant when they recognize the detrimental (or beneficial) effects of their fertility behavior and act accordingly. When children turn out to be a burden rather than a gift, the will of God is no longer seen in the same light and attitudes change. A change in attitude is not necessarily a prerequisite for a change in behavior as students of "cognitive dissonance" have shown. People frequently do what they feel they need to do in a given circumstance, and if this results in psychological conflict, they tend, however imperfectly, to change their attitudes, ideas, and values, or their behavior, to reduce internal dissonance. As discussed earlier, they attempt to adjust behavior and cognitions to form a psychologically consistent system; however, they can, if the stakes are sufficiently high, justify to themselves behavior which is inconsistent with expressed attitudes and values. If such behavior is continued, the system of attitudes and values is likely to change.

With few exceptions, peoples have been aware of the connection between intercourse and procreation. This would appear to be such a commonplace observation as not to be notable but for the fact that the connection need not be obvious. The practical universality of intercourse, even among the young, in many pre-industrial and primitive societies, the fact that an act of intercourse does not necessarily result in pregnancy, and the time interval between intercourse and the first definite signs of pregnancy may act to obscure the connection.

Marston Bates[4] cites the observation of Spencer and Gillen that among the very primitive Arunta,

The idea is firmly held that the child is not the direct result of intercourse, that it may come without this, which merely, as it were, prepares the mother for the reception and subsequent birth of a child, who in spirit form, inhabits one of the local totem centres.

But even the primitive Arunta saw as significant the fact that both sexual intercourse and the delivery of a baby involve the birth canal. Some modern anthropologists see denial of paternity by Australoids as a cultural repression of a recognizable fact to preserve shibboleths and the continuity of the totemic group.[5] The Dobu say that the Trobrianders, who deny the connection between intercourse and pregnancy, lie about this, and the issue is a sore point between the two peoples.[6]

Practically all people know that an abstinent woman does not get pregnant. But abstinence is not the only method of birth control known to most peoples, as has been recorded by Himes,[7] even where the practice of birth control is not prevalent. Indeed, some methods such as prolonged lactation were known to many peoples before they were known to modern scientists.

As a last resort people have been known to practice infanticide and, at times, not as a last resort as among the ancient Greeks and Romans, whose sensibilities were different from our own. One of the early signs that many English and French women of the eighteenth and nineteenth centuries did not want the children they bore was the practice of widespread though covert infanticide. Many infants were abandoned in the streets. Even if these found their way to a foundling home, they were almost as sure to die as if they had remained in the streets. Other mothers farmed out infants to wet nurses for rearing, in many of whose care the child did not long survive. Poor care and heavy use of opiates to keep infants quiet resulted in infant deaths without blame attaching itself to the parents.[8] In late eighteenth and nineteenth century France, the practice of working urban mothers handing over infants to wet nurses in the countryside led to abuses, child abandonment, and mortality on such a scale that vigorous, but perhaps ineffective, government intervention and regulation of the traffic was established, with an attendant bureaucracy.[9]

Some of the methods of controlling the number of offspring were cruel and callous. People tend to select and develop methods consistent with their values and circumstances. It would have been strange indeed if the ancient Romans and Greeks behaved more humanely in matters of birth control than they did with regard to sentient life in other contexts. Nor would it be surprising to learn that many devout Hindus abstain from sexual intercourse once they have fulfilled what they perceive to be their reproductive obligations.

Some of the ways of controlling fertility in a society may arise from its own complex of practices such as delaying marriage when livings are not available. And some contraceptive techniques may be invented locally. But, as is the case for much of a community's repertoire of techniques, contraceptive techniques are likely to have been learned from other peoples in the process we label diffusion. Few people have been so isolated that they have not been visited by traders, soldiers, and other travelers and do not number travelers among their own. What is learned and attended to from the outside are techniques which are usefully applied inside.

Parents have children for a number of reasons. One is for personal satisfaction, to achieve a sense of fulfillment and status in one's own eyes and those of others, or to express nurturing needs. Another, and for many a compelling reason, is for economic advantage and the assurance of the survival of the family. Then again, children may come as the unintended and often unwanted byproduct of sexual intercourse. While procreation can usually be left to nature, its prevention generally requires positive action. Thus, inertia and ineffective birth control result in a number of births that might not have otherwise occurred. But inertia and carelessness are also frequently a result of uncertainty or indifference as to the consequences of controlling fertility. As the consequences become more apparent and salient, couples can and do practice birth control more effectively.

The Effectiveness of Birth Control in Modern Society

American and European women have demonstrated the capacity to limit births even in the face of legal sanction against contraception and prevailing attitudes concerning size of family. About 44 percent of American women born between 1905–1909, the cohort passing through the depression of the 1930s in their prime reproductive years, had either no children (22 percent) or only one (22 percent). General attitudes about the role of women as mothers and homemakers, their need for children, and the undesirability of an only child were perhaps as strong then as they were during the 1940s and 1950s. Yet during a period of straitened economic conditions and with relatively limited birth control techniques such as condom, diaphragm, and withdrawal, the no-child and one-child family were prominent.

The tendency of couples to control their fertility became stronger as the need to do so increased. Studies showed that while American couples trying to prevent pregnancy but who wanted children may have been lackadaisical and ineffective in practicing birth control before the birth of their first child, they became increasingly more effective contraceptors as they approached the number of children they wanted. Based on a survey performed before the pill was generally available, Westoff and his colleagues reported that couples wanting two children and using condom, diaphragm, or coitus interruptus, experienced 21 contraceptive failures (pregnancies) per 100 women years of contraception from time of marriage to the birth of the first child, fewer than eight failures or pregnancies per 100 women years of contraception between the birth of the first and second child, and fewer than three failures per 100 women years of use between the birth of the second and third child. (More than 25 percent of contraceptors reported "taking chances".)[10]

The widespread effectiveness of birth control in the United States would appear to be contradicted by the findings of the 1965 National Fertility Survey of American married women. Thirty two percent of ever pregnant wives among couples who intended to have no more children reported that they had conceived at least one of their pregnancies at a time when either they or their husbands wanted no more children. (In more than 80 percent of these instances neither husband nor wife wanted more children.)[11] Based on these data, investigators concluded that 20 percent of children born between 1960–1965 were conceived when the pregnancy had not been intended by the parents. (A little more than 20 percent were unwanted if the criterion of unwantedness was the intention of only one parent; somewhat less than 20 percent were unwanted if the criterion was the intention of both parents.[12]

In addition to the estimated 20 percent of children conceived when their parents wanted no more chldren, 40 percent of wanted children were conceived at a time when parents, who though expecting to have more children in the future, had not intended to have them just then. These were labelled "timing failures."

The implications of the 1970 National Fertility Survey regarding the effect of modern contraception on the incidence of unwanted children appeared to be that the situation had improved. Ryder[13] reported that in 1970, 14 percent of couples who did not intend to have more children experienced a contraceptive failure during the first year of risk. By contrast, 26 percent of the couples who had intended to have children in the future, but not in a year, reported a contraceptive failure during the first year of risk. The failure rate declined in later years and older women were less subject to contraceptive failure than younger women. Ryder noted that the women who were married during 1954–1955 had more contraceptive failures in comparable periods than those married during 1961–1965. Part of the reason proposed was that the women married during the latter period had access to the pill, a surer contraceptive than other methods. But even among those in the later marriage cohorts who used the traditional contraceptives such as the condom, diaphragm, foam, douche, or the rhythm method, the failure rate was lower. Ryder concluded that 53 percent of the decline in prevention failures was due to the adoption of the pill.

The National Fertility Survey of 1970 provided the data for the estimate that the proportion of unwanted births in the preceding five years in the United States had decreased to 15 percent though 44 percent of births were still unplanned.[14] Since American married women surveyed in the latter half of the 1960s were intending to have fewer children than those surveyed earlier, they spent more time at risk of an unwanted pregnancy. Westoff[15] estimated that the risk of an unwanted pregnancy decreased some 36 percent from the five years preceding the 1965 survey to the five years preceding the 1970 survey. He attributed half of this decreased risk to the more effective use of contraception due mainly to increased use of pills, sterilization and IUD's.

The conclusions of Ryder, Westoff, and Bumpass are based on definitions of contraceptive failure which may subject their conclusions to misinterpretation. The particular definitions of contraceptive failure and unwanted births used in the 1965 and 1970 National Fertility Surveys did not include the dimension of intensity of motivation. More specifically they did not distinguish between unwanted pregnancies which occurred despite the actual practice of contraception and those which occurred when contraception was used irregularly or had been discontinued. The 1973 National Survey of Family Growth ascertained the use or non-use of contraception at the time that the unwanted pregnancy occurred. (Carelessness is, of course, not easily ascertained.) In this study, the contraceptive failure rate during the first year of use for those who did not want more children was only 4 percent from 1970 to 1973. While in the earlier National Fertility Survey the failure rate for whites was 12 percent compared to 35 percent for blacks, in this study (using the more rigid definitions of contraceptive failure) the rate for whites was 3.7 percent compared to 4.2 percent for blacks.[16]

The continuation rate for a contraceptive is often taken as a sign of its acceptability, a prerequisite for efficacy. But motivation is also involved— taking the pill day in and day out for years is no mean feat even if many manage to do it. Nor is having oneself sterilized an easy decision for many people. Both require considerable motivation which could, in the absence of these alternatives, result in the more efficient use of more traditional methods.

Attitudes towards pregnancy during the baby boom were obviously quite different from those before and after, and women married between 1951–1960 contributed much to the boom. Even when pregnancies were unwanted, there was likely to have been some ambivalence; the feeling of those not wanting any more children may have been relatively weak. Certainly the pill is a more effective contraceptive than conventional methods, but those women who used the pill may have been the same women who would have tried hard to make other contraceptives work were the pill not available. The elements of ambivalence and strength of feeling are too significant to be ignored, but are not easily studied.

Despite the differences in conceptualization of contraceptive failure and the failure rates reported in the 1970 National Fertility Survey and the 1973 National Survey of Family Growth, the proportions of births reported as unwanted in both surveys were roughly comparable. Thirteen percent of the women responding in the 1973 survey who gave birth that year reported that they did not want the pregnancy; another 7 percent were indeterminate in their response.[17]

Despite the differences between the English and Americans in contraceptive practices, the proportions of pregnancies reported as unwanted by English and American women are comparable. A 1970 national fertility survey in England and Wales[18] included more than 2,500 married women and cohabiting women, of whom 3 percent were widowed, divorced, or separated. Sixteen percent of the British women who gave birth in the year preceding the survey reported that when they found themselves to be pregnant, they regretted it then and for always. While the different definitions and ways of querying unwanted pregnancies make the American and British studies difficult to compare, the similarity of response was striking, considering the more primitive methods generally used by British women. Twelve percent of British ever married women under the age of 40 reported that they used withdrawal for contraception; only one percent of American married women under 40 did so. Twenty-four percent of the British ever married women reported the use of condoms; 8 percent of American married women did. Thirty-nine percent of American women, not pregnant and trying not to get pregnant, depended on pills, IUD's, or sterilization (male or female); only 27 percent of British women did so. A larger proportion (16 percent) of American married women from 16–40 were pregnant or planning pregnancy than were British ever married women (14 percent). Thus, the British ever married women with lesser access to birth control services, these not having been provided by the National Health Services at the time, and using more primitive techniques than the Americans, were able to maintain a lower birth rate with a comparable level of unwanted births. One need not compare sample surveys to see that low birth rates can be achieved with primitive methods. In 1970, the Belgians, reported to have relied mainly on withdrawal, had birth rates of around 14 per 1,000, though illegal abortions may have played some part in this.

Lest the high proportion of unwanted births for the American women surveyed in 1965, (20 percent, less than 15 percent more recently) be taken to indicate that contraception was not practiced effectively, consider the following: Where average completed family size includes three children per couple, and it is assumed that 20 percent of these were unwanted, then somewhat more than half a child per woman, on the average, was unwanted. If the average completed family size is two children, which appears to be the recent trend, and 15 percent of the births are unwanted, the latter amounts to an average of less than a third of an unwanted child per couple. Now, under the conditions of lactation and perinatal mortality, age of marriage, and related factors which prevailed, women could easily have had 12 or even more children on the average, if contraception were not practiced. Thus, contraception must have been practiced effectively, if not perfectly. Indeed, fertility rates could fall quite low, even below the replacement level, and the proportion of unwanted births still remain relatively high. Though easy access to effective birth control methods would likely reduce birth rates further still, the resulting reduction may not be very much in a low fertility society where motivation for low fertility is strong.

In any case, the categories "desired number of children", "unwanted children," etc., are such pallid reflections of reality, to say nothing about the depth of feelings involved, as to have little but superficial meaning. Highly sophisticated queries designed to elicit responses predictive of behavior may not touch on the factors which are actually salient. While people may be prevailed upon to hazard a notion as to the number of children they would like to have, or whether a given pregnancy was wanted or unwanted, the notion may include so many implicit or even unconscious reservations that the response obtained provides only a small portion of the pertinent information.

An account given by a woman in an interview[19] illustrated the poverty of the survey conceptualization of the unwanted child. During the early years of her marriage the woman had resolved not to have children and had resisted the various pressures directed to changing that resolve. Approaching thirty, she decided, for her own reasons, to have children. Had the woman, through some accident, given birth during her twenties, she would have been obliged to respond to the National Fertility Survey questionnaire that these births were unwanted then and would be unwanted in the future.

The use of the concept of unwanted births presumes, however, that once a decision to have no further pregnancies was reached, there would have been no change. The analysts of the National Fertility Survey considered that their estimates of unwanted births were conservative since some couples, having reconciled themselves to the unwanted child, perhaps even loving it, would forget or repress the circumstances of its birth. By the same token, however, the couples or individuals who regretted a more or less planned child, may come to regard that child as an accident, particularly when ambivalence about having a child was present at conception. Many life decisions relating to careers, marriage, residence, and the like, are made under ambiguous and ambivalent circumstances. There is no reason to believe that fertility decisions are more resolute and binding.

The consequences of having unwanted children are different from those of poor and ineffective action in other areas of behavior, and it would be remiss not to take note of this. The consequences involve a long term commitment to a being which needs considerable nurturing. While many people may adapt well to an unwanted pregnancy, others cannot. In both the American and British studies, unwanted births were more frequent among the young, presumably immature. They are also more frequent among the poor who are frequently not merely poor but also emotionally depressed.

In a Swedish study,[20] 120 children born to mothers whose request for abortion was refused, were followed until age 21. The proportion of these children using psychiatric services of one kind or another was twice that of the controls; four times as many needed public assistance, twice as many

were educationally subnormal, and more than twice as many were delin-
quents and criminals as compared to controls. The mothers involved may
have been inadequate as well. The controls were infants of the same sex born
in the same hospital. Had the controls been wanted children but born to
mothers of the same temperament and class characteristics as the subject
mothers, the outcomes for controls might not have been different from that
of subjects. In any case, whatever the implications of family planning
services for population growth, their value as a social welfare service
bringing us closer to the realization of the humane society is the issue at
hand. Regardless of the difficulties in arriving at more or less precise or
reliable estimates or even definitions of unwanted pregnancies, they do occur
and their social and personal impact considerably exceeds their demographic impact.

Udry and his associates evaluated the effect of subsidized family planning
services on reproductive behavior in the United States.[21] They examined,
through a regression analysis which included several control variables
(mean educational level, mean family income and other characteristics of the
counties), the effect of public family planning expenditures for physician-
administered contraception on various fertility indices, including unwanted
pregnancies for low income and other families in 16 counties. The research
included two surveys three years apart. Briefly, fertility rates in general and
the percentage of unwanted births decreased during the three years separating the interviews. But the amount of public money spent within each
county per poor woman did not affect the amount of these decreases, neither
among the poor nor among the non-poor. Women, including poor women,
in counties that spent a great deal of money on family planning tended to
switch from private facilities to public facilities for contraceptive services to
a greater extent than in the counties which spent less public money on family
planning. The poor were, of course, helped financially. The people of the
counties in the foregoing study obviously had private sector services available to them even though access to them involved a financial sacrifice which
was considerable to the poor.

In other times and places, even in the United States, services may not have
been so readily available, particularly for the poor, and the provision of
government assistance may have helped improve contraceptive practice. Not
surprisingly, other studies have reported considerable effects of the public
family planning services, including drops in the birth rate. (These are
recognized and cited in the report by Udry et al., noted above.) Yet it could
hardly be said that such declines would not have occurred in any case,
though perhaps at a slower pace. In a world where purveyors arise to take
advantage of every need, be it for narcotics or abortions, one cannot expect
contraceptives to be excluded. Public services are justified by improvement
in the welfare of individuals, and this is the measure of the value of publicly
financed family planning services.

Family Planning in Developing Countries

Many developing nations have officially adopted a population policy aimed
at reducing births and population growth rates. The stated objectives of

some are to help increase the rate of economic growth and mitigate the problems of unemployment, urban slums, civil disorder, hunger, and the other social ills purportedly aggravated by overpopulation. Population policies, of various types, apply to a sizeable portion of the population of developing countries, 91 percent in Asia, 48 percent in Africa and 13 percent in Latin America, comprising more than two-thirds of the people in less developed areas as of 1973. In addition, many nations not subscribing, officially at least, to antinatalist or Malthusian views, have been no less avid in the provision and promotion of birth control, the stated objectives being the improvement of health and free choice of family size.[22] In both cases the principal instrument of population policy has been the promotion and provision of birth control services. Countries with stated policy support for family planning services include 94 percent of the population in developing countries; those actually providing real programmatic support cover 78 percent of the people in developing countries.[23]

Until recently, practically all of the world's family planning programs espoused voluntary participation following the principal enunciated by the 1968 Nations Conference on Human Rights:

couples have the basic human right to decide freely and responsibly on the number and spacing of children and the right to adequate education in this respect.

This is, of course, a statement of human rights and not one of population policy. If implemented, prospective parents will be better able to control the size of their families, but they may still choose to have enough children to result in considerable population growth.

Surveys conducted in rural areas of developing countries in the 1970s reported that 50 percent of the persons with three living children, and 70 percent with four wanted no more.[24] Sub-Saharan Africans were exceptional in that they wanted large families. Similar findings were reported a decade earlier.[25]

In the drive to introduce family planning in less developed countries, literally hundreds of "K.A.P." surveys were performed to ascertain the knowledge, attitudes, and practices of people with regard to controlling their fertility. A great many of these surveys were performed by highly competent researchers under the aegis of prestigious institutions. They found that many people wanted to limit their fertility; in many areas couples wanted fewer children than they already had and would use contraceptive services if they were provided. Though the numbers of children wanted would still result in population growth, preventing unwanted children would diminish the rates significantly. These findings boded well for family planning programs and helped launch great drives and efforts to bring these services to people.

However, when services were made available in the 1960s, the patronage was disappointingly low in many areas. A characteristic comment was made by an Indian official (Gopalswami) in the early 1960s, "It is somewhat depressing but not exactly surprising that although ninety-two percent of the women were definitely [sic] desirous of limiting their families, only four percent did anything about it. The desire to limit families is there but it is not keen enough to move the people to change their accustomed conjugal habits."[26] The fact, however, was that in the area (Madras) that Gopalswami was referring to, people were limiting their fertility, though they were not using government services. The proportion of children relative to women in Madras and the estimated infant mortality rates were comparatively low for India.

Among family planning workers the discrepancy between K.A.P. survey findings and reality was known as "the Kap gap." The tendency was to attribute to gap to the lack of strength in the desire of people to contracept. While Gopalswami hoped that sterilization might prove successful where more conventional contraceptives did not, others looked to still further developments of a more acceptable contraceptive or some appealing method of delivery. J. M. Stycos, long involved in family planning and fertility research, noted that at the same time respondents in surveys express sentiments and reasons favorable to small families, they may also express reasons and sentiments favorable to large families, such as fear of children dying, support in old age, and the emotional satisfactions of chidren.[27] There is thus considerable ambivalence in responding to questions about the desired number of children. Stycos noted also that while poor women may on interview often express a desire for few children, most also note on further inquiry that they hadn't given the question any thought until they were asked.[28] One recalls Mamdani's respondent who gave the expected answer out of politeness.

Pessimism about birth control service acceptance was premature in the 1960s for with time the number of new acceptors of services rose both as a result of more countries instituting programs and the growth of established programs. Also, perhaps, family planners and family planning were becoming more acceptable and respectable in the eyes of the people. The number of new acceptors in developing countries' family planning programs rose from 2,484,000 in 1965 to 17,385,000 in 1975.[29] Sub-Saharan Africa lags in establishing programs and in program patronage which is consistent with its high fertility and the large families typically desired.

Reports of surveys conducted from 1974 to 1976 in five Asian countries (Pakistan, Nepal, Thailand, Malaysia, and Korea) under the auspices of the World Fertility Survey indicated that despite ongoing family planning programs in these countries, women are still having significantly more children than they say they want. Large proportions (40–60 percent) of married women who said that they wanted no more children either did not practice contraception or did not use efficient methods. Despite the fact that the levels of contraceptive practice and fertility varied considerably, in Korea, 46 percent of exposed women, and in Nepal only 3 percent, were practising contraception, the estimated unmet need for family planning services among these countries was remarkably constant. Westoff explained this by noting that as family planning and birth control increase, so do aspirations for fewer children and hence a need for additional services. Westoff added (perhaps as an afterthought) "and vice versa."[30] Indeed, the significant causal sequence may be that as more and more women (and men) aspire more and more intently to have fewer children, the practice of contraception increases and providers are encouraged and find it easier to increase the amount of services. In many countries where family planning programs were well accepted, birth rates were declining before the programs were under way and many people who used official services may have ben substituting these program services for other birth control methods. In some Latin American countries such as Chile and Colombia, one of the justifications for official sponsorship of family planning programs was the high incidence of poorly performed illegal abortions and the consequent morbidity and mortality. These showed the effort many people were making to avoid having children.

Thus, a number of eminent demographers and social analysts questioned the effectiveness of family planning programs in influencing population growth. In the view of these analysts, fertility behavior derives from the social cultural condition and milieu; a desire for smaller families will follow on social change, modernization, development, increased education and opportunities for women, and research is needed to elucidate the changes required. When people are moved to control fertility, they will find a way regardless of the presence or absence of government family planning services. Thus, the establishment of family planning programs may hasten fertility declines but little.[31]

Indeed, if for some reason the offered family planning services are unattractive, people may well turn elsewhere for help in controlling fertility. In Puerto Rico, a limited number of family planning service clinics were established by a voluntary association as early as the 1930s but were discontinued because of a lack of clientele as well as opposition from religious groups and other problems.[32] In the next three decades the expansion of family planning services was slow and sometimes retrograde as the private associations which sponsored these services were poorly supported and frequently uncertain of that support. More recently, the government of Puerto Rico was moved to press somewhat more vigorously for the reduction of births and the extension of family planning services.

In the interim, however, the birth rates in Puerto Rico declined markedly. While clinics offering the usual methods of birth control were ill attended, women increasingly were having themselves sterilized. In the late 1940s, 7 percent of women surveyed were reported to have been sterilized. A survey in the early 1950s indicated that over 16 percent of women were sterilized. A health and welfare survey in 1965 indicated that 34 percent of mothers, women with at least one child, and almost 47 percent between the ages of 35 and 39 had been sterilized.[33] This without any great fanfare.

When a well established and accepted family planning program such as that of South Korea did not provide a wanted service, people tended to look outside the purview of the official system. The results of a survey in Seoul, South Korea, showed that the proportion of women who had had recourse to illegal abortion had increased 72 percent, from 25 percent in 1964 to 43 percent in 1970; an estimated 17 percent of pregnancies ended in induced abortion in 1961 increasing to 40 percent in 1969. The increase was particularly marked among the poor and uneducated so that the former class difference in the use of abortion was significantly attenuated. Many aborted women were reported to have practiced contraception more regularly after the abortion than they did before it.[34]

Birth rates in the Dominican Republic declined from 51 per 1,000 in 1965 (with a total fertility rate estimated to be 7.4 children) to 36 per 1,000 in 1975 (and an estimated total fertility rate of 5.4 children). In 1968 the government initiated a family planning program which turned out to be very active, though it did not provide for sterilization. Yet 38 percent of women practicing contraception do so through sterilization by private physicians without the advantage of government subsidies.[35] Knowledge of effective family planning methods was fairly widespread (as shown by the Dominican Republic segment of the World Fertility Survey) attesting to the possible if not probable effectiveness of the family planning information and education services. Thus it might be said that even those who did not use the contraceptive services of the government program (and two-thirds of contraceptors obtained services elsewhere) may nonetheless have been influenced to control their fertility through the activities of the official program. On the other hand, had the government not established a family planning program, people would have likely found their way to contraception as have many others before them. Undoubtedly family planning programs have helped many people by making contraception easier and more accessible. Whether the facilitation of services significantly affected the levels of fertility control, and how much, are questions which are not easily answered.

A large number of evaluation studies have been performed on the impact of family planning programs on fertility. Some show very little impact of the programs even when fertility has declined. Reynolds traced the factors associated with the decline in Costa Rica's birth rate from over 48.3 births per 1,000 population in 1959 to 31.5 per 1,000 in 1971.[36] In the early stages of the decline, age at marriage increased as did the dissolution of unions; this was accompanied and followed by declines in marital fertility through traditional contraception, female sterilization, and birth control pills provided largely by the private commercial sector which obtained customers or clients by word of mouth without public information. Pills became increasingly important as a method of fertility control after 1964. Public family planning programs started extensive operations around 1968–1969, when birth rates had already declined to 35 per 1,000, and by 1971 were still serving less than 10 percent of women of reproductive age, though the proportions served had been increasing. Until 1966, practically all contraceptives were being supplied by the private sector, but with the establishment of a vigorous program many women appeared to be switching back and forth between the public and private birth control purveyors; thus, in effect, there may have been considerable substitution of one for the other. All in all, Reynolds concluded that the public program did not contribute much to the drop in fertility between 1959 and 1969.

A few studies, largely of small communities, showed rather dramatic declines in fertility upon the introduction of intensive family planning programs. These marked declines are not matched by the trends observed in other community studies. Nonetheless, it is not unreasonable to expect that providing family planning services where there are none will speed a decrease in fertility in areas where people are attempting to control births.

Freedman and Berelson are among the more prominent evaluators and advocates of the effectiveness of family planning as a partial population measure. They are aware of and sensitive to caveats, reservations, and qualifications that should attend research when the data are sparse, incomplete, and inaccurate. But it is not the quality of the data that should give rise to doubt as much as the underlying premises on whch their conclusions are based. In one of their many extensive studies, Freedman and Berelson classified a number of developing countries by social setting (infant mortality, school attendance, and gross domestic product) as a measure of proclivity to lower fertility. These countries were also classified by strength of family planning program effort. Both factors were found to be important in effecting a decline in fertility. Included in the classifications of high social setting and strong family planning effort were Costa Rica, Jamaica, Fiji, South Korea, Taiwan, Singapore, Barbados and Hong Kong—all highly circumscribed and densely populated. They also showed widely varying though declining birth rates. Venezuela, relatively high in per capita product, rich in oil and in land, was classified high on the social setting scale but weak in family planning programs. Venezuela's birth rate was noted as being high by Freedman and Berelson, but birth rates in Venezuela have been showing signs of falling. The countries classified as having both a low social setting and a weak family planning program included mostly African countries (not only poor but relatively sparsely populated) and also Bangladesh and Pakistan. These countries had birth rates in excess of 45 per 1,000. However, Egypt, which had also been classified among those countries with both a low social motivational level and a weak program had experienced a decline in fertility which brought its birth rate down to around 35 per 1000 by 1972, while Sri Lanka and Mauritius, credited with middle level social motivational settings and moderate program efforts have considerably lower birth rates.[37] We are not really aware of all the situational factors which lead people to reduce their fertility. The selection of what might be termed modernization variables to reflect the social setting conducive to fertility control indicates the narrowness of Freedman and Berelson's perspective.

In Freedman's and Berelson's analyses all the strong program efforts were found in the high social setting countries; these were also countries in which modernization tendencies and population pressure reinforced each other. Freedman and Berelson attributed the strong programs to the service and health infrastructures present in more developed areas. But these services and their infrastructures arose because of the demand and need for them. While Pakistan and Bangladesh's family planning programs are classified as weak, and India's as only moderately strong, these programs are among the oldest and most mature and have received considerable public and private fiscal support from both domestic and foreign sources. The ineffectiveness of their program operations is often blamed on administrative inefficiency, lack of motivation of program workers, and other organizational factors. These, however, are frequently a result of the poor reception the programs receive from the public they presume to serve, and such a reception may be demoralizing and discouraging. Were the programs in greater demand, much of the source of inefficiency, lack of motivation of workers, and paucity of support might well be eliminated.

Most of the world's nations have government-financed family planning services. These are of varying quality and accessibility, but as long as they expand in tune to demand, they can, if they wish, claim an important part in effecting fertility declines. Undoubtedly, the presence of a strong family planning service can and has facilitated fertility declines already in progress, and has appeared to increase the rate of those declines in a number of countries. But, suppose that an accelerated decline at one time may predispose a community to a decelerated decline in the future, as population pressure diminishes or as birth rates and fertility go lower and lower. Whatever the case, the demographic impact of family planning programs has not been so uniform or so dramatic as to obviate argument, often more sharp than illuminating, in their defense.

Whatever the demographic effects of family planning programs, the social impact is appreciable. Unwanted children, even if they are insufficient in number to have a marked effect on birth rates, can be very costly to society, out of all proportion to their contribution to population growth, particularly if they are associated with antisocial behavior. In addition, people in the past have employed brutal means in the absence of alternatives to avoid the burden of parenthood. The avoidance of this burden should not be so costly that it affects other areas of life.

Some Comments on Birth Control Policy

The principal components of deliberate population policy in most countries are family planning programs in antinatalist countries and family subventions and subsidies in pronatalist countries. Both are also tools of welfare policy and exist side by side in welfare states.

Some governments have been impatient and have tried to hurry the course of events. The response in India to relatively small financial incentives or payments to family planning acceptors did not satisfy some of the advocates of population control in Indira Gandhi's government. Despite declining fertility rates, fair program acceptance, and other needs, these advocates introduced coercive and drastic measures to induce people to curtail their fertility. They only succeeded in helping bring about the fall of Madame Gandhi's government in the election of 1977.[38]

In an experimental incentive program on Taiwan, educational costs of children for enrolled families which undertook to have no more than three children were subsidized. Ninety-eight percent of eligible families in the experimental township enrolled in the program. Fertility has been falling, but not more rapidly than in a similar control township without such an incentive program.[39]

Singapore has taken what is probably the most drastic action to date. Birth rates in Singapore had declined from over 45 per 1,000 in the early 1950s to 28.6 per 1,000 in 1966 when a government family planning program was established. During the next few years, birth and fertility rates continued to fall somewhat more rapidly to a level of 22.1 per 1,000 in 1970. In the following two years birth and fertility rates remained fairly stable, even increasing slightly in 1972 among older women, some of whom had postponed births they had intended to have. Both the total fertility rate and the average number of children desired had fallen to about three children per woman. In 1973 the decline in fertility resumed its course, with the gross reproduction rate declining some 8 percent, though the birth rate had dropped only 4 percent because of the higher proportion of young women coming into reproductive age.

In August 1973, the city state of Singapore put into effect legislation to discourage large families. These measures included higher fees for the delivery of higher birth order children, limitation of paid maternity leave to two births, income tax exemptions for the first three children only, elimination of housing subsidies and priorities for large families, and lower priority in the choice of primary school admission for children of fourth birth order and above. Perhaps the slight hesitation in the decline of birth rates and the large numbers of young women entering reproductive age influenced the government to adopt these coercive policies directed at achieving a two-child family norm. In any event, fertility resumed its decline in 1973 before the policies could have had significant impact in view of the nine months duration of pregnancy.

A survey of a large sample of Singapore married women in September 1973 showed that 22.4 percent of them were aware of the change in delivery fees; 81 percent were aware of the change in primary school registration priorities; and 69 percent were aware of the change in housing subsidy priorities for large families. Around 40 percent of the women had heard about the change in income taxes and paid maternity leave (most Singapore women do not work outside the home). Almost half the women said that the change in primary school registration priority would not influence them and more than half said that the other changes would have no influence on them, though 90 to 95 percent thought that other people would be influenced, an indication, perhaps, of their own hidden feelings.[40]

The decline in fertility rates continued more rapidly between 1973 and 1975, than formerly. The birth rate for 1974 was 19.5 per 1,000 and in 1975 it was 17.8 per 1,000. The restrictive policies may have been responsible for the difference in the pace of decline, but the difference may not be very significant as fertility rates were rapidly approaching rather low levels in any case. If these coercive policies are effective, it may be because they are consistent with the already existing trend in fertility behavior. At the same time, these policies may result in some disadvantages accruing to children of large families, a phenomenon whose negative aspects may well outweigh the small benefits the governments can anticipate from such a population policy.

The example of Romania approaches the issue from another direction. By 1966, the Romanian birth rate was 14.3 per 1,000 population; a principal method of birth control was cheap legal abortion readily and widely available. In October of 1966, the government, alarmed by the low birth rates, restricted the use of abortions, which had previously been available on request, to very narrowly defined circumstances, ceased importing contraceptives though locally manufactured condoms remained available, increased family child allowances and increased taxes on childless individuals. Nine months later the birth rate rose to around 39 per 1,000, somewhat lower than what might be expected in a non-contracepting population. Three months later birth rates began to decline. By 1968, the birth rate had fallen to about 27 per 1,000; in 1969 to about 23.7 per 1,000 and by 1973, it was reported to be around 19 per 1,000, and then between 19 and 20 for several years. The absence of easy abortions and the presence of more generous family allowances may have resulted in an increase in children among those to whom not having children was a marginally motivated decision. However, the trend towards lower birth rates would indicate that the experience of having more children is sufficiently onerous to many that they are now seeking contraceptives and abortions even though these may be more difficult to obtain than formerly.

There is little reason to think that in time Romanians will respond much differently to the legal difficulties in obtaining contraceptive services and abortions than did, for instance, the French. The fertility of the latter was relatively low (around 17 per 1,000 in 1973, and 15 per 1,000 in 1974), despite an attractive government system of family allowances under which having many children significantly increases the effective family income of a worker and until recently, laws against abortion. French birth rates might have been somewhat lower were it not for the handsome family allowances, but not much lower. Though family allowances may result in slightly higher birth rates than would otherwise be the case, they do not keep birth rates from falling to low levels. Sweden, offering a wide range of family allowances and maternity benefits, has a birth rate of 13 per 1,000; similarly, East and West Germany have birth rates of 10 per 1,000. Norway and The Netherlands had somewhat higher birth rates, 15 and 14 per 1,000 respectively in 1974.

Since the fear of having more children than are economically (and psychologically) tolerable is an important deterrent to fertility, family allowances which mitigate this fear may indeed be responsible for some small number of births which might not otherwise occur. And since people are imperfect in controlling their fertility, as they are in other areas of life, easy access to birth control may prevent some number of births which would otherwise occur. But family allowances and family planning services may be justified more on the basis of their contribution to the welfare of individuals and thence to society than on the basis of their effect on population. In the short run they may work. One can imagine incentive systems so attractive or penalties so coercive that they are difficult to resist. But the wealth or power to implement such schemes are limited. A rough estimate is that the effect of family planning incentive or disincentive schemes which are feasible do not usually extend beyond two or three points of the birth rate per 1,000 population, and perhaps a little more, but not for an appreciable period of time.

The experience of China would appear to contradict the notion that the government cannot effect much demographic change by its commitment to family planning in the form of promotion, suasion, coercion, and provision of services. Many experts affirm the success of China's fertility control program. Few of them will agree with each others estimates of population size (ranging, among a sample of four experts, from 850 million to 977.9 million), birth rates (ranging from 14 per 1,000 to 33.6 per 1,000) and death rates (ranging from 6.0 to 12.1).[41] Most agree, however, that birth rates have been falling as a result of fertility control programs. This may be true or it may be wishful thinking for there are no data by which to confirm or deny this phenomenon, information being based solely on enthusiastic hearsay.[42] Whatever the unknown facts of the case, it is incongruous that experts ready to attribute the drop in Chinese fertility to the official program and policy appear to forget that the changes in Chinese social and economic life in the past thirty years may also have had quite a lot to do with the decline in fertility.

The factors significant to population policy are those which affect the costs and benefits of children. These involve social and economic structures, tax systems, land tenure, income policy, equality of sexes, educational opportunities, and a host of other elements and issues which have considerable implications for justice and welfare, regardless of their relationship to population. Indeed, these are so much more important to human welfare that they should not (probably could not) become subordinate elements of population policy.

Notes

1. M. Zborowski and E. Herzog, *Life is With People: The Culture of the Shtetl* (New York: Schocken, 1962), pp. 285--87.

2. See R. G. Potter, "Changes of Natural Fertility and Contraceptive Equivalents," *Social Forces* 54:1 (September 1975), p. 40, Table 1.

3. J. Stoeckel and M. A. Chowdhury, "Pakistan: Response Validity in a KAP Survey," *Studies in Family Planning* 47 (November 1969), pp. 5--9; also L. Green "East Pakistan: Knowledge and Use of Contraceptives," *Studies in Family Planning* 39 (March 1969), pp. 9--14.

4. B. Spencer and F. J. Gillen, *The Arunta; A Study of a Stone Age People* (London: Macmillan, 1927); cited by M. Bates, *The Prevalence of People* (New York: Scribner's, 1955), p. 96.

5. M. F. Ashley-Montagu, *Coming Into Being Among the Australian Aborigines* (London: Routledge & Sons Ltd., 1937).

6. E. A. Hoebel, *Anthropology: The Study of Man*, 4th ed. (New York: McGraw-Hill, 1972), p. 376.

7. N. E. Himes, *Medical History of Contraception* (New York: Schocken Books, paperback, 1970).

8. W. L. Langer, "Checks on Population Growth, 1750--1850," *Scientific American* 226:2 (February 1972), pp. 93--99; also W. L. Langer, "Europe's Initial Population Explosion," *American Historical Review* 69:1 (October 1963), pp. 1--17.

9. G. D. Sussman, "The Wet Nursing Business in Nineteenth Century France," *French Historical Studies* 19 (1975), pp. 304--29.

10. C. F. Westoff, R. G. Potter and P. C. Sagi, *The Third Child* (Princeton, N.J.: Princeton University Press, 1963), pp. 41--42.

11. N. B. Ryder and C. F. Westoff, "Fertility Planning Status: United States, 1965," *Demography* 6:4 (November 1969), pp. 435--44.

12. L. Bumpass and C. F. Westoff, "The Perfect Contraceptive Population," *Science* 169 (September 18, 1970), pp. 1177--82.

13. N. B. Ryder, "Contraceptive Failure in the United States," *Family Planning Perspectives* 5:3 (Summer 1973), pp. 133--42.

14. See Report on the Commission on Population Growth and the American Future, *Population and the American Future* (Washington, D.C.: U.S. Government Printing Office, 1972), p. 97, Table 11.1.

15. C. F. Westoff, "The Modernization of U.S. Contraceptive Practice," *Family Planning Perspectives* 4:3 (July 1972), pp. 9--12.

16. B. Vaughan, J. Trussell, J. Mencken and E. F. Jones, "Contraceptive Failure Among Married Women in the United States, 1970--1973," *Family Planning Perspectives* 9:6 (November/December 1977), pp. 251--58.

17. National Center for Health Statistics, *Wanted and Unwanted Births Reported by Mothers 15--44 Years of Age: United States, 1973*, Advance Data No. 9, August 10, 1977 (U.S. Department of Health, Education and Welfare, Public Health Service.)

18. M. Bone, *Family Planning Services in England and Wales* (London: Her Majesty's Stationery Office, 1973), as reviewed by E. F. Jones, "Family Planning and Fertility: U.S. and U.K. Compared," *Family Planning Perspectives* 6:2 (Spring 1974), pp. 123--25.

19. Ingeborg Day, "Daughters and Mothers," *MS*, June 1975, pp. 51–53.

20. H. Forssman and I. Thuwe, "One Hundred and Twenty Children Born After Therapeutic Abortion Refused," *Acta Psychiatrica Scandinavia* 42 (1966), pp. 71--78.

21. R. Udry, K. E. Bauman and N. M. Morris, "The Effect of Subsidized Family Planning Services on Reproductive Behavior in the United States: 1969--1974," *Demography* 13:4 (November 1976), pp. 463--78.

22. D. Nortman, *Population and Family Planning Programs: A Factbook*, Reports on Population/Family Planning, No. 2 (New York: Population Council, December 1974); see also B. M. Stamper, *Population Policy in Development Planning*, Reports on Population/ Family Planning, No. 13 (New York: Population Council, May 1973).

23. W. B. Watson, ed., *Family Planning in the Developing World* (New York: Population Council, 1977), p. 6.

24. B. Berelson, *World Population: Status Report 1974*, Reports on Population/Family Planning, No. 15 (January 1974), p. 30.

25. B. Bereleson, "K.A.P. Studies on Fertility," in B. Berelson et al., eds., *Family Planning and Population Programs* (Chicago: University of Chicago Press, 1966), pp. 655--68.

26. R. A. Gopalswami, "Family Planning Outlook for Government Action in India," in C. V. Kiser, ed., *Research in Family Planning* (Princeton, N.J.: Princeton University Press, 1962), pp. 67--81.

27. J. M. Stycos, "Problem of Fertility Control in Underdeveloped Areas," *Marriage and Family Living* 25 (1963), pp. 5--13.

28. J. M. Stycos, *Human Fertility in Latin America* (Ithica, N.Y.: Cornell University Press, 1968), p. 160.

29. Watson, ed., *Family Planning in the Developing World*, op. cit. p. 5.

30. C. F. Westoff, "The Unmet Need for Birth Control in Five Asian Countries," pp. 9--18; and L. J. Cho "Fertility Preferences in Five Asian Countries," pp. 2--8 in *International Family Planning Perspectives and Digest* 4:1 (Spring 1978).

31. See K. Davis, "Population Policy: Will Current Programs Succeed?", *Science* 158 (November 1967), pp. 730--39; also P. M. Hauser, "On Non-Family Planning Methods of Population Control," in A. Bose, P. Desai and S. P. Jain, eds., *Studies in Demography* (Chapel Hill: University of North Carolina Press, 1970), pp. 353--68; also P. M. Hauser, "Family Planning and Population Programs: A Review Article," *Demography* 4:1 (1967), pp. 397--414.

32. J. N. Curt, "Puerto Rico," in B. Berelson et al., eds., *Family Planning and Population Programs* op. cit., pp. 227--233.

33. H. B. Presser, "Puerto Rico: The Role of Sterilization in Controlling Fertility." *Studies in Family Planning* 45 (September 1969), pp. 8--12; H. B. Presser, "The Role of Sterilization in Controlling Puerto Rican Fertility," *Population Studies* 23:3 (1969), pp. 343--61.

34. Population Chronicle No. 6, Population Council, September, 1971, "Abortion Rises 72 Percent in Six Years in Korea," p. 6, a report on a monograph by Dr. Sung Bong Hong, *Changing Patterns of Induced Abortion in Seoul, Korea.*

35. "30% Decline in Dom Rep. Birth Rate Ascribed to Voluntary Sterilization and F. P. Program," *International Family Planning Perspectives and Digest*, 4:1 (Spring 1978) pp. 25--27.

36. J. Reynolds, "Costa Rica: Measuring the Demographic Impact of Family Planning Programs," *Studies in Family Planning* 4:11 (November 1973), pp. 310--16.

37. R. Freedman and B. Berelson, "The Record of Family Planning Programs," *Studies in Family Planning*, 7:1 (January 1976).

38. L. C. Landman, "Birth Control in India: The Carrot and the Rod?", *Family Planning Perspectives* 9:3 (May/June 1977).

39. Watson, *Family Planning in the Developing World*, op. cit., p. 23.

40. W. F. Kee and S. Swee Hock, "Knowledge, Attitudes and Practice of Family Planning in Singapore," *Studies in Family Planning* 6:4 (April 1975), pp. 109--12.

41. *Family Planning Perspectives* 9:6 (November/December 1977), pp. 284--85.

42. See "Fertility Control and Public Health in Rural China: Unpublicized Problems," *Population and Development Review* 3:4 (December 1977), pp. 482--85; J. S. Aird, *Population Policy and Demographic Prospects in the People's Republic of China*, 1972 (reprinted by U.S. Department of HEW, NIH).

12

A Superfluity of People?

Introduction

A painful social problem is the presence of superfluous people who contribute little or nothing to their own welfare or that of others, a problem common to many civilizations. Tiberius Gracchus, more than a hundred years before the birth of Christ, protested:

The wild beasts that roam Italy have their dens and lairs to shelter them, but the men who fight and die for Italy have nothing but air and light. . . . They are called masters of the world, they have no clod of earth to call their own.[1]

John Winthrop wrote of England in 1629:

This lande growes wearye of her Inhabitants so as man which is the most pretious of all the Creatures is here more vile and base, then the earth they treade upon: so as children, neighbors and freindes (especially if they be poore) are rated the greatest burdens, which if things were right would be the cheifest earthly blessing.[2]

Winthrop, a Puritan reformer, despairing of setting things right, emigrated to become governor of the Massachusetts colony. Others wished for "times when our Country was not pestered with multitude, not overcharged with swarmes of people," as did an Englishman when England and Wales numbered fewer than five million people.[3] Whence came these swarms of people who wandered the roads and squatted in rural and urban slums with nothing to do but be a disturbance and nuisance, if not worse, to their more fortunate fellows?

In Rome, the superfluity of people in the times of the Gracchi was generated by the displacement of the small free farmers by slaves. The lands of the small farmers were devastated and they themselves were paupered in the wars which started Rome on the path of empire, and the large-scale taking of slaves. At the same time, the opportunity for the ambitious were expanded. Hardship purchases, foreclosures and other actions were employed by the wealthier and more powerful families to incorporate the small farms into latifundial estates manned by slaves. Small citizen farmers, unsuccessful in legal and extralegal actions to maintain their holdings, drifted into the cities and particularly to the capital city, where they swelled the early Roman proletariat. Rome was largely a seat of government, a parasite city with little commerce or industry. Its inhabitants lived off tribute, taxes and exactions from the provinces. Much of the day to day work could be done cheaply and effectively by imported slaves who were often manumitted when they lost their utility and thus were turned into proletarians. But the proletariat in the days of the Republic had votes which were useful to the politicians who vied with each other in providing bread and circuses which supplemented the meager fund of subsistence and amusement available to the proletariat. In the days of the Empire, the proletariat formed mobs and the combination of bread and circuses helped to prevent the more serious disorders this functionless class of people might have otherwise generated. The proletariat of Rome originated in expropriation and dislocation. Its number could not have been maintained by natural growth, for the mortality of Rome was too high for that.

Many of the superfluous Englishmen to whom Winthrop referred were also people displaced from their livelihoods by the rich and powerful. If we knew no facts other than that the English population increased perhaps some 25 percent during the late sixteenth and early seventeenth centuries, the problem would appear to be one of population exceeding resources. Many observers of that time thought so, but they also remarked on the forceable depopulation of the countryside wrought by enclosures (see Chapter 14).

. . . the people . . . do swarme in the land, as yong bees in a hive in June; in so much that there is very hardly roome for one man to live by another. The mightier like strong old bees thrust the weaker, as younger, out of their hives: Lords of Manors convert towneships in which were a hundred or two hundred communicants, to a shepheard and his dog.[4]

Whether England would have appeared to swarm with superfluous people during the seventeenth century were it not for the evictions of enclosures and the legal closing of wastes to internal colonization may be an academic question. The fact is that birth rates fell almost to the level of death rates in this period and the population stabilized until, in the eighteenth century, the opportunities for livelihood increased.

One simplistic view is that surpluses of people are generated by population growth in excess of the capacity of economic growth to absorb the increase. A Malthusian, accepting the institutional usages governing the economy as proper and efficient, tends to blame resource limitation for the inability of the economy to expand. A Marxist, confident of the productive capacity of labor and technology, tends to blame the inability of the economy to accomodate even a stationary or declining population on institutional constraints. Between these viewpoints are a variety of theorists who consider the inability of economies to accomodate everyone as a function of all three factors: population, resources and the intervening institutions.

The point of view proposed here is that the superfluities of people, which so often appeared to plague human society, have their origins in the structure of society and not in the resources available to it. The abstract notion that the proliferation of people will eventually exceed resources, or that population may grow more rapidly than resources can be expanded, is easy to conceive. But people are responsive, at least in the matter of fertility, to such constraints. And, they find it more difficult to cope with the constraints of human society than with those of nature. Their fertility behavior is thus, of necessity, more often directed towards coping with other humans.

Superfluous Labor in Industrial Societies

One need not be a Marxist to appreciate the paradox that under that highly productive system, capitalism, society has been often plagued with unemployment even as people need and want the goods and services which are not being produced because labor and factories lie idle. Workers are unemployed, not because of a lack of capital or resources, or a lack of need for goods and services, but because of a lack of effective demand. By demand, economists mean not only that a product or service is wanted, but that the want can be backed by payment. Malthus and Ricardo argued that a smaller labor force—that is, a smaller population—would result in less unemployment and higher wages in keeping with the law of supply and demand. (According to them, higher wages leads to population increase which leads to unemployment which in turn reduces wages.) But, they did not consider that a smaller population might exhibit a proportionately lesser demand for goods and services in an economy operating at a lower level with fewer opportunities for employment. Many economists felt, at the time, that the depression of the 1930's was being sustained by the then prevailing low birth rates which helped keep the economy stagnating through a diminished demand for goods and services.[5]

Marx saw surplus labor as inherent in the capitalist mode of production, the inevitable outcome of the "General Law of Capitalist Accumulation." In this formulation, capital accumulation leads to the redundancy of a large part of the labor force. Competition among capitalists forces them to keep costs (and prices) down; enterprises are thus obliged to operate more efficiently through the introduction of labor saving technologies and organization, increasing division of labor and economies of scale. More and more goods are produced by less and less labor.

The workers, as consumers, are a principal market for the goods they produce. Since, according to Marx, they do not receive the full value of the goods and services they produce, they cannot buy these back; inventories begin to accumulate. The surplus value, taken by capitalists, is in good part expended on further industrial expansion, providing employment for other workers. These workers are also purchasers and help to keep inventories moving, as does the expansion of markets into new areas. But the increase in effective demand for goods, in Marx's view, cannot keep pace with the growing efficiency of production under a capitalist system in which the workers do not receive full value of the goods they produce while the capitalists invest their portion only when profits are anticipated. The outcomes are accumulations of inventories, stoppages of production, and the collapse of the less efficient businesses, leading to increased monopoly, unemployment, and augmentation of the surplus labor force. Each economic system, according to Marx, has its own law of population and that peculiar to capitalism is that labor produces the means by which it is made superfluous. The size of the population and its growth rate affect only the volume of business which may be transacted.

Many of Marx's conclusions may appear to have been overdrawn. As industries have become more concentrated and firms larger, price competition among them has diminished. Workers have managed to maintain and increase their wages and better their working conditions through economic and political organization. Managers and bureaucrats have proliferated in the great oligopolies resulting from centralization of capital. The service sector of the economy, dominated by small firms in many areas, e.g. health care, legal services, and increasingly involving the government, has greatly expanded. The proliferations of functionaries, many of whom add little to productive capabilities, help consume the products of industry. Nonetheless, this is often not enough to support the required level of economic growth.

The great depression of the 1930's and the many preceeding economic crises appeared to validate Marx's analysis. At the depth of the depression, some 25 percent of the work force in the United States was unemployed; factories were idle though goods and services were needed. Farm produce was destroyed to maintain farm prices, and food production was curtailed while people went hungry.

The occurrence of business cycles and periodic recessions and depressions was accepted as a fact of life by most economists before the depression of the 1930's. They felt that these were in part due to the inventories, wages, prices, interest rates and investment which had gotten out of equilibrium with each other and an adjustment was needed. As prices fell, goods would move out of inventories; as wages and interest rates fell, it would again become profitable to employ labor and borrow to expand production. Eventually, production and economic growth would start up again. However, the depression of the 1930's appeared to presage a long, perhaps permanent period of chronic high unemployment despite efforts to get the economy going. The end of the decade of economic stagnation was brought about by the outbreak of World War II. Today, the solution of the laissez faire economists is not acceptable to most people, though some who are not threatened by unemployment and its problems, still advocate it. It is doubtful that even they could tolerate a great depression.

Out of the depression and the experience of World War II came the realization, formalized by Keynes, that a profit motivated economy, whatever else its advantages, would not operate automatically to maintain full employment and an equitable distribution of goods; that government intervention is required to keep the economy growing, to maintain full employment, and to provide for the welfare of those who fall out of it. Various mechanisms are employed to assure that the economy keeps expanding. Unemployment insurance cushions the drop in purchasing power and is a welfare mechanism as well. Through fiscal and monetary policies the government stimulates effective demand by lowering taxes, influencing the interest rate, and taking other actions which may increase the amount of money taxpayers can spend and corporations can invest. The government also increases its purchases of goods and services. Increasing capital investments not only creates a demand for labor in the process, but also, in time, increases the productivity of labor. Productivity is also increased by technological developments, a better educated labor force, and improved organization. New technologies resulting in new industries result in new employments, but the economy must keep on growing to maintain full employment and compensate for the effects of inequity, a resolution not without problems, inflation, waste, and pollution.

Superfluous People in Traditional Societies

As Boserup noted, population growth in pre-industrial subsistence societies resulted in the more intensive use of land and the application of more labor intensive technologies as land available per capita diminished. (see Chapter 6.) This served not only to increase production but employment as well. Geertz, in his book on "Agricultural Involution," described the changes in Javanese agriculture as population increased. The population of Java multiplied several times at least in the 150 years since the Dutch first noted that the island was overpopulated. As land suitable for cultivation became scarce in certain areas, its use was rotated among the families of villages and communities; thus, each family was guaranteed a living. Small razor-like sickles were used to harvest rice, assuring minimal loss of the crop and maximal employment. in the complexity of relationships which gave many access to land, there was no feeling that a superfluity of people existed. Few took the opportunity, as they were encouraged to do by successive governments, to emigrate to the outer islands of Indonesia which were sparsely settled and available for colonization.

Within many peasant village cultures, provision was often made through some institutional arrangement to assure that each member had access to some conventional level of sustenance. In India, the jajman-kamin system performed this function.[6] The farmers as jajmans, roughly translated as patrons, were under moral obligation to produce sufficient food and fiber for all. This was distributed in some customary manner to the kamin (or client) families of the different jatis (or subcastes) with whom the farmers were traditionally tied. These families performed village functions appropriate to their jati group: smith, leatherworker, launderer, sweeper, priest, and so on. The members of the lower jatis also served as agricultural labor in many areas. The pollution ascribed to their presence did not extend to the fields. The exchanges of goods and services were not on a quid pro quo basis, but each family discharged its traditional function as a matter of duty and traditional obligation, and received goods and services appropriate to its station as a matter or right. The duties of the lower jatis, the unclean castes, were onerous and degrading while the goods and services they received were paltry. But some mean level of subsistence was theirs. Since rights, obligations and associated relationships between families were inherited from generation to generation, there was considerable insurance against a family becoming superfluous in the economy. These traditional relationships survived the changes in patterns of land tenure introduced by the British raj; they held through famines, wars and other disasters. However, the growing cash nexus in agricultural production and distribution has attenuated, and it promises to eliminate the exchanges in the jajman-kamin relationships, if not the social and economic discrimination involved.

Not all peasant societies were as rigidly structured as that of India. The old Chinese peasant families could advance their status by buying land or seeing to the education of a son who might thus enter the bureaucracy and bestow favors on his family. By the same token, a family could lose their land through default, indebtedness, taxes, or hardship sales and lose their status and prerogatives with their land. To obtain and hold land, even as a tenant, a family had to produce a large surplus which required a number of children, some of whom would in their turn, find land hard to come by.

In peasant communities where cooperation and mutual aid and reciprocal obligations among households provided the poor with a meager security and subsistence, there was still considerable conflict. The Indian village described above was plagued by factions and conflicts. Two observers of the same village of Mexican peasants (Tepotzlan) reported opposing views of the life of its people. Redfield presented the village as a smoothly functioning and cooperative social and economic unit, providing reasonably for its members under the economic circumstances.[7] Lewis, observing the village seventeen years later, reported conflict, poverty, stealing, competitiveness, and hostility between and within families, and between the rich and poor, which reflected a contrasting view of the cooperativeness of the Tepoztecans and their adjustment to and satisfaction with life.[8] Part of the inconsistency in the two points of view may have been due, as Redfield later noted, to the changes which occurred in the seventeen years between the two studies, a declining sense of security among Tepoztecans as their contacts with urban ways increased.[9] Redfield felt, however, that the main reason for the difference in views was that while he focused on the joys and strengths of the Tepoztecan, Lewis focused on their sufferings and inadequacies. Cooperative institutions and personal satisfactions coexisted with competitiveness, hostility, and frustration, a combination of opposites.

Still changes had occurred in Mexico and in Tepoztlan between Redfield's observations in the 1920's, (even as he was making these observations) and those of Lewis in the 1940's. The reforms in Mexican rural economic structure which began with the revolutions in the 1910's doing away with the quasi-feudal organization of rural society were largely ended with the expiration of President Cardenas' term of office in 1940. Thereafter, land ownership, which previously tended towards equalization, became increasingly concentrated as commercial motives more and more dominated the rural economy.[10] Lewis noted that "The increasing exploitation of communal resources for commercial rather than for subsistence purposes, which was encouraged by the railroad and the highway, made for competition which did not exist before."[11] Although Lewis was talking about conflicts between villages, the commercial motive could have added much to the economic conflicts between villagers.

As Lewis noted further, conflicts and oppression among villagers existed in old times; in Diaz's time the caciques of Tepoztlan did not hesitate to exploit their weaker neighbors, and parallels can be found in other villages in other societies in other times. Commercialization did not introduce conflict into villages so much as to give it new dimensions, changing the rules and dissolving the ties that formerly bound villagers even as they contended with each other. The mutual aid and associated cooperative institutions of peasant societies were maintained not so much out of altruistic motives as out of the pragmatic need for cohesion in the face of pressures and threats from the outside world. Internal conflicts remained.

The transition from subsistence to commercial agriculture, as the markets for food and fiber became larger and as the farmers achieved more direct access to markets, was followed by weakening and eventual breakdown of the traditional order. During the 1920's, the village moneylenders in the subsistence economy areas of the Punjab were content to allow farmer debtors to hold and work their land, but in the prosperous areas of commercial farming, the moneylenders strove to promote default in order to take over land.[12] Proprietors held land subject to new laws and principles which did not recognize the rights and obligations of former times; the motive force for expanding production and employing labor had become not that of assuring subsistence to people as part of a system of rights and obligations but of making a profit. And, as noted earlier, the land taxes and other colonial exactions, which in former times necessitated production of a surplus and employment of labor, have decreased in many regions. Thus, employment opportunities on the land decreased relative to the size of populations.

The lack of economic opportunity in rural areas appears to be as much a problem in many Latin American and African countries where open land is readily available and could be brought into production if labor were expended on it, as in Asia where open land is limited and where increased agricultural output depends on more intensive cultivation. In India, where open land has been limited for decades, surveys of villages often note economic deterioration, landlessness, extensive poverty, etc. Such conditions were noted in similar surveys two and three generations ago when populations were smaller and little seems to have changed except that with increased commercialization of agriculture the livelihood of the lower castes is not as secure as it was in the past. While the relative economic condition of the poor has deteriorated, it is not so certain that their *absolute* economic condition has deteriorated, as evidenced by the conflicting conclusions of different reports and studies.[13] The increase in uncertainty of livelihood for some is more likely due to the changes in economic orientation towards the commercialization of agriculture, than to a paucity of resources.

Some observers have reported that the apparent low levels of unemployment observed in a number of villages of traditional non-industrial societies, at least in the recent past, was illusion. Work sharing practices which allowed people to do some little work to sustain themselves and their families, were often held to be a form of charity. As noted earlier, the term "hidden or disguised unemployment" or "underemployment" was used in this context to characterize the employment of more people than were needed to perform a task, or the employment of individuals in presumably unproductive or useless tasks. According to some economists, were the labor force smaller in such situations, the amount of production would not have decreased. Thus, a proportion of the work force was in actuality redundant, even if it did not appear to be so, while to output per worker was much lower than it needed to be and everyone was the poorer for it.[14]

This notion has been criticized for not taking into account the fact that not all people accept western values of efficiency and productivity. In many traditional societies, all who could, participated in producing the sustenance and services needed by the community. Moreover, since agricultural work is largely seasonal, the village work force has to be proportional to the seasonal work peaks, not to the average annual requirements for workers. Thus, for most of the year the work force of traditional villages may appear to be redundant. A number of agricultural economic analyses in developing countries including those of densely populated areas of India indicated that increased labor inputs resulted in increased output.[15] Schultz noted that reductions in the labor force, whether by mortality in the 1918 influenza epidemic in India, or by drafts of labor for non-agricultural work elsewhere, were followed by decreases in agricultural production.[16] As has been noted, agricultural production has increased with increased population, even with little technological advance.

Myrdal, in an extensive review of the underemployment of labor in south Asian societies, noted that for more than a century and a half, colonial administrators were concerned that their territories were overpopulated, their concerns stemming in no small part from the observations that the labor force used to produce a given product was overly large and underemployed. The presumption was that there was insufficient land and other resources to keep the work force busy. However, as populations grew, so did the product of the labor force, either through the bringing new lands into production or through intensification of work on the same land. Myrdal concluded that the concept of underemployment or hidden unemployment was not very useful in economic analysis since institutional factors, customs, tradition, and social structure, entered strongly into the determination of work patterns, valuation of leisure, levels of subsistence and payment for labor.[17]

Chayanov's rule, as it is called by Sahlins, characterizes the generation and apportionment of work in subsistence societies and states that "the greater the relative working capacity of the household, the less its members work."[18] The rule is based on Chayanov's observations that in several Russian peasant communities in tzarist times, the output per worker increased as the consumer/worker ratio of the household increased; the more consumers to be supported, the greater the intensity of work per worker; the more workers there were to produce what was needed, the less the intensity of work per worker. Whether or not the attitude of peasants towards work in a subsistence economy is more reasonable than ours, it is not a result of overpopulation.

Parkinson's Law[19], that work expands to occupy the time of the workers who are assigned to perform it, was designed for bureaucrats whose status and power depend on the number of workers and work jurisdictions they control regardless of their productivity and the utility of their output. Despite the increased productivity of labor since the depression of the 1930's when an 8-hour day became standard, partly as a labor sharing device, there has been little increase in leisure in the United States, until perhaps recently. The work time of housewives may have even increased despite washing machines, vacuum cleaners, dryers and other appliances.[20] Cleanliness and order beyond the requirements of hygiene, and less functional styles and fashions keep people busy and industry operating. Even leisure becomes equipment-intensive and expensive, and meeting these needs provides many jobs.

The concept of hidden unemployment is an ethnocentric one. The English industrialist of the eighteenth and nineteenth centuries, viewing the 40-hour week, restrictions on child labor, labor restrictive safety rules and similar labor legislation and practices of today, might have concluded that as a result, there is considerable hidden unemployment. Many of the personal services, and even professional services, which are reckoned into our economic product may, in the future, be deemed to have been unproductive and useless.

Urbanization in the Third World

While the populations of third world countries have been growing rapidly at around 2.5 percent a year, their cities have been growing twice as fast, fed by migration from the countryside as well as by births. Migration from the countryside to cities and consequent urban growth is heavier in Latin America and Africa where much potentially arable land lies unexploited, than in Asia where there is little vacant land available for settlement.[21]

The movement to cities, often attributed to overpopulation of the countryside, may in actuality reflect, as was noted earlier, the change in the economy from subsistence cultivation to one of commercial enterprise in agriculture as well as in newly developing industries. Nonetheless, the visible urban unemployment, the squatter settlements, the favelas, and shantytowns rising on the outskirts of many of the cities of the third world arouse considerable concern as a presage of things to come, the social disorganization which will attend population growth. Lacking sewage and water, educational, medical, police and other public services, filled with unemployed and underemployed, these areas appear to threaten the cities they surround, as the inner cities of the United States, having attracted the displaced poor of rural areas, appear to threaten the welfare of the communities around them.

McNamara noted that in 1950 there were 16 cities in the developing world with populations of a million or more; in 1975, there were 60 such cities, and he projected that the number will soon increase to 200. Half the increase was due to natural population growth in the cities; the other half to migration.[22] This movement to the cities, taken as an indication of the superfluity of labor on the land, was not considered a solution to the problem of population growth as jobs were not generated fast enough in the cities to accomodate the influx of migrants.

On the other hand, the economist W. A. Lewis[23] saw some advantage for capital accumulation and industrialization in the existence of a large labor surplus though not in the population growth which generated it. The surplus would facilitate payment of low wages just enough above the subsistence or institutional wage prevalent in the traditional agricultural sector to attract workers from rural areas. The low wages would, in turn, make higher profits possible; and since savings and capital accumulation are derived largely from profits, industrialization would proceed more rapidly than were there no labor surplus. Also, since much of the labor force in the agricultural sector is surplus, food production would not be much affected, a proposition which, as has been noted, is questionable. An historical analogy may be drawn with seventeenth and eighteenth century England, when enclosures forced many rural folk into the industrial towns, forcing entire families into the factories at abysmal wages. But the world has changed since those days.

Wages in the industrial sector of most developing nations are several times higher than those in the agricultural or subsistence sector, despite the apparent available surplus of labor. The differentials between urban and rural wages are increasing. Unions and political interests are often held responsible by economists for the relatively high wages in cities. But Horowitz, on the basis of her analysis, concluded that it was more profitable to pay higher wages because they result in increased productivity of workers, either through improvement in their nutrition and physical condition or through incentive effect, or for other reasons not specified.[24] The wages are thus maintained despite unemployment and labor surpluses.

In the cities of many contemporary developing countries, unemployment is found more frequently among the moderately educated young adults—for whom appropriate job opportunities are scarce, but who can afford to wait for a position consistent with their aspirations—than among the unskilled. The latter, which include a high proportion of family breadwinners, are able to find some small livings, many of which may be considered unproductive and marginal pursuits: hawking, personal services, coolie labor, and the like. One observer has noted that Haiti, a very poor rural populous nation, showed very little open unemployment, while its relatively wealthier neighbors, Jamaica, Puerto Rico, and others, showed high levels of unemployment. Per capita incomes in these latter countries have been growing as a result of economic development; but those choosing to work in the modern sector are subject to the risks of unemployment to a much greater degree than those who remain in the traditional, largely rural agricultural sectors. The pull is the relatively high wages offered (or enforced by unions) in the modern sector industries, such that the temporarily unemployed or occasionally employed are, over the long run, better off economically than those who remain in the rural areas.[25]

Thus, the recent heavy migration from rural to urban areas of developing nations may not be an indication that there is no room for the migrants on the land, as is often taken to be the case, but rather that many find urban occupations and incomes more attractive than rural, while commercialization of agriculture forces others off the land. This notion is supported by the fact that such movement is occurring in Latin America and Africa, where much of the potential agricultural land is unexploited, as well as in Asia where there is little potentially arable land open to settlement (though there remains considerable potential for the intensification of agriculture).

While the movement from the countryside to the city is often taken as an indication of the superfluity of labor on the land, the paradox is that the production of food and fiber needs to be increased and purported superfluous labor could be used to accomplish this. In some areas, relatively virgin territories need to be developed; in the more heavily settled areas, waterworks and the like need to be constructed, all possible with the investment of labor, as was done in the past in agricultural regions which are highly productive today. However, in the commercial economies dominating most of the world, industry and labor flows to meet a monetized demand rather than needs. Economic energy flows to meet the demand of those in the third world and elsewhere who are in a position to pay and to buy. Consequently, labor flows to the cities. This is not a new phenomenon. Malthus noted:

The superior encouragement that has been given to the industry of towns, and the consequent higher price that is paid for the labor of artificers, than for the labor of these employed in husbandry, are probably the reasons why so much soil in Europe remains uncultivated. Had a different policy been pursued throughout Europe, it might have been much more populous than at present, and yet not be more encumbered by its population.[26]

The government of Jakarta (Indonesia) in the late 1960's tried to limit further migration from the countryside and, in some cases, to forbid it by requiring residence permits purchased at high fees, removing sidewalk vendors, prostitutes, and loafers from the streets, and restricting other trades (such as pedicab drivers) from certain areas of the city.[27] Though migration to Jakarta was slowed, it continued nonetheless, and migrants also went to other towns. Migration to Jakarta was attractive because of the relatively higher incomes poor people could enjoy compared to what they could earn in the countryside.[28] Shantytowns proliferate in Africa and Latin America where urban living, even in shantytowns, may be more attractive because of higher wages while much rural land not intensively used may be closed to settlement because it is part of private holdings.

Many authorities regard the flow of people into the cities of the third world as a serious problem, thinking that somehow poor people can better take care of themselves economically in the country despite the increase in real earnings experienced by many of the poor when they move to the city. In some cases, the authorities may regard the poor as eyesores and would like to see them hidden away. What bothers many people is the threat of social disorganization frequently associated with urban life, particularly among poor people.

The distinction between the urban and rural way of life has a long history, sometimes to the advantage of the urban community as the creator of high culture, sometimes to the advantage of the rural community whose members are presumed to be more directly concerned with each other's welfare and needs though at the price of a demanding conformance. This distinction has given rise to the dichotomy of rural-urban or folk-urban types of communities, each with its characteristic way of life.

Some years ago, Wirth[29] proposed that the character of urban life may be explained on the basis of three variables, number, density of settlement, and heterogeneity of the urban population. Much earlier, in 1903, Simmel[30] pointed out that urban dwellers have so many more and frequent contacts with people than rural dwellers that they can maintain only superficial relations with most. Large and dense populations have been presumed to diminish the power of informal social controls and lead to increased reliance on more formal social controls, these being frequently less effectual in controlling antisocial behavior. Alienation, anomie, a lack of belonging or personal involvement, and other aspects of social and personal disorganization have frequently been considered to accompany life in cities and large settlements.

Milgram, following Simmel, proposed that

The principal point of interest for a social psychology of the city is that moral and social involvements with individuals is necessarily restricted. This is a direct and necessary function of excess of input over capacity to process. Such restriction of involvement runs a broad spectrum from refusal to become involved in the needs of another person, even when the person desperately needs assistance, through refusal to do favors to the simple withdrawal of courtesies. . . .[31]

Thus Milgram blamed the indifference of urban dwellers to each other on a need to moderate the stimulation of a great variety and frequency of person to person contact. But the indifference is more likely a result of the values embedded in the social structure and relations of the community, rural or urban. Villagers can also be insensitive to the plight of strangers.

Latane and Darley concluded, on the basis of their research on "bystander apathy," that bystanders who do not intervene to assist a person in distress do not necessarily do so out of indifference but out of indecision. They are not sure what response is appropriate; they are anxious not only because of the physical risk involved, but because of the liability which may follow, even though it be nothing more than to appear foolish as when one invades another's privacy.[32] In our malpractice and damage suit prone society, the penalty can be more substantial.

Indifference, lack of community, and anonymity are not necessary features of urban life; the city itself may not be regarded as a community by its inhabitants but as the place in which their community is located. Jane Jacobs[33] has pointed to the informal surveillance of city streets and other public places by inhabitants and shopkeepers in some of the older neighborhoods of New York City. The indigenous organization of such neighborhoods was contrasted with the breakdown which often occurred under the impact of planners. Shops were removed from residential areas; the latter were designed to insure privacy while at the same time accomodating large numbers of people. Even public places, hallways, streets, were designed to become so private that they are empty much of the time and escape the surveillance which hinders criminals. Jacobs' point was that the indigenous ways of coping with density led to greater security than the sophisticated approach taken by planners who treated density on some abstract level.

Hauser in his review of urban-rural and urban-folk dichotomies[34] noted that the prediction of community characteristics by size, density, and homogeneity was poor, a view shared in much of the research cited by him. He examined the characteristics and lifestyles of urban dwellers in Asian cities in which he had lived and found them not to conform with the expectations frequently held. Within the urban areas the actual communities in which people lived out their lives were homogeneous and closely knit. Oscar Lewis also noted that city life did not necessarily result in greater secularization, anonymity, breaking of family ties, etc. The poor folk of Mexico City were even more religiously Catholic than their village antecedents; extended family ties increased in the city and many village beliefs persisted.[35]

The capabilities of people in squatter settlements to maintain these as viable communities and develop them into cities and towns, is generally underestimated. The popular journals present photographic essays of dirty children, skinny adults, and shanties which evoke pity and horror. Yet a closer examination may reveal adaptive people, showing considerable enterprise, making progress.

Mangin reported on a long-term and intensive study of one such community on the fringes of Lima in Peru.[36] Most of the inhabitants of the barriada studied by Mangin, had been city dwellers who moved out to the shantytown because they could make a better life for themselves there than in the city's slums. Though their incomes were low, barriada families were relatively more stable than those of the old urban slum and rural areas; nor did they live the life of squalor or hopelessness associated with the "culture of poverty." With time and in the face of frequent official overt and violent objections, the inhabitants of the barriadas brought in water, built sewage systems, improved their houses, established stores and workshops; the barriada took on more and more the aspects of a well-established community. All this occurred within the framework of a democratic process, though personal power ploys and conflict intervened as might be expected. The squatters produced their own solution to the housing needs of new migrants and others, a solution that official agencies could not begin to tackle.

Papanek[37] in his survey of the poor of Jakarta reported that their neighborhoods, ill served by public services, were stable social organizations. Cooperative self help was nearly universal and the neighborhoods appeared to be comprised of villages transplanted to the urban environment. The majority had some education and were literate. Of the stigmata of the so-called "culture of poverty" (social disorganization, alienation, etc.), the only ones particularly evident were poverty itself and fear of the government, the latter with apparently good reason.

Slums are not unusual phenomena in urban history nor are the creation of the equivalent of favelas and shantytowns unique to the current population boom in developing countries. The conditions of these rapidly growing urban areas are gruesome, but hardly more so than the reports of observers of the slums of the same cities fifty years ago when their populations were smaller. Geddes' writing of his observations of Calcutta and Bombay in the 1920s and 1930s noted:

. . . under the full impact of the commercial and industrial revolution, these cities grew up almost unchecked by legislation of the kind which began to abate the horror of British ports, manufacturing towns and mines more than a century ago. . . .

and went on to describe horrors exceeding any noted today.[38] The slums of eighteenth and nineteenth century European cities, terrible as they were, appeared no worse than those in America where there was plentiful land and resources. Nor are contemporary seemingly irresolvable urban problems of considerable magnitude confined to developing countries. Description of the slums of Calcutta, its population expanded by an influx of refugees from the partition of India and by migrants from rural areas, are harrowing. So are descriptions of the slums of New York; a city which has not grown much in the last decades, but whose population has changed character as the displaced poor sought a place there. Cities of past ill repute such as Havana and Shanghai have changed considerably under the reforming zeal of revolutionary governments. Crime, vice, and violence have purportedly been eliminated though the cities have not lost in population.

The growth of cities is limited by the productivity of the rural sector which produces raw food and fiber. In the United States and western Europe the relatively small number of people engaged directly in agriculture supported by urban technology, provides food and fiber for a much larger population, up to 20 times its size. Davis discounted the capability of technology to significantly help increase food production in the third world in view of the scarcity of energy and fertilizer. He proposed that the density of agricultural settlement in Asia placed severe limitations on urban growth, for the farmers would not be able to produce a sufficient food surplus to support a large urban sector.[39] Among other factors, he noted the limitation of farm acreage in South Korea where the average farm decreased in size from .90 hectares in 1959 to .88 hectares in 1970, and in Taiwan where average farm size declined from 1.6 hectares in 1901–1910 to 1.2 hectares in 1950–1960. These were odd choices to illustrate the point, for both countries are often cited as models of modernization, industrialization, urbanization, food sufficiency, and declining birth rates in the third world.

In the colder climates of Europe and America of the past, increased agricultural production was often obtained by bringing more land under the plow. In South and East Asia today, increased agricultural production is often obtained by cropping the same piece of land more than once a year; in some areas three crops a year are possible. In Korea, approximately one and a half crops per year are produced on cultivated land; in Taiwan, up to 1.9 crops are produced.[40] In India, however, only about 15 percent of land is in effect double cropped though multiple cropping has been known together with the appropriate land management techniques in tropical lands, for thousands of years.[41] Thus, it is inappropriate to compare agricultural densities in Europe and North America with those of Asian tropical countries as indications of the future potential of agricultural production in Asia.

However, there is no reason why residential patterns of settlement need to follow the western trends if such turn out to be nonfunctional. Most people of developing nations are likely to remain in the rural agricultural sector for some time to come resulting in increasing density of rural areas. Kerala, the state with the highest rural population densities in India in 1961, may be a case in point. In the 1961 census, the population density of Kerala was reported as 1,127 persons per square mile, more than two and a half times the Indian average. About 85 percent of its population was reported living in rural areas making for an average rural density of about 1,000 persons per square mile. In one district (Allepey), with 83 percent of the population rural, the population density was 2,600 persons per square mile. Cultivated acreage per person or per household in Kerala was the smallest for Indian states.

Per capita income in Kerala for 1955–1956 was less than average for India, Rs.228 vs. Rs.255, but not much less. (The all-India per capita income included the relatively high incomes generated by commercial and industrial cities such as Bombay, Calcutta, Ahmedabad and others.) However, the productivity of agriculture in Kerala more than matched the average productivity of Indian agriculture. In 1960–1961, Kerala produced almost three times the average produce per acre (in Rs.) as did Indian agriculture in general.[42]

The 1961 census reported that 55 percent of Kerala males and 39 percent of Kerala females were literate, for an overall literacy rate of 47 per 100. In Allepey, the densest district, the overall literacy rate was 57 per 100. (The literacy rate for all India was 24 per 100.) Since the literacy rate is based on the total population, the rates for those over ten years old would be about 35 percent greater. Also, Kerala had the lowest infant mortality, two to three times the number of health and medical facilities per capita as did India; and a sex ratio of 1,022 females per 1,000 males (the highest of the states), an indication that females are not subject to the excessive female mortality characteristics of India, with a sex ration of 941 women to 1,000 males in 1961. The fertility of Kerala during the preceding decade had still been high, around 39 births per 1,000 population.

Reports from the 1971 census indicated that during the preceding ten years, the density of Kerala had increased to about 1,420 persons per square mile, an increase of 27 percent. Literacy had increased to some 60 percent of the total population (at least 75 percent of those over ten years of age). In general, the impression is of greater stability and less turbulence during the 1960s and early 1970s than in the 1950s. There are also various indications that fertility is declining rapidly in Kerala and that official birth control programs are being increasingly patronized. The death rate is 9 per 1,000 population; life expectancy in Kerala is 60 years, the highest in India. Kerala has the highest proportion of villages with protected water supplies and though they are poor, its people consume by and large nutritionally adequate diets even if not the most opulent.[43]

Urbanization is not the only resolution to high density in rural settlement. In some areas of the world, it may well be possible if not probable that densely populated rural communities will preserve much of their agrarian economies while developing amenities which were formerly available only to urban people.

Notes

1. Quoted in H. J. Muller, *Freedom in the Ancient World* (New York: Harper, 1961), p. 254.
2. Quoted in C. Bridenbaugh, *Vexed and Troubled Englishmen, 1590–1642* (New York: Oxford University Press, 1969), p. 397.
3. Ibid., p. 397.
4. Quoted in Bridenbaugh, op. cit., p. 397.
5. G. Myrdal, *Population, A Problem for Democracy* (Cambridge, Mass.: Harvard University Press, 1940); A. H. Hansen, "Economic Progress and Declining Population Growth," *American Economic Review* 29 (March 1939), pp. 1–15.

6. D. G. Mandelbaum, *Society in India*, 2 vols. (Berkeley: University of California Press, 1970).

7. R. Redfield, *Tepoztlan, A Mexican Village: A Study of Folk Life*, (Chicago: University of Chicago Press, 1930).

8. O. Lewis, *Life in a Mexican Village, Tepoztlan Restudied* (Urbana: University of Illinois Press, 1951).

9. R. Redfield, *The Little Community and Peasant Society and Culture* (Chicago: University of Chicago Press, 1960), pp. 135--7 (The Little Community).

10. R. Stavenhagen, "Social Aspects of Agrarian Structure in Mexico," in R. Stavenhagen, ed., *Agrarian Problems and Peasant Movements in Latin America* (New York: Doubleday Anchor, 1970); also E. H. and C. H. Jacoby, *Man and Land: The Essential Revolution* (New York: Alfred A. Knopf, 1971), p. 43.

11. Lewis, op. cit., p. 117.

12. M. Darling, *The Punjab Peasant in Prosperity and Debt* (Bombay: Oxford University Press, 1957), Chapter 12; cited by G. Myrdal, *Asian Drama*, 3 vols. (New York: Pantheon, 1968).

13. See, for instance, R. Cassen, "Welfare and Population: Notes on Rural India Since 1960," *Population and Development Review* Population Council, 6:1 (September 1975), pp. 33--70.

14. C. H. C. Kao, K. R. Anschel and C. K. Eicher, "Disguised Unemployment in Agriculture: A Survey," in C. K. Eicher and L. W. Witt, eds., *Agriculture in Economic Development* (New York: McGraw-Hill, 1964). See also Chapter 6, note 11.

15. M. Paglin, "Surplus Agricultural Labor and Development: Facts and Theories," *American Economic Review* (September 1965), pp. 815--34; C. H. Rao, *Agricultural Production Functions, Costs and Returns in India* (Bombay: Asia Publishing House, 1965).

16. T. W. Schultz, *Transforming Traditional Agriculture* (New Haven: Yale University Press, 1964), pp. 67--70.

17. See G. Myrdal, op. cit., Appendix 6, "A Critical Appraisal of the Concept and Theory of Underemployment," pp. 2041--61.

18. M. Sahlins, *Stone Age Economics* (Chicago: Aldine Atherton, 1972), p. 87; based on A. V. Chayanov, *The Theory of Peasant Economy* (Homewood, Ill.: R. D. Irwin, for the American Economic Association, 1966).

19. C. N. Parkinson, *Parkinson's Law* (Boston: Houghton Mifflin, 1957).

20. J. Vanek, "Time Spent in Housework," *Scientific American* 231:5 (November 1974), pp. 116--20.

21. For a more detailed analysis of relative rates of change in urban and rural populations of the different continents, see K. Davis, "Asia's Cities: Problems and Options," *Population and Development Review* 1:1 (September 1975), pp. 71--86.

22. R. S. McNamara, "Urban Poverty in Developing Countries: A World Bank Analysis," Address to the 30th Annual Meeting of the International Monetary Fund and the World Bank Group, Sept. 1, 1975.

23. W. A. Lewis, "Economic Development With Unlimited Supplies of Labor," in A. N. Agarwala and S. P. Singh, *The Economies of Underdevelopment* (London: Oxford University Press, 1958), pp. 400--49; originally published in *The Manchester School* 22 (May 1954), pp. 139--92; G. Ranis and J. C. H. Fei, "A Theory of Economic Development," *American Economic Review* 51:4 (September 1961), pp. 533--65.

24. See G. Horowitz, "Wage Determination in a Labor Surplus Economy. The Case of India," *Economic Development and Cultural Change* 22:4 (July 1974), pp. 666--72.

25. See G. M. Tidrick, "Wage Spillover and Unemployment in a Wage Gap Economy: The Jamaican Case," *Economic Development and Cultural Change* 23:2, (January 1975), pp. 306--24; R. G. Ridker and H. Lubell, eds., *Employment and Unemployment Problems of the Near East and South Asia*, 2 vols. (New Delhi: Vikas Publications, 1971, as reviewed by J. R. Eriksson in *Economic Development and Cultural Change* 23:1 (October 1974), pp. 193--97; R. A. Berry, "Open Unemployment as a Social Problem in Urban Colombia: Myth and Reality," *Economic Development and Cultural Change* 23:2 (January 1975), pp. 276--91.

26. T. R. Malthus, "An Essay on the Principle of Population," (London: 1798), in G. Himmelfarb, ed., *T. R. Malthus, On Population* (New York: Modern Library, 1961), "First Essay," p. 121.

27. G. F. Papenek, "The Poor of Jakarta," *Economic Development and Cultural Change* 24:1 (October 1975), pp. 1--28.

28. Ibid.

29. L. Wirth, *Community Life and Social Policy* (Chicago: University of Chicago Press, 1956), p. 117.

30. G. Simmel, *The Sociology of George Simmel*, K. H. Wolf, ed., (Glencoe, Ill.: The Free Press, 1950), pp. 409--16.

31. S. Milgram, "The Experience of Living in Cities," *Science* 167 (March 1970), pp. 1461--68.

32. B. Latane and J. M. Darley, "Bystander Apathy," *American Scientist* 57:2 (1969), pp. 244--68.

33. J. Jacobs, *The Death and Life of Great American Cities* (New York: Random House, 1961).

34. P. M. Hauser, "Observations on the Urban-Folk and Urban-Rural Dichotomies as Forms of Western Ethnocentrism," in P. M. Hauser and L. F. Schnore, eds., *The Study of Urbanization* (New York: Wiley, 1965), pp. 503--17.

35. O. Lewis, "Further Observations on the Folk-Urban Continuum and Urbanization with Special Reference to Mexico City," in P. M. Hauser and L. F. Schnore, eds., *The Study of Urbanization* op. cit., pp. 491--503.

36. W. Mangin, "Squatter Settlements," *Scientific American* 217:4 (October 1967), pp. 21--29.

37. Papenek, op. cit.

38. A. Geddes, "The Social and Psychological Significance of Variability in Population Changes with Examples from India, 1871--1941, *Human Relations* 1:2 (1947), pp. 181--205.

39. Davis, op. cit.

40. D. G. Dalrympler, *Survey of Multiple Cropping in Less Developed Nations*, Foreign Agricultural Economic Report No. 91 (Washington, D.C.: U.S. Department of Agriculture, Economic Research Service, October 1971).

41. Ibid., ch. 2.

42. India, National Council of Applied Economic Research, *Agricultural Income by States, 1960--61*, Occasional Paper No. 7 (New Delhi, 1963).

43. A. Berg, "The Trouble With Triage," *New York Times Magazine* June 15, 1975, pp. 21, 26--35; see also Indian Census 1961, 1971.

13

Other Purported Consequences of Population Growth

Density and Social Pathology

Overpopulation evokes visions of crowding and high densities. Calhoun studied rats and mice to determine the effect of crowding and density on behavior. He would confine a colony of rats (or mice) to a space large enough for them to carry on normally. The colony was provided with adequate food and water, permitting an increase in numbers through reproduction not limited by lack of sustenance. In time, density reached a level at which a variety of behavioral disorders appeared. Nesting and lactating behavior was disturbed; a high rate of infant mortality, maternal mortality and pregnancy failure ensued. Many males became sexually disoriented, others became abnormally aggressive, attacking and biting without provocation; others became quite apathetic and passive, never copulating, never fighting, totally withdrawn and isolated; huddling became so common that much of the available space was unused. The population of rats decreased and did not recover even when the population dwindled below the density at which the troubles had started. The integrity of the rat society had been destroyed in what Calhoun called a "behavioral sink."[1]

An example of a human society which reproduced itself into a "behavioral sink" is hard to find. But Calhoun found an analogy to his overpopulated rat and mice colonies in the Ik people described by Colin Turnbull.[2] These people, perhaps, the meanest on earth, live on an African mountain in Uganda, restricted there by the government which appropriated their former range for a wildlife preserve. The Ik take pleasure in each other's misfortunes, adding to them by persecuting one another indiscriminately without distinction of age, friendship, family, or stranger. Injured or feeble persons may be harried maliciously to a needless death. They steal food from each other; husband against wife and both against such children as are born. In many respects they exhibit the same characteristics as the individually and socially disorganized rats and mice of the behavioral sink. Calhoun proposed that these unfortunate people are an example of the future of the human race if breeding continues apace, the Ik being formerly a people able to roam free and now confined to a lesser space.[3]

The likeness of the Iks and Calhoun's rats is not strange; both were disorganized. But the Ik did not get that way through mindless breeding. They were put into a disorganized condition by other more powerful humans.

Up to recent times, the Ik appeared to have been a well organized and cooperative hunting and gathering people. Their present mountain home was formerly a temporary resting place in their nomadic wandering; it was otherwise economically insignificant. The most important area to them was the Kidepo Valley, rich in the wildlife from which they derived their livelihood. They were precipitously banished from the Valley on its conversion to a game reserve. They were obliged to make do with a mountain, having little knowledge of how to make a living from it, though this cannot entirely explain their failure to do so. Turnbull noted that there were other mountain people, not far distant, who had made the transition from hunting and gathering to hillside agriculture while maintaining the integrity of their society. Perhaps the reason they accomplished this was that they had made the change under their own impetus, developing institutions appropriate to a cultivating society as well as the necessary skills and knowledge. The Ik, on the contrary, lost their old institutional controls and developed no new ones. Instead, they resorted to the crassest forms of individualism and materialism, the immediate advantage of one over another becoming the guiding principle of behavior. Such cooperation as occurred was brittle and transient. In times of plenty, little food was stored for it would be stolen or even destroyed for spite. In times of dearth, they depended on government relief but had no way of distributing it among themselves. Those who got to the relief station first collected the rations, gorged themselves, and left nothing for others. Children were turned out to shift for themselves at an early age. The prospect for this society disappearing in a generation or two is substantial. The Ik are hardly crowded on their mountain. What appears obvious is that they lost their culture and sense of worthiness, becoming literally demoralized in the process.

Density cannot be blamed for the demoralized personal and social behavior of many if not all people placed in concentration camps, with little hope of survival or for the alcoholism and suicide rates of American Indians, forced onto reservations and bereft of human dignity. Indeed, most examples of the detrimental effects of density are of situations where people have been deliberately contained under oppressive conditions often designed to destroy the integrity of their culture. In contrast to the Ik, the transition from hunting to farming, though perhaps accompanied by some stress, did not result in obvious psychopathology among most of the myriads who made that transition in history.

That density affects human behavior adversely would appear to be common sense. Crime, mental illness, disease, family breakdown, and other forms of social pathology are more prevalent in certain crowded and densely populated sections of American cities than elsewhere. But these are also the poorer sections. Winsborough[4] critically examined the proposition that more densely populated neighborhoods (of Chicago) were subject to greater social pathology and illness (as measured by indices of infant mortality, tuberculosis rates, age-standardized public assistance rates, and child dependency) than were the less densely populated neighborhoods. He determined that when the socio-economic status of neighborhoods was controlled, only the infant mortality rate appeared related to density while tuberculosis rates, age-standardized death rates, and public assistance rates were lower in the denser neighborhoods. In different neighborhoods inhabited by people of the same social class, population density and social pathology are not consistently associated. Others have proposed that the important factor is not so much density as crowding—the number of people per room, etc.[5] But when social class and related factors are controlled the added effect of crowding appears to be small.

The actual advantages of population density have not escaped notice. Jonathan Freedman explored the issue of crowding and behavior and found that high density living in well planned urban complexes made possible the fulfillment of many human aspirations not otherwise satisfied. After reviewing a large body of research on the effects of population density he noted:

Large scale survey and demographic studies have generally failed to find an effect of density when other factors are controlled; observational studies in the field have produced mixed results; and controlled experimental studies have, with a few exceptions, found either no effects of density, or complex inconsistent effects.[6]

Many European cities with as great (or greater) densities as those of the United States show a fraction of the crime of the latter. Nor dos the quality of life in many European countries having greater density than the United States appear to be worse. The land area in these countries available for living and recreation is considerably less, yet living is no more stressful and is possibly less so due to the greater and more effective application of social and urban planning. One may point to various differences in the organization and composition of European communities, but this is exactly the point which needs to be attended to—not density.

Despite the difficulty in establishing a link between population density and quality of life, many observers still feel that there must be such a link even though it is not readily observed. Two noted analysts (Day and Day) call for more research and the development of better and more sophisticated measures of population density and its effects.[8]

The simple definitions and conceptions of population density may be inadequate and better ones may be needed. But the relationship between population density and social pathology or even quality of life are just not obvious. This does not imply that humans will live happily at any level of density but that people tend not to exceed the population densities with which they can effectively cope. The very rapid decline in the birth rates of eastern Europe, including European Russia, may, in good part, be due to the low priority given to housing development relative to industrial development while the aspirations of the population for living space and lifestyle had changed from those of their forebears. To put it another way, social or interpersonal relations in the modern family are such that crowding is not well tolerated and therefore avoided though this avoidance may involve not having children which people may otherwise wish to have. This was not so in the past.

On casual overview, the density of peoples within a settlement bore little relation to the land available for occupancy. Throughout history, settled peoples have tended to live closely packed. Farmers rarely lived on the land as in America and Scandinavia, but in villages and hamlets which, though inhabited by relatively small numbers of people, were often crowded. And within the villages, houses were small, one or two rooms to accomodate five or six people. Security appeared to lay in the huddling of the people, though there was plenty of room and the houses were of simple construction, not difficult to erect.

The space available on this planet for human settlement is finite and its boundaries well defined. The vision of humanity filling every nook and crevice of this space is easily evoked. The consequences presented are of people having to live in dangerous places, exhausting the land, leaving no room for those who look for solitude and the enjoyment of unspoiled nature, destroying the heritage of future generations, and living so close to each other that they become physically and mentally ill.

A scientist commenting on the storms which in late 1970 led to the death of hundreds of thousands of people of the coastal deltas and island of Bangladesh, proposed that had there been fewer people they would not have had to live in such a dangerous place.[8] This argument ignores completely the history of human settlement.

Many thousands of years ago, when there were possibly no more than five to ten millions of people, all the continents of the earth were inhabited. Some people lived in the frigid north, others in river valleys subject to the perils of flooding, still others lived in the shadow of volcanos; some lived in houses built on stilts over lakes and lagoons, others burrowed into cliffs, and yet still others moved to the high Andes and other mountains which required physiological adjustment to the low oxygen tensions of such high altitudes. In contemporary America, some wealthy people, whose alternatives are many, prefer to build houses precariously perched on cliffs and hurricane coasts and islands where the risk of destruction is appreciable. Large tracts of expensive and desired real estate in Florida were subjected to hurricanes 50 years ago. This did not discourage resettlement.

Consider Tristan de Cunha. In the 1960s, the several hundred inhabitants of this small and poorly endowed island in the South Atlantic were evacuated and relocated in England after their volcanic island home erupted and was covered with lava. They were presumably provided assistance in making the readjustment. After several years, with no sign of volcanic activity, practically all the former inhabitants elected to return to their primitive and precarious existence on Tristan de Cunha against the advice of the British government. The pace of life in England was perhaps too competitive for them. The people of Tristan preferred the risk of a total holocaust, of which they had had a preview, and the limitations of life on a small, bleak island to a life into which they did not fit and with which they could not cope.

The major forces which caused peoples to spread over the world were economic pressures, aggressive neighbors, or just the satisfactions of a nomadic life. When people were relatively few and communities or bands small, they ranged over large territories in the course of making a living. Hunters and gatherers, swidden cultivators and pastoral nomads left few exploitable areas untouched. The larger communities of settled cultivators, in effect, took up relatively less of the world's space for a long while. The settled communities still use only a small portion of the earth's land surface, though the wealthier citizens of the world still manage to roam all over.

Except for South America and Africa, few regions not now settled are suitable for farming. In Europe and Asia more than 80 percent of the potentially arable land is cultivated. In Latin America and Africa, one half the potentially arable land is cultivated.[9] Asian agricultural productivity (excluding Japan) is but a fraction of that of Europe, and increased food production will depend upon increasing yields per acre. Even if all potentially cultivable land on earth were eventually put to the plow, as much as three-quarters of the earth's land area could remain wilderness or potential wilderness if properly managed. This may be decreased somewhat if advances in technology make it feasible to farm desert areas which are not now considered to be potentially arable. The principal threat to these areas comes from the exploitation of the non-agricultural resources they may contain, a threat which stems more from economic growth than from population growth.

Population, Economic Growth, and the Environment

Few observers regard population size and growth as the sole or even the principal cause of environmental problems. Affluence and technology are recognized as contributing significantly to problems of pollution and environmental degradation. But many people believe that these problems are greatly exacerbated and their resolution impeded by excessive population and by population growth. If the population were not growing, resources would be exploited more slowly and the amount of pollution would be less. Thus, whatever the source of pollution, increased population is presented as a multiplier of the magnitude of the problem.

A model, defining the multiplier effect of population, was presented by Barry Commoner in an attempt to separate the effects on pollution of population growth, increased affluence taken as consumption per capita, and changes in technology. Increased consumption may reflect not only growing affluence but also changes in ways of living that do not imply enhanced welfare. Suburban sprawl may make it necessary for many people to drive cars. Commoner concluded that technological changes, not population or affluence, are the principal source of pollution.[10]

In the Commoner model, pollution = population × affluence × technology; the amount of pollution is considered to be the product of the impact of technology (for example, nitrogen oxide emissions per automobile mile traveled), affluence or consumption (automobile miles traveled per capita), and population. Nitrogen oxide emissions per mile are presumed to reflect the technological design of cars. The effects of changes may be evaluated as in the following example. Total nitrogen oxide emissions from automobiles increased 630 percent between 1946 and 1967. For every 100 cc of nitrogen oxide emissions in 1946, there were 730 in 1967. Nitrogen oxide emissions are estimated to have increased 158 percent per automobile mile driven.

Miles driven per capita increased 100 percent. Population increased 41 percent. Thus, in 1967, each automobile on the average emitted 2.58 times as much nitrogen oxide per mile driven as in 1946; each person drove twice as many miles on the average and there were 1.41 times as many people. The product

$$2.58 \times 2.00 \times 1.41 = 7.30$$

represents the volume of nitrogen oxide emissions in 1967 relative to that of 1946, an increase of 630 percent. If population had remained the same as in 1946, total nitrogen oxide emissions would have increased 416 percent, or 66 percent of the actual increase. But, if only the population had increased, the increase in nitrogen oxide would have amounted to 41 percent, or 6.5 percent of the actual total increase. Since the factors leading to increased pollution are multiplicative, there is no mathematically valid way of expressing precisely the relative contribution of each factor without reference to the others. Moreover, it is often difficult to distinguish between true affluence and the imperatives of travel and consumption of goods which originate in the way business is conducted and is thus a cost of production—even if an enjoyable one.

Erlich used the same formula, but held that, in any case, the increase in pollution would have been less by a considerable proportion had population not increased.[11] Regardless of the source of increased pollution, at some point the capacity of natural environmental systems to manage pollution becomes severely taxed. A body of water may be able to handle increasing waste effluents up to a point, after which its capacity to degrade the effluents breaks down. Similarly, artificial means of degrading pollution, as in sewage treatment, may become prohibitively expensive after some point is reached. Thus, the argument goes, even if the pollution resulting from increased population were small, there would appear to be considerable value attached to avoiding population growth. This belief may be illusory and the type of analysis which partitions pollution into the effects of population, affluence, and technology, treating these as independent factors may be, in many respects, misleading.

Population growth and its components, births, deaths, and immigration are not independent of the way people live. If people had smaller families, they might well use their surplus incomes to drive still fancier cars more miles; they could fly more air miles on more expensive and more frequent vacations and, thus, become more extravagant users of resources and producers of pollution. They may even have had fewer children in order to have the opportunity to use their surplus income in this manner. If they had large families, they might not be able to spend so much on automobiles, though they might spend more on other things. The increase of pollution is most marked in countries with low population growth rates where it far exceeds the increase in population.[12]

As was discussed in greater detail earlier, the decline in fertility and population growth in western countries was generally associated with increased income and consumption, with some exceptions. During the economic depression of the 1930s, when incomes fell, so did fertility, as many people tried to maintain their reference standard of living and consumption. During post-World War II baby boom, people found that with tastes based on the depression period and the improved economic conditions, they could have both an acceptable standard of living and children. During the 1960s, children, at least in quantity, lost value as well as becoming more costly. Fertility declined as incomes and standards of consumption increased. In a society in which consumption, including expenditures on children, is an important focus of lifestyle, a decrease in population growth and the implied lesser number of children per family is not likely to result in a decline of total consumption unless the family's income also declines. During the 1950s in the United States, a period of increasing fertility until after the middle of that decade, consumption of consumer durables hardly kept pace with increasing incomes. During the 1960s, a period of declining fertility, the purchase of durables increased twice as fast as incomes.

Freedman[13] reported that those Taiwan families who practiced birth control also spent more of their income on consumer durables. Among households with the same income, those which possessed more of such modern items as television sets, refrigerators, and electric rice cookers were also likely to have been more successful family planners as well as better savers. Those families which lived in the more traditional fashion were presumed more likely to have spent the excess of income over subsistence needs on ceremonials such as marriages, funerals, feasts, and other social cementing activities. Thus, lowering of fertility associated with the adoption of modern styles of living will not result in diminished demands on the environment if economic processes in the developing nations parallel those of the West.

The characteristics of economic growth differ as that growth serves to support in various combinations, an increasing population, a rising level of affluence, and full employment levels of economic activity. The first purpose, an increasing population, involves increasing outputs through increasing labor inputs with sufficient additional capital investment and technological innovation to escape the law of diminishing returns. The second, a rising level of affluence, and third, full employment, often linked in modern industrial society, involve increasing the productivity of labor, heavy capital investments, new technologies and materials frequently requiring intensive expenditures of energy and material resources while generating considerable nondegradable pollution in the process. Moreover, the realization of the third purpose depends upon maintaining an increasing level of economic activity. Profits or other incentives are needed to activate the system. One way to assure that the system operates profitably and continuously involves the production of waste, frequent changes in models, in technology, in materials, and through planned obsolescence and other designs to assure continuing purchases. Advertising and promotion create or reinforce anxieties and then palliate them by generating products and services otherwise having little utility. The generation of waste is not confined to private sector enterpreneurs; bureaucrats, professionals, and the military all generate useless work, products and services to enhance their statuses, but in doing so, they also generate employment.

Economic growth arising from the imperatives and dynamics of modern economic systems is more demanding of resources and the environment than those arising from population. Lower levels of population growth would not slow the assault on the environment by much: Were the population of Europe and the United States half their current size, the current state of resource depletion and environmental degradation might have been delayed no more than a decade or two, so rapid has been the increase in per capita resource utilization. The pace of resource utilization may not be as significant as the pace of compensatory action, reclamation, the development of alternative resources, particularly in the substitution of renewable for non-renewable resources. This does not occur in our society until the situation clearly demands it, that is to say, until it is profitable to do so or intolerable not to.

Schumacher[14] proposed a change in the technological style of production to one which is energy conserving, more labor intensive and yet would have little impact on the comforts and conveniences we enjoy. To this end, he assembled a staff of technologists to plan and develop new modes of production. Commoner and others have suggested the use of less destructive technologies, using the wind, sun, tides and other natural forces as sources of energy. Meritorious as many of these suggestions may be, the problem is not so much a lack of technological knowledge or ideas, but how to introduce them into a social and economic structure in which small decentralized operations, labor intensive technologies, increased costs, and the like are inconsistent with the incentives which energize the economy in capitalist, and also socialist economies. The issue is not technological but social.

An expanding economy not only helps to maintain full employment but also helps to compensate for inequities in wealth and income. With increasing productivity comes increasing per capita output and income. As per capita income increases, those who were not very well off may see their personal condition improving if everyone gets a share of the increase. This mitigates the resentment and conflict which would otherwise occur because of wide differences in income. The income of those who were better off also increases; otherwise they would see themselves as becoming relatively worse off, an eventuality they can resist, as they have the power to do so. From 1950--1970, average real per capita income in the United States increased around 55 percent, but by 1970 there was a slightly wider gap between the low income classes and the high income classes.[15]

Under the press of discontent with unequal income distribution and the need for employment security, the economy must keep expanding. Expansion in the service sector of the economy may help attain full employment, but since individuals measure their well-being by material possessions and energy usage, in housing and conveniences, in automobiles, in travel and the like, expansion must also occur in the industrial and related sectors. Increased costs of consumer durables associated with an expansion of pollution control industry are likely to spread to other sectors as people try to keep up. The intrinsic costs of pollution control may be small but are likely to be multiplied by the profiteering and encumbrances which tend to proliferate with opportunity in our society.

To resolve pollution by controls resulting in a slowdown in economic growth or increasing inflation may be self-defeating. Ignoring or just paying lip service, as is often done, to the needs and aspirations of the mass of people, will not in the long run help preserve the environment. Those whose livelihoods are threatened will perceive environmental controls as compatible only with the interests of a few and detrimental to themselves.

The problem of pollution is thus related to the hard fact that it is generated by activities which are of considerable profit to a small group, powerful enough to escape its impact, and represent employment opportunities to the larger number who are obliged to tolerate some level of discomfort or even peril, if they are to maintain their livelihood and living standards. To those whose livelihood is insecure, talk about the quality of life becomes somewhat empty. People may be moved to control pollution if and when the detriments exceed the benefits derived under the socio-economic order.

As was noted earlier settled communities, unlike small mobile communities which can move on after they have fouled an area, cannot depend on the unaided processes of nature to dilute and degrade their wastes quickly enough to avoid their noxious effects. The water supplies of peasant villages, no matter how small, were generally polluted and unsafe and the ground a reservoir of parasites. The cities of former times, more hazardous than the countryside, were the places where the science and technology of dealing with pollution arose. If urban mortality differentials of the eighteenth century and the conditions which gave rise to this mortality were projected into the future, the cities of today would not be in existence. (In rural Sweden of 1755–1756, life expectancy for males was 33, but in Stockholm it was reported to be 14 years.) Today, even the crowded dirty cities of third world countries are healthier places than their rural hinterlands, and the smoggy cities of the modern world are immeasurably healthier than the old horse-manured cities with their flies and other disease vectors. The difference between the cities of former times and those of today, is due to the control and management of larger quantities of less degradable wastes. The Thames became in effect an open sewer in the nineteenth century, but recently, with sewage treatment, the quality of the Thames, serving a much larger population than it did formerly, is improving.[16] Knowledge and technology have played a part in the improvement of conditions since those days and so has the increase in the power of many people to demand and realize more healthful circumstances for themselves.

Awareness, recognition and action to obviate noxious conditions are not merely matters of accumulating appropriate knowledge, though this is, of course, essential. Delays in accumulating such knowledge as well as acting on it may be due in large part to political and economic considerations. Political and economic power are not distributed uniformly, nor are the impacts of noxious products and techniques. If the people affected by "Minamata Disease" had been politically powerful, or if the owners and managers of the Chisso Corporation which discharged mercury wastes into Minamata Bay had suffered the consequent poisoning or had not profited thereby, "Minamata Disease" would not have reached such terrible and epidemic proportions before steps were taken to eliminate its cause.[17] By the same token, if miners had alternatives, they would not knowingly have had to expose themselves to a high risk of severely disabling accidents, occupational diseases, and death.

Concern about pollution and intervention to abate it have preceded the appearance of no-growth enthusiasts, and the success of such efforts has largely depended on how these efforts affected the overall welfare of the populace. An ordinance against the burning of sea coal was passed in London, a relatively small city during Elizabethan times, but was not consistently enforced for the simple reason that there was no other practicable way to keep warm. The other physical characteristics of life were not so pleasant for most people that coal dusts and smoke added much to their discomfort. An eminent success in recent times was the banning of D.D.T. The application of D.D.T. in malaria and typhus control programs in war-disordered Europe and in developing nations had saved the lives of millions of people, and contributed to the health and vigor of many more. In developed countries, D.D.T. was an important adjunct to economic growth in agriculture until it was replaced by other less stable, more degradable compounds though, as in the case of organic phosphates, these represent a health problem for the workers who use them. A number of years passed before the detrimental effects of D.D.T. on the reproduction of some wildlife was recognized, and it has not yet been shown to have had significant deleterious effects on humans. Nonetheless, in the United States, the use of D.D.T. has been severely restricted, banned in effect since 1972, and its concentration in biota is diminishing.[18] Whether the ban on D.D.T. would have held if the less stable substitutes had not been developed or if some situation had arisen, such as a typhus epidemic, in which the use of D.D.T. was essential, is questionable.

Had populations been smaller or agricultural growth slower, D.D.T. would still have been used since, as an effective weapon against pests, it increased agricultural efficiency. The accumulation of D.D.T. in the environment and its concentration in the environment would undoubtedly have been less rapid. But in all likelihood, so would the recognition of its ill effects and the action taken to obviate these effects. The generation of pollution depends on the levels and types of economic activity, the technologies involved and, to a lesser degree, on population size. The control of pollution requires intervention; nature's way of controlling pollution is often insufficient, while action to obviate pollution does not occur until the pollution becomes intolerable. Thus, the levels and types of pollution and actions to control them in various countries of similar economic characteristics but of differing population densities appear to be remarkably similar.

Adaptation, reclamation, and conservation do not occur automatically; they depend on human action and intervention. Environmentalists have contributed significantly to assuring that many areas of natural beauty are conserved and that some others given over to industry and business are so designed as to be healthful and pleasing to the aesthetic sensibilities as well as satisfying the economic appetites. They play a central role in identifying, drawing attention to problems and rallying support for the resolution of critical issues. But in the end, support for conservation and concern for the environment will depend on how these affect the general welfare including the provision of economic security within the framework of prevailing economic systems.

Population Growth and Economic Development

There are those who are concerned that population growth increases the pollution generated by the economy in industrialized countries. Others are concerned that the currently high population growth rates in the under-developed nations prevent their industrialization and slow down the increase in per capita income. The models used by analysts, largely economists, to describe the relationship between population and income growth in less developed countries assume that economic behavior follows rational patterns and define these patterns according to their own lights. These assumed rational behavior patterns are incompatible with social and economic realities, however, and the models illustrate an abstract and delusory way of thought.

The central focus of this group of models is the impact of population growth on savings and thus on capital accumulation. Since capital investment is required to develop industries, increase productivity and per capita income, as well as to provide jobs and mitigate the operation of the laws of diminishing returns, any phenomenon which inhibits savings and investment at household, corporate, and governmental levels will retard economic progress and industrialization. The approaches employed by these models attempt to measure abstractly what impact lower population growth and fewer births would have on savings and future per capita income. The models thus necessarily ignore the other values children may have for their parents and concentrate on estimating the economic effects of children on society. They do not succeed in that purpose.

One of the early models purported to estimate the present cash value of a birth (or a birth prevented). The estimated value of an individual's future consumption was subtracted from the estimated value of his or her future production, year by year, starting with the first year of life and ending with the estimated last year. Each presumptive future year's consumption and production was discounted at an appropriate rate to reflect the value it would have at the time of the estimate, that is, its "present value."

The justification for this procedure is that if one saves or invests a sum of money now, one expects to get back a larger sum of money in the future. Interest is thus an incentive for the lender to forego present consumption. The savings may be used in business and industry where its use will generate additional wealth. For instance, suppose one had ten dollars now and invested it with a return of 15 percent per annum. In ten years the ten dollars (with accumulated earnings or interest) would have increased to more than forty dollars. Thus, the present value of the future forty dollars, which might be received ten years from now, is only ten dollars. If the interest or discount rate were 10 percent instead of 15 percent the ten dollars would have grown to almost $26 dollars in 10 years. (Inflation complicates the business but it is ignored to simplify the exercise.)

Now let us suppose that the excess of production over consumption is $300 during the year of a worker's peak production age at 35 years. If the discount rate is 15 percent, not unusual for developing countries, the value of that year's excess discounted to the time of birth of that worker is only $22.50. If the worker were 50 years old when the $300 surplus was produced, its value discounted to the time of birth is practically zero. By this reasoning, it would hardly pay to invest anything at the time of a child's birth to assure its survival past age 50.

The cost of bearing and rearing a child is incurred early in its life and thus is not discounted by very much to arrive at the child's value at birth. On the other hand, the earnings of a worker, which occur later in life, are discounted heavily so as to appear to be of small worth at the time of birth. This type of analysis results in the conclusion that the present value of a birth is negative in developing societies where productivity is low. In developed societies where the costs of rearing and educating children is high and entry into the labor force is late, similar conclusions can be reached. The negative value of an individual at birth is frequently estimated as being quite large, up to several times the per capita annual income. Proponents of this type of analysis propose investing an amount up to the negative value of the birth to prevent it.

Other startling conclusions can be drawn from this type of cost benefit analysis. If the discount rate is taken to be 15 percent and the value of an individual's consumption is assumed to be constant over a lifetime, then a person's lifetime production (assumed to start at age 17 and constant thereafter) must be at least ten-fold that of lifetime consumption if the value of a new birth is to be at least zero (rather than negative). Even if it is assumed more realistically that a child's consumption is less than an adult's, lifetime production must be many times that of consumption. If account is taken of the fact that a person's production increases slowly to middle age, the total production over consumption must be further increased if that person's birth is to be worth something economically.[19]

Taking into account some of the criticisms raised by Ohlin and others, a variety of alternative models have been presented. These models purport to more directly and validly demonstrate mathematically and through simulation the effect on per capita income of increased savings and investment permitted by a lowering of the population growth rate. These models include the use of production functions to project the future of income given the various factors of production (such as labor and capital) which would be available under different conditions of fertility and population growth. Cobb-Douglas and Harrod-Domar production functions are used to project the future income benefits under various conditions. In their pioneering venture, Coale and Hoover employed a Harrod-Domar model to project growth in per capita income under different conditions of fertility and population growth. A series of subsequent models attempt greater precision, but the key element remains the assumed increase in savings, investments and capital accumulation which is presumed to result when there are fewer children.[20]

Intuitively, fewer children to support and educate would appear to make possible an increased rate of savings for parents and the state. Since children may not effectively enter the labor force until late adolescence, the loss of potential labor is not felt for some time. In the interim, the increased savings would make for increased capital investment leading to higher productivity per individual. Several observers have proposed that much of the labor force in less developed countries is currently redundant, anyway. Job sharing practices result in more workers performing a single job than is necessary.

While there was some argument as to which of the many models or formulations best reflected the economic benefits of lower population growth, all indicated considerable benefits. For despite differences in the structure of these models, all assumed that capital accumulation would be relatively greater, the lesser the rate of population growth. But whether these mathematical formulations reflect the realities of behavior and economic growth is another matter.

Parents in the developing countries continue to have children despite the economic models which show that they might do better in the long run by saving their money. Perhaps the models are ignored because peasant populations have little opportunity to save money in any case. If they can manage to produce more than their immediate needs, they stand little chance to realize a profit under existing market and related economic structures. The result is that savings are best accomplished through investing any surplus, over and above the families' needs, in children who will provide future security as well as contribute to the family's labor fund. On a day-to-day basis children do not cost much, and in traditional societies they become workers at an early age helping to support the family. If resources are insufficient for the additional labor to become an asset, fertility declines.

If there were fewer children, the rate of agricultural growth might actually decline if, as Boserup has noted, the impetus for agricultural growth in pre-industrial societies comes from the need to provide for a growing population. Much of the investment in expanding agriculture in pre-industrial societies comes in the form of the non-monetized labor of peasants. These include terracing of land, construction of feeder irrigation ditches, drainage canals, and other works. The labor comes from time which might have gone to leisure were it not for the pressure of population growth.

Children are a consumption good (giving pleasure to parents) as well as an economic good, an eventual factor of production, and a source of security. If fewer children were born, the potential savings might be applied not to increasing production but to alternative forms of consumption. The poor, in particular, find it difficult to save, their choices being which few of their many pressing needs will be satisfied. Significant savings comes largely from those who possess some wealth, from the profits of business enterprises themselves, and from the forced savings of government taxation and exactions.[21]

According to this view, if the government does not need to provide services for an increasing population, it can allocate a greater share of its income to investment in development, while investments in health and educational services could cover a greater proportion of the population. Whether the income generated or taxes collected by the government would be greater in a stationary population than when population and associated enterprises are growing may be questioned on empirical grounds.

Kuznets compared growth in per capita income with population growth within each of three groups of countries, African-Asian (excluding Japan), Latin American, and European. Each group could be said to represent, on the average, different levels of development. This division was necessary, for each group faces different types of economic problems. Within each group there was no relationship to be discerned between per capita income and population growth.[22] He suggested that demographic factors are not major in economic growth and that the key factors are institutional.[23]

In a prototype study published in 1958, Mexico was one of the case studies used to illustrate how rapid population growth would retard development.[24] In the interim, between 1950 and 1970, the population of Mexico doubled while the proportion of age eligible children attending school increased 72 percent, life expectancy increased 26 percent, and per capita income increased 89 percent. Population growth had had little deterrent effect on these indices. Easterlin, reviewing the economic experience of developing countries since 1957, noted that rather than population growth precluding economic growth, the surge in population growth in developing nations was frequently accompanied by unprecedented increases in per capita income.[25]

The developed countries of Europe did not experience such high population growth rates as are characteristic of the developing countries today. Nonetheless, in their long and difficult period of industrialization, capital was accumulated not so much by the savings of the general population or the government as by a ruthless exploitation of labor and colonial possessions, and by trade and business practices which are not likely to be tolerated today, even in authoritarian societies. One justification for the enclosures and eviction of cottagers and tenants from their holdings in pre-industrial England was that they would provide otherwise unwilling labor for the growing industries.

In the nineteenth century, France, with low levels of fertility and population growth, exhibited very sluggish economic growth compared to England and the United States, the latter having the highest population growth rates of the time due to immigration as well as relatively high fertility. In recent times, very high rates of economic growth, including that of per capita income, were evidenced by Brazil and Mexico, both with high fertility and population growth rates. Argentina and Chile, with much lower fertility rates than Brazil and Mexico and more developed economically to begin with, nonetheless showed much smaller economic growth rates. Unfortunately, many and even most people need not necessarily benefit when their nation shows considerable economic growth; obviously factors other than population are the more important determinants of economic growth.

Economists like to argue from the vantage point of *ceteris paribus*: that is, "all else being equal." Thus, among societies with equal propensities to consume, with equal motivation to produce, with equivalent value systems and the like, that society with lesser fertility and lesser population growth will save more than those societies with higher rates. If these conditions or assumptions are accepted, then the conclusions must logically follow. Keyfitz argued that the absence of a correlation between the rate of population growth and the rate of per capita income growth does not in itself invalidate the models which propose that high population growth slows economic development. He noted that other factors may be operating to mask the inhibitory effect of population growth on economic development. Thus, aggressive governments may be stimulating economic growth despite population growth, but were population growth lower, economic growth would be increased further still. Keyfitz proposed that the only way to disprove the model is to show that the factors operating to increase economic growth are related to characteristics derived from population growth.[26]

Simon, in an attempt to reconcile the discrepancy between the economic theory reflected in modeling and the empirical facts, presented a new model which incorporated, in addition to the mechanisms of savings discussed earlier, mechanisms through which high fertility and population growth stimulate economic growth. These new mechanisms include the effects of population pressure and the need to support a large family on the choices people make between leisure and work, economies of scale in social overhead capital, and other mechanisms by which population growth stimulated economic growth as documented by economic historians. Simon's model projects that at moderate growth rates (population doubling in, say, 50 years), the economy would perform better in the long run than it would at lower growth rates. In the short run (60 years or less), the stationary population would do only slightly better than the moderately growing population.[27] In contrast to the other models discussed, Simon's model would appear to fit, at least, the economic history of western European countries on whose experience it is partially based. Both the complex structure of the simulation model and parameters plugged into it are, however, based on limited data and observations and on assumptions which may not be pertinent in all circumstances and times. As with the "Limits to Growth" model discussed earlier, what comes out is what is put in and, in common with most economic analyses, the assumption of *ceteris paribus* is a necessary component of the model. In the real world things are rarely "equal," and the automatic assumption of equal social and political and economic institutions is futile. More to the point is that in different societies reproduction and population growth may have different significances for production and economic growth. Indeed, the reproduction of people, the production of economic goods and the patterns of savings may all stem in a unique and holistic pattern from the same ideological or institutional imperatives.

Consider the Hutterite communes of the American and Canadian prairies. The Hutterites, a fundamentalist Protestant sect of some 12,000 people in 1960, practice a primitive form of Christian communalism based on a productive and technologically advanced agricultural economy. They have had among the highest fertility and growth rates ever recorded and this seems to have had little impact on savings. The high growth rates of the Hutterites (more than 4 percent per annum with a doubling time of 16 years) required that they frequently capitalize new agricultural communes, purchase and develop land, as well as keep up with current technology in their agricultural operations. Savings, consumption, lifestyle, work organization, and fertility behavior spring from the same ethical base among the Hutterites.

Economists have presented evidence that the increase in production, even within a single country over a limited time, cannot be explained largely by the increase in labor and capital inputs, much less capital accumulation alone. There is a large residual which must be entered into the equation.[28] This residual is comprised of the manner in which the economy is organized, including technology, quality of the labor force (including education), industrial organization, and cultural values. Modelers have responded by making their models more complex, by including urbanization, educational levels, technological growth, and the like, as factors which are operated on and operate to increase wealth. Presumably, policymakers would give priority to those factors which are most cost effective in the models.[29] These complex models are difficult to evaluate and despite the great cost in developing them and running them on a computer, may be no more useful than the simple population growth-savings models which, incidentally, are still important and central subsystems in the more complex models. The principal failing of these models may well be in the predilection to exclude the non-quantifiable facts of life and these, such as the character of entrepreneurship and the perhaps hidden institutional patterns, may be the most important factors. It is difficult, if not impossible, to quantify the principal elements of economic progress. Even the measure of entrepreneurship may depend on the cultural context in which it occurs rather than on some intrinsic characteristic.

A case in point is the so-called dependency ratio: the proportion of the population in the non-working age groups, particularly the young, divided by the proportion of the population in the working age groups. Where the general levels of fertility are high, as in most third world countries, 40 percent or more of the population are under 15 years of age. This may be construed as a tremendous burden on the working adults, keeping them from saving and investing in the future, and keeping these countries in a backward economic condition. Yet, in the context of most high fertility societies, children do not cost much to rear and they become economically useful at an early age, often long before they reach fifteen years. Under the prevailing institutional structures of such countries, the only savings and investment open to parents is through having and rearing children. The thought of having a large number of dependents may disturb people in modern societies; it does not disturb people in "traditional" societies. The dependents more than pay for themselves. Most societies, past and present, have been so structured that the basic economic unit and the sole source of security was the family which had to be large, particularly under conditions of high mortality, to cope effectively with circumstances. The family maintained the integrity and viability of the societal infrastructure without which economic issues become moot.

Notes

1. J. B. Calhoun, "Population Density and Social Pathology," *Scientific American* 208:2 (February 1962), pp. 139–48; see also J. B. Calhoun, "Plight of the Ik and Kaiadilt is Seen as a Chilling Possible End for Man," *Smithsonian* 3:8 (November 1972), p. 27–32.
2. C. Turnbull, *The Mountain People* (New York: Simon & Schuster, 1972).

3. Calhoun, "Plight of the Ik and Kaiadilt," op. cit., p. 27–32.

4. H. H. Winsborough, "The Social Consequences of High Population Density," *Law and Contemporary Problems* 30:1 (Winter 1965), pp. 120–26.

5. O. R. Galle, W. R. Gove and J. M. McPherson, "Population Density and Pathology, What are the Relations for Man?", *Science* 176 (April 1972), pp. 23–29.

6. J. L. Freedman, "The Effects of Population Density on Humans," in J. T. Fawcett, ed., *Psychological Perspectives on Population* (New York: Basic Books, 1972), pp. 209–40; J. L. Freedman, *Crowding and Behavior: The Psychology of High Density Living* (New York: Viking Press, 1975).

7. A. T. Day and L. H. Day, "Cross National Comparison of Population Density," *Science* 181 (September 1973), pp. 1016–23.

8. G. Hardin, "Nobody Ever Dies of Overpopulation," *Science* 171 (February 1971), p. 527.

9. President's Science Advisory Committee, *The World Food Problem*, Report of the Panel on the World Food Supply, vol. 2 (Washington, D.C.: U.S. Government Printing Office, 1967), pp. 405–69; P. F. Low, "Prospects for Abundance: The Food Supply Question," in H. M. Bahr, B. A. Chadwick and D. L. Thomas, eds., *Population, Resources, and the Future* (Provo, Utah: Brigham Young University Press, 1972), Table 1, p. 66.

10. B. Commoner, *The Closing Circle* (New York: Bantam Books, 1972), p. 175.

11. "Critique of the Closing Circle," P. R. Ehrlich and J. P. Holdren, and response by B. Commoner, *Environment* 14:3 (April 1972), pp. 23–52; see also P. R. Ehrlich and J. P. Holdren, "Impact of Population Growth," *Science* 171 (1971), pp. 1212–17.

12. N. Lee and P. J. W. Saunders, "Pollution as a Function of Affluence and Population Increase," in P. R. Cox and J. Peel, eds., *Population and Pollution* (London: Academic Press, 1972), pp. 119–37.

13. D. S. Freedman, "The Relationship of Family Planning to Savings and Consumption in Taiwan," *Demography* 9:2 (August 1972), pp. 499–505; see also D. S. Freedman, "The Role of Consumption of Modern Durables in Economic Development," *Economic Development and Cultural Change* 19:1 (October 1970), pp. 25–48.

14. E. F. Schumacher, *Small is Beautiful* (New York: Harper & Row, 1973).

15. Herman P. Miller, *Rich Man, Poor Man*, (New York: Thomas Y. Crowell, 1971); also H. P. Miller, "Inequality, Poverty and Taxes," *Dissent* 23:1 (Winter 1975), pp. 40–49.

16. D. R. Arthur, "Katabolic and Resource Pollution in Estuaries," in P. R. Cox and J. Peel, eds., *Population and Pollution* (London: Academic Press, 1972), pp. 65–83.

17. W. E. and A. E. Smith, *Minamata* (New York: Hold, Rinehart and Winston, 1975).

18. U.S. Environmental Protection Agency, *D.D.T.—A Review of Scientific and Economic Aspects of the Decision to Ban its Use as a Pesticide*, (Springfield, Va.: U.S. Environmental Protection Agency, 1975).

19. G. Ohlin, *Population Control and Economic Development*, O.E.C.D. (Organization for Economic Cooperation and Development), 1967, for a short review of other flaws in these types of analyses.

20. For a review of these models see W. C. Robinson and D. E. Horlacher, "Population Growth and Economic Welfare," *Reports on Population/Family Planning No. 6* (New York: Population Council, 1971). Specific models are proposed by S. Enke, "The Gains to India from Population Control: Some Money Measures and Incentive Schemes," *Review of Economics and Statistics* 42:3 (1960), pp. 175–81; S. Enke, "Birth Control for Economic Development," *Science* 164 (1969), pp. 798–802; G. B. Simmons, *The Indian Investment in Family Planning: An Occasional Paper* (New York: Population Council, 1971); P. Demeny, "Investment Allocation and Population Growth," *Demography* 2 (1965): pp. 203–33. A pioneering venture in this area is that of A. J. Coale and E. M. Hoover, *Population Growth and Economic Development in Low Income Countries* (Princeton, N.J.: Princeton University Press, 1958).

21. The reader may also be interested in the exchange of opposing views of H. Leibenstein, "Pitfalls in Benefit-Cost Analysis of Birth Prevention," *Population Studies* 23:2 (1969), pp. 161–70; "More on Pitfalls," *Population Studies* 24:1 (1970), pp. 117–19; S. Enke, "Leibenstein on the Benefits and Costs of Birth Control Programs,' *Population Studies* 24:1 (1970), pp. 115–16.

22. S. Kuznets, "Population and Economic Growth," *Proceedings of the American Philosophical Society* 111:2 (1967), pp. 170–93.

23. S. Kuznets, "Demographic Aspects of Modern Economic Growth," *Proceedings of 2nd World Population Conference, Belgrade, 1965* (New York: United Nations, 1967).

24. Coale and Hoover, op. cit.

25. R. A. Easterlin, "Effects of Population Growth on the Economic Development of Developing Countries," *Annals of the American Academy of Political and Social Science* 369 (January 1967), pp. 98–108.

26. N. Keyfitz, "How Do We Know the Facts of Demography?", *Population and Development Review* 1:2 (December 1975), pp. 267–88.

27. J. L. Simon, "Population Growth May Be Good for LDC's in the Long Run: A Richer Simulation Model," *Economic Development and Cultural Change* 24:2 (January 1976), pp. 309–37.

28. S. Kuznets, *Modern Economic Growth* (New Haven: Yale University Press, 1966), pp. 80–81.

29. W. B. Arthur and G. McNicoll, "Large Scale Simulation Models in Population and Development: What Use to Planners," *Population and Development Review* 1:2 (December 1975), pp. 251–66.

14

Some Final Observations

A Misconstruction of History

Population growth often appears to threaten those who are well off, perhaps because change may be required to accomodate such growth. This anxiety may be needless, but history is often viewed from the perspective of these fears. "The poor increase like fleas and lice, and these vermin will eat us up unless we enclose . . . ." said an English gentleman of the seventeenth century when the population of England was less than a tenth its current size.[1] Recently, an American gentleman expressed the same opinion, sounding the alarm that our civilization may be doomed by the reproductive proclivities of other people.[2]

The inexorable progression to ruin as a result of uncontrolled breeding was the subject of an essay, "The Tragedy of the Commons" by Hardin,[3] which has gained a wide acceptance and a wider circulation among some academic and scientific circles. In this essay, an analogy is drawn between the effects of the production of children who will be supported by the earth's resources and the pasturing of livestock by herdsmen on a common pasture to which each has unlimited and unregulated access. When herdsmen and cattle are few and pastures are large, the herdsmen may do as they please; no matter how much livestock one herdsman puts on the pasture, others are not adversely affected since there is plenty for all. But when the pasture becomes crowded and the feed is consumed faster than it can be renewed, the destruction of the pasture becomes imminent. When a herdsman puts an additional animal on the pasture, the gain from the maintenance of that animal accrues solely to him, but the loss—because of depleted productivity of the pasture—is shared by all. Thus, if each herdsman acts independently, self-interest would dictate that each stock the pasture with as many animals

266

as possible. And the ultimate result of this aggregated behavior is the complete ruin of the pasture. Hardin asserted that this problem was resolved by the institution of private property wherein an owner accrues not only the benefits of a piece of land but also assumes the losses associated with its use. This is presumed to encourage conservation and increased productivity. (Hardin recognized that the owner of property may infringe on the common, as by dumping waste in the air or water, and that such pollution must be regulated.) Since no institution such as private property operates to control population growth, Hardin affirmed that some level of coercive control, agreed upon by democratic consensus would be justified because the major part of the cost of children is borne by the community and the commons.

An examination of the history of the commons and its enclosure in England reveals that "The Tragedy of the Commons" is a myth bearing little relationship to the realities of history. Even when much of the land was held in common, the people with access to these resources were aware of the need to conserve them and maintained institutions to assure this. Private property and associated power destroyed these institutions. The acceptance of the thesis of "The Tragedy of the Commons" by many scientists tells us something about how uncritical and prejudiced scientists can be regarding the institutions which sustain them.

The enclosure movement involved a change in the definition of prerogatives accruing to owners and to occupiers of land. The traditional view of ownership which existed before enclosure was defined by Tawney:

The owner is a trustee, whose rights are derived from the function which he performs and should lapse if he repudiates it. They are limited by his duty to the state; they are limited no less by the rights of his tenants against him. Just as the peasant may not cultivate his land in the way which he may think most profitable to himself, but is bound by the law of the village to grow the crops which the village needs and to throw his strips open after harvest to his neighbor's beasts, so the lord is required both by custom and by statute to forego the anti-social profits to be won by methods of agriculture which injure his neighbors and weaken the State.[4]

Christopher Hill noted that as late as the middle of the sixteenth century "the idea that men could 'use their possessions as they list' seemed to Crowley to be 'tantamount to atheism.'"[5]

The great majority of rural folk before and during the early part of the enclosure movement lived and worked on manorial estates and many of these practiced the open field system of cultivation.

Very simply, the open field system may be described thusly. A tract of arable land was divided into three large fields; one was used to plant a crop such as winter wheat; another field was planted to a crop such as peas or beans, or other legumes, and the third field lay fallow. Crops would be rotated among these fields each year. Each tenant had rights to several long strips in each field, evening out the quality of the land each received to work; but the farmer was not free to plant as he would. A court leet, or meeting of all the tenantry, presided over by the lord or his steward, debated and decided what each field would bear. After harvest the fields were thrown open, so the stock could graze on the stubble. Much of the manor was in waste which was used as a common pasture, but contrary to the implications of Hardin's plot, a tenant could not graze any number of beasts at will but was regulated by custom and court leet, the leet having enforcement power. The manor would likely include a woodland in which the peasant might gather fuel, though not fell trees, which was the lord's prerogative. Both lord and tenants were aware of the need to regulate land use. Open field agriculture was neither as unproductive nor as destructive as its opponents proposed. As Brailsford noted, the peasantry of the seventeenth century had learned to govern itself well.[6]

Although the great majority of rural folk in pre-industrial England lived within fielden parishes, many lived as squatters or cottagers, insecure in their rights, in the fens, forests, and wastes on sufferance of the owners or the local authorities. The squatters or cottagers were among the masterless men, as Christopher Hill has called them, people who had fallen out of the traditional order; they included vagabonds, out-of-work laborers, craftsmen and other such folk. These would eke out or supplement a small living from the common lands by herding a few cattle or sheep. It hardly entered the minds of such people to try to maximize their incomes as Hardin's fable would have it. To graze livestock on the common waste was a welfare prerogative of the poor, limited by the rights of other commoners and subject to the powers of the authorities who had jurisdiction.

Obligations to conserve accompanied the rights of usufruct almost universally. The fenmen who inhabited marshes were reputed to be among the most independent and irascible of commoners. They caught wild fowl and fish, and herded a few cattle or sheep, often going on stilts through the marshes to do so, and cut the marsh grass for fodder. Yet independent as they were, they were subject to manorial customs and laws paying rents in kind to landlords. A complex of rules and customs relating to fishing and other use rights, and allocating labor obligations of users for the maintenance of embankments and other structures kept many waterways navigable.[7] The fens were enclosed in Stuart and early Hanoverian times (1650–1800). The marshes were not destroyed nor the rivers polluted by the commoners, but by the enclosers who drained them and the industrialists who discharged factory wastes into them. The breakdown of the codes and customs which preserved the commons came not with population pressure. As we have seen fertility does respond to resource constraints. But the lust for power and wealth does not.

Henry VII ascended the English throne in 1485, a year often taken to mark the end of the middle ages, and the beginning of an accelerated commercialization of society. Many characteristics of modern economic enterprise existed to a degree prior to this date, and facets of feudal society survived much longer, some even to the present. Nonetheless, after this date encroachments on the commons are noted more often. Rowland Parker, tracing the history of an English village through 2,000 years, noted that between 1490 and 1540, entries of fines were becoming more frequent in the village record, such as a fine of 10 shillings assessed a butcher for overloading the village commons and pastures to the detriment of all tenants and residents. What is more, the fines were being ignored as they were not in the old days and the problem would increase in the sixteenth century. Parker discerned a growing tendency for people to feather their own nests without regard to the interests of others, behavior which was effectively inhibited in earlier times by neighbors and others.[8] The abuse of the commons may be attributed to the inadequacy of the system but, actually, it reflected the growing power of aggressive and enterprising people to arrogate to themselves the greater part of the usufruct of resources; finally, by enclosure, the same sorts of people could claim exclusive rights as with personal property. As the economy became commercialized and monetized, friends and neighbors lost their influence.

The official policy up to the end of the sixteenth century was largely opposed to enclosure, the consequent depopulation of the countryside, and the laying down of arable lands to grass in the face of a need for an increased food supply. In some parts of the country, the government was successful in returning to the plow, land which had been enclosed for sheep-folds. Such action may have slowed down the pace of enclosure, but the process continued inexorably as the chronicles of the time attest. By the seventeenth century, the policy of parliament and crown had changed. Wastes and fens were enclosed by commercial interests who obtained title with unlimited rights of proprietorship. Squatters and copyholders were evicted and the land closed to settlement. Much arable land was converted to sheepwalks to supply wool for the growing textile industry, much of it in Flanders, thus reducing the production of food.

The cost in human misery was high, due not so much to the growth of population, much of which occurred only after conditions improved, but to the manner in which social change was effected, causing so many to be displaced from their livelihoods. These included not only tenants and copyholders but other small farmers and yeomen whose titles were declared defective or who were obliged to sell for various reasons. Gregory King[9] estimated that, in 1688, the lower classes, which included 60 percent of English families, did not have incomes sufficient to support even their wretched standard of living but depended in some measure on alms and poor relief to supplement their earnings.

E. P. Thompson noted that the community structure and rights associated with copyhold and tenancy which were recognized and endorsed in the collective memory of the pre-industrial and self-governing village were not held to be necessarily valid in law, and many suffered as a result. Excluded from access to the commons, the working people were proletarianized, their livings subject to the decisions of others and those others were not kindly folk! Chambers, not an unfriendly critic of enclosure, wrote:

The appropriation to their own exclusive use of the whole of the common waste by the legal owners meant that the curtain which separated the growing army of labourers from utter proletarianization was torn down. It was, no doubt, a thin and squalid curtain . . . but it was real and to deprive them of it without providing a substitute implied the exclusion of the labourers from the benefits which their intensified labour alone made possible.[10]

Arthur Young, a prominent eighteenth century proponent of the new scientific agriculture and enclosure, had occasion for regret:

I had rather that all the commons of England were sunk in the sea, than that the poor should in future be treated on enclosing as they have generally been hitherto.

By nineteen out of twenty enclosure bills, the poor are injured, and some grossly injured.[11]

The customary behavior patterns which ordered rural society broke down under the onslaught of commercial interest. The ever diminishing commons became the last resort of those poor who obtained cottagers' rights to its use. And they, perhaps knowing that the days of commoner rights were numbered, did not give the commons the kind of care it once received. Cynicism was the order of the day.

> The law locks up the man or woman,
> Who steals the goose from off the common;
> But leaves the greater villain loose
> Who steals the common from the goose.[12]

Yet though many traditional controls which regulated status and behavior broke down, the age at marriage increased through the seventeenth and early part of the eighteenth centuries until conditions began to improve. The absence of livelihood inhibited marriages, and fertility rates were not much higher than mortality rates at the end of the seventeenth century.

Some historians do not share the harsh views generally held about the injustice of the enclosures, which occurred after 1750.[13] The land enclosed in these latter times was put to cultivation rather than in pasture as previously. Many of the dispossessed were absorbed into the agricultural labor force instead of being evicted and left to shift for themselves. New developments in agriculture led to increased food production. The justification for many historians of enclosure lay in the capacity of the commercial farmers to increase food production and release manpower in support of the industrialization of the country. The fact remained that the tenants never had much chance to respond to the change in market forces with increased productivity. They lost their lands not through economic failure but through the exercise of political power by the new proprietors. It must have been a poor comfort to the former tenant by right or yeoman to be able to hire on as occasional agricultural or factory labor, at minimal wages and with frequent bouts of unemployment and recourse to the poor law authorities. In former days the peasantry had shown their ready capability of adapting and responding to new circumstances. Indeed the open field system with its long narrow strips was a response to the development of the heavy, team-drawn plow and the need to increase food production earlier, in the middle ages. And many of the techniques and crops of the new agriculture were drawn from the gardening practices developed by peasants.

Whether the copyholding tenants or yeoman farmers could have increased food production as quickly as did the large commercial farmers must remain largely conjectural. But Hardin's parable of the commons and the enclosures which brought it to an end ignores the historical context. Instead, the parable is tailored to fit a preconception that human behavior in the aggregate is destructive unless regulated by a process which, democratic or not, is guided by an elite. The historical context, however, teaches another lesson. The tenants of pre-enclosure manorial estates, each with a stipulated access to common resources needed to act in concert and did so to conserve their common until the sanctions they possessed lost their force. The enclosers were not bound to consider the impact of their behavior on others, nor bound to conservation practices that were not profitable. The misery of the times was not due to the abuse of the commons by those who used it, but rather to the seizure of the commons by those with power.

The lesson of Hardin's "tragedy" was to be that if each person had children as it suited him or her personally, the world would become a miserable place. The lesson from the historical analogy he selected was, however, that misery resulted from the exercise of inordinate power and if the world has improved since then, it is because of limitations placed on the power one person may exercise over the livelihood of another.

Recapitulation and Conclusions

The drive for power and domination over resources and people is not self-limiting. There are few deterrents to the use of power if its expression is not contained by conscience or the capacity of others to resist—as individuals or in concert as a community. Powerful persons can frequently insulate themselves from the detrimental effects which may result from their social, political, and economic behavior. Even if they pollute the environment, their position permits them to live in a manner and style in which the noxious effects may be ignored.

On the other hand, the cost and consequences, good and bad, of children fall heavily on the parents or the family. Even with extensive welfare and educational services as in economically developed nations, the burden of children may be onerous to the parents.

In less developed countries the burden of childbearing and rearing falls almost entirely on family. Though the costs of rearing children in these countries are small, so are the resources available to parents and they are not protected against any detrimental consequences which may ensue. Thus, fertility tends to become self-limiting as both the personal and social consequences fall heavily on those whose behavior results in population growth.

It is not surprising then that social ills are often a consequence of the abuse of power by relatively small groups while population rarely, if ever, presses so heavily on resources that significant, lasting ill effects ensue. Despite abstract arguments that population pressure, resulting from growth or size and density, must eventually exacerbate societal ills, there is no indication that this occurs in the real world. The abstract arguments or models do not take into account human adaptability.

The seemingly widespread concern with population growth may be largely a reflection of the well articulated disquietude of elites. This concern often is a boon to many political leaders who then attribute the lack of progress in improving social welfare to fertility behavior. The Agency for International Development (U.S. Department of State) and the World Bank both state that population control is essential to economic development, and attribute many of the failures of economic development programs to excessive population growth. For many scientific and social welfare workers, concern with population is also a boon. The issue provides them with an area in which they can perform useful and personally rewarding work while avoiding conflict with the political and economic entities which support their status. Bachrach and Bergman, sympathetic to the population issue, have traced the manner in which a relatively small group of wealthy individuals, foundations, and sympathetic academic influentials have managed to dominate current population issues and studies in the United States through propaganda, financing of academic enterprises, and influencing of government policies.[14] The outcome is a bias in the formulation of population issues and research. This bias, whatever its justification, must detract from the objectivity with which events are viewed.

This is not to imply that cynical self-interest is the sole source of bias and concern with population growth. Indeed, the concern is frequently with the preservation of values, as well as the survival of the human species. Areas of undisturbed natural beauty, opportunities for solitude, freedom from oppressive crowds, assurance of subsistence, and a place in the world for all have long been aspirations of ordinary people as well as poets and philosophers. The more advantaged are in a position to enjoy the good things and may see them threatened by the changes implicit in population growth. The majority of people, however, are still faced with the problems of physical survival and the attainment of a sense of personal worth and dignity, which are prerequisites for a happy future. Their fertility behavior can be understood only in pursuance of these values under the conditions with which they must cope.

The resolution of societal ills will involve changes in the distribution of political power and in economic structures. The power of elites to limit access to resources and to use them principally as it profits them to do so will need to be contained. Priority will need to be given to food production to satisfy the needs of all people since, as is apparent, these needs are not satisfied under present market conditions despite considerable unused productive capacity. While real economic growth helps to mitigate insecurity and the effects of inequality in contemporary economies, the changes in technology introduced to increase productivity and growth frequently lead to pollution and resource depletion. Increased security and equity would not only serve to advance human welfare but environmental conservation as well. Much has been written by competent and cogent advocates of land reform, humane food production and distribution policies, equitable terms of trade for poor countries and other policies to help people and nations. The problem is not only to get such policies accepted but implemented in such a manner that the general public, not merely elites and functionaries, are the beneficiaries. But this book has almost run its course and though the directions advocated for human society are implicit in the preceding discussions, their explication and development must be reserved for future works.

Many of the promoters of population control are aware of the inequities and constraints with which people must cope, and they advocate a variety of reforms and services to mitigate those oppressive conditions. So did Malthus, but he is not known as a social reformer and rightly so. He contributed nothing to the knowledge of the causes of social and economic inequality; instead his work distracted from a focus on the central sources of human misery.

The welfare of future generations is not likely to depend on the numbers of people. Population, resources and technology maintain a dynamic balance as they change, moved by and compensating for socio-structural stress. The welfare of future generations will depend on a different legacy, the character of the institutional structures and the knowledge developed by preceding generations. Human societies have, in general, been fairly proficient in resolving technological problems; at least they have been more proficient in these areas than in others. They have been least proficient in coping with problems of power and inequity. The legacy that would most benefit future generations would be the resolution of the contradictions in social and economic organization which makes "social justice" sound utopian if not platitudinous while peace, equity, and security are made to appear incompatible with enterprise, productivity, and freedom.

Notes

1. Quoted by C. Hill, *The World Turned Upside Down* (New York: Viking Press, 1972), p. 42.

2. G. Hardin, "The Survival of Nations and Civilizations," *Science* 172 (1971), p. 1297.

3. G. Hardin, "The Tragedy of the Commons," *Science* 162 (1969), pp. 1243–48.

4. R. H. Tawney, *Religion and Rise of Capitalism* (1922) (New York: Penguin Books, 1947), p. 128.

5. C. Hill, *Reformation to Industrial Revolution: The Pelican Economic History of Britain*, vol. 2 (New York: Penguin Books, 1967), p. 27.

6. H. N. Brailsford, *The Levellers and the English Revolution* (Stanford, Cal.: Stanford University Press, 1961), pp. 420–25.

7. G. M. Trevelyan, *English Social History* (Harmondsworth: Penguin Books, 1967), p. 162; H. C. Darby, *The Medieval Fenland*, 1940.

8. R. Parker, *The Common Stream* (New York: Holt, Rinehart and Winston, 1975), pp. 112--13, 16.

9. P. Laslett, *The World We Have Lost* (New York: Scribners, 1965), Ch. 2, specifically the table, "Gregory King's Scheme of the Income and Expense of the Several Families of England Calculated for the Year 1688."

10. J. D. Chambers, "Enclosure and Labour Supply in the Industrial Revolution," *Economic History Review*, 2nd Series V (1952–3), p. 336; see also E. P. Thompson, *The Making of the English Working Class* (Penguin Books, Pelican Edition, 1963), Ch. 7, "The Field Labourers," pp. 232--58; Hill, *Reformation to Industrial Revolution* op. cit., pp. 268–74.

11. Quoted by Hill, *Reformation to Industrial Revolution*, op. cit., p. 270.

12. E. Ergang, *Europe From the Renaissance to Waterloo* (Boston: D. C. Heath, 1939), p. 569.

13. J. D. Chambers and G. E. Mingay, *The Agricultural Revolution, 1750--1880* (London: Batsford, 1966), Ch. 4.

14. P. Bachrach and E. Bergman, *Power and Choice: The Formulation of American Population Policy* (Lexington, Mass: Lexington Books, 1973).

Index

About the Author

Dr. Kleinman, whose professional training has been in public health, holds an M.P.H. in epidemiology and a Dr. P.H. in population planning. His academic work has also included graduate studies in statistics, sociology, psychology, economics, and other areas related to his principle interests. He has been engaged in public health administration, program development and evaluation, research and occasional teaching and lecturing at universities and colleges; was head of Research and Statistics, Bureau of Maternal and Child Health, California State Health Department; and was senior research associate at the Battelle Population Studies Center in Seattle. He has published in professional medical, public health, population and economic development journals.